Casenote® *Legal Briefs*

CONTRACTS

Keyed to Courses Using

Calamari, Perillo, Bender, and Brown's
Cases and Problems on Contracts

Sixth Edition

This publication is designed to provide accurate and authoritative information in regard to the subject matter covered. It is sold with the understanding that the publisher is not engaged in rendering legal, accounting, or other professional services. If legal advice or other expert assistance is required, the services of a competent professional person should be sought.

— From a Declaration of Principles adopted jointly by a Committee of the American Bar Association and a Committee of Publishers and Associates

About Wolters Kluwer Law & Business

Wolters Kluwer Law & Business is a leading global provider of intelligent information and digital solutions for legal and business professionals in key specialty areas, and respected educational resources for professors and law students. Wolters Kluwer Law & Business connects legal and business professionals as well as those in the education market with timely, specialized authoritative content and information-enabled solutions to support success through productivity, accuracy and mobility.

Serving customers worldwide, Wolters Kluwer Law & Business products include those under the Aspen Publishers, CCH, Kluwer Law International, Loislaw, Best Case, ftwilliam.com and MediRegs family of products.

CCH products have been a trusted resource since 1913, and are highly regarded resources for legal, securities, antitrust and trade regulation, government contracting, banking, pension, payroll, employment and labor, and healthcare reimbursement and compliance professionals.

Aspen Publishers products provide essential information to attorneys, business professionals and law students. Written by preeminent authorities, the product line offers analytical and practical information in a range of specialty practice areas from securities law and intellectual property to mergers and acquisitions and pension/benefits. Aspen's trusted legal education resources provide professors and students with high-quality, up-to-date and effective resources for successful instruction and study in all areas of the law.

Kluwer Law International products provide the global business community with reliable international legal information in English. Legal practitioners, corporate counsel and business executives around the world rely on Kluwer Law journals, looseleafs, books, and electronic products for comprehensive information in many areas of international legal practice.

Loislaw is a comprehensive online legal research product providing legal content to law firm practitioners of various specializations. Loislaw provides attorneys with the ability to quickly and efficiently find the necessary legal information they need, when and where they need it, by facilitating access to primary law as well as state-specific law, records, forms and treatises.

Best Case Solutions is the leading bankruptcy software product to the bankruptcy industry. It provides software and workflow tools to flawlessly streamline petition preparation and the electronic filing process, while timely incorporating ever-changing court requirements.

ftwilliam.com offers employee benefits professionals the highest quality plan documents (retirement, welfare and non-qualified) and government forms (5500/PBGC, 1099 and IRS) software at highly competitive prices.

MediRegs products provide integrated health care compliance content and software solutions for professionals in healthcare, higher education and life sciences, including professionals in accounting, law and consulting.

Wolters Kluwer Law & Business, a division of Wolters Kluwer, is headquartered in New York. Wolters Kluwer is a market-leading global information services company focused on professionals.

Format for the Casenote® Legal Brief

Nature of Case: This section identifies the form of action (e.g., breach of contract, negligence, battery), the type of proceeding (e.g., demurrer, appeal from trial court's jury instructions), or the relief sought (e.g., damages, injunction, criminal sanctions).

Fact Summary: This is included to refresh your memory and can be used as a quick reminder of the facts.

Rule of Law: Summarizes the general principle of law that the case illustrates. It may be used for instant recall of the court's holding and for classroom discussion or home review.

Facts: This section contains all relevant facts of the case, including the contentions of the parties and the lower court holdings. It is written in a logical order to give the student a clear understanding of the case. The plaintiff and defendant are identified by their proper names throughout and are always labeled with a (P) or (D).

Party ID: Quick identification of the relationship between the parties.

Concurrence/Dissent: All concurrences and dissents are briefed whenever they are included by the casebook editor.

Analysis: This last paragraph gives you a broad understanding of where the case "fits in" with other cases in the section of the book and with the entire course. It is a hornbook-style discussion indicating whether the case is a majority or minority opinion and comparing the principal case with other cases in the casebook. It may also provide analysis from restatements, uniform codes, and law review articles. The analysis will prove to be invaluable to classroom discussion.

Palsgraf v. Long Island R.R. Co.

Injured bystander (P) v. Railroad company (D)

N.Y. Ct. App., 248 N.Y. 339, 162 N.E. 99 (1928).

NATURE OF CASE: Appeal from judgment affirming verdict for plaintiff seeking damages for personal injury.

FACT SUMMARY: Helen Palsgraf (P) was injured on R.R.'s (D) train platform when R.R.'s (D) guard helped a passenger aboard a moving train, causing his package to fall on the tracks. The package contained fireworks which exploded, creating a shock that tipped a scale onto Palsgraf (P).

🏛 RULE OF LAW
The risk reasonably to be perceived defines the duty to be obeyed.

FACTS: Helen Palsgraf (P) purchased a ticket to Rockaway Beach from R.R. (D) and was waiting on the train platform. As she waited, two men ran to catch a train that was pulling out from the platform. The first man jumped aboard, but the second man, who appeared as if he might fall, was helped aboard by the guard on the train who had kept the door open so they could jump aboard. A guard on the platform also helped by pushing him onto the train. The man was carrying a package wrapped in newspaper. In the process, the man dropped his package, which fell on the tracks. The package contained fireworks and exploded. The shock of the explosion was apparently of great enough strength to tip over some scales at the other end of the platform, which fell on Palsgraf (P) and injured her. A jury awarded her damages, and R.R. (D) appealed.

ISSUE: Does the risk reasonably to be perceived define the duty to be obeyed?

HOLDING AND DECISION: (Cardozo, C.J.) Yes. The risk reasonably to be perceived defines the duty to be obeyed. If there is no foreseeable hazard to the injured party as the result of a seemingly innocent act, the act does not become a tort because it happened to be a wrong as to another. If the wrong was not willful, the plaintiff must show that the act as to her had such great and apparent possibilities of danger as to entitle her to protection. Negligence in the abstract is not enough upon which to base liability. Negligence is a relative concept, evolving out of the common law doctrine of trespass on the case. To establish liability, the defendant must owe a legal duty of reasonable care to the injured party. A cause of action in tort will lie where harm,

though unintended, could have been averted or avoided by observance of such a duty. The scope of the duty is limited by the range of danger that a reasonable person could foresee. In this case, there was nothing to suggest from the appearance of the parcel or otherwise that the parcel contained fireworks. The guard could not reasonably have had any warning of a threat to Palsgraf (P), and R.R. (D) therefore cannot be held liable. Judgment is reversed in favor of R.R. (D).

DISSENT: (Andrews, J.) The concept that there is no negligence unless R.R. (D) owes a legal duty to take care as to Palsgraf (P) herself is too narrow. Everyone owes to the world at large the duty of refraining from those acts that may unreasonably threaten the safety of others. If the guard's action was negligent as to those nearby, it was also negligent as to those outside what might be termed the "danger zone." For Palsgraf (P) to recover, R.R.'s (D) negligence must have been the proximate cause of her injury, a question of fact for the jury.

▶ ANALYSIS
The majority defined the limit of the defendant's liability in terms of the danger that a reasonable person in defendant's situation would have perceived. The dissent argued that the limitation should not be placed on liability, but rather on damages. Judge Andrews suggested that only injuries that would not have happened but for R.R.'s (D) negligence should be compensable. Both the majority and dissent recognized the policy-driven need to limit liability for negligent acts, seeking, in the words of Judge Andrews, to define a framework "that will be practical and in keeping with the general understanding of mankind." The Restatement (Second) of Torts has accepted Judge Cardozo's view.

▬▬■

Quicknotes

FORESEEABILITY A reasonable expectation that change is the probable result of certain acts or omissions.

NEGLIGENCE Conduct falling below the standard of care that a reasonable person would demonstrate under similar conditions.

PROXIMATE CAUSE The natural sequence of events without which an injury would not have been sustained.

▬▬■

Issue: The issue is a concise question that brings out the essence of the opinion as it relates to the section of the casebook in which the case appears. Both substantive and procedural issues are included if relevant to the decision.

Holding and Decision: This section offers a clear and in-depth discussion of the rule of the case and the court's rationale. It is written in easy-to-understand language and answers the issue presented by applying the law to the facts of the case. When relevant, it includes a thorough discussion of the exceptions to the case as listed by the court, any major cites to the other cases on point, and the names of the judges who wrote the decisions.

Quicknotes: Conveniently defines legal terms found in the case and summarizes the nature of any statutes, codes, or rules referred to in the text.

Wolters Kluwer Law & Business is proud to offer *Casenote® Legal Briefs*—continuing thirty years of publishing America's best-selling legal briefs.

Casenote® Legal Briefs are designed to help you save time when briefing assigned cases. Organized under convenient headings, they show you how to abstract the basic facts and holdings from the text of the actual opinions handed down by the courts. Used as part of a rigorous study regimen, they can help you spend more time analyzing and critiquing points of law than on copying bits and pieces of judicial opinions into your notebook or outline.

Casenote® Legal Briefs should never be used as a substitute for assigned casebook readings. They work best when read as a follow-up to reviewing the underlying opinions themselves. Students who try to avoid reading and digesting the judicial opinions in their casebooks or online sources will end up shortchanging themselves in the long run. The ability to absorb, critique, and restate the dynamic and complex elements of case law decisions is crucial to your success in law school and beyond. It cannot be developed vicariously.

Casenote® Legal Briefs represents but one of the many offerings in Legal Education's Study Aid Timeline, which includes:

- *Casenote® Legal Briefs*
- *Emanuel Law Outlines*
- *Examples & Explanations* Series
- *Introduction to Law* Series
- Emanuel *Law in a Flash* Flash Cards
- Emanuel *CrunchTime* Series

Each of these series is designed to provide you with easy-to-understand explanations of complex points of law. Each volume offers guidance on the principles of legal analysis and, consulted regularly, will hone your ability to spot relevant issues. We have titles that will help you prepare for class, prepare for your exams, and enhance your general comprehension of the law along the way.

To find out more about Wolters Kluwer Law & Business' study aid publications, visit us online at *www.wolterskluwerlb.com* or email us at *legaledu@wolterskluwer.com*. We'll be happy to assist you.

Get this Casenote® Legal Brief as an AspenLaw Studydesk eBook today!

By returning this form to Wolters Kluwer Law & Business, you will receive a complimentary eBook download of this Casenote® Legal Brief and AspenLaw Studydesk productivity software.* Learn more about AspenLaw Studydesk today at *www.wolterskluwerlb.com.*

Name	Phone ( )

Address	Apt. No.

City	State	ZIP Code

Law School	Graduation Date Month _____ Year _____

Cut out the UPC found on the lower left corner of the back cover of this book. Staple the UPC inside this box. Only the original UPC from the book cover will be accepted. (No photocopies or store stickers are allowed.)

> **Attach UPC inside this box.**

Email (Print legibly or you may not get access!)

Title of this book (course subject)

ISBN of this book (10- or 13-digit number on the UPC)

Used with which casebook (provide author's name)

Mail the completed form to: Wolters Kluwer Law & Business
Legal Education Division
130 Turner Street, Bldg 3, 4th Floor
Waltham, MA 02453-8901

* Upon receipt of this completed form, you will be emailed a code for the digital download of this book in AspenLaw Studydesk eBook format and a free copy of the software application, which is required to read the eBook.

For a full list of eBook study aids available for AspenLaw Studydesk software and other resources that will help you with your law school studies, visit *www.wolterskluwerlb.com.*

Make a photocopy of this form and your UPC for your records.

For detailed information on the use of the information you provide on this form, please see the PRIVACY POLICY at *www.wolterskluwerlb.com.*

A. Decide on a Format and Stick to It

Structure is essential to a good brief. It enables you to arrange systematically the related parts that are scattered throughout most cases, thus making manageable and understandable what might otherwise seem to be an endless and unfathomable sea of information. There are, of course, an unlimited number of formats that can be utilized. However, it is best to find one that suits your needs and stick to it. Consistency breeds both efficiency and the security that when called upon you will know where to look in your brief for the information you are asked to give.

Any format, as long as it presents the essential elements of a case in an organized fashion, can be used. Experience, however, has led *Casenote® Legal Briefs* to develop and utilize the following format because of its logical flow and universal applicability.

NATURE OF CASE: This is a brief statement of the legal character and procedural status of the case (e.g., "Appeal of a burglary conviction").

There are many different alternatives open to a litigant dissatisfied with a court ruling. The key to determining which one has been used is to discover *who is asking this court for what.*

This first entry in the brief should be kept as *short as possible.* Use the court's terminology if you understand it. But since jurisdictions vary as to the titles of pleadings, the best entry is the one that addresses who wants what in this proceeding, not the one that sounds most like the court's language.

RULE OF LAW: A statement of the general principle of law that the case illustrates (e.g., "An acceptance that varies any term of the offer is considered a rejection and counteroffer").

Determining the rule of law of a case is a procedure similar to determining the issue of the case. Avoid being fooled by red herrings; there may be a few rules of law mentioned in the case excerpt, but usually only one is *the* rule with which the casebook editor is concerned. The techniques used to locate the issue, described below, may also be utilized to find the rule of law. Generally, your best guide is simply the chapter heading. It is a clue to the point the casebook editor seeks to make and should be kept in mind when reading every case in the respective section.

FACTS: A synopsis of only the essential facts of the case, i.e., those bearing upon or leading up to the issue.

The facts entry should be a short statement of the events and transactions that led one party to initiate legal proceedings against another in the first place. While some cases conveniently state the salient facts at the beginning of the decision, in other instances they will have to be culled from hiding places throughout the text, even from concurring and dissenting opinions. Some of the "facts" will often be in dispute and should be so noted. Conflicting evidence may be briefly pointed up. "Hard" facts must be included. Both must be *relevant* in order to be listed in the facts entry. It is impossible to tell what is relevant until the entire case is read, as the ultimate determination of the rights and liabilities of the parties may turn on something buried deep in the opinion.

Generally, the facts entry should not be longer than three to five *short* sentences.

It is often helpful to identify the role played by a party in a given context. For example, in a construction contract case the identification of a party as the "contractor" or "builder" alleviates the need to tell that that party was the one who was supposed to have built the house.

It is always helpful, and a good general practice, to identify the "plaintiff" and the "defendant." This may seem elementary and uncomplicated, but, especially in view of the creative editing practiced by some casebook editors, it is sometimes a difficult or even impossible task. Bear in mind that the *party presently* seeking something from this court may not be the plaintiff, and that sometimes only the cross-claim of a defendant is treated in the excerpt. Confusing or misaligning the parties can ruin your analysis and understanding of the case.

ISSUE: A statement of the general legal question answered by or illustrated in the case. For clarity, the issue is best put in the form of a question capable of a "yes" or "no" answer. In reality, the issue is simply the Rule of Law put in the form of a question (e.g., "May an offer be accepted by performance?").

The major problem presented in discerning what is *the* issue in the case is that an opinion usually purports to raise and answer several questions. However, except for rare cases, only one such question is really the issue in the case. Collateral issues not necessary to the resolution of the matter in controversy are handled by the court by language known as *"obiter dictum"* or merely *"dictum."* While dicta may be included later in the brief, they have no place under the issue heading.

To find the issue, ask *who wants what* and then go on to ask *why did that party succeed or fail in getting it.* Once this is determined, the "why" should be turned into a question.

The complexity of the issues in the cases will vary, but in all cases a single-sentence question should sum up the issue. *In a few cases,* there will be two, or even more rarely, three issues of equal importance to the resolution of the case. Each should be expressed in a single-sentence question.

Since many issues are resolved by a court in coming to a final disposition of a case, the casebook editor will reproduce the portion of the opinion containing the issue or issues most relevant to the area of law under scrutiny. A noted law professor gave this advice: "Close the book; look at the title on the cover." Chances are, if it is Property, you need not concern yourself with whether, for example, the federal government's treatment of the plaintiff's land really raises a federal question sufficient to support jurisdiction on this ground in federal court.

The same rule applies to chapter headings designating sub-areas within the subjects. They tip you off as to what the text is designed to teach. The cases are arranged in a casebook to show a progression or development of the law, so that the preceding cases may also help.

It is also most important to remember to *read the notes and questions* at the end of a case to determine what the editors wanted you to have gleaned from it.

HOLDING AND DECISION: This section should succinctly explain the rationale of the court in arriving at its decision. In capsulizing the "reasoning" of the court, it should always include an application of the general rule or rules of law to the specific facts of the case. Hidden justifications come to light in this entry: the reasons for the state of the law, the public policies, the biases and prejudices, those considerations that influence the justices' thinking and, ultimately, the outcome of the case. At the end, there should be a short indication of the disposition or procedural resolution of the case (e.g., "Decision of the trial court for Mr. Smith (P) reversed").

The foregoing format is designed to help you "digest" the reams of case material with which you will be faced in your law school career. Once mastered by practice, it will place at your fingertips the information the authors of your casebooks have sought to impart to you in case-by-case illustration and analysis.

B. Be as Economical as Possible in Briefing Cases

Once armed with a format that encourages succinctness, it is as important to be economical with regard to the time spent on the actual reading of the case as it is to be economical in the writing of the brief itself. This does not mean "skimming" a case. Rather, it means reading the case with an "eye" trained to recognize into which "section" of your brief a particular passage or line fits and having a system for quickly and precisely marking the case so that the passages fitting any one particular part of

the brief can be easily identified and brought together in a concise and accurate manner when the brief is actually written.

It is of no use to simply repeat everything in the opinion of the court; record only enough information to trigger your recollection of what the court said. Nevertheless, an accurate statement of the "law of the case," i.e., the legal principle applied to the facts, is absolutely essential to class preparation and to learning the law under the case method.

To that end, it is important to develop a "shorthand" that you can use to make marginal notations. These notations will tell you at a glance in which section of the brief you will be placing that particular passage or portion of the opinion.

Some students prefer to underline all the salient portions of the opinion (with a pencil or colored underliner marker), making marginal notations as they go along. Others prefer the color-coded method of underlining, utilizing different colors of markers to underline the salient portions of the case, each separate color being used to represent a different section of the brief. For example, blue underlining could be used for passages relating to the rule of law, yellow for those relating to the issue, and green for those relating to the holding and decision, etc. While it has its advocates, the color-coded method can be confusing and time-consuming (all that time spent on changing colored markers). Furthermore, it can interfere with the continuity and concentration many students deem essential to the reading of a case for maximum comprehension. In the end, however, it is a matter of personal preference and style. Just remember, whatever method you use, underlining must be used sparingly or its value is lost.

If you take the marginal notation route, an efficient and easy method is to go along underlining the key portions of the case and placing in the margin alongside them the following "markers" to indicate where a particular passage or line "belongs" in the brief you will write:

N   (NATURE OF CASE)
RL   (RULE OF LAW)
I   (ISSUE)
HL   (HOLDING AND DECISION, relates to the RULE OF LAW behind the decision)
HR   (HOLDING AND DECISION, gives the RATIONALE or reasoning behind the decision)
HA   (HOLDING AND DECISION, APPLIES the general principle(s) of law to the facts of the case to arrive at the decision)

Remember that a particular passage may well contain information necessary to more than one part of your brief, in which case you simply note that in the margin. If you are using the color-coded underlining method instead of marginal notation, simply make asterisks or checks in the margin next to the passage in question in the colors that indicate the additional sections of the brief where it might be utilized.

The economy of utilizing "shorthand" in marking cases for briefing can be maintained in the actual brief writing process itself by utilizing "law student shorthand" within the brief. There are many commonly used words and phrases for which abbreviations can be substituted in your briefs (and in your class notes also). You can develop abbreviations that are personal to you and which will save you a lot of time. A reference list of briefing abbreviations can be found on page xii of this book.

C. Use Both the Briefing Process and the Brief as a Learning Tool

Now that you have a format and the tools for briefing cases efficiently, the most important thing is to make the time spent in briefing profitable to you and to make the most advantageous use of the briefs you create. Of course, the briefs are invaluable for classroom reference when you are called upon to explain or analyze a particular case. However, they are also useful in reviewing for exams. A quick glance at the fact summary should bring the case to mind, and a rereading of the rule of law should enable you to go over the underlying legal concept in your mind, how it was applied in that particular case, and how it might apply in other factual settings.

As to the value to be derived from engaging in the briefing process itself, there is an immediate benefit that arises from being forced to sift through the essential facts and reasoning from the court's opinion and to succinctly express them in your own words in your brief. The process ensures that you understand the case and the point that it illustrates, and that means you will be ready to absorb further analysis and information brought forth in class. It also ensures you will have something to say when called upon in class. The briefing process helps develop a mental agility for getting to the *gist* of a case and for identifying, expounding on, and applying the legal concepts and issues found there. The briefing process is the mental process on which you must rely in taking law school examinations; it is also the mental process upon which a lawyer relies in serving his clients and in making his living.

Abbreviations for Briefs

acceptance	acp	offer	O
affirmed	aff	offeree	OE
answer	ans	offeror	OR
assumption of risk	a/r	ordinance	ord
attorney	atty	pain and suffering	p/s
beyond a reasonable doubt	b/r/d	parol evidence	p/e
bona fide purchaser	BFP	plaintiff	P
breach of contract	br/k	prima facie	p/f
cause of action	c/a	probable cause	p/c
common law	c/l	proximate cause	px/c
Constitution	Con	real property	r/p
constitutional	con	reasonable doubt	r/d
contract	K	reasonable man	r/m
contributory negligence	c/n	rebuttable presumption	rb/p
cross	x	remanded	rem
cross-complaint	x/c	res ipsa loquitur	RIL
cross-examination	x/ex	respondeat superior	r/s
cruel and unusual punishment	c/u/p	Restatement	RS
defendant	D	reversed	rev
dismissed	dis	Rule Against Perpetuities	RAP
double jeopardy	d/j	search and seizure	s/s
due process	d/p	search warrant	s/w
equal protection	e/p	self-defense	s/d
equity	eq	specific performance	s/p
evidence	ev	statute	S
exclude	exc	statute of frauds	S/F
exclusionary rule	exc/r	statute of limitations	S/L
felony	f/n	summary judgment	s/j
freedom of speech	f/s	tenancy at will	t/w
good faith	g/f	tenancy in common	t/c
habeas corpus	h/c	tenant	t
hearsay	hr	third party	TP
husband	H	third party beneficiary	TPB
injunction	inj	transferred intent	TI
in loco parentis	ILP	unconscionable	uncon
inter vivos	I/v	unconstitutional	unconst
joint tenancy	j/t	undue influence	u/e
judgment	judgt	Uniform Commercial Code	UCC
jurisdiction	jur	unilateral	uni
last clear chance	LCC	vendee	VE
long-arm statute	LAS	vendor	VR
majority view	maj	versus	v
meeting of minds	MOM	void for vagueness	VFV
minority view	min	weight of authority	w/a
Miranda rule	Mir/r	weight of the evidence	w/e
Miranda warnings	Mir/w	wife	W
negligence	neg	with	w/
notice	ntc	within	w/i
nuisance	nus	without	w/o
obligation	ob	without prejudice	w/o/p
obscene	obs	wrongful death	wr/d

Table of Cases

The Agreement Process

Quick Reference Rules of Law

Lucy v. Zehmer

Purchaser of farm (P) v. Owners of farm (D)

Va. Sup. Ct. of App., 196 Va. 493, 84 S.E.2d 516 (1954).

NATURE OF CASE: Action for specific performance of a land sale contract.

FACT SUMMARY: Zehmer (D) claimed his offer to sell his farm to Lucy (P) was made in jest.

🏛 RULE OF LAW
If a person's words and acts, judged by a reasonable standard, manifest a certain intent, it is immaterial what may be the real but unexpressed state of that person's mind.

FACTS: Zehmer (D) and his wife (D) contracted to sell their 471-acre farm to Lucy (P) for $50,000. Zehmer (D) contended that his offer was made in jest while the three of them were drinking and that Zehmer (D) only desired to bluff Lucy (P) into admitting he did not have $50,000. Lucy (P) appeared to have taken the offer seriously by discussing its terms with Zehmer (D), by rewriting it to enable Mrs. Zehmer (D) to sign also, by providing for title examination, and by taking possession of the agreement. Lucy (P) offered $5 to bind the deal and the next day sold a one-half interest to his brother (P) in order to raise money.

ISSUE: Does the law impute to a person an intention corresponding to the reasonable meaning of his words and acts?

HOLDING AND DECISION: (Buchanan, J.) Yes. The existence of an offer depends upon the reasonable meaning to be given the offeror's acts and words. For the formation of a contract, the mental assent of the parties is not required. If the words and acts of one of the parties have but one reasonable meaning, his undisclosed intention is immaterial except when an unreasonable meaning which he attaches to his manifestations is known to the other party. Accordingly, one cannot say he was merely jesting when his conduct and words would warrant reasonable belief that a real agreement was intended. Reversed and remanded.

▌ ANALYSIS

Note that it is not what is said but how it is heard and reasonably understood. Mutual assent of the parties is required for the formation of a contract, but mental assent is not. Where one party can reasonably believe from the other party's acts and words that a real agreement is intended, the other party's real but unexpressed intention is immaterial. Mutual assent is an objective determination based upon what a reasonable man would believe. An offer is an expression of will or intention creating a power of acceptance upon the offeree. If the offer to sell the farm had been for a price of $50, the court could judge the ridiculousness of the offer in determining whether a reasonable man would believe it to be serious.

Quicknotes

MUTUAL ASSENT A requirement of a valid contract that the parties possess a mutuality of assent as manifested by the terms of the agreement and not by a hidden intent.

OFFER A proposed promise to undertake performance of an action, or to refrain from acting, that is to become binding upon acceptance by the offeree.

Balfour v. Balfour

Ill wife (P) v. Working husband (D)

C.A., 2 K.B. 571 (1919).

NATURE OF CASE: Appeal from award of support based on a contract.

FACT SUMMARY: Mr. Balfour (D), who worked in Ceylon, agreed to pay Mrs. Balfour (P), his wife, a specified monthly sum while she lived in England because of illness.

🏛 **RULE OF LAW**
An agreement is not a valid contract unless the parties intend that it can be sued upon (i.e., intend that it be "attended by legal consequences").

FACTS: Mr. Balfour (D) and Mrs. Balfour (P), husband and wife, lived together in Ceylon, where Mr. Balfour (D) worked, until 1915. In 1915, they came to England during Mr. Balfour's (D) vacation time. When Mr. Balfour (D) needed to return to his work in Ceylon, though, doctors advised Mrs. Balfour (P) to stay in England for a while because of her rheumatoid arthritis. Before leaving, however, Mr. Balfour (D) agreed to send Mrs. Balfour (P) a specified sum per month until she could again join him in Ceylon. Thereafter, though, differences arose between them, and Mr. Balfour (D) suggested that they permanently remain apart. In response, Mrs. Balfour (P) commenced proceedings for restitution of conjugal rights and for alimony in the amount which Mr. Balfour (D) had agreed to pay her monthly. The lower court held that Mr. Balfour (D) was under an obligation to support his wife and that the earlier agreement created a valid contractual agreement to pay her the specified monthly sum. After judgment for Mrs. Balfour (P), Mr. Balfour (D) appealed.

ISSUE: Must the parties to an agreement intend that it can be sued upon in order for such agreement to create a valid contract?

HOLDING AND DECISION: (Lord Atkin, J.) Yes. An agreement is not a valid contract unless the parties intend that it can be sued upon (i.e., intend that it be "attended by legal consequences"). Of course, a husband and wife do not usually intend that the agreements which they make between themselves will be accompanied by any legal consequences. Instead, they make such agreements on the basis of "natural love and affection" and normally intend that the terms of such agreements can be varied as performance proceeds or as disagreements develop. Here, therefore, it is presumed that Mr. (D) and Mrs. (P) Balfour, who made the agreement as husband and wife, did not intend that it could be sued upon. As such, it is not a contract. Judgment reversed.

⟩ ANALYSIS

This case illustrates the general rule that the parties to a contract must intend that it be accompanied by legal consequences. It further illustrates that when a husband and wife are living together, any agreement with respect to the wife's support is presumably based upon a "social obligation" (i.e., no legal consequences are intended, and, therefore, no contract is created). Note, though, that business arrangements between a husband and wife are presumably intended to create legal consequences. Note, also, that separation agreements are presumably intended to create legal consequences (i.e., are enforceable).

■═■

Quicknotes

ALIMONY Allowances (usually monetary) which husband or wife by court order pays to the other spouse for maintenance while they are separated, or after they are divorced (permanent alimony), or temporarily, pending a suit for divorce (pendente lite)

■═■

Texaco, Inc. v. Pennzoil Co.

Oil company (D) v. Oil company (P)

Tex. Ct. of App., 729 S.W.2d 768 (1987).

NATURE OF CASE: Appeal from award for tortious interference with contract.

FACT SUMMARY: Texaco, Inc. (D) contended there was insufficient evidence for the jury to find Pennzoil Co. (P) had entered into a binding agreement with Getty Oil when Texaco (D) made its contract to purchase Getty.

🏛 RULE OF LAW
Whether parties to an agreement intended to be bound by an unexecuted contract is a question of fact.

FACTS: Pennzoil Co. (P) and Getty Oil negotiated a purchase of Getty by Pennzoil (P). The terms were agreed to subject to approval by the respective boards of directors. A press release issued by both companies announced the agreed-upon terms and the ratification requirement. Before the boards met, a Memorandum of Agreement was signed which was also subject to board approval. Texaco, Inc. (D) made a counteroffer to Getty's board, which then repudiated the Memorandum of Agreement and agreed to sell to Texaco (D). Pennzoil (P) sued, contending Texaco (D) tortiously interfered with its contract with Getty. Texaco (D) defended on the basis that until the Memorandum of Agreement was approved, no binding contract existed, and, thus, no interference could be shown. The jury found for Pennzoil (P), and Texaco (D) appealed.

ISSUE: Is it a question of fact whether parties to an agreement intended to be bound by an unexecuted contract?

HOLDING AND DECISION: (Warren, J.) Yes. Whether parties to an agreement intended to be bound by an unexecuted contract is a question of fact. The formation of a valid contract depends on the objective intent of the parties as expressed outwardly in their words and deeds, and not merely on the form that agreement has taken. Under the relevant law, the parties have the power to freely obligate themselves in either a formal or informal manner. To determine intent, a court will look to the parties' outward expressions and not to their subjective or unexpressed intentions. Whether parties intended to be bound only by a formal, signed writing depends on (1) whether a party expressly reserves the right to be bound only when a written agreement is signed; (2) whether there was any partial performance by one party that the party disclaiming the contract accepted; (3) whether all essential terms of the alleged contract had been agreed upon; and (4) whether the complexity or magnitude of the transaction was such that a formal, executed writing would normally be expected. It is the jury's task to evaluate the credibility and weight of the conflicting evidence presented by both sides. Here, the press release was worded in indicative terms rather than hypothetical ones. In addition, statements in the transaction drafts were standard phrases in common business usage and not preconditions to formation. The record as a whole demonstrates that legally and factually sufficient evidence exists to support the jury's finding that the parties had reached an objective agreement on all the essential terms of the transaction and therefore intended to be bound. Judgment affirmed upon remittitur filing reducing punitive damages from $3 million to $1 million.

▶ ANALYSIS

This case represents the largest jury verdict in the history of the civil justice system. Pennzoil (P) was awarded over $10 billion in compensatory and punitive damages, although the award was reduced by the trial court.

Quicknotes

COUNTEROFFER An offer made by the offeree, which has the effect of rejecting the offer deemed unsatisfactory and of proposing a different offer.

PUNITIVE DAMAGES Damages exceeding the actual injury suffered for the purposes of punishment of the defendant, deterrence of the wrongful behavior or comfort to the plaintiff.

REMITTITUR The authority of a court to reduce the amount of damages awarded by the jury.

TORTIOUS INTERFERENCE WITH CONTRACTUAL RELATIONSHIP An intentional tort, whereby a defendant intentionally elicits the breach of a valid contract resulting in damages.

Hawkins v. McGee

Patient (P) v. Physician (D)

N.H. Sup. Ct., 84 N.H. 114, 146 A. 641 (1929).

NATURE OF CASE: Appeal from decision to set aside verdict for breach of warranty of success of an operation.

FACT SUMMARY: Hawkins (P) sued McGee (D) for not making his hand perfect after McGee (D) operated on it.

🏛 RULE OF LAW
The true measure of a buyer's damages is the difference between the value of the goods as they would have been if the warranty as to the quality had been true and the actual value at the time of sale, including any incidental consequences within the contemplation of the parties when they made their contract.

FACTS: Dr. McGee (D) was to remove scar tissue from the right palm of Hawkins (P) and then graft skin from the chest of Hawkins (P) and place it on his palm. McGee (D) stated that the hospital stay should be three to four days, and a few days after that Hawkins (P) could return to work with a 100 percent perfect hand. At trial, McGee (D) argued that even if this statement was made, no reasonable man would understand this as an intention to enter into a contractual relationship. The trial court allowed the jury to consider pain and suffering due to the surgery and the positive ill effects of the surgery. The verdict was in favor of Hawkins (P), but McGee (D) moved to set aside the verdict, because the damages were excessive. The trial court found the damages to be excessive and set aside the verdict, unless Hawkins (P) remitted all sums over $500. When Hawkins (P) refused, the verdict was set aside. Hawkins (P) appealed.

ISSUE: Is the true measure of a buyer's damages the difference between the value of the goods as they would have been if the warranty as to the quality had been true and the actual value at the time of the sale?

HOLDING AND DECISION: (Branch, J.) Yes. The true measure of damage is the difference between the value of the goods as they would have been if the warranty as to the quality had been true and the actual value at the time of the sale, including any incidental consequences within the contemplation of the parties when they made their contract. Therefore, the true measure of damages in the present case is the difference between the value to Hawkins (P) of a perfect hand, such as promised by McGee (D), and the value of the hand in its present condition. Included are any incidental consequences fairly within the contemplation of the parties when they made

the contract. Any other damages are not to be given. Suffering does not measure this difference in value. Pain is incident to a serious operation. Submitting to the jury as a separate element of damage any change for the worse in the condition of the hand was erroneous and misleading. Instead, damages might properly be determined for McGee's (D) failure to improve the condition of the hand. It is unnecessary to consider whether the evidence justified the trial court's finding that damages greater than $500 were excessive. New trial ordered.

▶ ANALYSIS

Prior to a third trial over damages, McGee (D) notified his malpractice insurer, United States Fidelity and Guaranty Co., that he wanted to pay $1,400 to Hawkins (P) to settle the case. He was going to look to them for payment. When the company refused, McGee (D) brought suit, but the court found in favor of the insurance company, having concluded that its policy did not cover special contracts to cure. *McGee v. United States Fidelity & Guaranty Co.*, 53 F.2d 953 (1st Cir. 1931). The insurance company denied coverage as the verdict was for breach of contract and not the tort of malpractice, and its defense was sustained.

■═■

Quicknotes

BREACH OF WARRANTY The breach of a promise made by one party to a contract on which the other party may rely, relieving that party from the obligation of determining whether the fact is true and indemnifying the other party from liability if that fact is shown to be false.

CONSEQUENTIAL DAMAGES Monetary compensation that may be recovered in order to compensate for injuries or losses sustained as a result of damages that are not the direct or foreseeable result of the act of a party, but that nevertheless are the consequence of such act and which must be specifically pled and demonstrated.

CURE In a commercial transaction, the seller has a right to correct a delivery of defective goods within the time originally provided for performance as specified in the contract.

■═■

Sullivan v. O'Connor

Patient (P) v. Plastic surgeon (D)

Mass. Sup. Jud. Ct., 363 Mass. 579, 296 N.E.2d 183 (1973).

NATURE OF CASE: Appeal from verdict for plaintiff in action for medical malpractice and breach of contract.

FACT SUMMARY: [O'Connor (D), a doctor, promised to improve Sullivan's (P) appearance by cosmetic surgery. In fact, O'Connor's (D) efforts left Sullivan (P) with more of a disfigurement than previously.]

🏛 RULE OF LAW
A physician who promises to improve the appearance of a patient through plastic surgery can be sued for breach of contract where the result is not as promised.

FACTS: [Alice Sullivan (P), an entertainer, sued her surgeon after the results of the cosmetic surgery on her nose were less than optimal. After two operations, Sullivan's (P) nose looked worse than it had previously. As a result of the surgery, the nose was disfigured, apparently permanently. Sullivan (P) sued to recover damages from O'Connor (D), alleging both breach of contract and medical malpractice. A jury trial resulted in a verdict for Sullivan (P) on the malpractice claim and for O'Connor (D) on the breach of contract claim and awarded damages.]

ISSUE: Can a physician who promises to improve the appearance of a patient through plastic surgery be sued for breach of contract where the result is not as promised?

HOLDING AND DECISION: (Kaplan, J.) Yes. A physician who promises to improve the appearance of a patient through plastic surgery can be sued for breach of contract where the result is not as promised. Because contracts involving promises by physicians are necessarily predicated on matters which can be no more certain than medical science itself, they are often deemed unenforceable on grounds of public policy. Some decisions recognize and enforce them, however, though the decisions in which they have been enforced are strained. Courts tend not to want to enforce them because of the uncertainties, but sometimes do in order to maintain a check on medical professionals in an effort to hinder charlatans who might make medical promises that can't be kept. The middle road is the wisest: allow such lawsuits, but insist on clear proof.

▶ ANALYSIS

Ordinarily, a nonbreaching party is entitled to recover such compensatory damages as will place him in the same situation as he would have enjoyed had the contract never been breached. Under some circumstances, the nonbreaching party will be awarded restitution only of whatever he has given in performance of the contract, i.e., he will be restored to the position he occupied prior to execution.

◼▬◼

Quicknotes

BREACH OF CONTRACT Unlawful failure by a party to perform its obligations pursuant to contract.

CONTRACTUAL OBLIGATION A duty that someone agrees to perform pursuant to a contract.

EXPRESS PROMISE The expression of an intention to act, or to forbear from acting, granting a right to the promisee to expect and enforce its performance.

MEDICAL MALPRACTICE Conduct on the part of a doctor falling below that demonstrated by other doctors of ordinary skill and competency under the circumstances, resulting in damages.

NEGLIGENCE Conduct falling below the standard of care that a reasonable person would demonstrate under similar conditions.

◼▬◼

Leonard v. Pepsico, Inc.

Consumer (P) v. Company (D)

88 F. Supp. 2d 116 (S.D.N.Y. 1999), *aff'd per curiam*, 210 F.3d 88 (2d Cir. 2000).

NATURE OF CASE: Defense motion for summary judgment.

FACT SUMMARY: Leonard (P) brought suit against Pepsico, Inc. (D) for refusing to comply with terms of an alleged contract.

🏛 RULE OF LAW

An advertisement is not an enforceable offer when it could not be considered by an objective reasonable person as a true offer, rather than as an obvious joke.

FACTS: Leonard (P), after viewing a television commercial from Pepsico, Inc. (D) offering a Harrier Jet Fighter for 7,000,000 "Pepsi points," raised $700,000 (the equivalent of such points) which he proffered to Pepsico (D) as an "acceptance" of its "offer," demanding the Harrier. Pepsico (D) refused to supply the Harrier, arguing that its commercial was obviously done in jest and that no reasonable person could possibly have considered it a real offer. Leonard (P) brought suit on the alleged contract, and Pepsico (D) moved for summary judgment.

ISSUE: Is an advertisement an enforceable offer when it could not be considered by an objective reasonable person as a true offer, rather than as an obvious joke?

HOLDING AND DECISION: (Wood, J.) No. An advertisement is not an enforceable offer when it could not be considered by an objective reasonable person as a true offer, rather than as an obvious joke. A purported offeree's understanding of a television commercial as a true and valid offer must be based on a reasonable person standard. In this case, no objective person could reasonably have concluded that the commercial actually offered consumers a Harrier Jet Fighter. Offering consumers a Harrier Jet Fighter for 7,000,000 "Pepsi points," as did the television commercial, clearly was "done in jest." Obviously, it would be preposterous reasonably to believe that Pepsico (D) would or could award to a consumer a $23 million high-powered military attack aircraft. In light of the "obvious absurdity of the commercial," Pepsico's (D) commercial did not constitute an offer. Defense motion for summary judgment granted.

▶ *ANALYSIS*

The *Leonard* case explains that if it is objectively clear that an offer was not serious, then no offer has been made.

Quicknotes

MOTION FOR SUMMARY JUDGMENT Judgment rendered by a court in response to a motion by one of the parties, claiming that the lack of a question of material fact in respect to an issue warrants disposition of the issue without consideration by the jury.

OFFER A proposed promise to undertake performance of an action, or to refrain from acting, that is to become binding upon acceptance by the offeree.

SPECIFIC PERFORMANCE An equitable remedy whereby the court requires the parties to perform their obligations pursuant to a contract.

■▬■

Hoffman v. Horton

Auction bidder (P) v. Property owner (D)

Va. Sup. Ct., 212 Va. 565, 186 S.E.2d 79 (1972).

NATURE OF CASE: Auction contract.

FACT SUMMARY: The auctioneer missed a bid and closed the auction.

> ## 🏛 RULE OF LAW
> Where a bid is missed or is made simultaneous with the falling of the auctioneer's hammer, he may, in his discretion, reopen the bidding.

FACTS: Horton's (D) property was being sold at auction in a foreclosure sale. The auctioneer (D) had received a bid of $177,000 from Hoffman (P) and, hearing no other bids, struck his hand with his fist to signify that the sale was complete. The auctioneer (D) was immediately notified that he had missed a bid made prior to striking his hand. The auctioneer (D) reopened the auction over Hoffman's (P) protest, and Hoffman (P) finally bought it for $194,000. Hoffman (P) brought suit to recover the difference between $194,000 and $177,000, i.e., $17,000, alleging that his offer of $177,000 had been accepted and a contract formed the instant the auctioneer struck his hand. The court found against Hoffman (P) on the ground that the Uniform Commercial Code (U.C.C.) granted an auctioneer discretion to reopen the bidding if he has missed a bid or one is made while his gavel is falling for the final time.

ISSUE: Does an auctioneer have discretion to reopen bidding at a land sale where a bid has been missed or is made simultaneously with the closing of the sale?

HOLDING AND DECISION: (Carrico, J.) Yes. The U.C.C. does not apply to the sale of real property. However, we are willing to adopt its theory and apply it to such sales. Where the auctioneer misses a bid or one is made prior to or simultaneous with closing of the bidding, an auctioneer has the discretion to reopen the bidding. We do not find that discretion was abused herein. Judgment affirmed.

> ## ▶ ANALYSIS
> U.C.C. § 2-328(2) covers auctions and sales dealing with personal property, and the rules are the same as announced in *Hoffman*. Because of the special nature of auctions and the fact that no injury is suffered by the bidder (i.e., reliance), the mistake is rectified at once, and acceptance of the offer was based on a mistake. There is also an implied condition to the offer that it be accepted only if it is the highest bid.

■■■

Quicknotes

FORECLOSURE SALE Termination of an interest in property, usually initiated by a lienholder upon failure to tender mortgage payments, resulting in the sale of the property in order to satisfy the debt.

■■■

Lonergan v. Scolnick

Interested buyer (P) v. Property seller (D)

Ca. Dist. App. Ct., 129 Cal. App. 2d 179, 276 P.2d 8 (1954).

NATURE OF CASE: Appeal from judgment for defendant in action for breach of contract.

FACT SUMMARY: Scolnick (D) sold his property before Lonergan (P) had a chance to respond to a letter asking for an immediate decision on the property.

RULE OF LAW
No contract is formed if the party knows or has reason to know that the other party does not intend to enter into a binding agreement without some further assurance.

FACTS: Scolnick (D) advertised real property for sale. Lonergan (P) wrote him to inquire where the property was located and what its price was. Scolnick (D) advised him of price and location and that he needed a decision soon since he had another interested party. Lonergan (P) visited the property but wrote Scolnick (D) to make certain that this was where the property was located. Scolnick (D) agreed to the escrow agent chosen by Lonergan (P) and stated that it was probably Scolnick's (D) property which Lonergan (P) had visited. Scolnick (D) stated that he needed an immediate decision from Lonergan (P) as to whether he wanted the property. Before Lonergan (P) even received the letter, Scolnick (D) had sold the property to a third party. Lonergan (P) sued, and Scolnick (D) stated that the correspondence merely constituted preliminary negotiations and no unequivocal offer had ever been made by Scolnick (D).

ISSUE: Is a contract formed if the party knows or has reason to know that the other party does not intend to enter into a binding agreement without some further assurance?

HOLDING AND DECISION: (Barnard, J.) No. No contract is formed if the party knows or has reason to know that the other party does not intend to enter into a binding agreement without some further assurance. An acceptance and an offer must be unequivocal and show that the parties intended them to constitute a present, binding agreement. Where further assurances are requested, a party knows or should know that the response is not an offer or acceptance but is merely part of the preliminary negotiations. Scolnick (D), based on his response, did not treat Lonergan's (P) letter as an offer, and his response was not acceptance, but merely a request for a definite offer. The newspaper advertisement was merely a solicitation of offers. No contract was formed. Judgment for Scolnick (D) affirmed.

ANALYSIS

In *Fairmont Glass Works*, 51 S.W. 196 (1899), the plaintiff inquired as to the defendant's lowest price on 10 loads of Mason jars. The reply was "$4.50 to $5.00 for immediate acceptance." The defendant refused to fill plaintiff's subsequent order. The court held that the defendant's reply was not a quotation of prices but a definite offer to sell. "For immediate acceptance" was deemed to constitute an offer to sell at these prices.

Quicknotes

BREACH OF CONTRACT Unlawful failure by a party to perform its obligations pursuant to contract.

Fairmount Glass Works v. Crunden-Martin Woodenware Company

Glass company(D) v. Jar buyer (P)

Ky. Ct. of App., 106 Ky. 659, 51 S.W. 196 (1899).

NATURE OF CASE: Appeal from judgment for plaintiff in action to recover damages for breach of contract for sale of goods.

FACT SUMMARY: Crunden-Martin Woodenware Company (Cruden-Martin) (P) requested by letter of Fairmount Glass Works (Fairmount) (D) the lowest price it could give on Crunden-Martin (P) order for Mason jars, which prices Fairmount (D) gave to Crunden-Martin (P) but whose order Fairmount (D) then refused to fill.

🏛 RULE OF LAW
Where prices are requested on an order and the vendor quotes those prices to the vendee, the vendor has offered to fill the order and is obligated to fill the order upon receipt within a reasonable time of vendee's acceptance.

FACTS: Crunden-Martin Woodenware Company (Crunden-Martin) (P) requested of Fairmount Glass Works (Fairmount) (D) by letter dated April 20, 1895, the lowest price at which Fairmount (D) could fill Crunden-Martin's (P) order for ten carloads of Mason jars. Fairmount (D) answered by letter dated April 23, 1895, with its prices for different sizes of jars with terms and conditions "for immediate acceptance." Crunden-Martin (P) telegraphed a reply on April 24, 1895, to "enter order ten carloads as per your quotation. Specifications mailed." The same day, Fairmount (D) telegraphed back it could not fill the order; its output was sold out. Fairmount (D) then received by mail Crunden's (P) specifications calling for "strictly first quality goods," which Fairmount (D) contended was not an acceptance of their offer (if the court found an offer) as made.

ISSUE: Where prices are requested on an order and the vendor quotes those prices to the vendee, has the vendor offered to fill the order and become obligated to fill the order upon receipt within a reasonable time of vendee's acceptance?

HOLDING AND DECISION: (Hobson, J.) Yes. Where prices are requested on an order and the vendor quotes those prices to the vendee, the vendor has offered to fill the order and is obligated to fill the order upon receipt within a reasonable time of vendee's acceptance. The quotation of prices "for immediate acceptance" upon vendee's order was more than a simple quotation of prices; it was an offer. The true meaning of the correspondence is determined by reading it as a whole. After vendee had accepted the terms, the vendor could not withdraw its offer. Vendor's use of the term "for immediate acceptance" when considered with previous communication indicates an intent to make an offer to vendee, who could then accept or reject within a reasonable time. Vendor's claim that vendee's specifications, which were received after vendor withdrew its offer, were not within the terms of vendee's telegraphed acceptance fails as vendor did not state this objection in its withdrawal of its offer. Judgment affirmed.

▶ ANALYSIS

Ordinarily, the mere quotation of prices is not an offer to sell at those prices but rather an invitation to make an offer. Where the evidence shows the intent of the parties to be otherwise, that is to say, that an offer was intended, the general rule will not be followed. The existence of an offer is determined by considering what a reasonable man would believe from his consideration of the words and acts of the other party. It is also suggested that the court is holding the vendee's price inquiry upon an order as a strong basis for vendee's reliance on the vendor's price quotation. Where the price quotation is unsolicited or in response to the general question of what the vendor's lowest price would be, the vendee lacks the reliance seen in this case.

Quicknotes

BREACH OF CONTRACT Unlawful failure by a party to perform its obligations pursuant to contract.

Haines v. City of New York

Developer (P) v. City government (D)

N.Y. Ct. of App., 41 N.Y.2d 769, 364 N.E.2d 820 (1977).

NATURE OF CASE: Appeal from judgment for plaintiff in action to compel performance.

FACT SUMMARY: An action was brought to require the City of New York (D) to build a new sewage treatment plant for the benefit of additional users of the system.

🏛 RULE OF LAW
Where no duration is specified, the court may determine the intentions of the parties in order to ascertain the proposed term of the contract.

FACTS: The City of New York (the City) (D), pursuant to a statutory authorization, entered into a contract to construct a sewage system consisting of a plant, sewer mains, and laterals. All construction costs and subsequent maintenance, operation, and repair were to be borne by the City (D). The contract was executed in 1924. By the 1970s, the flow through the plant was at its maximum capacity. Any increase in usage would have rendered the purification treatment nugatory and would have interfered with the quality of the water leaving the treatment plant. Haines (P) sought approval to develop his land into a subdivision. The City (D) refused permission on the ground that the sewage plant could not handle the increased flow. Haines (P) brought suit, alleging that the City's (D) obligation under the contract was perpetual and that it was obligated to construct additional plants under it if usage required. The trial court and appellate court held for Haines (P). The City (D) appealed.

ISSUE: Where a contract does not contain a clause specifying its duration, may the courts determine the parties' intent in order to ascertain the term and scope of the contract?

HOLDING AND DECISION: (Gabrielli, J.) Yes. Where no duration is specified, the court may determine the intentions of the parties in order to ascertain the proposed term of the contract. Unless a contract specifically states that it is to be perpetual, no such intention will be presumed. Where no duration is specified, the court must inquire into the intentions of the parties and the facts surrounding the execution of the contract to ascertain the term intended by them. Where duration can be fairly and reasonably fixed by implication, a contract will not be deemed terminable at will. Where no duration is specified, it will normally be presumed that the parties intended it to continue for a reasonable time. Under the circumstances herein, this would be until the City (D) no longer needed or desired the water purity that the plant was designed to insure. The City (D), however, obligated itself to build only one plant and to expand it for future needs. The City (D) cannot be required to build additional plants under the agreement or to reduce the water purity requirement to handle additional needs. Judgment modified to reflect judgment for City (D).

▶ ANALYSIS

Contracts of agency or employment are deemed terminable at will where no duration is specified. *Clark Paper & Mfg. Co. v. Stenacher*, 236 N.Y. 312, 140 N.E. 708 (1923). A contract will never be deemed to be perpetual in duration absent a clear, unequivocal promise in the contract. *Mitler v. Freideberg*, 32 Misc. 2d 78, 222 N.Y.S.2d 480 (1961). Rather, as was held in *Haines*, the court will attempt to determine the intention of the parties. 1 Williston, *Contract* § 38.

■=■

Wagenseller v. Scottsdale Memorial Hospital

Terminated employee (P) v. Supervisor (D)

Az. Sup. Ct., 147 Ariz. 370, 710 P.2d 1025, en banc (1985).

NATURE OF CASE: Appeal of summary judgment dismissing action for wrongful termination.

FACT SUMMARY: Wagenseller (P) allegedly was fired for refusing to join her supervisor in committing acts of indecent exposure during a camping trip.

RULE OF LAW
An employer may terminate an at-will employee for good cause or no cause but not for cause contrary to public policy.

FACTS: Wagenseller (P) worked at Scottsdale Memorial Hospital (the Hospital) (D). Her supervisor was Smith (D). According to Wagenseller (P), her relationship with Smith (D) began to deteriorate when, on a camping trip, Wagenseller (P) refused to join in a skit wherein the participants "mooned" the audience. Wagenseller (P) alleged that this led to her termination. She sued Smith (D) and the Hospital (D). The trial court entered summary judgment dismissing the action, holding that, as an at-will employee, Wagenseller (P) could be fired for any reason. The court of appeals affirmed. The Arizona Supreme Court granted review.

ISSUE: May an employer terminate an at-will employee for any cause?

HOLDING AND DECISION: (Feldman, J.) No. An employer may terminate an at-will employee for good cause or no cause but not for cause contrary to public policy. Originally, the doctrine of at-will employment gave employers the right to terminate for any reason. Increasingly, courts have recognized that this area of law involves a balancing of the employer's interest in its ability to manage itself against society's interest in a stable work force and the prevention of acts contrary to public policy. When an employer fires an employee for reasons inimical to public policy, society is hurt. Therefore, the proper balance is to permit an employer to fire for no cause or good cause but not for "bad" cause. As to what defines public policy, one must consult statutes, the constitution, as well as prior judicial decisions. The public policy must be truly public and not a private or proprietary interest for the courts to apply this exception to "at-will" employment. To permit an employer to fire an employee for refusing to break a law would certainly be contrary to the policy expressed in that law. Here, "mooning" arguably constitutes indecent exposure, which is a violation of the criminal code. Wagenseller (P) may not be fired for refusing to violate this law, and therefore, this action must be tried on the merits. This decision does not, however, create a new employment contract between the parties. Termination for a reason which may violate public policy is simply not a right inherent in the existing contract. Affirmed in part, reversed in part, and remanded.

ANALYSIS

The court considered two other theories presented by Wagenseller (P). The first involved her contention that her firing was contrary to procedures outlined in the employment manual, which was part of an implied-in-fact contract. The court agreed that she should be permitted to litigate this. The court rejected, however, her contention that every employment relationship contained an implied-in-law covenant of good faith. This, said the court, would essentially abrogate the at-will doctrine, which it declined to do.

Quicknotes

AT-WILL EMPLOYMENT The rule that an employment relationship is subject to termination at any time, or for any cause, by an employee or an employer in the absence of a specific agreement otherwise.

PUBLIC POLICY Policy administered by the state with respect to the health, safety and morals of its people in accordance with common notions of fairness and decency.

WRONGFUL TERMINATION Unlawful termination of an individual's employment.

Joseph Martin, Jr., Delicatessen, Inc. v. Schumacher

Landlord (P) v. Tenant (D)

N.Y. Ct. App., 52 N.Y.2d 105, 417 N.E.2d 541 (1981).

NATURE OF CASE: Appeal from denial of specific enforcement.

FACT SUMMARY: Schumacher (D) sought to enforce a lease provision which stated that the lease may be renewed at a rental "to be agreed upon."

🏛 RULE OF LAW
A real estate lease provision calling for the renewal of the lease at a rental to be agreed upon is unenforceable due to its omission of a material term.

FACTS: Schumacher (D) leased a store from Martin (P) for a five-year term at a specified rental. A clause in the lease provided that Schumacher (D), as tenant, was entitled to renew the lease for an additional five-year term at a rental "to be agreed upon." Schumacher (D) gave timely notice of his desire to exercise his privilege of renewal, and Martin (P) responded that the price would be $900 a month, almost double the current rent. Schumacher (D) hired an appraiser, who placed the fair market value of the store at $545 a month. Schumacher (D) then filed suit for specific performance. Martin (P) brought a separate eviction action, and the trial court ruled in his favor, holding that the lease provision was only an agreement to agree and therefore unenforceable. On appeal, the court expressly overruled an established line of precedents and held that Schumacher (D) should be able to prove whether a binding agreement by the parties was intended. Martin (P) appealed.

ISSUE: Is a real estate lease provision calling for the renewal of the lease at a rental to be agreed upon unenforceable due to its omission of a material term?

HOLDING AND DECISION: (Fuchsberg, J.) Yes. A real estate lease provision calling for the renewal of the lease at a rental to be agreed upon is unenforceable due to its omission of a material term. It is a well-settled principle of law that a court may enforce a contract only where the terms of that contract are sufficiently certain and specific. Otherwise, a court would be forced to impose its own conception of what the parties should or might have agreed upon, rather than attempting to implement the bargain actually made. For that reason, a mere agreement to agree on a material term in the future without any details as to the methods of ascertaining that term cannot be enforced since the court, rather than the parties, would be creating the agreement. A real estate lease which provides for a renewal term at a rental to be agreed upon is nothing more than an agreement to agree and, hence, cannot be enforced due to its omission of a material term. Reversed.

CONCURRENCE: (Meyer, J.) While the majority was correct in its decision in the instant case, it goes too far in suggesting that such a lease provision would never be enforceable.

DISSENT IN PART: (Jasen, J.) Although the renewal clause was unenforceable due to its uncertainty, Schumacher (D) should have been able to prove his entitlement to renewal of the lease on other grounds.

▶ ANALYSIS

The difficulty courts have in enforcing contracts which are left incomplete by the parties is illustrated by the case of *Ansorge v. Kane,* 244 N.Y. 395 (1927). The parties had agreed on a sale of land and had specified the price and the amount which was to be paid in cash up front. The manner of the deferred payments was "to be agreed upon." When the seller reneged, the buyer sought specific performance. In denying the remedy, the court held that an agreement to agree upon such a material term as contract payments rendered the contract unenforceable. However, the court stated that had the contract been absolutely silent regarding the payments, rather than saying they would be as agreed upon, the contract could have been enforced using reasonable and customary payment terms.

Quicknotes

FAIR MARKET VALUE The price of particular property or goods that a buyer would offer and a seller would accept in the open market following full disclosure.

SPECIFIC PERFORMANCE An equitable remedy whereby the court requires the parties to perform their obligations pursuant to a contract.

BMC Industries, Inc. v. Barth Industries, Inc.

Eyeglass lens manufacturer (P) v. Equipment manufacturer (D)

160 F.3d 1322 (11th Cir. 1998).

NATURE OF CASE: Appeal from denial of defendant's post-trial motions in breach of contract action.

FACT SUMMARY: BMC Industries, Inc. (P) sued Barth Industries, Inc. (Barth) (D) for breach of contract when Barth (D) failed to deliver automated machinery. The trial court held the Uniform Commercial Code (U.C.C.) did not apply to the contract between the parties because it was a contract for services. On appeal, the court reconsidered the applicability of the U.C.C.

> ## ⚖ RULE OF LAW
> The court considers the "predominant factor," or the purpose of the contract, when evaluating the applicability of the U.C.C. to a contract involving both goods and services.

FACTS: BMC Industries, Inc. (BMC) (P) manufactured lenses used in eyeglasses. Competitors used foreign labor, so BMC (P) decided to automate portions of its manufacturing process. BMC (P) sought to accomplish this by contracting with Barth Industries, Inc. (Barth) (D) for the "design, manufacture, and installation" of automated manufacturing equipment. Barth (D) was to deliver the equipment on a certain date, but failed to do so. Eighteen months after the scheduled delivery date, BMC (P) sued Barth (D) for breach of contract. Barth (D) countersued for breach of contract and the case went before a jury. The jury returned a verdict for BMC (P) and awarded damages of $3 million. Barth (D) moved for judgment as a matter of law and for a new trial, both of which were denied. Barth (D) appealed the denial of both motions.

ISSUE: Does the court consider the "predominant factor," or the purpose of the contract, when evaluating the applicability of the U.C.C. to a contract involving both goods and services?

HOLDING AND DECISION: (Tjoflat, J.) Yes. The court considers the "predominant factor," or the purpose of the contract, when evaluating the applicability of the U.C.C. to a contract involving both goods and services. The U.C.C. Article 2 only applies to contracts involving the sale of goods but many contracts are hybrid contracts involving the sale of both services and goods. Many courts consider the "predominant factor", or purpose, of the hybrid contract to determine if the U.C.C. Article 2 should apply to the contract. The determination of the type of contract is generally a fact question, but if the terms of the contract are undisputed, it becomes a legal question. The court must then find the primary purpose of the contract. If the primary purpose of the contract is for services, the

U.C.C. does not apply. Courts look to the contractual language and the billing method when applying the "predominant factor" test. First, the language may refer to the parties as "buyer" and "seller", which implies a contract for goods. Second, the billing method may result in greater payment for services rendered, which implies a contract for services. In the present case, the design and manufacture implied a contract for services to the trial court. In applying the "predominant factor" test, however, the contract appears to be one for goods. The language includes a title of "Purchase Order" which is typically goods, and the parties refer to themselves as "buyer" and "seller." The parties contemplated payment on a delivery schedule of the completed machines rather than upon completion of the design and manufacturer's services. Finally, the BMC-Barth contract had to rely at least in part on services because no company had ever automated this type of manufacturing before, so the design and manufacturer's services were essential. The finished product was the purpose, however. The U.C.C.'s Article 2 should apply to this contract. Denial of Barth's (D) motion for judgment as a matter of law is affirmed. Denial of Barth's (D) motion for a new trial is reversed based on the U.C.C. contract issues and remanded for retrial on claims against Barth and counterclaims based on the U.C.C.

▶ ANALYSIS

Courts typically apply the "gravamen" test or the "predominant factor" test. The gravamen test involves the courts looking to the portion of the contract which is the subject of the complaint to determine if it involves goods or services. More jurisdictions employ the "predominant factor" test because it considers the entire contract and not just one portion out of context.

■≡■

Quicknotes

BREACH OF CONTRACT Unlawful failure by a party to perform its obligations pursuant to contract.

GRAVAMEN The material part of a cause of action setting forth the injury that is sought to be redressed.

■≡■

Southwest Engineering Co. v. Martin Tractor Co., Inc.

Contracting purchaser (P) v. Breaching supplier (D)

Kan. Sup. Ct., 205 Kan. 684, 473 P.2d 18 (1970).

NATURE OF CASE: Action in damages for breach of contract.

FACT SUMMARY: Martin Tractor Co., Inc. (D) refused to fill Southwest Engineering Co.'s (P) order, alleging that the mode of payment had not been decided and, therefore, no contract existed.

🏛 RULE OF LAW
Once a contract is found to exist, the court may supply missing terms.

FACTS: Southwest Engineering Co. (Southwest) (P) needed a generator and other equipment. Southwest (P) entered into an agreement with Martin Tractor Co., Inc. (Martin) (D) to supply the equipment. One of Martin's (D) officers agreed to supply the generator for $21,500, which included a 10 percent discount and the additional equipment at Martin's (D) cost. A memorandum was prepared by Martin's (D) officer, and he printed his name at the top. Martin (D) subsequently refused to perform, and Southwest (P) had to purchase the items elsewhere at a higher cost. At trial for the difference, Martin (D) alleged that the contract violated the Statute of Frauds because the memorandum was not signed and did not contain needed terms. Martin (D) also claimed that the method of payment could not be agreed upon by the parties, and this prevented a finding that a contract existed. The court found for Southwest (P).

ISSUE: If a contract is found to exist, may the court provide missing terms?

HOLDING AND DECISION: (Fontron, J.) Yes. Once a contract is found to exist, the court may supply the missing terms. The Uniform Commercial Code (U.C.C.) provides a framework to fill in missing terms, as does prior common law. For example, where the method of payment is in dispute, the U.C.C. § 2-310 states that the normal method of payment is upon delivery. U.C.C. § 2-204(3) states that even though one or more terms are left open, the contract will not fail for indefiniteness if the parties intended to enter into a contract and there is a reasonably certain basis for giving an appropriate remedy. The memorandum contains the essential terms of sale and is binding. Affirmed.

▶ ANALYSIS

A "signing" is merely required for authentication. A billhead or letterhead, logo, etc., are sufficient so long as they tend to indicate that the memorandum is legitimate. "Quantity" is generally the one term the U.C.C. will not attempt to supply. If there is no basis for determining the amount of goods covered by the contract, no contract exists. A special exception is made in requirements and output contract since quantity may be determined by implying good faith and reasonableness into the contract.

■═■

Quicknotes

BREACH OF CONTRACT Unlawful failure by a party to perform its obligations pursuant to contract.

■═■

Copeland v. Baskin Robbins U.S.A.

Purchaser (P) v. Seller (D)

Cal. Ct. App., 96 Cal. App. 4th 1251, 117 Cal Rptr. 2d 875 (2002).

NATURE OF CASE: Action for breach of contract.

FACT SUMMARY: Copeland (P) brought a breach of contract action against Baskin Robbins (D) on the theory that an enforceable contract was formed by the parties' agreement to agree on a mutual purchase arrangement.

⚖ RULE OF LAW
A contract to negotiate an agreement can be formed and breached like any other contract.

FACTS: Baskin Robbins (D) publicly announced its intentions to close one of its manufacturing plants and Copeland (P) expressed an interest in acquiring it, provided Baskin Robbins (D) would agree to purchase ice cream he manufactured at the plant. The parties reached a tentative agreement that Copeland (P) would purchase the plant and Baskin Robbins (D) would purchase seven million gallons of ice cream from Copeland (P) over a three-year period. This duel purchasing arrangement is known as "co-packing" and was considered critical to Copeland (P). The agreement was confirmed in letters between the parties and Copeland (P) submitted a $3,000 deposit to Baskin Robbins (D). Negotiations broke down, however, over the additional terms for the purchase of the ice cream, including the price, flavor, quality control standards, trademark protection and who would bear the loss from spoilage. Baskin Robbins (D) returned Copeland's (P) deposit and informed Copeland (P) that it would continue negotiations on the sale of the plant and the lease of the plant's assets, but not on the part of the agreement for purchase of the ice cream. Copeland (P) sued alleging Baskin Robbins (D) breached the contract by refusing to reach agreement on the terms for the co-packing agreement. The trial court granted Baskin Robbins's (D) motion for summary judgment finding that the essential elements of the co-packing deal were never agreed upon, and, consequently, there was no enforceable contract.

ISSUE: Can a contract to negotiate an agreement be formed and breached like any other contract?

HOLDING AND DECISION: (Johnson, J.) Yes. A contract to negotiate an agreement can be formed and breached like any other contract. It is still a general rule that where the essential elements of a promise are reserved for future agreement that no legal obligation arises until that future agreement is reached. However, persons are free to enter into contracts for anything that does not involve illegal or immoral subject matter, and a valid contract to negotiate the remaining terms of a contract can be entered into by the parties. This is distinguishable from an unenforceable "agreement to agree" for two reasons. First, a contract to negotiate terms of an agreement is not of the same substance as a mere "agreement to agree" in that such a contract is discharged as long as the parties negotiate in good faith. Second, performance is ascertainable in that sufficient terms of the negotiation can be articulated creating the required substantive elements of the contract. In this instance, where the negotiations concern the sale of goods, the correspondence between the parties sufficiently identified the subject matter as more than just an "idea," and binds the parties to complete the negotiations. Consequently, the covenant of good faith and fair dealing applies. Sound public policy reasons exist for protecting parties from bad faith practices during business negotiations. Negotiations today are extremely complex and are often reached on a piecemeal basis through a series of communications. These slow forming contracts are time consuming and costly and the parties' investments should be protected from bad faith dealing. However, damages lie only on the basis of reliance theory because expectation damages are not ascertainable. Here, Copeland (P) cannot recover because there is no way to know what the ultimate terms of the agreement would have been if there had ever been an agreement. Judgment affirmed.

▶ ANALYSIS

This decision attempts to reach an equitable result by recognizing the complexity and cost associated with modern business negotiations while balancing available damages should a party succeed on this theory of breach. It should be noted that the court of appeals still affirmed the trial court's grant of summary judgment to Baskin Robbins (D). The court of appeals found that the proper measure of damages for breach of a contract to negotiate would be reliance damages, or those damages incurred by the plaintiff's reliance on the defendant to negotiate in good faith. This measure of damages would encompass the plaintiff's out-of-pocket costs in conducting the negotiations and potentially lost opportunity costs. Expectation damages cannot be recovered as there is no adequate way of predicting the terms of the final agreement or if such a final agreement would have been reached. In this instance, Copeland (P) failed to establish reliance damages and summary judgment was still appropriate.

■=■

Continued on next page.

Quicknotes

EXPECTATION DAMAGES Damages awarded in actions for non-performance of a contract, which are calculated by subtracting the injured party's actual dollar position as a result of the breach from that party's expected dollar position had the breach not occurred.

■━■

Oglebay Norton Co. v. Armco, Inc.

Shipping company (P) v. Mining company (D)

Ohio Sup. Ct., 52 Ohio St. 3d 232, 556 N.E.2d 515 (1990).

NATURE OF CASE: Appeal from a judgment ordering specific performance of a long-term shipping contract.

FACT SUMMARY: When Oglebay Norton Co. (Oglebay) (P) and Armco, Inc. (D) could not agree on a shipping rate under their long-term contract, Oglebay (P) sought a declaratory judgment from the court that the contract rate was the correct rate, or, alternatively, that the court would set a reasonable rate.

🏛 RULE OF LAW
If the parties intend to conclude a contract for the sale of goods where the price is not settled, the price is a reasonable price at the time of delivery if the price is to be fixed in terms of an agreed standard set by a third person or agency and is not so set.

FACTS: Oglebay Norton Co. (Oglebay) (P) and Armco, Inc. (D) had a long-term contract for Oglebay (P) to ship iron ore for Armco (D). The price was established by reference to the regular rates as published in Skillings Mining Review. The contract was modified four times during the next 23 years, requiring substantial capital investment by Oglebay (P). When the parties were not able to agree on a rate after Skillings ceased publishing, Oglebay (P) sought a declaratory judgment that the contract rate was the correct rate or, alternatively, for the court to declare a reasonable rate. The court set the rate for that season at $6.25 per gross ton, requiring notification of the court if the parties could not agree on a future rate. A court-appointed mediator would then help them reach a mutual agreement. The court of appeals affirmed. Armco (D) appealed.

ISSUE: If the parties intend to conclude a contract for the sale of goods and the price is not settled, is the price a reasonable price at the time of delivery if the price is to be fixed in terms of an agreed standard set by a third person or agency and is not set?

HOLDING AND DECISION: (Per curiam) Yes. If the parties intend to conclude a contract for the sale of goods and the price is not settled, the price is a reasonable price at the time of delivery if the price is to be fixed in terms of an agreed standard set by a third person or agency and it is not so set. In this case, the undisputed dramatic changes in the market prices of Great Lakes shipping rates and the length of the contract would make it impossible for a court to award Oglebay (P) accurate damages due to Armco's (D) breach. Thus, specific performance of the contract is necessary. Moreover, ordering the parties to mediate for the duration of the contract is proper, given their unique business relationship, and their intent to be bound. Affirmed.

▶ ANALYSIS

The fourth modification, in 1980, of the contract at issue here extended it to the year 2010. To meet Armco's (D) requirements, Oglebay (P) then began a $95 million capital improvement program. The parties were unable to agree on a rate after a serious downturn in the iron and steel industry in 1984. In the face of those changed circumstances, Armco (D) had argued that the complete breakdown of the primary and secondary contract pricing mechanisms rendered the 1957 contract unenforceable.

■■■

Quicknotes

DAMAGES Monetary compensation that may be awarded by the court to a party who has sustained injury or loss to his person, property or rights due to another party's unlawful act, omission or negligence.

SPECIFIC PERFORMANCE An equitable remedy whereby the court requires the parties to perform their obligations pursuant to a contract.

■■■

Eckles v. Sharman

Basketball bankruptcy trustee (P) v. Basketball coach (D)

548 F.2d 905 (10th Cir. 1977).

NATURE OF CASE: Appeal from award for breach of contract.

FACT SUMMARY: The trial court entered a directed verdict holding Sharman (D) had, as a matter of law, breached his contract because the portions not agreed to by the parties were not material.

🏛 RULE OF LAW
Whether contract terms are material to the parties' agreement is a question of fact and not proper for a directed verdict.

FACTS: Sharman (D) contracted to coach the Los Angeles Stars of the American Basketball League. The team was sold to Mountain States Sports, and pursuant to the sales agreement, Mountain States was not obligated to assume the Sharman (D) contract unless he agreed to move with the team. The contract included a provision for Sharman (D) to be given a pension, yet no specifics on this point were ever agreed upon. It also allowed Sharman (D) an option to purchase a percentage of the team. No agreement was ever made concerning the pension and option clauses. Sharman (D) resigned as coach and contracted to coach the Los Angeles Lakers of the National Basketball Association. Mountain States declared bankruptcy, and Eckles (P), the trustee, sued Sharman (D) and the Lakers (D) for breach and inducement to breach. Sharman (D) contended that the contract was invalid because of the lack of agreement on the pension and option clauses. The court directed a verdict for Eckles (P), declaring as a matter of law, these two provisions were not material and did not invalidate the contract. Sharman (D) and the Lakers (D) appealed.

ISSUE: Is it a question of fact whether terms of a contract are so material as to render the agreement unenforceable if they are not agreed upon?

HOLDING AND DECISION: (Breitenstein, J.) Yes. It is a question of fact whether particular contract provisions are so material as to render the contract unenforceable in the absence of an agreement on those provisions. In this case, the jury could have found that Sharman (D) would not have intended to be bound by the contract if the pension and option provisions were not worked out. Whether the parties intended the contract to be enforceable in the absence of agreement on these points was not a question of law and should have been decided by the jury. Retrial ordered.

▶ ANALYSIS

The main issue in this case was the intent of the parties. This is inherently a question of fact. The court erred in directing a verdict of liability, holding as a matter of law, the parties' intent was not to invalidate the entire contract without agreement on the two provisions.

■■■

Quicknotes

BREACH OF CONTRACT Unlawful failure by a party to perform its obligations pursuant to contract.

DIRECTED VERDICT A verdict ordered by the court in a jury trial.

ISSUE OF MATERIAL FACT A fact that is disputed between two or more parties to litigation that is essential to proving an element of the cause of action or a defense asserted, or which would otherwise affect the outcome of the proceeding.

■■■

Broadnax v. Ledbetter

Good citizen (P) v. Texas sheriff (D)

Tex. Sup. Ct., 100 Tex. 375, 99 S.W. 1111 (1907).

NATURE OF CASE: Certified question to the state supreme court.

FACT SUMMARY: [A Texas sheriff (D) offered a reward for the capture and return to jail of an escaped prisoner. The plaintiff (P) returned the prisoner, but the sheriff (D) refused to pay. The plaintiff sued.]

🏛 RULE OF LAW
An enforceable contract is not formed where one party offers a reward for a service, but the party that performs the service doesn't know about the reward.

FACTS: [A Texas sheriff (D) offered a reward for the capture and return to jail of an escaped prisoner. The plaintiff (P) returned the prisoner, but the sheriff (D) refused to pay. The plaintiff (P) sued. The Court of Civil Appeals of the Third Supreme Judicial District certified a question to the Texas Supreme Court.]

ISSUE: Is an enforceable contract formed where one party offers a reward for a service, but the party that performs the service doesn't know about the reward?

HOLDING AND DECISION: [Judge not stated in casebook excerpt.] No. An enforceable contract is not formed where one party offers a reward for a service, but the party that performs the service doesn't know about the reward. A mere offer or promise to pay does not give rise to a contract, because a contract requires an assent or meeting of two minds. A contract is therefore not formed until the offer is accepted, and if there is no knowledge of the offer, there can be no acceptance, and therefore, no contract. The value of the service to the offeror is not the test; he's only responsible if he induces others to act because of his offer, and the acting upon this inducement is what supplies the mutual assent and the consideration. Finally, public policy does not warrant a finding here that the contract should be enforced, on grounds that it will help fight crime. People cannot be moved to action by offers of rewards that they don't know about, so that public policy argument is flawed.

▶ *ANALYSIS*

It might seem unfair that the plaintiff in this case does not receive the reward, since he performed the service called for, but fairness is irrelevant in this case. The simple fact is that acceptance cannot occur without knowledge of the offer. Because there can be no contract without acceptance, there also can be no breach.

Quicknotes

ACCEPTANCE Assent to the specified terms of an offer resulting in the formation of a binding agreement.

OFFER A proposed promise to undertake performance of an action, or to refrain from acting, that is to become binding upon acceptance by the offeree.

MCC-Marble Ceramic Center, Inc. v. Ceramica Nuova d'Agostino

Signing party (P) v. Drafting party (D)

144 F.3d 1384 (11th Cir. 1998).

NATURE OF CASE: [Nature of case not stated in casebook excerpt.]

FACT SUMMARY: MCC-Marble Ceramic Center, Inc. (P) sought not to be bound to the terms written on the reverse side of a contract which its agent, Monzon, signed, and which were in the Italian language.

🏛 RULE OF LAW
Parties who sign contracts are bound by them regardless of whether they have read or understood their terms.

FACTS: Monzon, MCC-Marble Ceramic Center, Inc.'s (MCC's) (P) agent, signed a contract while in Italy. Above the signature line was a provision incorporating the terms located on the reverse side of the form. The contract's terms were in the Italian language and Monzon neither spoke nor read Italian.

ISSUE: Are parties who sign contracts bound by them regardless of whether they have read or understood their terms?

HOLDING AND DECISION: [Judge not stated in casebook excerpt.] Yes. Parties who sign contracts are bound by them regardless of whether they have read or understood their terms. An individual who by occupation is experienced in commercial transactions cannot sign a contract and expect not to be bound solely because he did not understand its terms. This conclusion is consistent with the Convention on International Sale of Goods (CISG).

▌ ANALYSIS

This is a portion of the footnote 9 of the court of appeal's opinion. MCC (P) opposed the enforcement of certain terms of the parties' agreement located on the reverse side of a pre-printed form, which were incorporated by a provision located above the signature line.

■═■

Quicknotes

CONTRACT An agreement pursuant to which a party agrees to act, or to forbear from acting, in exchange for performance on the part of the other party.

■═■

Carlill v. Carbolic Smoke Ball Co.

Influenza sufferer (P) v. Smoke ball company (D)

C.A., 1 Q.B. 256 (1893).

NATURE OF CASE: Appeal from damages award in breach of contract action.

FACT SUMMARY: The Carbolic Smoke Ball Co. (D) advertised a reward to any person contracting influenza after using the Carbolic Smoke Ball (D) but refused to pay such reward to Carlill (P) when she caught the influenza after using the ball.

> ## 🏛 RULE OF LAW
> An advertised reward to anyone who performs certain conditions specified in the advertisement is an offer, and the performance of such conditions is an acceptance which creates a valid contract.

FACTS: The Carbolic Smoke Ball Co. (D) advertised in various newspapers a reward to any person who contracted influenza, colds, or any disease caused by taking cold after having used the Carbolic Smoke Ball three times daily for two weeks according to printed directions on each ball. Carlill (P) used the ball as directed but still caught the influenza. Thereafter, Carlill (P) brought an action against the Carbolic Smoke Ball Co. (D) to recover damages for breach of contract. After Carlill (P) was awarded damages in the amount of the original advertised reward, the Carbolic Smoke Ball Co. (D) brought this appeal.

ISSUE: Is an advertised reward to anyone who performs certain conditions specified in the advertisement an offer such that the performance of such conditions is an acceptance which creates a valid contract?

HOLDING AND DECISION: (Lord Lindley, J.) Yes. An advertised reward to anyone who performs certain conditions specified in the advertisement is an offer, and the performance of such conditions is an acceptance which creates a valid contract. Advertisements that state price, quantity, and use words of promise are considered offers. Furthermore, since such an advertisement requests deeds, not words, an offeree need not give notice that he is going to perform the required deeds. Here, the advertisement clearly offered a reward to anyone who performed certain specified conditions. As such, when Carlill (P) performed these conditions, she was entitled to the reward. Furthermore, there is no basis to the Carbolic Smoke Ball Co.'s (D) contention that there was no consideration for its promise. Any acceptance of the Company's (D) offer benefited it by stimulating sales of the smoke ball, and, furthermore, Carlill (P) was inconvenienced by using the ball. Affirmed.

CONCURRENCE: (Lord Bowen, J.) An offeror can eliminate the requirement for notice by expressly stating a particular mode of acceptance. The offeree must then merely comply with the indicated method for the offer to become binding. The advertisement here expressly stated that performance of the deeds was the mode of acceptance. Performance thus becomes sufficient acceptance and the offeror is bound.

▶ ANALYSIS

This case illustrates a case in which an advertisement is considered an offer (i.e., when there is no problem as to quantity because the ad specifies a reward to anyone who uses the product). The ordinary advertisement, though, which states that an item has been reduced in price, is not considered an offer because no quantity of the item is specified. Instead, such advertisements are generally held to represent only an intention to sell or a preliminary proposal inviting offers. Note, also, that this case illustrates the general rule that no notice is required before performance of an act specified in a unilateral contract. There are three different views, though, regarding notice after such performance: (1) No notice is required unless requested by the offeror; (2) notice is required if the offeree knows that the offeror has no adequate means of learning of the performance within a reasonable time; and (3) notice is always required.

Quicknotes

ACCEPTANCE Assent to the specified terms of an offer, resulting in the formation of a binding agreement.

UNILATERAL CONTRACT An agreement pursuant to which a party agrees to act, or to forbear from acting, in exchange for performance on the part of the other party.

Leonard v. Pepsico, Inc.

Pepsi points collector (P) v. Soda company (D)

88 F. Supp. 2d 116 (S.D.N.Y. 1999), *aff'd per curiam,* 210 F.3d 88 (2d Cir. 2000).

NATURE OF CASE: Motion for summary judgment

FACT SUMMARY: [Leonard (P) sought to enforce an alleged contract with Pepsico, Inc. (D) to provide him a Harrier Jet in exchange for Leonard's 7,000,000 Pepsi Points.]

🏛 RULE OF LAW
An offer for a reward becomes binding when the offeree performs the requested actions to claim the reward but the same is not true when the offer is an advertisement to receive offers.

FACTS: [Leonard (P), after viewing a television commercial from Pepsico, Inc. (D) offering a Harrier Jet Fighter for 7,000,000 "Pepsi points," raised $700,000 (the equivalent of such points) which he proffered to Pepsico (D) as an "acceptance" of its "offer," demanding the Harrier. Pepsico (D) refused to supply the Harrier, arguing that its commercial was obviously done in jest and that no reasonable person could possibly have considered it a real offer. Leonard (P) brought suit on the alleged contract, and Pepsico (D) moved for summary judgment.]

ISSUE: Does an advertisement to receive offers become binding in a similar fashion to an offer for a reward?

HOLDING AND DECISION: (Wood, J.) No. An offer for a reward becomes binding when the offeree performs the requested actions to claim the reward but the same is not true when the offer is an advertisement to receive offers. Leonard (P) argues that his situation is the same as that in *Carlill v. Carbolic Smoke Ball Co.*, 1 Q.B. 256 (Court of Appeal, 1892). In *Carbolic Smoke Ball*, the company advertised a money reward if anyone using the smoke ball contracted influenza. Carlill used the smoke ball, got influenza, and sought to collect her reward. The court there held that she was entitled to the money because she performed the requested actions set forth in the offer and the offer thus became binding upon the company. Leonard (P) relies on this and other cases involving offers of rewards. Pepsico (D), however, did not promise a reward of the Harrier Jet if an offeree performed certain actions. Pepsico (D) merely advertised a catalog of items that could be reviewed if a person collected Pepsi Points and abided by the terms of the Order Form. In fact, Leonard (P) admitted that the Harrier Jet was not even included in the catalog. A typical advertisement, as here, is an offer to negotiate for the purchase of goods rather than a promise of a reward. Leonard (P) cannot demonstrate the offer of a reward in this case.

▶ ANALYSIS

Pepsico (D) may have lost this case if it had plainly offered a Harrier Jet if an individual collected a certain number of Pepsi Points. The advertisement, though, was clearly not meant to be taken seriously and simply directed individuals to collect Pepsi Points for the opportunity to redeem something from a catalog. The opinion removing this case from the realm of a binding offer may have single-handedly saved viewers from hours of additional disclaimers attached to each and every advertisement.

■≡■

Quicknotes

SUMMARY JUDGMENT Judgment rendered by a court in response to a motion made by one of the parties, claiming that the lack of a question of material fact in respect to an issue warrants disposition of the issue without consideration by the jury.

■≡■

Day v. Caton

Wall builder (P) v. Neighbor (D)

Mass. Sup. Jud. Ct., 119 Mass. 513, 20 Am Rep. 347 (1876).

NATURE OF CASE: Action on a contract to recover the value of one-half of a party wall built upon and between adjoining estates.

FACT SUMMARY: Day (P) erected a valuable party wall between his and his neighbor's (D) land, but the neighbor (D), who knew of the construction and said nothing, refused to pay for one-half of the wall's construction.

🏛 RULE OF LAW
If a party voluntarily accepts and avails himself of valuable services rendered for his benefit when he has the option to accept or reject them, even if there is no distinct proof that they were rendered by his authority or request, a promise to pay for them may be inferred.

FACTS: Day (P) claimed he had an express agreement with the adjacent landowner, Caton (D), that in return for Day's (P) construction of a brick party wall upon and between their adjoining properties, Caton (D) would pay him one-half the value for the wall. When Caton (D) denied that any express agreement had ever been reached concerning payment for the party wall, Day (P) sued to enforce the alleged agreement.

ISSUE: If a party voluntarily accepts and avails himself of valuable services rendered for his benefit when he has the option to accept or reject them, even if there is no distinct proof that they were rendered by his authority or request, may a promise to pay for them be inferred?

HOLDING AND DECISION: (Devens, J.) Yes. If a party voluntarily accepts and avails himself of valuable services rendered for his benefit when he has the option to accept or reject them, even if there is no distinct proof that they were rendered by his authority or request, a promise to pay for them may be inferred. Where one person knows that another is conferring a valuable benefit on him and allows him to do so without objection, then a jury may infer a promise of payment. Silence may be interpreted as assent in the face of facts which fairly call upon one to speak. The question is one for the jury. Exceptions overruled.

▎ANALYSIS

Section 72(1)(a) of the Restatement (Second) of Contracts is in accord with the present decision. However, where one family member renders services to another family member, the presumption is that the services were made without expectation of payment. This is a rebuttable presumption.

■══■

Quicknotes

REBUTTABLE PRESUMPTION A rule of law, inferred from the existence of a particular set of facts that is conclusive in the absence of contrary evidence.

■══■

Wilhoite v. Beck

Cousin's executor (D) v. Host family (P)

Ind. App. Ct., 141 Ind. App. 543, 230 N.E.2d 616 (1967).

NATURE OF CASE: Appeal from the denial of a claim against decedent's estate.

FACT SUMMARY: Lawrence, a second cousin, lived with Beck (P) for 20 years.

🏛 RULE OF LAW
Where no gift presumption is present, a court may find an implied contract for services.

FACTS: Lawrence, apparently without invitation, came to the Beck (P) household to live. Lawrence resided with the Becks (P) for more than 20 years. They were second cousins. There was no express agreement that Lawrence was to pay for her board and room. Lawrence did state, on a number of occasions, that she did not accept charity and that the Becks (P) "would be taken care of" or words to that effect. Lawrence kept to herself, not taking part in the Becks' (P) family life. Lawrence worked during most of this time and was described as a highly independent woman. When Lawrence died, she left the residue of her estate in equal shares to several cousins, including the Becks (P). The Becks (P) submitted a claim to Lawrence's executor, Wilhoite (D), for services rendered Lawrence. The claim was rejected on the ground that services rendered family members were presumed to be gifts in the absence of an express contract or a clear and convincing showing that no gift was intended. The Becks (P) appealed the denial, alleging that there was an implied contract to pay for the room and board, and no gift had ever been intended.

ISSUE: Where there is no gift presumption to overcome, is a contract to pay for goods and services implied?

HOLDING AND DECISION: (Faulconer, J.) Yes. As a general rule, acceptance of goods and services implies a promise to pay for them. Where the services or goods are given to close family members, however, the law presumes a gift in the absence of clear and convincing evidence to the contrary, e.g., an express promise. Second cousins are not deemed to constitute a close family relationship, and the gift presumption is not present herein. Nor did Lawrence become a close part of the Becks' (P) family so as to create such a presumption. The evidence concerning Lawrence's independence, her refusal to accept charity, her promises that the Becks (P) "would be taken care of," etc., are sufficient to find that no gift was ever intended. Lawrence's will left all of her cousins an equal share of her estate. There is no showing that this was intended to compensate the Becks (P) for their services. The claim should be allowed. Affirmed.

▶ ANALYSIS

The closer the family relationship is the greater the presumption of a gift and the more difficult the burden of overcoming this presumption. 58 *Am. Jur.*, Work and Labor, § 11. Courts may find an implied contract to pay for the services or may grant the reasonable value of such services in quantum meruit to avoid unjust enrichment. *Wainwright Trust Co., Admr. v. Kind*er, 69 Ind. App. 88 (1918).

Quicknotes

DECEDENT A person who is deceased.

QUANTUM MERUIT Equitable doctrine allowing recovery for labor and materials provided by one party, even though no contract was entered into, in order to avoid unjust enrichment by the benefited party.

Miller v. NBD Bank, N.A.

[Parties not identified.]

Ind. Ct. App., 701 N.E.2d 282 (1998).

NATURE OF CASE: [Nature of case not stated in casebook excerpt.]

FACT SUMMARY: [Facts not stated in casebook excerpt.]

RULE OF LAW
In a suit or proceeding in which an executor or administrator is a party, involving matters that took place during the decedent's lifetime, any necessary party to the issue or record whose interest is adverse to that of the estate is not a competent witness as to such matters against the estate.

FACTS: [Facts not stated in casebook excerpt.]

ISSUE: In a suit or proceeding in which an executor or administrator is a party, involving matters that took place during the decedent's lifetime, is any necessary party to the issue or record whose interest is adverse to that of the estate a competent witness as to such matters against the estate?

HOLDING AND DECISION: [Judge not stated in casebook excerpt.] No. In a suit or proceeding in which an executor or administrator is a party involving matters that took place during the decedent's lifetime, any necessary party to the issue or record whose interest is adverse to that of the estate is not a competent witness as to such matters against the estate. This rule is codified in Indiana Code § 34-1-14-6 (repealed, now codified at Indiana Code § 34-54-2-4), commonly referred to as the Dead Man's Statute. The statute's purpose is to prevent the testifying as to acts or statements of a decedent in order to prevent fraud. The statute does not preclude the admission of evidence; rather, it prohibits a particular class of witnesses from testifying as to claims asserted against an estate.

▶ ANALYSIS

This excerpt from the *Miller* case is included as a response to the holding in *Wilhoite v. Beck*, 230 N.E.2d 616 (1967). There the court affirmed the trial court's judgment compensating Beck $11,368 for room, board and care and companionship allegedly owed. Although the court declined to set forth a general rule for a finding of an implied contract to reimburse such costs, the court stated that the facts and circumstances presented warranted such a judgment.

Quicknotes

DECEDENT A person who is deceased.

ESTATE ADMINISTRATOR A person designated by a court to effectuate the disposition of a decedent's estate.

EXECUTOR A person designated by an individual to effectuate the disposition of the individual's property pursuant to a testamentary instrument after the individual's death.

Hobbs v. Massasoit Whip Co.

Eel skin deliverer (P) v. Retainer (D)

Mass. Sup. Jud. Ct., 158 Mass. 194, 33 N.E. 495 (1893).

NATURE OF CASE: Exceptions to jury instructions in action for breach of contract.

FACT SUMMARY: Hobbs (P) sent Massasoit Whip Co. (D) eel skins which it retained until they were subsequently destroyed.

🏛 RULE OF LAW
Under appropriate circumstances, silence alone may constitute an acceptance, and a valid contract is formed.

FACTS: Hobbs (P) sent eel skins to Massasoit Whip Co. (Massasoit) (D). Massasoit (D) retained the skins but never used them. There was no contract between the parties, and Massasoit (D) never formally accepted the skins. The skins were subsequently destroyed, and Hobbs (P) sued for their value. At trial, Hobbs (P) introduced evidence that he had previously sent skins to Massasoit (D) under similar circumstances on four or five occasions. They had always been accepted and paid for by Massasoit (D) so long as they were at least 22 inches long. Massasoit (D) alleged that mere silence cannot create a contract, and no duty can be created requiring Massasoit (D) to respond or return the skins. At trial, the judge instructed the jury that it should find for plaintiff if the defendant, suspecting that the sender believes that the defendant accepts the skins, does nothing and fails to notify the sender of the non-acceptance, even in the absence of a contract.

ISSUE: Where appropriate, can silence by one party be deemed an acceptance?

HOLDING AND DECISION: (Holmes, J.) Yes. Under appropriate circumstances, silence alone may constitute an acceptance, and a valid contract is formed. A prior course of dealings may render silence an acceptance. Here, receipt of the skins and their retention, based on the prior dealings of the parties, constitutes a valid acceptance. Silence was sufficient conduct to manifest acceptance or assent to a contract under such circumstances. The judge did not mean to create a new rule that a sender can impose a notice-duty on a stranger by merely sending goods. The jury likely did not interpret the instruction in such a manner. Exceptions overruled.

▌ ANALYSIS

It is the overt manifestation of intent to contract rather than a party's subjective intent which controls. *O'Donnell v. Clinton*, 145 Mass. 461, 14 N.E. 747. While silence cannot create or impose a duty on strangers by the unilateral delivery of goods, a prior course of dealings, plus retention of the goods, may create a manifestation of assent. If the prior relationship would not create a presumption of assent, it may be disregarded by the courts. *Bushel v. Wheeler*, 15 Q.B. 442.

■=■

Quicknotes

ACCEPTANCE Assent to the specified terms of an offer, resulting in the formation of a binding agreement.

BREACH OF CONTRACT Unlawful failure by a party to perform its obligations pursuant to contract.

COURSE OF DEALING Previous conduct between two parties to a contact which may be relied upon to interpret their actions.

JURY INSTRUCTIONS A communication made by the court to a jury regarding the applicable law involved in a proceeding.

■=■

Petterson v. Pattberg

Executor (P) v. Holder of mortgage (D)

N.Y. Ct. App., 248 N.Y. 86, 161 N.E. 428 (1928).

NATURE OF CASE: Action for breach of contract.

FACT SUMMARY: Pattberg (D) offered to discount the mortgage on J. Petterson's estate on the condition that it be paid on a certain date. Pattberg (D) then sold the mortgage before Petterson (P), as executor of the estate, had paid him.

🏛 RULE OF LAW
An offer to enter into a unilateral contract may be withdrawn at any time prior to performance of the act requested to be done.

FACTS: Pattberg (D) held a mortgage on property belonging to J. Petterson's estate. Petterson (P) was executor of that estate. Pattberg (D) offered to discount the amount of the mortgage on the condition that it be paid on a certain date. Before that date Petterson (P) went to Pattberg's (D) home and offered to pay him the amount of the mortgage. Pattberg (D) told Petterson (P) that he had already sold the mortgage to a third person.

ISSUE: Can an offer to enter into a unilateral contract be withdrawn prior to performance of the act requested to be done?

HOLDING AND DECISION: (Kellogg, J.) Yes. An offer to enter into a unilateral contract may be withdrawn at any time prior to performance of the act requested to be done. Here, Pattberg's (D) offer proposed to Petterson (P) the making of a unilateral contract, the gift of a promise (to discount the mortgage) in exchange for the performance of an act (payment by a certain date). Pattberg (D) was free to revoke his offer any time before Petterson (P) accepted by performing the act. He revoked the offer by informing Petterson (P) that he had sold the mortgage. An offer to sell property may be withdrawn before acceptance without any formal notice to the person to whom the offer is made. It is sufficient if that person has actual knowledge that the person who made the offer has done some act inconsistent with the continuance of the offer, such as selling the property to a third person. Reversed.

DISSENT: (Lehman, J.) The issue in this case is whether the mortgage payment was a condition precedent to Pattberg's (D) promise to accept payment and provide a discount. Pattberg's (D) offer to accept the mortgage payment became binding when Petterson (P) arrived with payment. Consideration for Pattberg's (D) offer to accept Petterson's (P) payment was for Petterson (P) to actually make the payment. It is absurd to presume that Pattberg (D) intended to induce Petterson (P) to pay the mortgage

and then refuse that offered payment. Petterson's (P) payment was admittedly only a written intention to pay but he had an ability to pay when the offer was made. The letter should be interpreted as plain language and the promise should be enforced.

▶ ANALYSIS

Other facts in *Petterson* which do not appear in the opinion may have influenced the court. The trial record shows that Pattberg (D) was prevented from testifying as to a letter sent to J. Petterson (P), in which the offer was revoked. The record also suggests that Petterson (P) knew of the sale of the mortgage. Note, 1928, 14 *Cornell L.Q.* 81. The Restatement (Second) of Contracts provides, "Where an offer invites an offeree to accept by rendering performance, an option contract is created when the offeree begins performance." Actual performance is necessary. Preparations to perform, though they may be essential to performance, are not enough. However, they may constitute justifiable reliance sufficient to make the offeror's promise binding under § 90.

■━■

Quicknotes

BREACH OF CONTRACT Unlawful failure by a party to perform its obligations pursuant to contract.

REVOCATION The cancellation or withdrawal of some authority conferred or an instrument drafted, such as the withdrawal of a revocable contract offer prior to the offeree's acceptance.

UNILATERAL CONTRACT An agreement pursuant to which a party agrees to act, or to forbear from acting, in exchange for performance on the part of the other party.

■━■

Brackenbury v. Hodgkin

Daughter (P) v. Mother (D)

Me. Sup. Jud. Ct., 116 Me. 399, 102 A. 106 (1917).

NATURE OF CASE: Defendants' appeal in action in equity to secure reconveyance of real property, to restrain and enjoin Hodgkin (D) from further prosecution of his action, and to obtain adjudication as to who holds legal title to this real property in question.

FACT SUMMARY: Sarah Hodgkin (D) wrote her daughter and son-in-law, the Brackenburys (P), that if they would move to Maine from Missouri and take care of her for the rest of her life, she would leave the Brackenburys (P) her farm. The Brackenburys (P) moved to Maine, but Sarah (D) revoked her offer, and executed and delivered a deed to the property to her son, Walter Hodgkin (D), who then attempted to evict the Brackenburys (P).

RULE OF LAW

Where an offer invites a (continuing) performance, an option contract is created when the offeree begins the invited performance.

FACTS: Sarah Hodgkin (D), owner of the farm on which she lived, was the mother of six adult children, one of whom, Walter, was a defendant and another, a daughter, was a plaintiff. Sarah (D), a widow, wrote her daughter and son-in-law, the Brackenburys (P), asking them to move from Missouri to Maine, to move onto her farm and care for her for the rest of her life. The Brackenburys (P) were to pay moving expenses and to have use and income of the farm, together with the use of the household goods, with certain exceptions. Sarah (D) was to have what rooms she required. Sarah's (D) letter closed as follows: "you to have the place when I have passed away." The Brackenburys (P) moved to Maine as requested and began living on the farm and caring for Sarah (D). Friction developed between the parties after a few weeks. Sarah (D) then executed and delivered the deed to the farm to her son, Walter (D), who took the deed with full knowledge of the agreement existing between the parties. Walter (D) immediately served notice to quit upon the Brackenburys (P), who refused to remove themselves from the premises. The trial court found for the Brackenburys (P) and Walter (D) appealed.

ISSUE: When a continuing performance is invited, is an option contract created when the offeree begins performance rather than when he completes performance?

HOLDING AND DECISION: (Cornish, C.J.) Yes. An option contract is created when the offeree begins the invited continuing performance. Sarah's (D) offer was in writing, and its terms cannot be disputed. Neither an acceptance in words nor a counter-promise was required

by the Brackenburys (P). The offer was the basis of a unilateral contract as it required nothing more than an act (by the Brackenburys (P)) for the promise (of Sarah (D)). Accordingly, no other acceptance is necessary other than performance of the act. The Brackenburys (P) have continued to perform so far as they have been permitted to do so by Sarah (D). Appeal dismissed.

ANALYSIS

In this case, an option contract was formed. That occurs where performance cannot be completed in a single brief act but is continuing over a period of time. For example, the well-known Brooklyn Bridge hypothetical where A offers B $100 if B walks across the Brooklyn Bridge raises the problem of what happens if B begins to walk across but finds A has withdrawn his offer before B can reach the other end. Originally, the view was that the completed performance, i.e., having walked across the bridge, was the act desired by the offeror, and there could be no acceptance until the act was completed. Note, also, that this offer would be a unilateral contract requiring an act for a promise. Today, this view has changed. A, by having required a continuing performance by B, has created an option contract. Under the Restatement (Second), § 45, the theory is raised which limits revocability of any offer inviting a series of acts or even a single act to the time before the offeree has begun performance, in that an offer for an act may be regarded as continuing by implication a collateral offer to keep the main offer open if the offeree will start in performance of the act. Therefore, Sarah (D) in her offer may be implied to have said, "If you move to my farm and care for me, I promise not to revoke my offer within the time that it is reasonable for you to complete." In this case, that was Sarah's (D) lifetime. A way in which Sarah (D) might have successfully evicted the Brackenburys (P) would have arisen if she could have shown that the Brackenburys (P) had failed to care for her properly, hence breaching the contract.

■━■

Quicknotes

OPTION CONTRACT A contract pursuant to which a seller agrees that property will be available for the buyer to purchase at a specified price and within a certain time period.

REVOCATION The cancellation or withdrawal of some authority conferred or an instrument drafted, such as

Continued on next page.

the withdrawal of a revocable contract offer prior to the offeree's acceptance.

SPECIFIC PERFORMANCE An equitable remedy whereby the court requires the parties to perform their obligations pursuant to a contract.

UNILATERAL CONTRACT An agreement pursuant to which a party agrees to act, or to forbear from acting, in exchange for performance on the part of the other party.

■▬■

Motel Services, Inc. v. Central Maine Power Co.

Construction company (P) v. Power company (D)

Me. Sup. Jud. Ct., 394 A.2d 786 (1978).

NATURE OF CASE: Appeal from judgment for defendant in breach of contract suit.

FACT SUMMARY: Motel Services, Inc. (P) brought suit against Central Maine Power Co. (CMP) (D) seeking to recover a promotional allowance it claimed CMP (D) erroneously paid to the Waterville Housing Authority.

🏛 RULE OF LAW
A unilateral contract is formed where an offer requests not a promise to perform in accordance with its terms, but complete performance.

FACTS: Motel Services, Inc. (P) and Waterville Housing Authority (WHA) entered into an agreement whereby Motel Services (P) would build two housing projects for WHA on a "turnkey" basis. Motel Services (P) later sought to change the construction specifications to provide for an electrical rather than oil heating system. Motel Services (P) sought the change in order to qualify for an $8,000 promotional allowance given by Central Maine Power Co. (CMP) (D) to the owner of a home "initially built or converted to the use of electricity as the primary method of heating." Motel Services (P) along with CMP (D) demonstrated to the WHA and the Federal Department of Housing and Urban Development (HUD) that electric heating was more economical and promised to reduce its contract price by $16,000 if the change was approved. The WHA and HUD both agreed to the modification. After the electrical system was installed, Motel Services (P) conveyed the premises to WHA. A CMP (D) employee prepared and sent the appropriate forms for the receipt of the allowance—and eventually sent the allowance—to the WHA, the owner, on the date of the project's completion. Motel Services (P) brought this action against CMP (D), claiming it was entitled to the allowance. CMP (D) sued WHA (D) in a third-party action, which was dismissed. Judgment was entered in favor of CMP (D) and Motel Services (P) appealed.

ISSUE: Is a unilateral contract formed where an offer requests not a promise to perform in accordance with its terms, but complete performance?

HOLDING AND DECISION: (Pomeroy, J.) Yes. A unilateral contract is formed where an offer requests not a promise to perform in accordance with its terms, but complete performance. The lower court correctly characterized CMP's (D) marketing policy as an offer to enter into a unilateral contract. The general rule is that contracts are presumed to be bilateral; however, that presumption is rebutted by the offer, which requested complete performance in accordance with its terms, not just a promise to perform. Here it is clear that when Motel Services (P) undertook installment of the heating system in accordance with CMP's (D) policy, this constituted acceptance of the offer. Its failure to notify CMP (D) of acceptance did not affect its validity. While CMP's (D) offer was rendered irrevocable upon acceptance, payment of the allowance was still contingent upon completion of the required performance. CMP (D) set forth two grounds on which it contends Motel Services (P) failed to complete performance: (1) it did not complete the final steps necessary to claim the allowance (i.e., filling out the required forms); and (2) Motel Services (P) was no longer the owner of the buildings. The first argument fails since had CMP (D) provided Motel Services (P) with the forms, it would have fulfilled this requirement. Where the offeree of a unilateral contract is prevented from completing performance as a result of the offeror's conduct, such failure is not a defense to an action by the offeree on the contract. Second, the failure of Motel Services (P) to retain its status as owner of the properties does not preclude recovery. CMP's (D) offer was expressly limited to acceptance by "owners." Motel Services (P), at the time it undertook to perform the requested acts, was the owner of the buildings and accepted the offer. Judgment for Motel Services (P). Remanded.

▌ ANALYSIS

As a general rule, the offeror is considered "the master of his offer." As such he may dictate the means of acceptance, such as designation of the person or class of persons who may accept the offer.

■—■

Quicknotes

BILATERAL CONTRACT An agreement pursuant to which each party promises to undertake an obligation, or to forbear from acting, at some time in the future.

BREACH OF CONTRACT Unlawful failure by a party to perform its obligations pursuant to contract.

UNILATERAL CONTRACT An agreement pursuant to which a party agrees to act, or to forbear from acting, in exchange for performance on the part of the other party.

■—■

Horton v. DaimlerChrysler Financial Services Americas, L.L.C.

Debtor (P) v. Creditor (D)

262 S.W.3d 1 (2008).

NATURE OF CASE: Appeal of summary judgment.

FACT SUMMARY: Larry D. Horton (P) sued his creditor, DaimlerChrysler Financial Services Americas, L.L.C. (DaimlerChrysler) (D) for breach of contract when DaimlerChrysler (D) failed to remove negative information from Horton's (P) credit report.

🏛 RULE OF LAW
Unless otherwise indicated, an offer may be accepted in any manner reasonable under the circumstances.

FACTS: Larry D. Horton (P) owed money to Daimler-Chrysler Financial Services Americas, L.L.C. (Daimler-Chrysler) (D). DaimlerChrysler's agent, Commercial Recovery Systems, Inc. (Commercial) (D) offered Horton (P) a settlement providing that DaimlerChrysler (D) would accept $1000 as full and final settlement of the $25,000 owed, and that all derogatory credit information about the account will be removed, if the offer was accepted by June 30, 2003. Horton (P) sent the $1000 in two payments, the first on June 18 and the second on July 2, 2003. With the second check, Horton (P) included terms of his own, which essentially stipulated that the check was tendered with the understanding that it was to be accepted in full and complete satisfaction of all sums due and owing, and in complete release with regard to his account. Commercial (D) accepted both checks. When Horton (P) applied in 2005 to purchase a house and a new truck, he discovered that his credit report still contained negative information about the account, and he sued Daimler-Chrysler (D) and Commercial (D) for breach of contract. DaimlerChrysler (D) and Commercial (D) moved for summary judgment, denying that a contract was formed by Commercial's (D) offer, since Horton (P) failed to accept the offer by tendering the $1000 by the date specified–June 30. The trial court granted the motion. Horton (P) appealed on grounds that there were genuine issues of material fact concerning whether the acceptance of the checks was a waiver or modification of the time limitations contained in the original offer.

ISSUE: Unless otherwise indicated, may an offer be accepted in any manner reasonable under the circumstances?

HOLDING AND DECISION: (Morriss, C.J.) Yes. Unless otherwise indicated, an offer may be accepted in any manner reasonable under the circumstances. Commercial's (D) offer specified the terms of payment, but it did not specify a particular manner of acceptance of the offer. It

provides that "(t)his offer will be extended through June 30, 2003, after which time the full balance will be due." That language refers to the length of time the offer will remain open for acceptance, not the manner by which the offer could be accepted. The plain language of the offer does not specify a manner of acceptance. Because of that, the offer could be accepted in any manner reasonable under the circumstances, and Horton's (P) act of tendering the first check on June 18 was a clear, unequivocal act indicating acceptance. The contract was formed at that point. And while Horton (P) clearly breached the contract by not tendering the second payment on time, whether DaimlerChrysler (D) and Commercial (D) waived the payment due date is a question of fact for the trial court. Reversed and remanded.

▶ ANALYSIS

Note that an affirmative act—not a verbal response—constituted the acceptance in this case. Where there is an affirmative act that constitutes the required performance set forth in the offer, courts will usually find acceptance.

■▬■

Quicknotes

ACCEPTANCE Assent to the specified terms of an offer resulting in the formation of a binding agreement.

BREACH OF CONTRACT Unlawful failure by a party to perform its obligations pursuant to contract.

■▬■

Fujimoto v. Rio Grande Pickle Co.

Prospective buyer of land (P) v. Seller of land (D)

414 F.2d 648 (5th Cir. 1969).

NATURE OF CASE: Appeal from award for plaintiffs in action for breach of contract.

FACT SUMMARY: Fujimoto (P) and Bravo (P) signed employment contracts with Rio Grande Pickle Co. (D) and retained the contracts in their possession.

🏛 RULE OF LAW
Where the mode of acceptance is not specified, any act that clearly conveys acceptance is sufficient to create the contract.

FACTS: Fujimoto (P) and Bravo (P) held important positions with Rio Grande Pickle Co. (Rio Grande) (D). Fujimoto (P) and Bravo (P) were unhappy with their pay and threatened to quit. Rio Grande (D) sent each of them a new employment contract providing for a bonus of 10 percent of the profits of the company (D). Fujimoto (P) and Bravo (P) each signed and retained the contracts. They continued to work for Rio Grande (D) for 14 additional months. On at least one occasion, the terms of the bonus were discussed with an officer of Rio Grande (D). The bonus was never paid, and Fujimoto (P) and Bravo (P) brought suit for breach of contract. While the contract never specified how acceptance was to be communicated to Rio Grande (D), it argued that since the contracts had never been returned to it, there had been no acceptance.

ISSUE: Where the mode of acceptance is not specified, will overt acts that clearly manifest acceptance be sufficient to bind the parties?

HOLDING AND DECISION: (Goldberg, J.) Yes. An offeror may specify an exclusive mode of acceptance, a nonexclusive mode of acceptance, or no mode of acceptance. If no mode of acceptance is specified, any reasonable mode in accordance with usage and custom of men in similar situations is sufficient to bind the parties. Rio Grande (D) offered the contract in order to retain Fujimoto (P) and Bravo (P). Where no mode of acceptance is specified, any overt act clearly manifesting acceptance is sufficient to bind the parties. Here, Fujimoto (P) and Bravo (P) remained with Rio Grande (D) for 14 additional months and discussed the bonus with an officer of Rio Grande (D). This is sufficient to clearly bring home to Rio Grande (D) that its offer had been accepted. Judgment affirmed in part and reversed and remanded in part.

▶ ANALYSIS

The method of acceptance must be reasonable based on the nature of the offer. If no time is specified in which the offer must be received, a commercially reasonable time is inferred under the Uniform Commercial Code (U.C.C.) or by the courts. A mode of acceptance as speedy and secure as the method in which the offer was conveyed is normally acceptable. Corbin on Contracts, § 67.

■■■

Quicknotes

ACTION TO QUIET TITLE Equitable action to resolve conflicting claims to an interest in real property.

BREACH OF CONTRACT Unlawful failure by a party to perform its obligations pursuant to contract.

MAILBOX RULE Common law rule that acceptance of an offer is binding upon dispatch at which time an enforceable contract is formed so long as it complies with the requirements for acceptance.

■■■

Cantu v. Central Education Agency

Teacher (P) v. School district (D)

Tex. Ct. App., 884 S.W.2d 565 (1994).

NATURE OF CASE: Appeal from district court's judgment affirming a final order by the State Commissioner of Education.

FACT SUMMARY: Cantu (P) challenged the State Commissioner of Education's decision that her resignation became effective on the date when the superintendent mailed her a letter of acceptance.

🏛 RULE OF LAW
Acceptance of an offer by mail is impliedly authorized if reasonable under the circumstances.

FACTS: Cantu (P) was a special education teacher employed by the San Benito Consolidated Independent School District. Immediately prior to the beginning of the school year Cantu (P) delivered by hand a letter of resignation to her supervisor. The resignation letter was passed on to the superintendent of schools, the person with the authority to accept such resignations. The superintendent mailed Cantu (P) a properly addressed and stamped letter of acceptance. The day after the superintendent mailed the letter of acceptance, Cantu (P) hand-delivered another letter withdrawing her resignation. The superintendent responded by hand-delivering a copy of the mailed letter to Cantu (P) informing her that her resignation had already been accepted. Cantu (P) brought an administrative action against the Central Education Agency (D), and the State Commissioner of Education concluded that the acceptance of the resignation was effective upon the mailing of the acceptance letter. The district court agreed.

ISSUE: Is acceptance of an offer by mail impliedly authorized if reasonable under the circumstances?

HOLDING AND DECISION: (Smith, J.) Yes. Acceptance of an offer by mail is impliedly authorized if reasonable under the circumstances. The legal axiom that "the offeror is the master of his offer" articulates the power of the offeror to set conditions for acceptance. When parties communicate at a distance, however, a rule of law is required to establish the point at which a contract is formed. Such a rule of law helps to allocate the risk of loss and the inconvenience of the parties. The mailbox rule makes acceptance effective at the instant of a properly executed dispatch. Cantu (P) claims that she did not expressly authorize acceptance by mail and that, therefore, she was first in time to rescind her resignation. However, this court chooses to follow the Restatement (Second) of Contracts approach where acceptance by any medium reasonable under the circumstances is effective upon dispatch, absent an express contrary instruction in the offer. The

school received Cantu's (P) resignation by letter, and though it was hand-delivered, it is reasonable under these circumstances to mail acceptance when the parties were operating at a distance and the offer came in the form of a letter. There was no contrary instruction for acceptance expressed in the letter of resignation and the mailbox rule applies under these circumstances. The judgment of the district court is affirmed.

▶ ANALYSIS

The U.C.C. and the courts have continually expanded the number of terms to a contract that can be filled in, or supplied, by operation of law. The mailbox rule is one such bright-line rule designed to eliminate disputes that develop between parties when the process of offers and counter-offers are occurring over a distance. In this instance, a letter communicated the offer of resignation and it was reasonable to assume the acceptance would be in the same form. These rules only fill in the gaps when the parties fail to expressly provide the terms, thus, they do not impinge on the right of freedom of contract. If a party wishes for acceptance to take a particular form, other than the one implied, then the method of acceptance should be expressly provided.

■=■

Quicknotes

ACCEPTANCE Assent to the specified terms of an offer resulting in the formation of a binding agreement.

MAILBOX RULE Common law rule that acceptance of an offer is binding upon dispatch at which time an enforceable contract is formed so long as it complies with the requirements for acceptance.

■=■

Swift & Co. v. Smigel

Seller of merchandise (P) v. Mental patient (D)

N.J. Super. Ct., App. Div., 115 N.J. Super. 391, 279 A.2d 895 (1971).

NATURE OF CASE: Action on an account.

FACT SUMMARY: Smigel (D), an incompetent, was guarantor on goods sold on credit to the Pine Haven Nursing Home and Sanitarium.

🏛 RULE OF LAW
If a creditor does not know or have reason to know of the offeror's adjudicated mental incompetence, a subsequent acceptance of an offer creates a valid contract.

FACTS: Smigel (D), an adjudicated mental incompetent, was a continuing guarantor on credit sales made by Swift & Co. (P) to the Pine Haven Nursing Home and Sanitarium. The guarantee agreement had been entered into before Smigel (D) had been adjudicated an incompetent and was of a continuing nature covering future deliveries until revoked. Smigel (D) died, and Pine Haven went bankrupt. Swift (P) sued the estate (D) on the guarantee contract, and the action was dismissed because the court found that the incompetency of the offeror revoked the offer whether or not the offeree had notice of the incompetency.

ISSUE: Does incompetency of the offeror automatically revoke the offer?

HOLDING AND DECISION: (Conford, J.) No. Since this is a matter of first impression, we will attempt to formulate a rule which protects the reasonable expectations of the parties. It would be unfair to penalize a party dealing in good faith with one who is not known to be mentally incompetent. Rather, we adopt the rule that where the offeree does not know or have reason to know that the offeror has been judged legally incompetent, acceptance of the offer creates a valid contract. While unnecessary to our consideration herein, we reserve the question of the effect of incompetency on executory-contracts. Here, the contract was fair and executed. We remand for a determination of whether Swift (P) knew or should have known of Smigel's (D) incompetence and whether Smigel (D) was legally incompetent to enter into the contract even if Swift (P) had actual or constructive knowledge. Reversed and remanded.

▌ *ANALYSIS*

The same rationale used in *Swift* has been applied where the offeror has died before the acceptance, 1 *Corbin, Contracts* (1963) § 54. If the offer is for personal services or an agency relationship, the death or incapacity of the offeror will terminate the offer since it is personal to the offeror. 1 *Corbin, Contracts*. In such cases, the offeree or the estate cannot be bound.

■=■

Quicknotes

EXECUTORY CONTRACT A contract in which performance of an obligation has yet to be rendered.

GUARANTOR A party who agrees to be liable for the debt or default of another.

■=■

Ardente v. Horan

Prospective home buyer (P) v. Homeowners (D)

R.I. Sup. Ct., 117 R.I. 254, 366 A.2d 162 (1976).

NATURE OF CASE: Action to specifically enforce an agreement.

FACT SUMMARY: Ardente (P) asserted that he had accepted the Horans' (D) offer to sell their home and that a contract had thus been formed, but the Horans (D) insisted he had made only a counteroffer.

RULE OF LAW
An acceptance that is equivocal or upon condition or with a limitation is a counteroffer and requires acceptance by the original offeror before a contractual relationship can exist.

FACTS: The Horans (D) offered their home for sale, and Ardente (P) made a $250,000 bid that was communicated to them through their attorney. The attorney advised Ardente (P) that the bid was acceptable to the Horans (D) and prepared a purchase and sale agreement that was forwarded for Ardente's (P) signature to his attorney. Ardente (P) executed the agreement after investigating certain title conditions. His attorney sent it to the Horans (D) along with a $20,000 check and a letter from Ardente's (P) attorney stating his client's concern that certain items remain with the real estate as they would be difficult to replace (dining room set and tapestry in dining room, fireplace fixtures, and sun parlor furniture). It stated, "I would appreciate your confirming that these items are a part of the transaction." The Horans (D) refused to include the items and did not sign the agreement, which their attorney returned along with the check. Ardente (P) filed an action for specific performance, arguing that a contract had been formed. In granting summary judgment for the Horans (D), the court held the aforementioned letter was a conditional acceptance amounting to a counteroffer which was not accepted by the Horans (D).

ISSUE: Is a conditional acceptance treated as a counteroffer that must itself be accepted?

HOLDING AND DECISION: (Doris, J.) Yes. To be effective, an acceptance must be definite and unequivocal. An acceptance that is equivocal or upon condition or with a limitation is a counteroffer and requires acceptance by the original offeror before a contract arises. However, an acceptance may be valid despite conditional language if the acceptance is clearly independent of the condition. Ardente's (P) acceptance was not clearly independent of the condition and thus operated as a counteroffer that was not accepted by the Horans (D). Thus, no contract was formed. Affirmed and remanded.

ANALYSIS

Restatement (Second) of Contracts § 39, Comment (b) indicates that an offeree can state he is holding the offer under advisement but if the offeror desires to close the bargain immediately, he makes a counteroffer. In this way, the original offer remains open for its original term, but the counteroffer is nonetheless introduced. Thus, the counteroffer does not kill the original offer.

Quicknotes

ACCEPTANCE Assent to the specified terms of an offer, resulting in the formation of a binding agreement.

COUNTEROFFER An offer made by the offeree, which has the effect of rejecting the offer deemed unsatisfactory and of proposing a different offer.

SPECIFIC PERFORMANCE An equitable remedy whereby the court requires the parties to perform their obligations pursuant to a contract.

SUMMARY JUDGMENT Judgment rendered by a court in response to a motion by one of the parties, claiming that the lack of a question of material fact in respect to an issue warrants disposition of the issue without consideration by the jury.

Dorton v. Collins & Aikman Corp.

Carpet retailer (P) v. Carpet manufacturer (D)

453 F.2d 1161 (6th Cir. 1972).

NATURE OF CASE: Action to compel arbitration.

FACT SUMMARY: Collins & Aikman Corp.'s (D) acceptance form contained a compulsory arbitration clause, while Dorton's (P) order form did not.

🏛 RULE OF LAW
An arbitration provision may be deemed a nonmaterial alteration of the contract in certain circumstances.

FACTS: Dorton (P) orally ordered carpeting from Collins & Aikman Corp. (D). Collins & Aikman's (D) acceptance form contained a compulsory arbitration clause. Acceptance of an order, according to Collins & Aikman's (D) form, was subject to all terms and conditions of the form. Dorton (P) sued Collins & Aikman (D), and it attempted to obtain a stay of the proceedings pending arbitration as required under its form. The district court held that the language of the form did not make acceptance of all its provisions a condition precedent to the formation of a contract. It, therefore, found that the contract was controlled by Uniform Commercial Code (U.C.C.) § 2-207(3), where the conduct of the parties is such as to indicate that a contract has been formed. The court found, as a matter of law, that terms on an acceptance could not force arbitration on a party.

ISSUE: May an arbitration provision be deemed a nonmaterial alteration of the contract in certain circumstances?

HOLDING AND DECISION: (Celebreeze, J.) Yes. An arbitration provision may be deemed a nonmaterial alteration of the contract in certain circumstances. U.C.C. § 2-207 was adopted to prevent the operation of the common law mirror image rule. An acceptance and offer need not exactly match to find the existence of a valid contract. Traditionally, written offers and acceptances contain numerous provisions favorable to the drafter. In recognition of this fact, a contract is found where essential terms are present or inferable. Inconsistent terms do not become a part of the contract. If specific acceptance of the buyer's or seller's terms is made a condition precedent to the formation of the contract, no contract is formed absent an assent. Even in such cases, a contract may be formed by the actions if the parties and terms which materially alter the contract are deleted. We do not find that Collins & Aikman's (D) form requires acceptance of all terms as a condition precedent to formation of a contract. This must be specifically and unequivocally stated. Therefore, the question is whether the arbitration clause materially alters the contract as formed under U.C.C. § 2-207(3).

Arbitration clauses have gained wide acceptance, and we do not find that they constitute a per se material alteration. We remand for such a finding. Also, there was no evidence adduced to indicate that the oral offer did not contain an arbitration provision. [Remanded.]

▌ ANALYSIS

Under the common law, silence is not deemed to be consent. The U.C.C. alters this approach and would allow nonmaterial terms to become part of the contract unless they are objected to by the other party within 10 days of receipt. U.C.C. § 2-207(2). Prior to *Dorton*, an arbitration provision was specifically found to constitute an unreasonable additional term which does not become a part of the contract unless specifically consented to by the other party. Thus, there is a split in the courts.

Quicknotes

ACCEPTANCE Assent to the specified terms of an offer, resulting in the formation of a binding agreement.

ARBITRATION CLAUSE Provision contained in a contract pursuant to which both parties agree that any disputes arising thereunder will be resolved through arbitration.

CONDITION PRECEDENT The happening of an uncertain occurrence, which is necessary before a particular right or interest may be obtained or an action performed.

MIRROR-IMAGE RULE The common law rule that for acceptance to be effective the offeree must accept each and every term of the offer.

OFFER A proposed promise to undertake performance of an action, or to refrain from acting, that is to become binding upon acceptance by the offeree.

Diamond Fruit Growers, Inc. v. Krack Corp.

Tubing supplier (D) v. Cooling unit manufacturer (P)

794 F.2d 1440 (9th Cir. 1986).

NATURE OF CASE: Appeal from award of indemnity on a written contract.

FACT SUMMARY: Metal-Matic (D) contended that it effectively disclaimed responsibility to Krack (P) for incidental damages caused by its defective tubing by including such disclaimers in its sales receipt.

🏛 RULE OF LAW
Uniform Commercial Code (U.C.C.) § 2-207 holds that the exchange of differing purchase orders constitutes a binding contract only as to those portions upon which the orders agree.

FACTS: Over the course of many years, Krack (P) ordered tubing from Metal-Matic (D) pursuant to purchase orders sent by both parties. The purchase orders sent by Metal-Matic (D) contained a disclaimer of liability to Krack (P) for any incidental damages caused by any defect in the tubing. Krack's (P) purchase order did not contain this provision. Diamond sued Krack (P) for damages to fruit caused by a toxic leak in the tubing. Krack (P) filed a third-party complaint against Metal-Matic (D), who defended on the basis of the disclaimer. The trial court denied Metal-Matic's (D) motion for directed verdict. The jury held Metal-Matic (D) 30 percent responsible, and it appealed, after unsuccessfully moving for judgment n.o.v.

ISSUE: Is the exchange of differing purchase orders between merchants a binding agreement only as to those provisions on which the orders agree?

HOLDING AND DECISION: (Wiggins, J.) Yes. U.C.C. § 2-207 holds that the exchange of differing purchase orders constitutes a binding contract only as to those portions upon which the orders agree. This is changed only upon an affirmative acquiescence to the terms of the differing order. In this case, while some discussions occurred concerning the disclaimer, no affirmative adoption occurred on the part of Krack (P). As a result, the disclaimer was not agreed to and did not become a part of the contract. Affirmed.

▶ ANALYSIS

U.C.C. § 2-207 represents a statutory departure from the common law mirror image rule where any slight deviation from the offer constituted a rejection. Differing orders can constitute an agreement but only on like terms. This rule is consistent with public policy because neither party gets its way merely because it sent the last form.

Quicknotes

BATTLE OF THE FORMS Refers to the exchange of forms, pursuant to a contract for the sale of goods, between a buyer and seller.

U.C.C. § 2-207 Provides that a definite expression of acceptance sent within a reasonable time operates as an acceptance even though it states terms additional to or different from those offered, unless acceptance is expressly made conditional on assent to the additional terms.

ProCD, Inc. v. Zeidenberg

Software manufacturer (P) v. Purchaser (D)

86 F.3d 1447 (7th Cir. 1996).

NATURE OF CASE: Appeal from an order in favor of defendant in a case alleging breach of the terms of a shrinkwrap or end user license.

FACT SUMMARY: When Zeidenberg (D), a customer, bought and then resold the data compiled on its CD-ROM software disk, ProCD, Inc. (P) sued for breach of contract.

🏛 RULE OF LAW
A buyer accepts goods when, after an opportunity to inspect, he fails to make an effective rejection.

FACTS: ProCD, Inc. (P) compiled information from over 3,000 telephone directories into a computer database which it sold on CD-ROM disks. Every box containing the disks declared that the software came with restrictions stated in an enclosed license. This license, which was encoded on the CD-ROM disks as well as printed in the manual, and which appeared on a user's screen every time the software ran, limited use of the application program and listings to non-commercial purposes. Zeidenberg (D) bought a ProCD (P) software package but decided to ignore the license and to resell the information in the database. Zeidenberg (D) also made the information from ProCD's (P) database available over the Internet for a price, through his corporation. ProCD (P) sued for breach of contract. The district court found that placing the package of software on the shelf was an "offer" which the customer "accepted" by paying the asking price and leaving the store with the goods. A contract includes only those terms which the parties have agreed to and one cannot agree to secret terms. Thus, the district court held that buyers of computer software need not obey the terms of shrinkwrap licenses. Such licenses were found to be ineffectual because their terms did not appear on the outsides of the packages. ProCD (P) appealed.

ISSUE: Does a buyer accept goods when, after an opportunity to inspect, he fails to make an effective rejection?

HOLDING AND DECISION: (Easterbrook, J.) Yes. A buyer accepts goods when, after an opportunity to inspect, he fails to make an effective rejection under § 2-602 of the Uniform Commercial Code. A vendor, as master of the offer, may invite acceptance by conduct, and may propose limitations on the kind of conduct that constitutes acceptance. ProCD (P) proposed a contract that a buyer would accept by using the software after having an opportunity to read the license at leisure. Zeidenberg (D) did this, since he had no choice when the software splashed the license across his computer screen and would not let

him proceed without indicating acceptance. The license was an ordinary contract accompanying the sale of products and was therefore governed by the common law of contracts and the Uniform Commercial Code. Transactions in which the exchange of money precedes the communication of detailed terms are common. Buying insurance and buying a plane ticket are two common examples. ProCD (P) extended an opportunity to reject if a buyer should find the license terms unsatisfactory. Zeidenberg (D) inspected the package, tried out the software, learned of the license, and did not reject the goods. Reversed and remanded.

▶ ANALYSIS

The sale of information contained in computer databases presented new challenges to courts. Some courts found that the sale of software was the sale of services, rather than of goods. This case treated the sale of software as a sale of goods governed by Article 2 of the Uniform Commercial Code.

■■■

Quicknotes

CD-ROM Compact disc read-only memory.

INSPECTION OF GOODS The examination of goods, which are the subject matter of a contract for sale, for the purpose of determining whether they are satisfactory.

REJECTION The refusal to accept the terms of an offer.

SHRINKWRAP LICENSE Terms of restriction packaged inside a product.

U.C.C. § 2-602 Provides that a rejection after an opportunity to inspect may be effective unless the buyer manifests acceptance in the manner invited by the offeror.

■■■

Hill v. Gateway 2000, Inc.

Consumer (P) v. Company (D)

105 F.3d 1147 (7th Cir. 1997).

NATURE OF CASE: Appeal of denial of a motion to compel arbitration.

FACT SUMMARY: Hill (P) brought a RICO suit against Gateway 2000, Inc. (Gateway) (D) after purchasing a mail order computer. Gateway (D) moved to compel arbitration. The request was denied, and Gateway (D) appealed.

RULE OF LAW
Terms sent in the box with a product that state that they govern the sale unless the product is returned within 30 days are binding on a buyer who does not return the product.

FACTS: Hill (P) purchased a computer from Gateway 2000, Inc. (Gateway) (D) through a telephone order and subsequently brought suit against Gateway (D), in which a civil Racketeer Influenced and Corrupt Organizations Act (RICO) claim and other claims were asserted. Gateway (D) thereupon sought enforcement of an arbitration clause which had been included in the terms sent to Hill (P) in the box in which the computer was shipped. The federal district court denied the arbitration request, and Gateway (D) appealed.

ISSUE: Are terms sent in the box with a product that state that they govern the sale unless the product is returned within 30 days binding on a buyer who does not return the product?

HOLDING AND DECISION: (Easterbrook, J.) Yes. Terms sent in the box with a product that state that they govern the sale unless the product is returned within 30 days are binding on a buyer who does not return the product. The Hills (P) conceded noticing the statement of terms but denied reading it closely enough to discover the agreement to arbitrate. An agreement to arbitrate must be enforced except upon such grounds as exist at law or in equity for the revocation of any contract. A contract need not be read to be effective. People who accept products take the risk that the unread terms may in retrospect prove unwelcome. Terms inside Gateway's (D) box stand or fall together. If they constitute the parties' contract because the Hills (P) had an opportunity to return the computer after reading them, then all must be enforced. The court rejects Hills' (P) argument that the provision in the box should be limited to executory contracts and to licenses in particular. Both parties' performance of this contract was complete when the box arrived at their home. The case does not depend on the fact that the seller characterized the transaction as a license rather than as a contract, but rather treated it as a contract for the sale of goods and reserved the question whether for other purposes a "license" characterization might be preferable. All debates about characterization to one side, the transaction here was not executory. Vacated and remanded for arbitration.

ANALYSIS

While observing that the federal Magnuson-Moss Warranty Act requires firms to distribute their warranty terms on request, the court noted that the Hills (P) did not contend that Gateway (D) would have refused to enclose the remaining terms also. Concealment would be bad for business, scaring some customers away and leading to excessive returns from others. Second, said the court, shoppers can consult public sources (computer magazines, the web sites of vendors) that may contain this information. Third, they may inspect the documents after the product's delivery. In this case, the Hills (P) took the third option. By keeping the computer beyond 30 days, the Hills (P) accepted Gateway's (D) offer, including the arbitration clause.

Quicknotes

ARBITRATION An agreement to have a dispute heard and decided by a neutral third party, rather than through legal proceedings.

ARBITRATION CLAUSE Provision contained in a contract pursuant to which both parties agree that any disputes arising thereunder will be resolved through arbitration.

RICO Racketeer Influenced and Corrupt Organization laws; federal and state statutes enacted for the purpose of prosecuting organized crime.

Klocek v. Gateway, Inc.

Consumer (P) v. Computer vendor (D)

104 F. Supp. 2d 1332 (D. Kan. 2000).

NATURE OF CASE: Motion to dismiss on the ground that claims brought by the purchaser of a computer must be arbitrated pursuant to the vendor's standard agreement included with the computer.

FACT SUMMARY: Klocek (P) purchased a computer from Gateway, Inc. (D), which included a copy of its Standard Terms and Conditions Agreement (Standard Terms) with the computer. The Standard Terms provided that they would be accepted by the purchaser if the computer was kept beyond five days and also provided for arbitration of any claims arising from the agreement. Klocek (P) sued Gateway (D) for breach of contract and of warranty. Gateway (D) moved to dismiss, asserting that the claims had to be arbitrated under the Standard Terms agreement.

🏛 RULE OF LAW
Terms shipped with a computer do not become part of the sales contract where the vendor does not expressly make its acceptance conditional on the buyer's assent to the additional shipped terms and where the buyer does not expressly agree to the terms.

FACTS: Klocek (P) purchased a computer from Gateway, Inc. (D), which included a copy of its Standard Terms and Conditions Agreement (Standard Terms) in the box that contained the computer battery power cables and instruction manuals. The Standard Terms provided in bold type that they would be accepted by the purchaser if the computer was kept beyond five days. Paragraph 10 of the Standard Terms provided for arbitration of any claims arising from the agreement. Klocek (P) sued Gateway (D) for breach of contract and of warranty, and Gateway (D) moved to dismiss, asserting that the claims had to be arbitrated under the Standard Terms agreement.

ISSUE: Do terms shipped with a computer become part of the sales contract where the vendor does not expressly make its acceptance conditional on the buyer's assent to the additional, shipped, terms, and where the buyer does not expressly agree to the terms?

HOLDING AND DECISION: (Vratil, J.) No. Terms shipped with a computer do not become part of the sales contract where the vendor does not expressly make its acceptance conditional on the buyer's assent to the additional, shipped, terms and where the buyer does not expressly agree to the terms. Gateway (D) bears an initial burden of showing that it is entitled to arbitration. To do so, it must demonstrate that an enforceable agreement to arbitrate exists. When deciding if such an agreement exists, the court applies state law contract formation principles. Here, the Uniform Commercial Code (U.C.C.) governs the parties' transaction under both Kansas and Missouri law. The fact that Klocek (P) paid for and received a computer is evidence of a contract for the sale of a computer. Here, the issue is whether terms received with a product become part of the parties' agreement—an issue not decided by either Kansas or Missouri state courts. Authority from other courts is split, and seems to depend on whether the court finds that the parties formed their contract before or after the vendor communicated its terms to the purchaser. Gateway (D) urges following the approach taken by the Seventh Circuit, which enforced an arbitration clause in a situation similar to the one in this case. The Seventh Circuit reasoned that by including the license with the software, the vendor proposed a contract that the buyer could accept by using the software after having an opportunity to read the license. The Seventh Circuit, however, concluded, without support, that U.C.C. § 2-207 was irrelevant because the case involved only one written form, and that the vendor was the master of the offer. The Missouri or Kansas courts would not follow this reasoning because nothing in the language of § 2-207 precludes its application in a case that involves only one form. By its terms, § 2-207 applies to an acceptance or written confirmation. Therefore, the state courts would apply § 2-207 to the facts of this case. In addition, in typical consumer transactions, it is the purchaser who is the offeror, and the vendor is the offeree. Here, Gateway (D) has provided no evidence that would support a finding that it was the offeror—and therefore could propose limitations on the kind of conduct that constituted acceptance. Instead, the court assumes that plaintiff offered to purchase the computer and that Gateway (D) accepted plaintiff's offer. Under § 2-207, the Standard Terms are either an expression of acceptance or written confirmation. The Standard Terms are only a counteroffer if Gateway (D) first requires Klocek's (P) agreement to additional or different terms. Gateway (D) did not require Klocek (P) to accept the Standard Terms prior to completing the sale and has failed to demonstrate that Klocek (P) agreed to the Standard Terms or even knew of the five-day review-and-return period. Any additional or different terms did not automatically become a part of the Standard Terms because Klocek (P) is not a merchant and is required to expressly assent to the new terms. The fact that Klocek (P) kept the computer past five days was insufficient to demonstrate that he expressly agreed to the

Continued on next page.

Standard Terms. Therefore, Gateway (D) has not shown that Klocek (P) agreed to the arbitration provision, and its motion to dismiss is overruled.

▶ ANALYSIS

The decision in this case would find support from legal commentators who have found that software shrinkwrap agreements are a form of adhesion contracts and who have criticized the line of cases that support such agreements, such as those in the Seventh Circuit, on the ground that they ignore the issue of informed consumer consent. Nonetheless, several courts have followed the Seventh Circuit line of cases.

■━■

Quicknotes

ACCEPTANCE Assent to the specified terms of an offer, resulting in the formation of a binding agreement.

ARBITRATION CLAUSE Provision contained in a contract pursuant to which both parties agree that any disputes arising thereunder will be resolved through arbitration.

BREACH OF CONTRACT Unlawful failure by a party to perform its obligations pursuant to contract.

BREACH OF WARRANTY The breach of a promise made by one party to a contract that the other party may rely on a fact, relieving that party from the obligation of determining whether the fact is true and indemnifying the other party from liability if that fact is shown to be false.

COUNTEROFFER A statement by the offeree which has the legal effect of rejecting the offer and of proposing a new offer to the offeror.

■━■

Specht v. Netscape Communications Corp.

User (P) v. Software program provider (D)

306 F.3d 17 (2d Cir. 2002).

NATURE OF CASE: Motion to compel arbitration.

FACT SUMMARY: Specht (P) downloaded from the Internet free software from Netscape Communications Corp. (Netscape) (D). When an issue arose as to Specht's (P) use of the software, Netscape (D) moved to compel arbitration.

🏛 RULE OF LAW
Where consumers are urged to download free software, mere reference to the existence of license terms on a submerged screen does not place consumers on inquiry notice or constructive notice of terms.

FACTS: Specht (P) downloaded from the Internet free software from Netscape Communications Corp. (Netscape) (D). Specht (P) then brought suit against Netscape (D), alleging that usage of the software transmitted to Netscape (D) private information about the user's file transfer activity on the Internet in violation of federal statute. Netscape (D) moved to compel arbitration, arguing that Specht's (P) downloading of the Netscape (D) software constituted acceptance of the compulsory arbitration provision contained in the online licensing agreement.

ISSUE: Where consumers are urged to download free software, does mere reference to the existence of license terms on a submerged screen place consumers on inquiry notice or constructive notice of terms?

HOLDING AND DECISION: (Sotomayor, J.) No. Mere reference to the existence of license terms on a submerged screen does not place consumers on inquiry notice or constructive notice of terms. The download webpage screen was printed in such a manner that it tended to conceal the fact that it was an express acceptance of Netscape's (D) rules and regulations. There is no reason to assume that viewers will scroll down to subsequent screens simply because screens are there. Netscape (D) relies on cases that involve shrinkwrap licensing that placed consumers on inquiry notice. Those cases, *Hill v. Gateway 2000, Inc.*, 105 F.3d 1147 (7th Cir. 1997) and *ProCD, Inc. v. Zeidenberg*, 86 F.3d 1447 (7th Cir. 1996) do not help Netscape (D) because the licensing in those cases was conspicuous. Specht (P) was responding to an offer that did not carry an immediate visible notice of the existence of license terms or require unambiguous manifestations of assent to those terms. The uncontested evidence revealed that Specht (P) was unaware that Netscape (D) intended to attach license terms to the use of the downloaded software.

The district court's denial of the motion to compel arbitration is affirmed.

▶ ANALYSIS

As noted by the court in *Specht*, when products are "free" and users are invited to download them in the absence of reasonably conspicuous notice that they are about to bind themselves to contract terms, the transactional circumstances cannot be fully analogized to those "in the paper world" of arm's-length bargaining.

■══■

Quicknotes

CONSTRUCTIVE NOTICE Knowledge of a fact that is imputed to an individual who was under a duty to inquire and who could have learned of the fact through the exercise of reasonable prudence.

INQUIRY NOTICE The communication of information that would cause an ordinary person of average prudence to inquire as to its truth.

■══■

Beall v. Beall

Land purchaser (P) v. Landowner (D)

Md. Ct. of Special App., 45 Md. App. 489, 413 A.2d 1365 (1980).

NATURE OF CASE: Appeal from dismissal of complaint in action for specific performance.

FACT SUMMARY: Beall (P) wanted to buy Beall's (D) land pursuant to an alleged option contract. Beall (D) refused to sell and Beall (P) sought specific performance of the option contract.

⚖ RULE OF LAW
An option unsupported by consideration transforms into an offer revocable at any time by the offeror.

FACTS: Calvin Beall and his wife, Cecelia (D), owned land surrounded on three sides by Calvin's mother, Pearl's, farm and worked her land. Carlton Beall (P), Calvin's second cousin, purchased Pearl's farm. Carlton (P) agreed to permit Calvin to continue farming the land in exchange for Calvin paying property taxes. Calvin and Cecelia (D) also gave Carlton (P) a three-year option contract to purchase their land. Pursuant to the option, as consideration, Calvin and Cecelia received $100.00. A second five-year option was signed before the end of the first option but no new consideration was recited or paid. Carlton (P) did not exercise that option either. Prior to the end of the five years, Calvin and Cecelia (D) executed another extension for three years but did not recite or receive additional consideration. Calvin died leaving the land to Cecelia (D). Carlton (P) then elected to exercise the option and prepared to close on Cecelia's (D) land, but Cecelia (D) refused to sell. Carlton (P) sued Cecelia (D) for specific performance of the option contract. The trial judge dismissed the complaint for lack of consideration in the extensions to the option contract. Carlton (P) appealed.

ISSUE: Does an option unsupported by consideration transform into an offer revocable at any time by the offeror?

HOLDING AND DECISION: (Moore, J.) Yes. An option unsupported by consideration transforms into an offer revocable at any time by the offeror. An option only becomes an irrevocable, binding agreement upon payment of consideration. The lack of an option contract, however, may still leave an offer and acceptance resulting in an enforceable contract. Calvin and Cecelia (D) did not receive additional consideration for the two extensions on the option contract, so it is arguably invalid. Cecelia (D) received no benefit for the additional extensions. The original offer, however, to sell the land to Carlton (P) may remain. Calvin and Cecelia (D) had to revoke the offer prior to Carlton's (P) acceptance, but the trial court did not delve into the existence of a valid offer or valid

acceptance. Reversed (on other grounds) and remanded for new trial.

▶ ANALYSIS

Carlton (P) waited ten years before accepting Calvin and Cecelia's (D) offer to sell their property for $28,000.00. Carlton's (P) ability to accept expired upon Calvin's death, however, because an offer expires with the offeror's death or incapacity.

■══■

Quicknotes

CONSIDERATION Value given by one party in exchange for performance, or a promise to perform, by another party.

OPTION CONTRACT A contract pursuant to which a seller agrees that property will be available for the buyer to purchase at a specified price and within a certain time period.

SPECIFIC PERFORMANCE An equitable remedy whereby the court requires the parties to perform their obligations pursuant to a contract.

■══■

Consideration

Quick Reference Rules of Law

Kim v. Son

Lender (P) v. Debtor (D)

2009 WL 597232 (2009) (unpublished opinion).

NATURE OF CASE: Appeal of trial court judgment.

FACT SUMMARY: J. Jinsoo Kim (P) tried to enforce as a contract a gratuitous promise to repay a loan written by his friend, Son (D), in Son's own blood.

> 🏛 **RULE OF LAW**
> Where consideration is lacking, a contract does not exist.

FACTS: J. Jinsoo Kim (P) loaned the won equivalent of $170,000 to his friend, Son (D), which Son (D) invested in two businesses that failed. One night at a sushi bar after too many drinks, Son (D) asked the waiter for a safety pin, used it to prick his finger, and wrote a promissory note with his blood. The rough translation of the note reads, "Sir, please forgive me. Because of my deeds you have suffered financially. I will repay you to the best of my ability." At some point the same day, Son (D) also wrote in ink, "I hereby swear (promise) that I will pay back to the best of my ability, the estimated amount of 170,000,000 wons to Kim." A year later, Kim (P) sued Son (D), alleging that Son (D) defaulted on the promissory note. There was a bench trial, and the court ruled in Son's (D) favor. The court ruled that the blood agreement was not an enforceable contract because there was no evidence Son (D) agreed to personally guarantee the loan, and because the note lacked consideration. As such, it was a gratuitous promise, not an agreement. Kim (P) appealed. [The decision also notes that in the opening of his brief, Kim (P) states, "Blood may be thicker than water, but here it's far weightier than a peppercorn," which is apparently a reference to *Hobbs v. Duff*, 23 Cal. 596 (1863), which held that "What is a valuable consideration? A peppercorn. . . ."]

ISSUE: Where consideration is lacking, does a contract exist?

HOLDING AND DECISION: (O'Leary, J.) No. Where consideration is lacking, a contract does not exist. [The court offers no rationale beyond restating the facts listed above and affirming the trial court's determination that the promise was gratuitous, and that because there was no consideration, there was no contract.]

> ▶ **ANALYSIS**
>
> This is a straightforward illustration of the rule that without consideration, a contract is not formed. A promise alone, however serious or zealously offered, cannot be enforced if it is gratuitous. Of course, if the loan had been given in reliance on a promise, the outcome would have been different. Because the promise to repay came after the loan, and because the loan was given without a promise to repay in exchange, the promise is gratuitous.

Quicknotes

CONSIDERATION Value given by one party in exchange for performance, or a promise to perform, by another party.

GRATUITOUS PROMISE Promise made by someone who has not received consideration for it, which makes the promise unenforceable as a legal contract.

Hamer v. Sidway

Assignee of nephew (P) v. Executor (D)

N.Y. Ct. App., 124 N.Y. 538, 27 N.E. 256 (1891).

NATURE OF CASE: Appeal from denial of damages in an action for breach of contract.

FACT SUMMARY: Sidway's (D) decedent promised to pay $5,000 to Hamer's (P) assignor if he would forbear from the use of liquor, tobacco, swearing, or playing cards or billiards for money until his 21st birthday.

🏛 RULE OF LAW
In general, a waiver of any legal right at the request of another party is a sufficient consideration for a promise.

FACTS: Story, of whose estate Sidway (D) was executor, agreed with his nephew, William, that he, Story, would pay him $5,000 if he refrained from drinking liquor, using tobacco, swearing, or playing cards or billiards for money until his 21st birthday. Upon turning 21, William wrote Story saying that he had fulfilled his part of this deal and was entitled to the money. Story replied that William had in fact earned the money, but because Story feared that William might squander it, Story told William that he would keep the money set aside for him at interest. William agreed to this arrangement. Story died 12 years later without having paid over the $5,000. William assigned his right in the money to his wife who, in turn, assigned her right to Hamer (P), who brought this action for breach of contract when Sidway (D) refused to pay on the ground that William gave no consideration nor did he suffer a detriment, but rather that his health and habits were benefited. Hamer (P) appealed judgment for Sidway (D).

ISSUE: Generally, is a waiver of any legal right at the request of another party a sufficient consideration for a promise?

HOLDING AND DECISION: (Parker, J.) Yes. Generally, a waiver of any legal right at the request of another party is a sufficient consideration for a promise. Valuable consideration may consist of either some right, interest, profit, or benefit accruing to the one party, for whom forbearance, detriment, loss, or responsibility is given, suffered, or undertaken by the other. To follow Sidway's (D) contention would be to leave open to controversy whether a consideration was erased by the degree a detriment is given by a promisee also benefited him. "The order appealed from should be reversed and the judgment of the Special Term affirmed with costs payable out of the estate."

▶ ANALYSIS

The trust question was raised above because a pure contract action would have been barred by the running of the statute of limitations while an action on a trust would not have been so barred. "Consideration means not so much that one party is profiting as that the other abandons some legal right in the present or limits his legal freedom of action in the future as an inducement for the promise of the first." Pollock, *Contracts*, 166. Abstinence from liquor or giving up the use of liquor has independently been held to be sufficient consideration for a promise.

■═■

Quicknotes

BREACH OF CONTRACT Unlawful failure by a party to perform its obligations pursuant to contract.

CONSIDERATION Value given by one party in exchange for performance, or a promise to perform, by another party.

TRUST The holding of property by one party for the benefit of another.

■═■

Kirksey v. Kirksey

Sister-in-law (P) v. Brother-in-law (D)

Ala. Sup. Ct., 8 Ala. 131 (1845).

NATURE OF CASE: Appeal damages award to plaintiff in breach of promise action.

FACT SUMMARY: Kirksey (D) promised "Sister Antillico" (P) a place to raise her family "[i]f you come down and see me."

🏛 RULE OF LAW
To be legally enforceable an executory promise must be supported by sufficient, bargained-for consideration.

FACTS: Kirksey (D) wrote to "Sister Antillico" (P) a letter containing the following clause: "If you will come down and see me, I will let you have a place to raise your family." Antillico (P) moved sixty miles to Kirksey's (D) residence where she remained for over two years. Kirksey (D) then required her to leave although her family was not yet "raised." Antillico (P) contends that the loss which she sustained in moving was sufficient consideration to support Kirksey's (D) promise to furnish her with "a place" until she could raise her family. Antillico (P) received damages of $200 and Kirksey (D) appealed.

ISSUE: Is a promise on the condition, "If you will come down and see me," given as a bargained exchange for the promisee's "coming down and seeing" the promisor?

HOLDING AND DECISION: (Ormond, J.) No. Such a promise is a promise to make a gift. Any expenses incurred by the promisee in "coming down and seeing" are merely conditions necessary to acceptance of the gift. In this case, Kirksey (D) did not appear to be bargaining either for Sister Antillico's presence or for her sixty-mile move. Instead, Kirksey (D) merely wished to assist her out of what he perceived as a grievous and difficult situation. Reversed.

▌ ANALYSIS

This well-known case demonstrates the court's insistence on finding a bargained-for exchange before it will enforce an executory promise. A promise to make a gift is generally not legally binding until it is executed. Compare Williston's famous hypothetical in which a benevolent man says to a tramp: "If you go around the corner to the clothing shop there, you may purchase an overcoat on my credit." This hypothetical highlights the conceptual problem of the present case in that it is unreasonable to construe the walk around the corner as the price of the promise, yet it is a legal detriment to the tramp to make the walk. Perhaps a reasonable (though not conclusive) guideline is the extent to which the happening of the condition will benefit the promisor. The present case might be decided differently today under the doctrine of promissory estoppel which had not yet been developed in 1845.

∎▬∎

Quicknotes

CONDITION Requirement; potential future occurrence upon which the existence of a legal obligation is dependent.

GIFT A transfer of property to another person that is voluntary and which lacks consideration.

PROMISSORY ESTOPPEL A promise that is enforceable if the promisor should reasonably expect that it will induce action or forbearance on the part of the promisee, and does in fact cause such action or forbearance, and it is the only means of avoiding injustice.

∎▬∎

Pennsy Supply, Inc. v. American Ash Recycling Corp.

Subcontractor (P) v. Supplier (D)

Pa. Super. Ct., 895 A.2d 595, *appeal denied,* 907 A.2d 1103 (2006).

NATURE OF CASE: Appeal from dismissal of complaint in breach of contract action.

FACT SUMMARY: Pennsy Supply, Inc. (Pennsy) (P), subcontractor on a paving job, used American Ash Recycling Corp's (Ash's) (D) product to complete its job. The product proved defective and was classified as hazardous waste. Ash (D) refused to remove and dispose of the product and Pennsy (P) sought to recover its costs for doing so.

> 🏛 **RULE OF LAW**
> Consideration exists when a promisor benefits, a promisee suffers a detriment, and the promise was not gratuitous, even if the parties do not bargain for the consideration.

FACTS: Pennsy Supply, Inc. (Pennsy) (P) was the paving subcontractor on a school construction project. The project contract required Pennsy (P) to use certain materials in completing its paving, but substitution of AggRite, manufactured by American Ash Recycling Corp. (Ash) (D), was allowed. The contract included a letter from Ash (D) promoting free AggRite on a first come, first serve basis. Pennsy (P) ordered 11,000 tons of AggRite to complete its paving. Just over one year after completing the job, the pavement developed extensive cracks. Pennsy (P) remedied the cracks at no cost. The remedy included removing and disposing of the AggRite, which the Pennsylvania Department of Environmental Protection classified as a hazardous waste product. Pennsy (P) requested Ash (D) arrange to remove and dispose of the AggRite, but Ash (D) did not do so. Pennsy (P) then filed a breach of contract action against Ash (D) seeking to recover $251,940.20 in remedial costs and $133,777.48 in removal and disposal costs. Ash (D) filed demurrers to all counts; the trial court sustained the demurrers and dismissed the complaint. Pennsy (P) appealed.

ISSUE: Does consideration exist when a promisor benefits, a promisee suffers a detriment, and the promise was not gratuitous, even if the parties do not bargain for the consideration?

HOLDING AND DECISION: (Melvin, J.) Yes. Consideration exists when a promisor benefits, a promisee suffers a detriment, and the promise was not gratuitous, even if the parties do not bargain for the consideration. The trial court did not find sufficient consideration to support the existence of a contract between Pennsy (P) and Ash (D). Pennsy (P) alleged that Ash (D) induced Pennsy (P) to use AggRite to avoid disposal costs associated with Ash's

(D) hazardous waste product. Thus, Ash (D) allegedly benefited from Pennsy's (P) use of its product and Pennsy (P) suffered a detriment. Justice Oliver Wendell Holmes, Jr. classified consideration as "the promise must induce the detriment and the detriment must induce the promise." The purpose for the promise is what distinguishes consideration from gift. The trial court believed that the complaint demonstrated only that Ash (D) made a conditional gift of the AggRite to Pennsy (P). On the contrary, the complaint alleged that Ash (D) actively promoted its AggRite to avoid disposal costs. This can be viewed as an allegation of consideration. The consideration need not have been bargained for by the parties for a contract to exist. Reversed and remanded.

▶ *ANALYSIS*

A contract does not exist without consideration, but this case demonstrates that the parties do not necessarily have to bargain for the consideration. Ash (D) promised free product perhaps to avoid disposal costs, Pennsy (P) accepted the free product and ended up spending hundreds of thousands of dollars to dispose of the product, and consideration is born to support a contract between the parties. Ash (D) appealed this case to the Pennsylvania Supreme Court, but the appeal was denied.

■■■

Quicknotes

BREACH OF CONTRACT Unlawful failure by a party to perform its obligations pursuant to contract.

CONSIDERATION Value given by one party in exchange for performance, or a promise to perform, by another party.

DEMURRER The assertion that the opposing party's pleadings are insufficient and that the demurring party should not be made to answer.

■■■

Gottlieb v. Tropicana Hotel and Casino

Gambling club member (P) v. Promoter (D)

109 F. Supp. 2d 324 (E.D. Pa. 2000).

NATURE OF CASE: Summary judgment motion in breach of contract action.

FACT SUMMARY: Gottlieb (P) contends that Tropicana Hotel and Casino (D) breached a promotional contract by refusing to pay the grand prize she allegedly won.

🏛 RULE OF LAW
Minimal detriment to a participant in a promotional contest is sufficient consideration for a valid contract.

FACTS: Ms. Gottlieb (P), a Pennsylvania resident, was a member of the Tropicana Hotel and Casino's (Tropicana's) (D) "Diamond Club." Tropicana (D) is located in Atlantic City, New Jersey. Membership in the Diamond Club is free, but in order to join, Ms. Gottlieb (P) had to provide her name, address, telephone number, and e-mail address. This information was entered into the casino's computer database, and an identification number and membership card was issued to Ms. Gottlieb (P). The card must be "swiped" in a machine each time a member plays a game at the casino, and the casino tracks information about the member's gambling habits to tailor its promotions. Ms. Gottlieb (P) alleges that on a visit to the casino she participated, as a member of the Diamond Club, in one of Tropicana's (D) promotional games called the "Fun House Million Dollar Wheel Promotion" ("Million Dollar Wheel"). When her turn came to play, she swiped her Diamond Club membership card and spun the wheel. Ms. Gottlieb contends that the wheel landed on the $1 million grand prize, but that immediately thereafter a casino attendant swiped another card through the machine, reactivated the wheel, and the prize was changed to two show tickets. Tropicana (D) claims the wheel never landed on the $1 million prize, that their attendant did not intervene, and that Ms. Gottlieb simply won the lesser prize. Ms. Gottlieb (P) brought suit contending that Tropicana (D) breached its contract to pay out on the promotion. Tropicana (D) claimed there was insufficient consideration to support a breach of contract claim and moved for summary judgment.

ISSUE: Is minimal detriment to a participant in a promotional contest sufficient consideration for a valid contract?

HOLDING AND DECISION: (Bartle, J.) Yes. Minimal detriment to a participant in a promotional contest is sufficient consideration for a valid contract. Although this action was brought under diversity jurisdiction, both Pennsylvania and New Jersey law require adequate consideration in order to form an enforceable contract so no conflict of law analysis need be applied to evaluate Tropicana's summary judgment motion with regard to the claim of breach. Similarly, both states recognize that minimal detriment to a participant in a promotional contest is sufficient consideration for a valid contract. Consideration is a bargained-for exchange, and it may take the form of either a detriment to the promisee or a benefit to the promisor. Ms. Gottlieb (P) had to travel to the casino to participate in the promotion, wait her turn and submit her Diamond Club card to allow the casino to track her gambling habits. Ms. Gottlieb (P), through her participation in the promotion, became part of the entertainment for all those present. These detriments to Ms. Gottlieb (P), even though minimal in nature, were given at the inducement of the promise given by Tropicana (D) in exchange for the chance to win the $1 million grand prize. Tropicana's motives in offering the promotion were not altruistic and the promotion was designed to increase patronage and excitement within the casino. Finding that sufficient consideration was given to form a valid contract, summary judgment for Tropicana (P) must be denied and the parties may litigate their factual dispute as to whether Ms. Gottlieb (P) won the $1 million dollar prize.

▶ ANALYSIS

The court does not spell out a bright-line test for determining the adequacy of consideration, or what distinguishes "nominal" consideration which is inadequate for contract formation, from "minimal detriment." The court leaves this determination open for a case-by-case determination. It should be noted, however, that this ruling is applicable only to the summary judgment motion. Whether or not the plaintiff succeeds on her claim remains open to litigation and the plaintiff must still satisfy the burdens of proof and persuasion to prevail on the merits of her claim.

■=■

Quicknotes

BREACH OF CONTRACT Unlawful failure by a party to perform its obligations pursuant to contract.

DIVERSITY JURISDICTION The authority of a federal court to hear and determine cases involving $10,000 or more and in which the parties are citizens of different states, or in which one party is an alien.

Continued on next page.

SUMMARY JUDGMENT Judgment rendered by a court in response to a motion made by one of the parties, claiming that the lack of a question of material fact in respect to an issue warrants disposition of the issue without consideration by the jury.

■══■

Fiege v. Boehm

Supposed father (D) v. Pregnant woman (P)

Md. Ct. App., 210 Md. 352, 123 A.2d 316 (1956).

NATURE OF CASE: Appeal from damage award to plaintiff in breach of contract action.

FACT SUMMARY: Fiege (D) promised to pay money if Boehm (P) would refrain from instituting bastardy proceedings, but Fiege (D), after blood tests, determined that Boehm's (P) bastardy claim was invalid and refused to pay.

🏛 **RULE OF LAW**
One party's promise not to assert a claim which she reasonably believes in good faith to be valid but which in fact is invalid may serve as consideration for a return promise by another party.

FACTS: Boehm (P), an unmarried woman, became pregnant and believed in good faith that Fiege (D) was the father. Fiege (D) promised to pay expenses incident to the birth and make regular payments for the raising of the child on condition that Boehm (P) would not institute bastardy proceedings against him. Subsequent to the child's birth, Fiege (D) had blood tests made which demonstrated that he could not have been the father. Fiege (D) then stopped making payments, whereupon Boehm (P) unsuccessfully instituted criminal bastardy proceedings against him. Boehm (P) sought to recover the balance of the expenses as promised. The jury awarded Boehm (P) $2,415.80 in damages. The trial court overruled Fiege's (D) motion for new trial and entered judgment on the jury's verdict. Fiege (D) appealed.

ISSUE: May one party's promise not to assert a claim which she reasonably believes in good faith to be valid but which in fact is invalid serve as consideration for a return promise by another party?

HOLDING AND DECISION: (Delaplaine, J.) Yes. One party's promise not to assert a claim which she reasonably believes in good faith to be valid but which in fact is invalid may serve as consideration for a return promise by another party. Although forbearance to assert a claim known to be invalid will not support a return promise, if the parties to a settlement agreement reasonably believe in good faith that the claim forgone is valid or if there is at least a bona fide dispute, the forbearance is consideration for a return promise. The subjective requisite that the claim be bona fide is combined with the objective requisite that the claim has a reasonable basis of support. In this case, no evidence suggests that Boehm (P) made her accusation in bad faith. Affirmed.

▶ **ANALYSIS**

Basic public policy underlies this decision. The law seeks to encourage out-of-court settlements which are not coerced. Such settlements (1) tend to promote goodwill, (2) are much less expensive for the parties to pursue than a full-blown court battle, and (3) help relieve unnecessary (and expensive) congestion on court dockets. However, a settlement based on forbearance to assert a claim known to be invalid is likely to be coercive and in bad faith, and courts will not enforce it.

■━■

Quicknotes

FORBEARANCE TO ASSERT CLAIM Refraining from the assertion of a legal claim upon the date at which it becomes due.

■━■

Schwartzreich v. Bauman-Basch, Inc.

Employee designer (P) Contracting employer (D)

N.Y. Ct. App. 231, N.Y. 196, 131 N.E. 887 (1921).

NATURE OF CASE: Appeal from reinstatement of damage award to plaintiff in action for breach of employment contract.

FACT SUMMARY: Schwartzreich's (P) employment contract was renegotiated to prevent him from taking a new position.

🏛 RULE OF LAW
Where an existing contract is terminated by the mutual consent of the parties, a subsequent contract is binding even if no new consideration is present.

FACTS: Bauman-Basch, Inc. (Bauman) (D) hired Schwartzreich (P) as a designer. Schwartzreich (P) received a better offer from a third party. Schwartzreich (P) informed Bauman (D) that he intended to leave unless Bauman (D) matched the new salary offer. Bauman (D) acceded, and a new contract for a higher salary was executed. Bauman (D) subsequently refused to pay Schwartzreich (P) the higher salary, alleging that the new "contract" had no consideration since Schwartzreich (P) was already obligated to perform the same duties at a lower price during the remaining term of the contract. Evidence at trial on the breach of contract alleged by Schwartzreich (P) was in conflict as to why the contract had been renegotiated and as to whether the other contract had been rescinded. The judge instructed the jury that the new contract would be valid if the old contract had first been mutually rescinded. The jury returned a verdict for Schwartzreich (P) but the trial judge set it aside and dismissed the complaint for lack of evidence of cancellation of the first contract. On appeal, the dismissal was reversed but reinstated the jury verdict instead of granting a new trial.

ISSUE: Where an existing contract is terminated by the mutual consent of the parties, is a subsequent contract binding even if no new consideration is present?

HOLDING AND DECISION: (Crane, J.) Yes. Where an existing contract is terminated by the mutual consent of the parties, a subsequent contract is binding even without the presence of additional consideration. The mutual promise to rescind the old contract is sufficient consideration to support the new one. If Bauman (D) had elected to stand on the original contract, it could have sued Schwartzreich (P) for damages if he breached it. Having elected to rescind the old contract and enter a new one, Bauman (D) is bound by its terms. Judgment affirmed.

▶ ANALYSIS

A contract modification which has the effect of altering the obligation of only one of the parties is ordinarily deemed unenforceable unless supported by a new consideration. This is because the party whose obligation has not been altered had a preexisting duty to perform in accordance with the original agreement and thus has given no consideration for the modification. In this situation, each party's relinquishment of his right to enforce the original contract constitutes adequate consideration for the modification.

■■■

Quicknotes

CONSIDERATION Value given by one party in exchange for performance, or a promise to perform, by another party.

■■■

Angel v. Murray

Taxpayer (P) v. City treasurer (D)

R.I. Sup. Ct., 113 R.I. 482, 322 A.2d 630 (1974).

NATURE OF CASE: Appeal from judgment for plaintiff in action for breach of contract.

FACT SUMMARY: Maher (D) asked for $10,000 more per year to collect refuse even though his contract with the city to provide this service had not yet expired.

🏛 RULE OF LAW
Where unanticipated circumstances or conditions have occurred, the parties to a contract may voluntarily increase the amount of compensation due even if no additional consideration is given.

FACTS: Maher (D) entered into a five-year contract with the city to provide it refuse collection services. A totally unanticipated growth in construction increased the number of units from which Maher (D) had to collect refuse by 20–25 units per year. Maher (D) requested an additional $10,000 per year for the remainder of the contract because of this unexpected increase. The Council discussed the matter at a public meeting and agreed to give Maher (D) $10,000 for that year, and an additional $10,000 was given him the following year. Apparently, Angel (P), a taxpayer, and others (P) brought a civil action against Maher (D) and Murray (D), the City Treasurer, to compel Maher (D) to repay the $20,000 in additional compensation received by him. Angel (P) alleged that there was no new consideration to support the modification since Maher (D) was already under a duty to collect the refuse. The trial judge found for Angel (P) and Maher (D) appealed.

ISSUE: Where unanticipated circumstances or conditions have occurred, may the parties to a contract voluntarily increase the amount of compensation due even if no additional consideration is given?

HOLDING AND DECISION: (Roberts, C.J.) Yes. Where unanticipated circumstances or conditions have occurred, the parties to a contract may voluntarily increase the amount of compensation due even if no additional consideration is given. The preexisting duty rule has, in the past, been used to hold such contracts invalid for lack of consideration. A modification of a contract is itself a contract which must be supported by consideration. We find that where the parties voluntarily agree to modify an existing contract, without coercion or duress, because of unanticipated conditions or circumstances, the modification is valid. There is no reason to prevent the parties from

modifying their contractual agreements. The new contract is valid. Judgment reversed and remanded.

▌ *ANALYSIS*

Some courts have gone through elaborate attempts to avoid the preexisting duty rule by first finding a rescission and then a new contract. *Linz v. Schuck*, 106 Md. 220, 67 A. 286 (1907). Many jurisdictions no longer temper application of the preexisting duty rule along the lines mentioned in *Angel*. Modifications made before the contract is fully executed on either side will be upheld if equitable and free from coercion. Restatement (Second) of Contracts § 89D(a).

Quicknotes

CONSIDERATION Value given by one party in exchange for performance, or a promise to perform, by another party.

PREEXISTING DUTY RULE A common law doctrine that renders unenforceable a promise to perform a duty, which the promisor is already legally obligated to perform, for lack of consideration.

Kibler v. Frank L. Garrett & Sons, Inc.

Farmer (P) v. Buyer (D)

Wash. Sup. Ct., 73 Wash. 2d 523, 439 P.2d 416, en banc (1968).

NATURE OF CASE: Action in damages for breach of contract.

FACT SUMMARY: Kibler (P), while disputing the amount due him on a contract, accepted a check marked "payment in full."

🏛 RULE OF LAW
If acceptance of a check in full satisfaction of a disputed debt is not adequately brought home to the creditor, no binding accord and satisfaction will be found.

FACTS: Kibler (P) agreed to harvest wheat for Frank L. Garrett & Sons, Inc. (Garrett) (D). Their contract called for Kibler (P) to receive a minimum of 18 cents per bushel. Kibler (P) harvested the wheat and charged Garrett (D) 20 cents per bushel, totaling $876. Garrett (D) sent Kibler (P) a check for $444. In fine print, the check stated that it was in full payment of the account. Kibler (P) cashed the check without realizing that the payment was to be in full payment of his contract charge. Garrett (D) alleged that by cashing the check an accord and satisfaction had been reached. Kibler (P) sued for the balance due under the contract, alleging that he had inadequate notice of the proposed accord and would not have accepted the lesser amount if he had known.

ISSUE: Must the debtor clearly inform the creditor that he will pay no more than what is offered and that this is to be in full satisfaction of the debt?

HOLDING AND DECISION: (Rosellini, J.) Yes. Before a debt may be extinguished through an accord and satisfaction, there must be a good-faith dispute of the amount and the creditor must specifically agree to accept a lesser amount than his claim in full satisfaction of the debt. The debtor must bring to the attention of the creditor his intention not to pay any more than what is being offered and that the offer is in full satisfaction of the debt. Unless this fact is clearly established, there has been no binding accord and satisfaction. A creditor may not be tricked into receiving a lesser amount for a valid debt. There must be a meeting of the minds of the parties as to a settlement of the creditor's claim. The notation on the back of the check, in fine print, was insufficient to establish that Kibler (P) had read it and accepted the partial payment as full satisfaction. Reversed and remanded.

DISSENT: (Hale, J.) The printed notation on the check, standing alone, was insufficient to comprise an accord and satisfaction. However, the facts and circumstances surrounding the delivery and cashing of the check, factual determinations by the trial court to which this court should defer, support the conclusion that Kibler (P) knowingly accepted the check as full payment and satisfaction of the debt. After revising his demand for payment twice, Kibler (P) had established an unliquified and uncertain debt. Once Garrett (D) responded with a counteroffer and a check clearly intended to serve as payment in full, any person would understand that cashing the check would constitute acceptance and total satisfaction of the debt. This court should affirm the trial court's decision to dismiss.

▶ ANALYSIS

An accord and satisfaction is a contractual agreement. The burden which the payer bears to reasonably bring home his intention regarding a payment is yet another example of the court's insistence on finding a "meeting of the minds" in every contract. Note the court's emphasis on the favor which it would give to genuine (as opposed to inadvertent) settlements.

■■■

Quicknotes

ACCORD AND SATISFACTION The performance of an agreement between two parties, one of which has a valid claim against the other, to settle the controversy.

■■■

Roth Steel Products v. Sharon Steel Corp.

Purchaser (P) v. Supplier (D)

705 F.2d 134 (6th Cir. 1983).

NATURE OF CASE: Appeal of award of damages for breach of contract.

FACT SUMMARY: Roth Steel Products (P) contended that certain contractual modifications insisted upon by Sharon Steel Corporation (D) were done in bad faith.

🏛 RULE OF LAW
A party seeking to modify a contract must do so for commercially reasonable reasons and in good faith.

FACTS: Sharon Steel Corp. (Sharon) (D), during a period of time in which the steel industry was "slow," negotiated with Roth Steel Products (Roth) (P) to sell the latter certain types of steel on a monthly basis at prices below Sharon's (D) published prices. About six months later, a variety of factors caused the supply of steel to lessen substantially, leading to price increases. Sharon (D) announced that it would no longer sell steel at below-published prices. Roth (P), having no alternative supply source, agreed. Subsequently, Sharon (D) often delivered in an untimely fashion, ascribing this to material shortages and regulatory problems, although significant quantities were sold in transactions not covered by federal price ceilings. Roth (P) eventually sued for breach. The trial court found that Sharon's (D) insistence on a modification was not done in good faith and awarded damages. Sharon (D) appealed.

ISSUE: Must a party seeking to modify a contract do so for commercially reasonable reasons and in good faith?

HOLDING AND DECISION: (Celebrezze, J.) Yes. A party seeking to modify a contract must do so for commercially reasonable reasons and in good faith. Article 2 of the Uniform Commercial Code (U.C.C.) leaves intact these two requirements found in common law. Whether a request for modification is commercially reasonable comes down to a question of whether the presence of unforeseeable contingencies will cause the party seeking modification to suffer a loss under the contract. This would belie the trial court's finding that the request was not commercially justifiable. However, it appears that Sharon (D) exploited Roth's inability to obtain alternate supplies, in essence forcing the modification upon Roth (P). This constitutes duress, which justifies the district court's finding of lack of good faith. Since this requirement for modification was absent, the district court properly found the modification to have been invalid. Affirmed in part, vacated in part, and remanded.

▶ ANALYSIS

The common law looked disfavorably upon contractual modifications. The dual conditions of commercial justification and good faith were required. Also required was consideration; the party against whom modification was sought had to obtain a benefit above and beyond that to which he was already entitled for a modification to be enforceable.

Quicknotes

GOOD FAITH An honest intention to abstain from any unconscientious advantage of another.

Ridge Runner Forestry v. Ann M. Veneman, Secretary of Agriculture

Company (P) v. Administrative agency (D)

287 F.3d 1058 (Fed. Cir. 2002).

NATURE OF CASE: Appeal from a decision of the Department of Agriculture Board of Contract Appeals.

FACT SUMMARY: Ridge Runner Forestry (P) brought suit against the Secretary of Agriculture (D) to enforce a Tender Agreement.

RULE OF LAW
A valid contract cannot be based upon an illusory promise.

FACTS: Ridge Runner Forestry (Ridge Runner) (P) is a Pacific Northwest fire protection company that entered into an agreement with the Forestry Service to provide equipment during emergencies. The agreement was entitled the Pacific Northwest Interagency Engine Tender Agreement (Tender Agreement), and provided that Ridge Runner (P) would furnish equipment to the government when requested "to the extent the contractor is willing and able at the time of the order." After four years of not receiving any government orders, Ridge Runner (P) sued, alleging the Forest Service had violated an implied duty of good faith and fair dealing by systematically excluding their company from providing services to the government. The Department of Agriculture Board of Contract Appeals (the Department) granted the Secretary of Agriculture's (D) motion to dismiss finding there was no enforceable contract.

ISSUE: Can a valid contract be based upon an illusory promise?

HOLDING AND DECISION: (Mayer, C.J.) No. A valid contract cannot be based upon an illusory promise. To be enforceable, a contract must have sufficient consideration to ensure the mutuality of obligation and sufficient definiteness to provide a basis for determining if a breach occurred and for determining the appropriate remedy. An illusory promise is one that takes the form of a promise, but does not place any limitation on the freedom of the alleged promisor. An illusory promise leaves the alleged promisor, free to subject his action to his own future will as if no words were exchanged between the parties. Neither party in this instance made anything more than an illusory promise. The government, unable to foresee its actual needs, maintained its option to secure firefighting services from any contractor it desired. Ridge Runner (P) would merely be considered should an emergency arise. As for Ridge Runner (P), the company was not obligated to provide the requested equipment, but merely to provide equipment if it was "willing and able." Neither party was bound to a definite obligation nor was consideration exchanged to make the Tender Agreement enforceable. The court affirms the Department's decision to dismiss.

ANALYSIS

This case is a classic example of form over substance. An agreement to make a future agreement for unspecified or quantified services and equipment is simply too deficient of essential contractual terms to be made enforceable. Even the Uniform Commercial Code, with its many gap-filling provisions, cannot supply enough of the missing terms to correct the illusory nature of this tender agreement.

■=■

Quicknotes

ILLUSORY PROMISE A promise that is not legally enforceable because performance of the obligation by the promisor is completely within his discretion.

■=■

Wood v. Lucy, Lady Duff-Gordon

Marketer (P) v. Fashion designer (D)

N.Y. Ct. App., 222 N.Y. 88, 118 N.E. 214 (1917).

NATURE OF CASE: Appeal in action for damages for breach of a contract for an exclusive right.

FACT SUMMARY: Wood (P), in a complicated agreement, received the exclusive right for one year, renewable on a year-to-year basis if not terminated by 90 days' notice, to endorse designs with Lucy, Lady Duff-Gordon's (Lucy's) (D) name and to market all her fashion designs for which she would receive one-half of the profits derived. Lucy (D) broke the contract by placing her endorsement on designs without Wood's (P) knowledge.

🏛 RULE OF LAW
While an express promise may be lacking, the whole writing may be "instinct with an obligation"—an implied promise—imperfectly expressed so as to form a valid contract.

FACTS: Lucy (D), a famous-name fashion designer, contracted with Wood (P) that for her granting to him an exclusive right to endorse designs with her name and to market and license all of her designs, they were to split the profits derived by Wood (P) in half. The exclusive right was for a period of one year, renewable on a year-to-year basis, and terminable upon 90 days' notice. Lucy (D) placed her endorsement on fabrics, dresses, and millinery without Wood's (P) knowledge and in violation of the contract. Lucy (D) claims that the agreement lacked the elements of a contract as Wood (P) allegedly is not bound to do anything.

ISSUE: If a promise may be implied from the writing even though it is imperfectly expressed, is there a valid contract?

HOLDING AND DECISION: (Cardozo, J.) Yes. While the contract did not precisely state that Wood (P) had promised to use reasonable efforts to place Lucy's (D) endorsement and market her designs, such a promise can be implied. The implication arises from the circumstances. Lucy (D) gave an exclusive privilege and the acceptance of the exclusive agency was an acceptance of its duties. Lucy's (D) sole compensation was to be one-half the profits resulting from Wood's (P) efforts. Unless he gave his efforts, she could never receive anything. Without an implied promise, the transaction could not have had such business efficacy as they must have intended it to have. Wood's (P) promise to make monthly accounts and to acquire patents and copyrights as necessary showed the intention of the parties that the promise has value by showing that Wood (P) had some duties. The promise to pay Lucy (D) half the profits and make monthly accounts was a promise to use reasonable efforts to bring profits and revenues into existence. Reversed.

▶ ANALYSIS

A bilateral contract can be express, implied in fact, or a little of each. The finding of an implied promise for the purpose of finding sufficient consideration to support an express promise is an important technique of the courts in order to uphold agreements which seem to be illusory and to avoid problems of mutuality of obligation. This case is the leading case on the subject. It is codified in Uniform Commercial Code § 2-306 (2) where an agreement for exclusive dealing in goods imposes, unless otherwise agreed, an obligation to use best efforts by both parties.

■━■

Quicknotes

BILATERAL CONTRACT An agreement pursuant to which each party promises to undertake an obligation, or to forbear from acting, at some time in the future.

IMPLIED PROMISE A promise inferred by law from a document as a whole and the circumstances surrounding its implementation.

■━■

Mezzanotte v. Freeland

Property purchaser (P) v. Property owner (D)

N.C. Ct. App., 20 N.C. App. 11, 200 S.E.2d 410 (1973).

NATURE OF CASE: Action for specific performance and damages.

FACT SUMMARY: Mezzanotte (P) made the land sale contract contingent on his being able to obtain a second mortgage at terms favorable to him.

🏛 RULE OF LAW
There is no want of mutuality where one party's discretion may be exercised only in good faith.

FACTS: Mezzanotte (P) entered into a contract to purchase real property from Freeland (D). The contract was contingent upon Mezzanotte's (P) being able to secure a second mortgage from the North Carolina National Bank "on such terms and conditions as are satisfactory." Freeland (D) subsequently sought to avoid the contract. Mezzanotte (P) sued for specific performance and damages. Freeland (D) alleged that the contingency on obtaining a second mortgage to Mezzanotte's (P) satisfaction rendered the contract illusory since there was a lack of mutuality of obligation. Mezzanotte (P) alleged that he could have rejected a proffered second mortgage from the bank only if he acted in good faith, and this requirement was sufficient to constitute mutuality.

ISSUE: If a discretionary power is conditioned on its being exercised in good faith, does mutuality of obligation exist?

HOLDING AND DECISION: (Baley, J.) Yes. Both parties remain mutually obligated to contract even though one party reserves a discretionary power if it can be exercised only in good faith. Mezzanotte (P) could not successfully avoid liability if he refused to accept a commercially reasonable second mortgage. The promise is not illusory if it is conditioned on the power being exercised only in good faith. The contract is valid. Affirmed.

▶ ANALYSIS

Mutuality of obligation has become a disfavored concept in most jurisdictions. Contracts will be invalidated only if the court finds the contract wholly illusory. Requirements of good faith are implied under the Uniform Commercial Code and by decisional law in most contracts to avoid the mutuality problem. *Sheldon Simms Co. v. Wilder*, 108 Ga. App. 4, 131 S.E.2d 854 (1963).

■══■

Quicknotes

GOOD FAITH An honest intention to abstain from any unconscientious advantage of another.

SPECIFIC PERFORMANCE An equitable remedy whereby the court requires the parties to perform their obligations pursuant to a contract.

■══■

Miami Coca-Cola Bottling Co. v. Orange Crush Co.

License purchaser (P) v. Licensor (D)

296 F. 693 (5th Cir. 1924).

NATURE OF CASE: Appeal from dismissal of action for specific performance and injunctive relief.

FACT SUMMARY: Miami Coca-Cola Bottling Co. (P) could cancel its contract with Orange Crush Co. (D) at any time, while Orange Crush (D) was bound to perform indefinitely.

RULE OF LAW
Where one party's obligation may be terminated at any time, mutuality of performance will allow the other party to terminate at any time regardless of its contractual obligation.

FACTS: Orange Crush Co. (D) agreed to give Miami Coca-Cola Bottling Co. (Coca-Cola) (P) an exclusive right to sell Orange Crush in a designated territory and to supply it with concentrates and advertising. The agreement was in the form of a perpetual license. Coca-Cola (P) agreed to sell Orange Crush and operate a bottling company for its production as well as using its best efforts to sell it. Coca-Cola (P) was free to terminate the relationship at any time. Orange Crush (D) informed Coca-Cola (P) that it was terminating the license. Coca-Cola (P) sued to enjoin cancellation and to compel performance. The court found that the contract was unenforceable for want of mutuality of performance.

ISSUE: Will specific performance be denied for want of mutuality of performance?

HOLDING AND DECISION: (Bryan, J.) Yes. Specific performance of a contract will be denied for want of mutuality of performance. There must be a promise for a promise. Here, Coca-Cola (P) may terminate the contract at any time. Under such circumstances, Orange Crush (D) cannot be held liable on its perpetual license promise. Affirmed.

▶ ANALYSIS

A few jurisdictions would not void Orange Crush's (D) obligation for lack of mutuality. Its promise would be enforceable based on other consideration in the contract, e.g., setting up a bottling company, best efforts, etc. Most jurisdictions, however, require that there must be mutuality between specific terms, e.g., time or remedies. *Marble Co. v. Ripley*, 10 Wall. 339 (1870). Absent such mutuality, the term will not be deemed binding. *Willard Sutherland & Co. v. U.S.*, 262 U.S. 489 (1923).

Quicknotes

INJUNCTIVE RELIEF A court order issued as a remedy, requiring a person to do, or prohibiting that person from doing, a specific act.

MUTUALITY OF PERFORMANCE The requirement for a valid contract that the parties be required to perform.

SPECIFIC PERFORMANCE An equitable remedy whereby the court requires the parties to perform their obligations pursuant to a contract.

Texas Gas Utilities Company v. S.A. Barrett

Gas provider (P) v. Gas purchaser (D)

Texas Sup. Ct., 460 S.W.2d 409 (1970).

NATURE OF CASE: Appeal from denial of damages for breach of contract.

FACT SUMMARY: The trial court found Texas Gas Utilities Company (P) could not recover for breach as the contract was unenforceable due to a lack of mutuality of obligation.

🏛 RULE OF LAW
Mutuality of obligation is essential to the enforcement of a contract.

FACTS: S.A. Barrett (Barrett) (D) contracted to purchase natural gas from Texas Gas Utilities Company (Texas Gas) (P) pursuant to written contract. The contract required Texas Gas (P) to provide ways and means for the provision of natural gas yet included a clause which stated it assumed no obligation regarding the quality or amount of gas to be delivered. Barrett (D) failed to make timely payments, and Texas Gas (P) sued. The jury found that the contract was unenforceable because it lacked mutuality of obligation, and a verdict for Barrett (D) was returned. The court of appeals affirmed, and Texas Gas (P) appealed.

ISSUE: Is mutuality of obligation essential to enforcement of a contract?

HOLDING AND DECISION: (Steakley, J.) Yes. Mutuality of obligation is essential to the enforceability of a contract. Mutuality of obligation provides the consideration necessary for a valid agreement. In this case, Texas Gas (P) was obligated to provide and maintain facilities and equipment for the supplying of gas to Barrett (D). As a result, a mutual obligation existed, creating a valid contract. Reversed and remanded.

▶ ANALYSIS

Mutuality is a basic element of any contract. It is what distinguishes a promise from an enforceable agreement. The mutual expectation of detriment or waiver of advantages is the element granting enforceability to contracts.

■=■

Quicknotes

MUTUALITY OF OBLIGATION Requires that both parties to a contract are bound or else neither is bound.

■=■

Wiseco, Inc. v. Johnson Controls, Inc.

Seller (P) v. Buyer (D)

2005 WL 2931896 (6th Cir. 2005) (unpublished opinion).

NATURE OF CASE: Appeal of summary judgment.

FACT SUMMARY: Johnson Controls, Inc. (JCI) (D), which manufactured metal headrest stays for DaimlerChrysler vehicles, outsourced manufacturing work to Wiseco, Inc. (P) under a requirements contract. After JCI (D) terminated its orders for certain parts, Wiseco (P) sued for breach of contract.

RULE OF LAW

Under a requirements contract, a buyer is only obligated to order from a seller such actual output or requirements as may occur in good faith, provided that no quantity is unreasonably disproportionate to any stated estimate may be tendered or demanded.

FACTS: Johnson Controls, Inc. (JCI) (D) produced metal headrest stays for DaimlerChrysler vehicles. One of JCI's (D) plants decided to out-source the manufacturing operation for one of the parts of the headrest to Wiseco, Inc. (P). Under the terms of the deal, Wiseco (P) would prepare for the job at its own expense and would produce around 4,000 parts per day. Actual requirements would be set by DaimlerChrysler's needs. Wiseco (P) bought and prepared equipment to handle the manufacturing work, and for six months produced approximately 4,000 parts per day. Six months after production began, JCI (D) told Wiseco (P) that it soon would be terminating orders of the part, and over the next six months, JCI's (D) requirements for the part decreased substantially. JCI (D) said that the decline in requirements for the part stemmed from DaimlerChrysler's changes in vehicle models, which did not use the part Wiseco (P) had been hired to make, but instead starting using a different part. Wiseco (P) sued JCI (D) for breach of contract, and the district court granted summary judgment for JCI (D), concluding that JCI (D) reduced its requirements in good faith.

ISSUE: Under a requirements contract, is a buyer only obligated to order from a seller such actual output or requirements as may occur in good faith, provided that no quantity is unreasonably disproportionate to any stated estimate may be tendered or demanded?

HOLDING AND DECISION: (Sutton, J.) Yes. Under a requirements contract, a buyer is only obligated to order from a seller such actual output or requirements as may occur in good faith, provided that no quantity is unreasonably disproportionate to any stated estimate may be tendered or demanded. Under the Uniform Commercial Code (U.C.C.), as adopted in Kentucky, a requirements contract demands that the buyer order from the seller "such actual output or requirements as may occur in good faith, except that no quantity unreasonably disproportionate to any state estimate . . . may be tendered or demanded." Whether a breach occurred in this case depends in part on Kentucky's understanding of the good faith required by the U.C.C., and relevant case law suggests that the good-faith requirement places constraints on the buyer: The buyer may not purchase the good in question from another seller, the buyer may not "merely have had second thoughts" about the terms of the contract, and the buyer assumes the risk of small changes in his circumstances. At the same time, the buyer does not act in bad faith if it reduced its requirements for "business reasons . . . independent of the terms of the contract or any other aspect of its relationship with the seller." JCI (D) argues that once DaimlerChrysler ceased to have requirements for the part in question, that became a good-faith reason for shrinking orders, and the change in orders accordingly did not amount to a breach of contract. Wiseco (P) argued that the allegedly different part is substantially the same part, but all evidence suggests that that's not true. Wiseco (P) also has presented no evidence that the two parts are essentially one and the same, and JCI (D), by contrast, introduced evidence about the differences between the parts. Wiseco (P) has not met its burden of establishing a triable issue of fact that JCI (D) reduced requirements under the contract in bad faith simply by identifying the existence of a part that succeeded the one Wiseco (P) originally contracted to produce. Affirmed.

ANALYSIS

This case illustrates a fact-driven legal issue: "bad faith." What constitutes "bad faith" is determined largely by case law. The U.C.C. goes as far as it can in defining the phrase, but it is really the court interpretation of the phrase, and its application to the facts, that gives the phrase meaning. This case is easy from that perspective, because there is no evidence of bad faith. It is cases in which there is some evidence of wrongdoing that the full ambiguity of the word "bad faith" is understood, because not all wrongdoing amounts to bad faith.

Quicknotes

BAD FAITH Conduct that is intentionally misleading or deceptive.

BREACH OF CONTRACT Unlawful failure by a party to perform its obligations pursuant to contract.

Summits 7, Inc. v. Kelly

Employer (P) v. Former employee (D)

Vt. Sup. Ct., 178 Vt. 396, 886 A.2d 365 (2005).

NATURE OF CASE: Defendant's appeal from injunction.

FACT SUMMARY: Defendant was plaintiff's at-will employee and signed a noncompetition agreement. After her employment ended, defendant began working for a competitor within the restricted geographic area and during the restricted time. Plaintiff obtained an injunction against defendant working for the competitor.

🏛 RULE OF LAW
Continued employment is sufficient consideration to enforce a non-competition agreement.

FACTS: Staci Lasker (f/k/a Staci Kelly) (D) worked for Summits 7, Inc. (Summits) (P). During her employment, Lasker (D) executed a noncompetition agreement with restrictions on her post-Summits' employment. Lasker's (D) employment with Summits (P) ended and she began working for a competitor within the geographically restricted area. Summits (P) filed for an injunction to prevent Lasker (D) employment based on the noncompete agreement. The court granted the injunction, finding sufficient consideration for the noncompete agreement in Lasker's promotions and raises. Lasker (D) appealed.

ISSUE: Is continued employment sufficient consideration to enforce a non-competition agreement?

HOLDING AND DECISION: (Allen, C.J.) Yes. Continued employment is sufficient consideration to enforce a non-competition agreement. The trial court's reliance on Lasker's (D) promotions and raises is erroneous, because those were rewarded to Lasker (D) for her performance. Lasker's continued employment, however, is sufficient consideration to enforce the noncompetition agreement. In an at-will employment situation, continued employment is sufficient consideration no matter when the noncompetition agreement is signed provided a company does not act in bad faith in terminating employment immediately after the noncompete agreement is executed. Affirmed.

DISSENT: (Johnson, J.) This agreement should be stricken for lack of consideration. The consideration of continued employment is illusory in this case. After Lasker (D) worked for Summits (P) for one year as an at-will employee, Summits (P) requested Lasker (D) execute the noncompetition agreement. Lasker's (D) "consideration" was simply continued employment but now with a highly restricted ability to find employment after she left Summits (P). The noncompetition agreement covered two and a half states, and was for a term of one year after leaving Summits

(P). Courts should closely scrutinize covenants not-to-compete because of the unequal bargaining power of the parties. Here, Lasker (D) could face possible dismissal or sign the overly restrictive covenant. The employee should receive an additional benefit to sign the covenant.

▶ ANALYSIS

Other jurisdictions do not consider continued employment to be sufficient consideration to support a covenant not to compete executed after employment has begun. The employee should receive an additional benefit, such as a promotion. The court in this case, however, completely dismissed the idea of a promotion as an additional benefit because it served as a reward for Lasker's (D) abilities on the job. Independent consideration is recommended despite this court's dismissal of it and promotions or salary raises often serve well as independent consideration.

Quicknotes

AT-WILL EMPLOYMENT The rule that an employment relationship is subject to termination at any time, or for any cause, by an employee or an employer in the absence of a specific agreement otherwise.

CONSIDERATION Value given by one party in exchange for performance, or a promise to perform, by another party.

INJUNCTION A court order requiring a person to do, or prohibiting that person from doing, a specific act.

NONCOMPETE CLAUSE A provision, typically contained in an employment contract or a contract for the sale of a business, pursuant to which the promisor agrees not to compete with the promisee for a specified time period and/or within a particular geographic area.

Moral Obligation and Consideration

Quick Reference Rules of Law

Sheldon v. Blackman

Promisee (P) v. Promisor's administrator (D)

Wis. Sup. Ct., 188 Wis. 4, 205 N.W. 486 (1925).

NATURE OF CASE: Appeal from the denial of a claim against decedent's estate.

FACT SUMMARY: Wilkinson gave Sheldon (P) a promissory note for past services rendered and stated that the value of subsequent services could be claimed against his estate.

🏛 RULE OF LAW
A contract, especially one founded partially on moral consideration, is not void merely because the services rendered were worth less than the contractual amount agreed upon by the parties.

FACTS: Wilkinson promised to leave all of his property to Sheldon (P) when he and his wife died if she would care for them. Mutual wills were executed to this effect. Sheldon (P) cared for both Wilkinsons for more than 30 years. After his wife's death, Wilkinson gave Sheldon (P) a promissory note for $30,000 for past services rendered, payable by his estate. Wilkinson apparently was afraid his will might be contested and desired to make certain Sheldon (P) was adequately compensated for her services in any event. The note stated that any subsequent services rendered could be claimed against his estate. Wilkinson died, and his will was held invalid. Sheldon (P) filed a claim against the estate (D) based on the note and subsequent services rendered. The claim was denied. Sheldon (P) appealed, and Blackman (D), the administrator, alleged that the note was unenforceable for want of consideration. It was alleged that the original oral contract with Wilkinson violated the Statute of Frauds since there was real property in the estate. Since, at maximum, Sheldon (P) could claim only for six-years services because of the statute of limitations, the consideration for the note was deemed inadequate.

ISSUE: May a party freely place any value he wishes on services rendered him where there are moral considerations present?

HOLDING AND DECISION: (Jones, J.) Yes. Wilkinson and his wife had the benefit of 30-years personal service from Sheldon (P). Wilkinson was under a moral obligation to compensate Sheldon (P) for her services even if barred in part by the statute of limitations and the Statute of Frauds. A party may freely place any value he wishes on services rendered to him, especially when there are moral considerations involved. The fact that the services are worth considerably less than the amount paid for them is immaterial. There is no failure or inadequacy of consideration. Whether motivated by generosity or moral obligations, a freely entered into contract where there are no allegations of fraud or undue influence is valid. Judgment for Sheldon (P) is affirmed.

▶ ANALYSIS

Generally, courts will not be receptive to nonparties to a contract who complain of want or failure of consideration. Parties should be free to value services in any manner they wish, and defenses based on consideration are normally personal to the parties. Where the value of services is indeterminate, indefinite, or largely a matter of opinion, the party being benefited should be deemed best able to value them.

■=■

Quicknotes

MORAL CONSIDERATION An inducement to enter a contract, which is not enforceable at law but is made based on a moral obligation and may be enforceable in order to prevent unjust enrichment on the part of the promisor.

■=■

Banco do Brasil S.A. v. State of Antigua and Barbuda

Banking corporation (P) v. Sovereign nation (D)

N.Y. App. Div., 268 A.D.2d 75, 707 N.Y.S.2d 151 (2000).

NATURE OF CASE: Appeal of decision to deny defendant's motion to dismiss.

FACT SUMMARY: The State of Antigua and Barbuda (D) sought dismissal of a breach of contract claim by raising the affirmative defense of the statute of limitations.

🏛 RULE OF LAW

The statute of limitations can be revived under the General Obligations Law when a party provides written acknowledgment of a debt and the written statement does not contradict the party's prior intention to pay.

FACTS: In 1981, Banco do Brasil (Banco) (P), a Brazilian banking corporation, entered into a loan agreement with the State of Antigua and Barbuda (the State) (D). The principal amount of the loan was $3 million. The Ministry of Finance for the State (D) agreed to act as guarantor and executed promissory notes on behalf of the State (D). The State (D) failed to repay the loan within the time specified in the promissory notes, but in 1985, the State (D) confirmed its obligation in writing and requested a new schedule for repayment. Again the State (D) failed to pay, and in 1997, they confirmed by letter the principal and interest remaining to be paid. The State (D) again failed to repay their debt and Banco (P) brought an action for breach of the loan agreement. The State (D) filed a motion to dismiss arguing the six-year statute of limitations had passed, but the trial court found that the 1989 and 1997 letters revived the statute of limitations under the General Obligations Law § 17-101. The State (D) appealed.

ISSUE: Can the statute of limitations be revived under the General Obligations Law when a party provides written acknowledgment of a debt and the written statement does not contradict the party's prior intention to pay?

HOLDING AND DECISION: (Lerner, J.) Yes. The statute of limitations can be revived under the General Obligations Law, § 17-101, when a party provides written acknowledgment of a debt and the written statement does not contradict the party's prior intention to pay. The writing becomes evidence of the new or continued contract to pay. The State's (D) 1997 letter acknowledged the debt and did not contradict the State's (D) intention to pay that debt. The trial court correctly applied this provision of the General Obligations Law and their decision is affirmed.

▶ ANALYSIS

This case is distinguishable from those involving a gratuitous promise, or ones involving past consideration. The original contract was valid and enforceable and the loan was premised on the future performance of repayment. The agreement was executed between sophisticated business parties who are presumed to know the law of contracts. The defendant could have let repayment lapse and allowed the statute of limitations to expire; however, the defendant revived the terms of the valid contract with its subsequent letters acknowledging its unpaid debt. The social policy behind the statute is to discourage those who would fraudulently promise repayment, inducing the other party to forgo legal action until the statute of limitation passed, and then argue the plaintiff's claim was time-barred once the plaintiff realized the true intentions of the defaulting party.

■=▪

Quicknotes

STATUTE OF LIMITATIONS A law prescribing the period in which a legal action may be commenced.

■=▪

Harrington v. Taylor

Injured rescuer promisee (P) v. Rescued promisor (D)

N.C. Sup. Ct., 225 N.C. 690, 36 S.E.2d 227 (1945).

NATURE OF CASE: Appeal in action to enforce a contract.

FACT SUMMARY: In gratitude for Harrington's (P) efforts in saving his life, Taylor (D) promised to pay her for her injuries.

🏛 RULE OF LAW
Gratitude for a gratuitous act is insufficient consideration to enforce a promise.

FACTS: Harrington (P) prevented Taylor (D) from being killed by his wife. Harrington (P) was severely injured. The next day, Taylor (D) promised to pay Harrington (P) for her injuries. Taylor (D) paid a small amount and then refused to make further payments. Harrington (P) sued for breach of contract, and Taylor (D) alleged that the contract was unenforceable for lack of consideration. The trial court found for Taylor (D) and Harrington (P) appealed.

ISSUE: Is gratitude for a gratuitous act sufficient consideration to enforce a contract?

HOLDING AND DECISION: (Per curiam) No. Gratitude or moral obligations arising from a gratuitous, humanitarian act are not sufficient considerations to enforce a contract. No matter how much we personally find Taylor's (D) refusal to pay improper, as a matter of law, the promise to pay for Harrington's (P) injuries is unenforceable. Affirmed.

▶ ANALYSIS

If the original act was not intended to be gratuitous, an implied contract may be found. For example, if an unconscious person is brought to a hospital and is given care for his injuries, there is an implied promise to pay for these services. In cases of rescue, the act is gratuitous. The rescuer is not presumed to have expected payment for his actions. Therefore, there is no, present consideration to support the subsequent promise to pay.

■=■

Quicknotes

CONSIDERATION Value given by one party in exchange for performance, or a promise to perform, by another party.

■=■

Webb v. McGowin

Crippled savior (P) v. Grateful pedestrian (D)

Ala. Ct. App., 27 Ala. App. 82, 168 So. 196, *cert. denied*, 232 Ala. 374, 168 So. 199 (1935).

NATURE OF CASE: Action on appeal to collect on a promise.

FACT SUMMARY: Webb (P) saved the now-deceased J. McGowin from grave bodily injury or death by placing himself in grave danger and subsequently suffering grave bodily harm. J. McGowin, in return, promised Webb (P) compensation. McGowin's executors (D) refused to pay the promised compensation.

🏛 RULE OF LAW
A moral obligation is sufficient consideration to support a subsequent promise to pay where the promisor has received a material benefit.

FACTS: Webb (P), while in the scope of his duties for the W. T. Smith Lumber Co., was clearing the floor, which required him to drop a 75-lb. pine block from the upper floor of the mill to the ground. Just as Webb (P) was releasing the block, he noticed J. McGowin below and directly under where the block would have fallen. In order to divert the fall of the block, Webb (P) fell with it, breaking an arm and leg and ripping his heel off. The fall left Webb (P) a cripple and incapable of either mental or physical labor. In return for Webb's (P) act, J. McGowin promised to pay Webb (P) $15 every two weeks for the rest of Webb's (P) life. J. McGowin paid the promised payments until his death eight years later. Shortly after J. McGowin's death, the payments were stopped, and Webb (P) brought an action against N. McGowin (D) and J. F. McGowin (D) as executors of J. McGowin's estate for payments due him. The executors (D) of the estate were successful in obtaining a nonsuit against Webb (P) in the lower court. Webb (P) appealed.

ISSUE: Is a moral obligation sufficient consideration to support a subsequent promise to pay where the promisor has received a material benefit?

HOLDING AND DECISION: (Bricken, J.) Yes. A moral obligation is sufficient consideration to support a subsequent promise to pay where the promisor has received a material benefit. This is true even where no prior obligation or liability existed. Obligation occurs when the services are not gratuitous and the promisor makes such an express promise as here. Reversed and remanded.

CONCURRENCE: (Samford, J.) The strict letter of the law might prohibit Webb's (P) recovery, but the result reached here is a just one.

▶ ANALYSIS

In most cases where the moral obligation is asserted, the court feels that the promise ought not to be enforced; instead of going into the uncertain field of morality, the court chooses to rely upon the rule that moral obligation is not a sufficient consideration. On the other hand, in cases where the promise is one which would have been kept by most citizens and the court feels that enforcement is just, a few courts will enforce the promise using the *Webb v. McGowin* rule. In general, the *Webb v. McGowin* rule is the minority rule and the *Mills v. Wyman*, 20 Mass. 3 Pick. 207 (1825), rule is the majority rule.

Quicknotes

CONSIDERATION Value given by one party in exchange for performance, or a promise to perform, by another party.

MORAL CONSIDERATION An inducement to enter a contract, which is not enforceable at law but is made based on a moral obligation and may be enforceable in order to prevent unjust enrichment on the part of the promisor.

PECUNIARY Monetary; relating to money.

CHAPTER 4

Promissory Estoppel

Quick Reference Rules of Law

Feinberg v. Pfeiffer Co.

Long-time employee (P) v. Employer (D)

Mo. Ct. App., 322 S.W.2d 163 (1959).

NATURE OF CASE: Action to recover damages for breach of a promise.

FACT SUMMARY: Pfeiffer Co. (D) promised to pay Feinberg (P) an annuity when Feinberg (P) retired, and Feinberg (P) relied on this promise to her detriment.

🏛 RULE OF LAW
A promise that the promisor should reasonably expect to induce action or forbearance of a definite and substantial character on the part of the promisee and that does induce such action or forbearance is binding if injustice can be avoided only by enforcement of the promise.

FACTS: Feinberg (P) was a long-time employee of Pfeiffer Co. (D). In view of Feinberg's (P) ability and length of service, Pfeiffer (D) promised her that if she ever chose to retire, Pfeiffer (D) would pay her $200 per month for the rest of her life. After working another year and a half, Feinberg (P) chose to retire and began receiving the promised $200 payments. Later, the payments were stopped, and Feinberg (P), who could no longer work, sought to recover on Pfeiffer's (D) promise.

ISSUE: If an employer promises an employee, upon retirement, a stipend for the rest of his life, and if the employee retires in reliance on that promise, is the promise binding on the employer?

HOLDING AND DECISION: (Doerner, Commr.) Yes. A promise that the promisor should reasonably expect to induce action or forbearance of a definite and substantial character on the part of the promisee and that does induce such action or forbearance is binding if injustice can be avoided only by enforcement of the promise. (Restatement of Contracts, § 90) The second illustration cited in the comments to Restatement § 90 is precisely applicable to the present case. "A promises to pay B an annuity during B's life. B thereupon resigns a profitable employment, as A expected that he might. B receives the annuity for some years, in the meantime becoming disqualified from again obtaining good employment. A's promise is binding." The fact that, in the illustration, B became "disqualified" from obtaining other employment before A discontinued the payments whereas Feinberg (P) did not discover that she had cancer and was therefore unemployable until after Pfeiffer (D) had discontinued its payments is immaterial. The reference to the disability in the illustration has to do with the prevention of injustice, and the injustice would occur regardless of when the disability occurred. Affirmed.

▶ ANALYSIS

Note that, in the present case, if Feinberg (P) were still healthy and able to work, the decision would have been different. In that situation, it would not be the case that injustice could be avoided only by enforcement of the promise. Note additionally that if Feinberg (P) had continued to work for Pfeiffer (D) until she became physically unable to continue and was forced to retire, she could probably not recover on Pfeiffer's (D) promise. Her retirement would not have been in reliance on Pfeiffer's (D) promise as the doctrine of promissory estoppel requires.

Quicknotes

PROMISSORY ESTOPPEL A promise that is enforceable if the promisor should reasonably expect that it will induce action or forbearance on the part of the promisee, and does in fact cause such action or forbearance, and it is the only means of avoiding injustice.

RELIANCE Dependence on a fact that causes a party to act or refrain from acting.

Conrad v. Fields

Debtor (D) v. Creditor (P)

2007 WL 2106302, (unpublished opinion), (2007).

NATURE OF CASE: Appeal from trial court judgment.

FACT SUMMARY: Walter R. Fields (D) agreed to pay to Marjorie Conrad (P) her tuition and expenses associated with attending law school. When he failed to pay, she sued.

🏛 RULE OF LAW
The elements of a promissory estoppel claim are (1) a clear and definite promise, (2) the promisor intended to induce reliance by the promise, (3) the promisee relied to the promisee's detriment, and (4) the promise must be enforced to prevent injustice.

FACTS: Walter R. Fields (D) was a friend of Marjorie Conrad (P) and a wealthy man. He was philanthropic, and sometimes paid education costs of others. He suggested that Conrad (P) attend law school and offered to pay for it. Conrad (P) accepted the offer, quit her job, and enrolled. Fields (D) made two tuition payments, but stopped payment on the second, and at some point told Conrad (P) that his assets had been frozen by the Internal Revenue Service. Until it was sorted out, he said, he would not be able to pay her expenses. They exchanged a few emails, and in one, Fields (D) wrote, "to be clear and in writing, when you graduate law school and pass your bar exam, I will pay your tuition." Later, he told Conrad (P) that he would not pay her expenses, and he threatened to get a restraining order if she continued to try to communicate with him. Conrad (P) filed a lawsuit, claiming that she relied to her detriment on Fields's (D) promise. The trial court awarded her damages in the amount of $87,314.63 under the doctrine of promissory estoppel.

ISSUE: Are the elements of a promissory estoppel claim (1) a clear and definite promise, (2) the promisor intended to induce reliance by the promise, (3) the promisee relied to the promisee's detriment, and (4) the promise must be enforced to prevent injustice?

HOLDING AND DECISION: (Peterson, J.) Yes. The elements of a promissory estoppel claim are (1) a clear and definite promise, (2) the promisor intended to induce reliance by the promise, (3) the promisee relied to the promisee's detriment, and (4) the promise must be enforced to prevent injustice. In her pleadings, Conrad (P) stated that based on the assurance and inducement of Fields (D), she made the decision to quit her job and enroll in law school, and that Fields (D) was aware of that fact. She testified to the same facts in court, and the trial court found her testimony credible. Fields's (D) expensive home and car, of which Conrad (P) was aware, made it appear as if he was fully capable of keeping his promise to pay her law school expenses, and Fields (D) reasonably should have expected his promise to induce action by Conrad (P). And because he told her his financial problems were temporary, and that he'd pay her expenses upon her graduation, she was not aware until after she graduated that she would suffer damages, and did not have an opportunity to mitigate damages. Finally, receiving a law degree was the expected and intended consequence of Fields's (D) promise, and though she benefited from attending law school, the debt she incurred in reliance on Fields's (D) promise is a detriment to her. Affirmed.

▶ ANALYSIS

This case illustrates the application of the elements of the theory of promissory estoppel to a particular set of facts in which the court finds detrimental reliance, even though the promisee also receives benefit. If there is detrimental reliance, whatever benefit also accrued is usually irrelevant.

Quicknotes

DETRIMENTAL RELIANCE Action by one party, resulting in loss, which is based on the conduct or promises of another.

PROMISSORY ESTOPPEL A promise that is enforceable if the promisor should reasonably expect that it will induce action or forbearance on the part of the promisee, and does in fact cause such action or forbearance, and it is the only means of avoiding injustice.

Salsbury v. Northwestern Bell Telephone Co.

Guarantor (P) v. Pledgor (D)

Iowa Sup. Ct., 221 N.W.2d 609 (1974).

NATURE OF CASE: Appeal in declaratory judgment action.

FACT SUMMARY: Northwestern Bell Telephone Co. (D) wrote a letter pledging $15,000 to a college supported by Salsbury (P). After the college folded, Salsbury (P) still sought payment of the $15,000.

🏛 RULE OF LAW
A charitable subscription binds the subscriber even without proof of consideration or detrimental reliance.

FACTS: Northwestern Bell Telephone Company (Northwestern Bell) (D) wrote a letter pledging a $15,000 contribution to Charles City College. Northwestern Bell (D) did not fill out a pledge card, although college personnel typed the information concerning the contribution onto a pledge card and retained the card for their records. The pledge was then assigned to a supplier of materials and, in order to secure credit from that supplier, Salsbury (P), chairman of the college's board of trustees, executed a personal guaranty. The obligation was secured by various subscription pledges, which were assigned by the supplier to a company which, after settling with Salsbury (P), reassigned the pledges to him. Northwestern Bell (D) refused to pay its pledge because the college folded after operating for only a short time, and Salsbury (P) sued for a declaratory judgment that the pledge was binding upon Northwestern Bell (D). The trial court ruled in favor of Salsbury (P). Northwestern Bell (D) appealed, contending that the obligation was unenforceable because it had not been supported by consideration.

ISSUE: Does a charitable subscription constitute a binding obligation even if it was not supported by consideration?

HOLDING AND DECISION: (Harris, J.) Yes. A charitable subscription binds the subscriber even without proof of consideration or detrimental reliance. This is the rule adopted by the tentative draft of the Restatement (Second) of Contracts § 90. In the past, courts desiring to bind charitable subscribers have resorted to the spurious argument that the promises of other subscribers constitute the consideration for a pledge. But, this theory unrealistically assumes that the subscriptions of two or more subscribers are given in exchange for one another. More recent cases have elected to enforce charitable pledges on a promissory estoppel theory. But this approach, of course, requires a finding of detrimental reliance on the part of the recipient of the pledge. In view of the public interest in assuring the enforceability of promises to contribute to charitable pursuits, the better rule is that subscriptions such as Northwestern Bell's (D) should be deemed binding without reference to consideration or reliance. Affirmed.

▶ ANALYSIS

Some of the better reasoned cases pertaining to charitable subscriptions have been reluctant to accept the argument that policy considerations merit a relaxation of the typical rules of contract law. (See, e.g., *Mount Sinai Hospital of Greater Miami, Inc. v. Jordan*, 290 So. 2d 484 [Fla. 1974].) Cases rejecting the policy argument generally insist upon a showing of consideration or detrimental reliance as a condition to the enforcement of a charitable pledge. The cautionary function of consideration, i.e., to prevent hasty and intemperate decisions from having a binding effect, may be particularly important in the context of charitable subscriptions.

━━■

Quicknotes

CONSIDERATION Value given by one party in exchange for performance, or a promise to perform, by another party.

DECLARATORY JUDGMENT An adjudication by the courts which grants not relief but is binding over the legal status of the parties involved in the dispute.

DETRIMENTAL RELIANCE Action by one party, resulting in loss, that is based on the conduct or promises of another.

━━■

Drennan v. Star Paving Co.

General contractor (P) v. Paving company (D)

Cal. Sup. Ct., 51 Cal. 2d 409, 333 P.2d 757 (en banc) (1958).

NATURE OF CASE: Appeal of an award of damages for breach of contract.

FACT SUMMARY: Drennan (P) sued Star Paving Co. (Star) (D) to recover damages when Star (D) could not perform the paving work at the price quoted in its subcontracting bid.

🏛 RULE OF LAW
Reasonable reliance on a promise binds an offeror even if there is no other consideration.

FACTS: In formulating a bid to the Lancaster School District, Drennan (P), a general contractor, solicited bids for subcontracting work. Star Paving Co. (Star) (P), a paving company, submitted the lowest paving bid, and Drennan (P) used that bid in formulating its bid to the school district. Using Star's (D) subcontracting bid of $7,131.60, Drennan (P) was awarded the general contract. Star (D) then told Drennan (P) that it made a mistake and could not do the work for less than $15,000. Star (D) refused to do the work, and Drennan (P) found a substitute company that did the work for $10,948.60. Drennan (P) sued Star (D) for the difference, claiming that Drennan (P) had reasonably relied on Star's (D) offer. Star (D) claimed that it had made a revocable offer. The trial court ruled in favor of Drennan (P) on the grounds of promissory estoppel, and Star (D) appealed.

ISSUE: Does reasonable reliance on a promise bind the offeror even if there no other consideration?

HOLDING AND DECISION: (Traynor, J.) Yes. Reasonable reliance on a promise binds the offeror even if there is no other consideration. Section 90 of the Restatement of Contracts provides that when a promise is made that induces action or forbearance of the promisee, the promissor is bound if injustice would result from nonenforcement. In the case of a unilateral offer, the offeror is bound to the promise if it produces reasonable reliance. Star (D) made a promise to Drennan (P) of a certain price. Star's (D) bid was the lowest, and Drennan (P) reasonably relied on it in formulating its bid and winning the contract. As a result, Drennan (P) was obligated to do the work at the price quoted and even had to put up a bond. Star (D) should have known such a result would occur if Star's (D) bid was accepted. The absence of consideration is not fatal to Star's (D) initial promise, as Drennan (P) substantially changed its position in reliance on Star (D). Injustice can only be avoided by the enforcement of Star's (D) subcontracting promise. Affirmed.

▶ ANALYSIS

Such reasonable reliance cases are often called firm offers. Firm offers can sometimes be implied promises to hold an offer open and have received criticism on the grounds that one party (the subcontractor) is bound while the other party (the general contractor) is not. Nonetheless, the modern trend is to enforce such promises.

Quicknotes

CONSIDERATION Value given by one party in exchange for performance, or a promise to perform, by another party.

FIRM OFFER Under the Uniform Commercial Code, refers to a signed, written offer to enter into a contract for the sale of goods that is irrevocable for a specified period of time, or if no time is stated, then for a reasonable time period not exceeding three months.

PROMISSORY ESTOPPEL A promise that is enforceable if the promisor should reasonably expect that it will induce action or forbearance on the part of the promisee, and does in fact cause such action or forbearance, and it is the only means of avoiding injustice.

RELIANCE Dependence on a fact that causes a party to act or refrain from acting.

Cosgrove v. Bartolotta

Promisee (P) v. Promisor (D)

150 F.3d 729 (7th Cir. 1998).

NATURE OF CASE: Appeal of trial court judgment.

FACT SUMMARY: Bartolotta (D) asked to borrow $100,000 from Cosgrove (P) in order to open a restaurant, in return for which Bartolotta (D) promised to repay the loan with interest and give Cosgrove (P) an ownership interest in the restaurant. Bartolotta (D) found other financing and cut Cosgrove (P) out of the deal, and Cosgrove (P) sued.

RULE OF LAW

(1) The reliance that makes a promise legally enforceable under the doctrine of promissory estoppel must be induced by a reasonable expectation that the promise will be carried out.

(2) Where a plaintiff has a good claim for either breach of contract or promissory estoppel, restitution is an alternative method of computing damages.

FACTS: Bartolotta (D) asked to borrow $100,000 from Cosgrove (P) in order to open a restaurant, in return for which Bartolotta (D) promised to repay the loan with interest and give Cosgrove (P) an ownership interest in the restaurant. Cosgrove (P) was an experienced corporate lawyer, and he performed some services to get the project off the ground in reliance on the promise of a share in the restaurant. He was ready and willing to make the loan, but Bartolotta (D) found other financing and cut Cosgrove (P) out of the deal. Cosgrove (P) never made the loan, but sued. The jury awarded damages in the amount of $135,000.

ISSUE:

(1) Must the reliance that makes a promise legally enforceable under the doctrine of promissory estoppel be induced by a reasonable expectation that the promise will be carried out?

(2) Where a plaintiff has a good claim for either breach of contract or promissory estoppel, is restitution an alternative method of computing damages?

HOLDING AND DECISION: (Posner, C.J.)

(1) Yes. The reliance that makes a promise legally enforceable under the doctrine of promissory estoppel must be induced by a reasonable expectation that the promise will be carried out. A promise that is vague and conditional may have sufficient expected value to induce a reasonable person to invest time and effort in trying to maximize the likelihood that the promise will be carried out. But if a person invests time and effort knowing that

he is investing for a chance, rather than relying on a firm promise that a reasonable person would expect to be carried out, he cannot plead promissory estoppel. In this case, the jury found that Bartolotta (D) was definite in promising Cosgrove (P) an ownership interest in the restaurant, and that Cosgrove (P) invested time and effort in the venture, along with the pledge to lend $100,000, because he had already been firmly promised a share. The promise was contingent only on his honoring his pledge. And while he never loaned the money, he did render professional services in reliance. In addition, the pledge itself put him at risk, because he would have been bound by the doctrine of promissory estoppel had Bartolotta (D) relied on it.

(2) Yes. Where a plaintiff has a good claim for either breach of contract or promissory estoppel, restitution is an alternative method of computing damages. Restitution in this context is not an alternative theory of liability, but an alternative method of computing damages. If it had been too difficult to value the restaurant, or to determine how large an ownership interest in it Cosgrove (P) had been promised, or to determine what it cost him in foregone opportunities, the value of his services was an alternative. But alternative and cumulative are not synonyms, and in this case, the $135,000 awarded by the jury was a cumulative figure representing the estimated value of what would have been his share in the business ($117,000), the value for his services ($17,000), and a kill fee ($1,000). The damages awarded by the jury were excessive. But since Bartolotta (D) didn't raise an objection to the verdict on this ground, the point is waived. Affirmed in part and reversed in part.

▶ ANALYSIS

One of the more interesting aspects of this case was the court's discussion of restitution, and the fact that the damages awarded by the jury were likely excessive. The defendant failed to raise the issue on appeal, and the issue is therefore waived, as the court pointed out, but the court nevertheless took a position on the issue. It obviously was to make the larger point of law that restitution in this context is an alternative theory of damages. If the reliance measure of damages (the detriment to Cosgrove (P) as a result of reliance) and the expectation measure of damages (the value of the promise) were too difficult to nail down, the value of his services could have been used as a measure of damages. But the court

Continued on next page.

pointedly stated that all three are not meant to be comput-
ed and added together as damages, which is what the
jury did.

■■■■

Quicknotes

PROMISSORY ESTOPPEL A promise that is enforceable if
the promisor should reasonably expect that it will induce
action or forbearance on the part of the promisee, and
does in fact cause such action or forbearance, and it is
the only means of avoiding injustice.

RESTITUTION The return or restoration to rightful owner
to prevent unjust enrichment.

■■■■

CHAPTER 5

Parol Evidence and Interpretation

Quick Reference Rules of Law

Mitchill v. Lath

Property buyer (P) v. Ice house owner (D)

N.Y. Ct. App., 247 N.Y. 377, 160 N.E. 646 (1928).

NATURE OF CASE: Appeal in action for specific performance.

FACT SUMMARY: Mitchill (P) bought some property from Lath (D) pursuant to a full and complete written sales contract. She sought to compel Lath (D) to perform on his parol agreement to remove an ice house on neighboring property.

RULE OF LAW
An oral agreement is permitted to vary from a written contract only if it is collateral in form, does not contradict express or implied conditions of the written contract, and consists of terms which the parties could not reasonably have been expected to include in the written contract.

FACTS: Mitchill (P), through a contract executed by her husband, bought some property from Lath (D). The written contract of sale was completely integrated. Lath (D) then made an oral agreement with Mitchill (P) that in consideration of her purchase of the property, he would remove an ice house which he maintained on neighboring property and which Mitchill (P) found objectionable.

ISSUE: Will an oral agreement which is not collateral, which contradicts express or implied conditions of a written contract, or which consists of terms which the parties could reasonably have been expected to embody in the original writing be permitted to vary a written contract?

HOLDING AND DECISION: (Andrews, J.) No. An oral agreement is permitted to vary from a written contract only if it is collateral in form, does not contradict express or implied conditions of the written contract, and consists of terms which the parties could not reasonably have been expected to include in the original writing. Here, the parol agreement does not meet these requirements since it is closely related to the subject of the written contract. It could also be said to contradict the conditions of the written contract. Reversed and dismissed.

DISSENT: (Lehman, J.) Additional terms cannot modify the written agreement here, but the parol agreement is collateral to the written agreement. The issue is whether the written agreement's obligation is increased by the oral agreement, which depends on three conditions: (1) whether the agreement is a collateral one; (2) that the parol agreement tracks the terms of the written agreement; and (3) whether the written agreement is complete. Parol evidence must be introduced to ascertain whether the parties contemplated the removal of an ice house after conveying land. The issue is whether the parties considered the written agreement complete by deliberately leaving out the ice house removal or whether the ice house removal constituted an enforceable, collateral agreement. The written contract here is not broad enough to cover the removal of the ice house from another parcel of property and parol evidence regarding that other agreement should be admitted.

ANALYSIS

Uniform Commercial Code (U.C.C.) § 2-202 provides, "Terms with respect to which the writings of the parties agree or which are set forth in a writing intended by the parties as a final expression of their agreement may not be contradicted by evidence of any prior agreement or of a contemporaneous oral agreement but may be explained or supplemented by course of dealing or usage of trade, or by course of performance, and by evidence of consistent additional terms unless the court finds the writing to have been intended as a complete and exclusive statement of the terms of the agreement." The section, according to the official commentator, conclusively rejects any assumption that, because a writing is final in some respects, it is to be interpreted as including all matters agreed upon by the parties.

■=■

Quicknotes

COLLATERAL AGREEMENT An agreement, that is made prior to or contemporaneous with a written agreement, which is admissible in evidence as long as it is consistent with the written document.

EXPRESS CONDITION A condition that is expressly stated in the terms of a written instrument.

IMPLIED CONDITION A condition that is not expressly stated in the terms of an agreement, but which is inferred from the parties' conduct or the type of dealings involved.

■=■

Lee v. Joseph E. Seagram & Sons, Inc.

Distributor (P) v. Company (D)

552 F.2d 447 (2d Cir. 1977).

NATURE OF CASE: Action for damages on an oral contract.

FACT SUMMARY: Joseph E. Seagram & Sons (Seagram) (D) orally promised to set Lee's (P) sons up in a distributorship as part of the consideration for the sale of Lee's (P) business to Seagram (D) under a written contract.

🏛 RULE OF LAW
A collateral oral agreement not covering or contradicting the terms of the contemporary written agreement may be proved by parol unless the written agreement is deemed completely integrated.

FACTS: Lee (P) agreed to sell his distributorship to Seagram & Sons (D). Lee (P) had had a long, close association with Seagram (D) and had been one of its officers. Lee (P) had begun the distributorship, partially at Seagram's (D) request and also to give his sons some experience in the business. As part of the sale, Seagram (D) orally promised to set the sons up in a distributorship as soon as one opened. The written sales contract did not refer to the oral agreement and did not cover this point in any manner. Seagram (D) refused to perform the contemporary oral contract, and Lee (P) brought suit. The contract was not deemed to be completely integrated, i.e., it admitted a statement that no contemporary or prior oral promises or warranties were made, and parol evidence was permitted since the oral contract did not contradict or alter the written contract. Seagram (D) did not refute the evidence as to the oral agreement. Seagram's (D) only contention on appeal was that parol evidence should not have been admitted to prove its existence.

ISSUE: Where a written contract is not integrated, may parol evidence be admitted to establish the existence of a contemporary oral agreement which neither alters nor contradicts the terms of the written contract?

HOLDING AND DECISION: (Gurfein, J.) Yes. The Parol Evidence Rule was adopted to prevent the fraudulent assertion of oral promises not contained in the written contract. If the writing contains an integration clause or the asserted oral promises vary or contradict the reasonable, unambiguous construction of written clauses, parol evidence is barred. The rule does not bar parol evidence as to contemporary oral contracts which neither vary nor contradict the written contract if it has no integration clause. Normally, the subject of the oral agreement must be something which the parties would not necessarily have included in the written contract. Here, there was a long and close association between the parties; the distributorship could reasonably be considered the subject of a second contract since the parties were different, i.e., the sons. The lack of an integration clause where one is customary is also evidence that the oral agreement was valid. Judgment denying Seagram's motion for summary judgment is affirmed.

▶ ANALYSIS

Integration is more easily inferred in simple contracts, e.g., the sale of land. *Mitchell v. Lath*, 247 N.Y. 377, 160 N.E. 646 (1928). In more complex cases, in which customary business practices may be more varied, an oral agreement can be treated as separate and independent of the written contract, even though a strong integration clause is present. *Gem Corrugated Box Corp. v. National Kraft Container Corp.*, 427 F.2d 499 (2d Cir. 1970). Agreements not covered under the written contract are far more likely in such situations.

Quicknotes

CONTEMPORANEOUS At the same time.

INTEGRATION CLAUSE A provision in a contract stating that the document represents the total and final expression of the parties' agreement.

PAROL EVIDENCE RULE Doctrine precluding parties to an agreement from introducing evidence of prior or contemporaneous agreements in order to repudiate or alter the terms of a written contract.

George v. Davoli

Purchaser (P) v. Seller (D)

City Ct. of Geneva, NY, 91 Misc. 2d 296, 397 N.Y.S.2d 895 (1977).

NATURE OF CASE: Action for breach of contract.

FACT SUMMARY: George (P) brought suit after Davoli (D) refused to honor a purchase agreement which permitted return of the jewelry purchased and partial refund of the purchase price.

🏛 RULE OF LAW
Oral testimony is admissible to supplement the missing terms of a written agreement when the supplemental terms are not inconsistent with the agreement and the writing was not intended to be an exclusive statement of the agreement's terms.

FACTS: George (P) and Davoli (D) entered into a written agreement for the purchase of Indian jewelry for the sum of $500. The agreement allowed George (P) to return the merchandise if the jewelry was found to be unacceptable, and Davoli (D) was thereby obligated to refund $440 of the purchase price. The written agreement was silent as to the time frame in which the jewelry could be returned to the seller. George (P) declined to testify at trial; however, Davoli (D) testified that in conjunction with the written agreement, the parties had agreed orally that the offer for accepting return of the merchandise would last only until the following Monday. George (P) attempted to return the jewelry on the following Wednesday and Davoli (D) refused to accept the return.

ISSUE: Is oral testimony admissible to supplement the missing terms of a written agreement when the supplemental terms are not inconsistent with the agreement and the writing was not intended to be an exclusive statement of the agreement's terms?

HOLDING AND DECISION: (Brind, J.) Yes. Oral testimony is admissible to supplement the missing terms of a written agreement when the supplemental terms are not inconsistent with the agreement and the writing was not intended to be an exclusive statement of the agreement's terms. Under the Uniform Commercial Code (U.C.C.) if the parties do not agree on a time frame for returning goods, then they must be returned "seasonably." See U.C.C. § 2-326 and 2-327. Under the present circumstances, seasonable return would commonly be within one week. However, U.C.C. § 2-202, the parol evidence rule, allows a court to accept oral testimony (extrinsic evidence) supplementing a written agreement when, as noted above, the supplemental terms are not inconsistent with the agreement, and the written agreement was not intended to be an exclusive statement of the agreement's terms. In this instance, the supplemental

terms do not, in any way, contradict or negate any of the terms of the written agreement, and the written agreement left open the time period for return. Because George (P) elected not to testify or offer any rebuttal evidence to Davoli's (D) testimony, the court accepts the testimony and finds the parol evidence rule allows Davoli's (D) testimony to supplement the written contract. George (P) simply failed to return the merchandise in a timely manner under the terms of the agreement and the case is dismissed.

▶ ANALYSIS

The parol evidence rule is designed to simplify litigation of contract disputes and it protects the parties from evidence intended to contradict the terms of the contract that the parties had thought they had entered. The court appropriately notes that the U.C.C.'s gap-filling measures apply when the parties fail to place certain terms in their contracts, i.e., what constitutes a "seasonable return." In this instance, however, the parties supplied the term absent from the written agreement in a contemporaneous oral agreement. The extrinsic evidence of the oral agreement does not contradict any of the written terms of the agreement and no evidence is presented to rebut the oral agreement. This case not only illustrates the importance of memorializing all of the terms of an agreement in writing but also demonstrates the strong public policy embodied in the U.C.C. to ensure the enforceability of contracts in instances where terms have been omitted.

■━■

Quicknotes

PAROL EVIDENCE RULE Doctrine precluding parties to an agreement from introducing evidence of prior or contemporaneous agreements in order to repudiate or alter the terms of a written contract.

■━■

Val-Ford Realty Corp. v. J.Z.'s Toy World, Inc.

[Parties not identified.]

N.Y. Sup. Ct., App. Div., 231 A.D.2d 434, 647 N.Y.S.2d 488 (1996).

NATURE OF CASE: Appeal from denial of motion for summary judgment.

FACT SUMMARY: Plaintiff sought recovery of rent due pursuant to a written lease agreement; defendants objected on the basis that the agreement was not really a contract, but was intended to defraud plaintiff's construction lender into advancing additional funds.

🏛 RULE OF LAW
Parol evidence is admissible in order to prove that an agreement purporting to be a contract is not really a contract.

FACTS: [Facts not stated in casebook excerpt.]

ISSUE: Is parol evidence admissible in order to prove that an agreement purporting to be a contract is not really a contract?

HOLDING AND DECISION: (Cahn, J.) Yes. Parol evidence is admissible in order to prove that an agreement purporting to be a contract is not really a contract. Plaintiff seeks to recover rent due pursuant to a written lease agreement executed by the corporate defendant and guaranteed by the individual defendant. The defendants admit executing such documents, but claim that the purpose was to defraud plaintiff's construction lender into advancing additional funds and were not intended by the parties to be enforceable. This parol evidence offered by defendants raises issues of credibility inappropriate for summary judgment. Parol evidence as a general rule is inadmissible to modify or add to terms of an integrated agreement. However, it may be admissible to prove that a purported contract is actually not a contract. Denial of plaintiff's motion for summary judgment affirmed.

▶ ANALYSIS

The Parol Evidence Rule is a doctrine precluding parties to an agreement from introducing evidence of prior or contemporaneous agreements in order to repudiate or alter the terms of a written contract.

■═■

Quicknotes

PAROL EVIDENCE Evidence given verbally; extraneous evidence.

■═■

Pacific Gas & Elec. Co. v. G.W. Thomas Drayage & Rigging Co.

Turbine owner (P) v. Repair company (D)

Cal. Sup. Ct., 69 Cal. 2d 33, 442 P.2d 641, en banc (1968).

NATURE OF CASE: Action for damages for breach of a contract.

FACT SUMMARY: G.W. Thomas Drayage & Rigging Co. (Thomas) (D) contracted to repair Pacific Gas & Elec. Co.'s (Pacific's) (P) steam turbine and to perform work at its own risk and expense and to indemnify Pacific (P) against all loss and damage. Thomas (D) also agreed not to procure less than $50,000 insurance to cover liability for injury to property. But when the turbine rotor was damaged, Pacific (P) claimed it was covered under that policy while Thomas (D) said it was only to cover injury to third persons.

🏛 RULE OF LAW
The test of admissibility of extrinsic evidence to explain the meaning of a written instrument is not whether it appears to the court to be plain and unambiguous on its face, but whether the offered evidence is relevant to prove a meaning to which the language of the instrument is reasonably susceptible.

FACTS: G.W. Thomas Drayage & Rigging Co. (Thomas) (D) contracted to replace the upper metal cover on Pacific Gas & Elec. Co.'s (Pacific's) (P) steam turbine and agreed to perform all work "at [its] own risk and expense" and to "indemnify" Pacific (P) against all loss, damage, expense, and liability resulting from injury to property arising out of or in any way connected with performance of the contract. Thomas (D) agreed to obtain not less than $50,000 insurance to cover liability for injury to property. Pacific (P) was to be an additional named insured, but the policy was to contain a cross-liability clause extending the coverage to Pacific's (P) property. During the work, the cover fell, damaging the exposed rotor in the amount of $25,144.51. Thomas (D) during trial offered evidence to prove by its conduct under similar contracts entered into with Pacific (P) that the indemnity clause was meant to cover injury to third person's property only, not to Pacific's (P).

ISSUE: Was Thomas's (D) offered evidence relevant to proving a meaning to which the language of the instrument was susceptible?

HOLDING AND DECISION: (Traynor, C.J.) Yes. While the trial court admitted that the contract was "the classic language for a third party indemnity provision," it held that the plain language of the contract would give a meaning covering Pacific's (P) damage. However, this admission by the court clearly shows the ambiguous nature of the agreement and the need for extrinsic evidence in order to clarify the intentions of the parties. Extrinsic evidence for the purpose of showing the intent of the parties could be excluded only when it is feasible to determine the meaning of the words from the instrument alone. Rational interpretation requires at least an initial consideration of all credible evidence to prove the intention of the parties. Reversed.

▶ ANALYSIS

This case strongly disapproves of the "plain meaning rule" which states that if a writing appears clear and unambiguous on its face, the meaning must be determined from "the four corners" of the writing without considering any extrinsic evidence at all. The trial court applied this rule. However, the rule, while generally accepted but widely condemned, would exclude evidence of trade usage, prior dealings of the parties, and even circumstances surrounding the creation of the agreement. Uniform Commercial Code (U.C.C.) § 2-202 expressly throws out the plain meaning rule. Instead, it allows use of evidence of course of performance or dealing to explain the writing "unless carefully negated." Here, Mr. C.J. Traynor greatly expanded the admission of extrinsic evidence to show intent. When he says it should not be admitted only when it is feasible "to determine the meaning the parties gave to the words from the instrument alone," he is saying in all practicality that extrinsic evidence to show intent should be admissible in just about any case, that rarely will the instrument be so exact as to clearly show intent.

■■■

Quicknotes

EXTRINSIC EVIDENCE Evidence that is not contained within the text of a document or contract but which is derived from the parties' statements or the circumstances under which the agreement was made.

FOUR CORNERS The express terms of a written document.

PAROL EVIDENCE RULE Doctrine precluding parties to an agreement from introducing evidence of prior or contemporaneous agreements in order to repudiate or alter the terms of a written contract.

■■■

Trident Center v. Connecticut General Life Insurance Co.

Commercial group (P) v. Lender (D)

847 F.2d 564 (9th Cir. 1988).

NATURE OF CASE: Appeal from a dismissal of contract action.

FACT SUMMARY: The district court dismissed Trident Center's (Trident) (P) declaratory relief action, ruling that the contract was clear and did not allow for prepayment of a loan, which Trident (P) sought to establish by parol evidence.

🏛 RULE OF LAW
Parol evidence is admissible to raise an ambiguity in a contract even where the writing itself contains no ambiguity.

FACTS: Trident Center (Trident) (P), an enterprise consisting of an insurance company and two large, sophisticated law firms, entered into a loan agreement with Connecticut General Life Insurance Co. (Connecticut) (D). The written agreement provided Trident (P) would borrow $56 million to construct an office building. The loan was to be paid off over a period of time; however, the contract precluded full repayment within the first 12 years. Because of a drop in interest rates, Trident (P) sought to repay the loan in full after four years. It claimed, despite the clear language of the contract, that the parties intended to allow prepayment at any time if a penalty was paid. Trident (P) brought a declaratory relief action requesting a court interpretation of the contract. Trident (P) unsuccessfully sought to present parol evidence of the meaning of the contract while admitting the language was unambiguous. The court dismissed the action, and Trident (P) appealed.

ISSUE: Is parol evidence admissible to show an ambiguity even in an otherwise unambiguous contract?

HOLDING AND DECISION: (Kozinski, J.) Yes. Parol evidence is admissible to show an ambiguity even in an otherwise unambiguous contract. Because language cannot infallibly communicate the true meaning or intent of parties to a contract, parol evidence must be allowed where such intent is in issue. Thus, it was error to deny use of such evidence and to dismiss the action. Reversed.

▶ ANALYSIS

This case does not represent the traditional common law view of the parol evidence rule. The opinion is very critical of the outcome which is mandated by the law of California, where the case arose. The opinion foresees considerable litigation invited by this decision and a breakdown in the finality of a written agreement.

Quicknotes

AMBIGUITY Language that is capable of more than one interpretation.

PAROL EVIDENCE RULE Doctrine precluding parties to an agreement from introducing evidence of prior or contemporaneous agreements in order to repudiate or alter the terms of a written contract.

Raffles v. Wichelhaus

Cotton seller (P) v. Cotton buyer (D)

Ex. 2 H. & C. 906, 159 Eng. Rep. 375 (1864).

NATURE OF CASE: Action for damages for breach of a contract for the sale of goods.

FACT SUMMARY: Raffles (P) contracted to sell cotton to Wichelhaus (D) to be delivered from Bombay at Liverpool on the ship "Peerless." Unknown to the parties was the existence of two different ships carrying cotton, each named "Peerless" arriving at Liverpool from Bombay, but at different times.

🏛 RULE OF LAW
Where neither party knows or has reason to know of the ambiguity, or where both know, or have reason to know, the ambiguity is given the meaning that each party intended it to have.

FACTS: Raffles (P) contracted to sell Wichelhaus (D) 125 bales of Surat cotton to arrive from Bombay at Liverpool on the ship "Peerless." Wichelhaus (D) was to pay 17 pence per pound of cotton within an agreed upon time after the arrival of the goods in England. Unknown to the parties, there were two ships called "Peerless" each of which was carrying cotton from Bombay to Liverpool. One ship was to sail in October by Wichelhaus (D) for delivery of the goods while Raffles (P) had expected the cotton to be shipped on the "Peerless" set to sail in December. As Wichelhaus (D) could not have the delivery he expected, he refused to accept the later delivery.

ISSUE: Did a latent ambiguity arise showing there had been no meeting of the minds, hence, no contract?

HOLDING AND DECISION: (Per curiam) Yes. While the contract did not show which particular "Peerless" was intended, the moment it appeared two ships called "Peerless" were sailing from Bombay to Liverpool with a load of cotton, a latent ambiguity arose, and parol evidence was admissible for the purpose of determining that both parties had intended a different "Peerless" to be subject in the contract. When there is an ambiguity, it is given the meaning that each party intended it to have. However, if different meanings were intended there is no contract if the ambiguity relates to a material term. Consequently, there was no meeting of the minds, and no binding contract. Judgment for defendants.

▶ ANALYSIS

When there is no integration of the contract, the standard for its interpretation is the meaning that the party making the manifestation should reasonably expect the other party to give it, i.e., a standard of reasonable expectation. This case illustrates an exception to this rule. Where there is an ambiguity, if both parties give the same meaning to it, there is a contract. If the parties each give a different meaning to the ambiguity, then there is no contract as occurred here. The ambiguity struck at a material term as payment was to be made within an agreed upon time after delivery. The parties could not even agree on the time of delivery. The other exception occurs when one party has reason to know of the ambiguity and the other does not, so it will bear the meaning given to it by the latter, that is the party who is without fault. Note that under Uniform Commercial Code (U.C.C.) § 2-322, delivery "exship," it would make no difference which ship would be carrier of the goods and the case would have gone the other way. However, Restatement (First) § 71 would appear to follow the general rule of the present case.

■━■

Quicknotes

AMBIGUITY Language that is capable of more than one interpretation.

MATERIAL TERMS OF CONTRACT A fact without the existence of which a contract would not have been entered.

MUTUAL ASSENT A requirement of a valid contract that the parties possess a mutuality of assent as manifested by the terms of the agreement and not by a hidden intent.

■━■

Nanakuli Paving and Rock Co. v. Shell Oil Co.

Concrete purchaser (P) v. Seller (D)

664 F.2d 772 (9th Cir. 1981).

NATURE OF CASE: Appeal from judgment n.o.v. denying damages for breach of contract.

FACT SUMMARY: Shell Oil Co. (D) contended it had not breached a supply contract as its course of conduct established the unwritten terms of the agreement.

RULE OF LAW
Trade usage and past course of dealings between contracting parties may establish terms not specifically enumerated in the contract, so long as no conflict is created with the written terms.

FACTS: Nanakuli Paving and Rock Co. (Nanakuli) (P) entered into a contract to purchase its requirements of concrete from Shell Oil Co. (Shell) (D). The contract was in effect for several years and renewed several times. Nanakuli (P) sued over a long-term supply contract, contending Shell (D) had failed to protect it from price increases. It argued that although such protection was not enumerated in the contract, it was part of the trade usage in concrete and thus implied in the contract. Further, Shell (D) had previously performed this service. Shell (D) argued the contract did not call for such, and its past conduct did not constitute a practice of protection. Rather it was a temporary waiver of the contract price. The trial court granted Shell (D) judgment n.o.v., and Nanakuli (P) appealed.

ISSUE: May trade custom and usage and past course of dealings establish contract terms?

HOLDING AND DECISION: (Hoffman, J.) Yes. Trade usage and past course of dealings between contracting parties may establish terms not specifically enumerated in the contract, so long as no conflict is created with the written terms. There was substantial evidence that the jury could rely upon in finding a consistent course of conduct including price protection. Further, the jury could have found that Shell (D) breached commercially reasonable standards in failing to provide adequate notice of the price increase. As a result, the entry of judgment n.o.v. was improper. Reversed.

CONCURRENCE: (Kennedy, J.) Juries should not be allowed to import good-faith concepts unless the concept is based on a well-established practice of which the parties had adequate notice. This case is not about generally unfair dealing but about the price increase.

ANALYSIS

The Parol Evidence Rule precludes extraneous evidence of contract terms unless such terms are ambiguous. The price protection term was so prevalent in the concrete trade that it was reasonable to find that the parties impliedly incorporated it into the contract. This was supported by Shell's (D) past history of price protection.

Quicknotes

COURSE OF DEALING Previous conduct between two parties to a contract which may be relied upon to interpret their actions.

JUDGMENT N.O.V. A judgment entered by the trial judge reversing a jury verdict if the jury's determination has no basis in law or fact.

REQUIREMENTS CONTRACT An agreement pursuant to which one party agrees to purchase all his required goods or services from the other party exclusively for a specified time period.

TRADE USAGE A course of dealing or practice commonly used in a particular trade.

CHAPTER 6

Capacity of Parties

Quick Reference Rules of Law

Pettit v. Liston

Minor motorcycle purchaser (P) v. Motorcycle seller (D)

Or. Sup. Ct., 97 Or. 464, 191 P. 660 (1920).

NATURE OF CASE: Appeal from dismissal of complaint in action for rescission.

FACT SUMMARY: Pettit (P), a minor, purchased a motorcycle on a time installment plan and, after using it for a while, attempted to return it and rescind the contract.

🏛 RULE OF LAW
A minor may not disaffirm a contract after paying all or a portion of the purchase price, having had the use or benefit of the product, without allowing the seller to retain funds to compensate it for any decline in value or damages.

FACTS: Pettit (P), a minor, purchased a motorcycle from Liston (D) on an installment purchase contract. Pettit (P) paid $125 down and was to pay $25 per month. Pettit (P) kept the motorcycle for over a month, then returned it, damaged, demanding his money back. Pettit (P) sued Liston (D) for the return of his $125.00. Liston (D) answered and Pettit (P) demurred. The court overruled the demurrer, Pettit (P) stood by the demurrer, and the court dismissed the petition. Pettit (P) appealed.

ISSUE: May a minor disaffirm a contract after paying all or a portion of the purchase price, having had the use or benefit of the product, without allowing the seller to retain funds to compensate it for any decline in value or damages?

HOLDING AND DECISION: (Bennett, J.) No. A minor may not disaffirm a contract after paying all or a portion of the purchase price, having had the use or benefit of the product, without allowing the seller to retain funds to compensate it for any decline in value or damages. If the minor has been dealt with fairly by the retailer, he should be liable for any decline in value of the product due to his use. This protects the minor from being taken advantage of by sellers, allows him to escape his contractual obligations because of his minority, and still allows a seller to be protected from loss for dealing with a minor. If the minor has paid all or a portion of the purchase price, the seller should be permitted to retain a sufficient amount to recompense it for losses based on use, damage, depreciation, etc. Affirmed.

▶ *ANALYSIS*

Generally, most jurisdictions have allowed minors to disaffirm their contracts either during their minority or when they reach their majority. An exception to this general rule is made where necessities of life, e.g., food and lodging, are given to the minor on credit. These contracts may not be disaffirmed. The rationale is that credit should freely be given in such situations for the benefit of the minor's necessities. To encourage such credit transactions, the minor is obligated to repay.

■══■

Quicknotes

RESCISSION The canceling of an agreement and the return of the parties to their positions prior to the formation of the contract.

■══■

Ortelere v. Teachers' Retirement Board

Husband beneficiary (P) v. Regulatory board (D)

N.Y. Ct. App., 25 N.Y.2d 196, 303 N.Y.S.2d 362, 250 N.E.2d 460 (1969).

NATURE OF CASE: Action to void a contract.

FACT SUMMARY: Mrs. Ortelere changed her teacher's retirement option while she was mentally ill.

RULE OF LAW
A contract by a mentally ill party who is unable to act rationally is deemed voidable where the other party knows or has reason to know of the illness.

FACTS: Mrs. Ortelere, a teacher, took a leave of absence for a nervous breakdown. Her psychiatrist diagnosed her condition as melancholic psychosis, and he suspected the existence of cerebral arteriosclerosis. The condition rendered her unable to act rationally or to make decisions. While ill, Mrs. Ortelere decided to retire. She requested information concerning her teacher retirement fund options. She changed her payment option from one granting unexpended benefits to be paid to her husband to one granting her maximum benefits during life, nothing being due after her death. She also borrowed the maximum amount from the fund. Mrs. Ortelere died one month later. She had been happily married for 38 years. Her husband (P) had quit his job to care for her, and they were of modest means. Her husband (P) offered to return the loan proceeds to the retirement system and requested that they reinstate the original option chosen since his wife was mentally ill at the time the new option was decided upon by her. The Teachers' Retirement Board (the Board) (D) refused, and at trial to void the selection, the court found that Mrs. Ortelere was not "legally" insane, and it found for the Board (D). Mr. Ortelere (P) argued that the definition of "legal" insanity was too restrictive, that the Board (D) knew it was dealing with a mentally ill party, and that no injury had been suffered by the Board (D).

ISSUE: Should a contract by a mentally ill party who is unable to act rationally be deemed voidable where the other party knows or has reason to know of the illness?

HOLDING AND DECISION: (Breitel, J.) Yes. A contract by a mentally ill party who is unable to act rationally is deemed voidable where the other party knows or has reason to know of the illness. It is time to depart from the old-fashioned standard that a contract will be voidable only if the party is wholly and absolutely incompetent to comprehend and understand the nature of the transaction or is under a delusion peculiar to the nature of the transaction. If (1) one party is mentally ill, (2) the illness renders him/her incapable of acting in a reasonable manner, and (3) the other party knows or has reason to know of the illness, the contract may be voided. The avoidance of duties under this test by persons who have understanding depends on balancing competing policy considerations, i.e., stability of contracts versus protection of the mentally ill. Where the other party knows of the illness, the balance will normally be in favor of the mentally ill party. Here, the system was designed to aid and protect retiring teachers. No payments had been made under the new option. No injury would be suffered by the Board (D) or the system if the loan was repaid and the original option was reinstated. Under the circumstances herein, a new trial will examine whether the election of benefits is voidable under the Restatement standards. Reversed and remanded.

DISSENT: (Jasen, J.) The husband (P) has failed to prove that his wife was incompetent with respect to her option selection. Her selection was a reasonable choice, and the letter she sent to the Board (D) established that she fully understood the nature of the contract. The previous rule concerning mental illness has been workable, and this is not the appropriate case to change the rule. The evidence herein indicated Mrs. Ortelere's decision was rational and necessary, and it did not establish an inference of her mental incompetence.

ANALYSIS

The Restatement also prescribes a test of competency when the other party does not know or have reason to know of the illness. "The power of avoidance under Subsection (1) terminates to the extent that the contract has been so performed in whole or in part or the circumstances have so changed that avoidance would be inequitable. In such a case a court may grant relief on such equitable terms as the situation requires." Restatement (Second) of Contracts, § 18c(2).

Quicknotes

CAPACITY TO CONTRACT The legal and physical ability to enter into a contractual agreement, typically characterized by the ability to understand the consequences of one's actions.

VOIDABLE CONTRACT A valid contract which may be legally voided at the option of one of the parties.

Avoidance for Misconduct or Mistake

Quick Reference Rules of Law

Gallon v. Lloyd-Thomas Co.

Immigrant employee (P) v. Employer (D)

264 F.2d 821 (8th Cir. 1959).

NATURE OF CASE: Appeal in action for duress.

FACT SUMMARY: Gallon (P) agreed to a modification of his employment contract after being placed in fear of deportation.

🏛 RULE OF LAW
A contract made under duress is voidable and may be ratified by plaintiff after the duress has been removed.

FACTS: Gallon's (P) work with Lloyd-Thomas Co. (D) had been unsatisfactory. Goran, an officer of Lloyd-Thomas (D), informed Gallon (P) that he was being investigated by the Justice Department. Gallon (P) had applied to become a permanent resident of the United States on the basis of his marriage to a U.S. citizen. Gallon (P) was, at the time, allegedly already married to a citizen of Great Britain. A meeting was held between Gallon (P), Goran, and another officer of Lloyd-Thomas (D), Gatenbey. After numerous threats and arguments, Gallon (P) had been completely broken down. Goran and Gatenbey agreed to see if they could stop the investigation and prevent Gallon's (P) deportation. Several days later, based on his fear of deportation and the promise to have the investigation stopped, Gallon (P) agreed to a new contract under which he had to repay his $15,000 in overdrafts on his drawing account and under which he lost his credits and moneys due on prior jobs for Lloyd-Thomas (D). Gallon (P) was represented by an attorney at the time the contract was signed. Gallon (P) subsequently related what had happened to the attorney and asked him whether or not he could be deported. During a seven-month period, Gallon (P) never objected to the contract, fulfilled all duties under it, and received his pay and benefits. Gallon (P) subsequently quit and sued for damages. From an award of actual and punitive damages, Lloyd-Thomas (D) appealed, alleging that there was no duress, and, even if duress had existed, Gallon (P) had subsequently ratified it. The court entered a judgment n.o.v. because, although the contract was entered into under duress, the plaintiff subsequently ratified it.

ISSUE: May a contract obtained through duress, be subsequently ratified through plaintiff's actions?

HOLDING AND DECISION: (Matthes, J.) Yes. A contract obtained through duress is voidable rather than void. A plaintiff may, by his subsequent actions after the duress has been dispelled, ratify the contract making it valid. Silence, retention of the benefits, or other implied or overt manifestations of assent are sufficient to constitute ratification. Here, Gallon (P) remained with Lloyd-Thomas (D) for approximately seven months under the new contract. Gallon (P) never complained about or mentioned the contract to any of Lloyd-Thomas's (D) management, even though he wrote six letters to its home office during this period. After Gallon's (P) discussion with his attorney and the passage of time, the duress must be deemed to have been dispelled. Retention of the benefits of the contract plus silence constituted ratification. Affirmed.

▶ ANALYSIS

Duress involves the rendering of one party's will subservient to that of another so that there is no free, voluntary choice. Duress is normally found only where there is a threat of physical injury or of similar tortious conduct. Threats of economic reprisals, etc., generally will not be deemed sufficient to constitute duress, though a minority of jurisdictions will allow such a defense.

■■■

Quicknotes

DURESS Unlawful threats or other coercive behavior by one person, that causes another to commit acts that he would not otherwise do.

JUDGMENT N.O.V. A judgment entered by the trial judge reversing a jury verdict if the jury's determination has no basis in law or fact.

■■■

Austin Instrument, Inc. v. Loral Corp.

Precision parts subcontractor (P) v. Radar set producer (D)

N.Y. Ct. App., 29 N.Y.2d 124, 324 N.Y.S.2d 22, 272 N.E.2d 533 (1971).

NATURE OF CASE: Appeal in action to recover damages for breach of contract.

FACT SUMMARY: Austin Instrument, Inc. (P) threatened to withhold delivery of precision parts unless Loral Corp. (D) would raise the contract price.

🏛 RULE OF LAW
A contract modification is voidable on the ground of duress when the party claiming duress establishes that its agreement to the modification was obtained by means of a wrongful threat from the other party which precluded the first party's exercise of free will.

FACTS: Loral Corp. (D) was under contract to produce radar sets for the government. The contract contained a liquidated damage clause for late delivery and a cancellation clause in case of default by Loral (D). Loral (D), which did a substantial portion of its business with the government, awarded Austin Instrument, Inc. (Austin) (P) a subcontract to supply some of the precision parts. Subsequently, Austin (P) threatened to cease delivery of the parts unless Loral (D) consented to substantial increases in the subcontract price. After contacting 10 manufacturers of precision gears and finding none who could produce the parts in time to meet its commitment to the government, Loral (D) acceded to Austin's (P) demand.

ISSUE: Is a contract modification voidable on the ground of duress, when the party claiming duress establishes that its agreement to the modification was obtained by means of a wrongful threat from the other party which precluded the first party's exercise of free will?

HOLDING AND DECISION: (Fuld, C.J.) Yes. A contract modification is voidable on the ground of duress when the party claiming duress establishes that its agreement to the modification was obtained by means of a wrongful threat from the other party which precluded the first party's exercise of free will. Loral (D) has made out a classic case of economic duress in that: (1) Austin (P) threatened to withhold delivery of "needful goods" unless Loral (D) agreed, (2) Loral (D) could not obtain the goods from another source of supply, and (3) the ordinary remedy of an action for breach of the original subcontract would not be adequate [since so much was riding on Loral's (D) own general contract with the government]. Austin's (P) threat deprived Loral (D) of its free will. Affirmed as modified.

DISSENT: (Bergan, J.) In applying the law of duress, the majority necessarily overturned crucial findings of fact by the lower courts.

▶ ANALYSIS

Although it has generally been held that a threat to breach a contract does not constitute economic duress, courts have recently begun to hold that various kinds of unethical business compulsion do constitute duress. The present case is an example of this trend. Note that even under the Uniform Commercial Code (which recognizes modification without consideration—§ 2-209) the requirement of good faith is ever present.

Quicknotes

CONSIDERATION Value given by one party in exchange for performance, or a promise to perform, by another party.

DURESS Unlawful threats or other coercive behavior, by one person that causes another to commit acts that he would not otherwise do.

ECONOMIC DURESS A defense to an action that a party was unlawfully coerced into the performance of an action by another due to fear of imminent economic loss and was not acting in accordance with his own free volition in performing the action.

GOOD FAITH An honest intention to abstain from any unconscientious advantage of another.

LIQUIDATED DAMAGES An amount of money specified in a contract representing the damages owed in the event of breach.

Francois v. Francois

Wealthy ex-husband (P) v. Scheming ex-wife (D)

599 F.2d 1286 (3d Cir. 1979), *cert. denied* 444 U.S. 1021 (1980).

NATURE OF CASE: Appeal from order rescinding property settlement agreement.

FACT SUMMARY: Jane Francois (D) contended that the trial court erred in invalidating a property settlement agreement between her and her ex-husband, Victor Francois (P), on the basis of undue influence.

> ## 🏛 RULE OF LAW
> A party who exploits his position of confidence and trust for his advantage over another in contractual relations has exercised undue influence which renders the contract voidable.

FACTS: Jane Francois (D) married Victor Francois (P), a man much older and more financially independent than she. Throughout the marriage, Jane (D) successfully persuaded Victor (P) to assign control of his assets to her. Ultimately, she decided to divorce and consulted an attorney, who drafted a property settlement agreement which was extremely disadvantageous to Victor (P). Jane (D) told Victor (P) that unless he signed the agreement, there was no hope for the marriage. Jane's (D) attorney advised Victor (P) to seek advice of counsel, and a lawyer in the same building was asked to read the agreement on Victor's (P) behalf. The lawyer advised Victor (P) against signing it, yet to save the marriage Victor (P) signed it. He then, pursuant to the agreement, assigned his ownership of certain real property to Jane (D). Approximately one year later, Jane (D) divorced Victor (P), who then sued to rescind the agreement on the basis it was voidable due to undue influence. The trial court invalidated the agreement and ordered the property reconveyed to Victor (P). Jane (D) appealed.

ISSUE: Is the exploitation of a confidential and trusting relationship to gain an advantage in contractual relations undue influence, rendering the agreement voidable?

HOLDING AND DECISION: (Rosenn, J.) Yes. The exploitation of a confidential and trusting relationship in order to gain an advantage in contractual arrangements is undue influence, rendering the agreement voidable. The evidence clearly supports the finding that a relationship of trust and confidence existed between the parties and that Jane (D) often influenced Victor (P) to act in detriment to his financial interests. By forcing him to sign the agreement under the belief he could save his marriage, Jane (D) exercised undue influence in the making of the contract. Thus, the agreement was voidable. Affirmed.

▶ ANALYSIS

The court pointed out that merely because the parties are married at the time of the undue influence does not automatically render the contract voidable. It must be affirmatively shown that a relationship of trust existed at the time which allowed the influence to be undue.

■■▬■

Quicknotes

UNDUE INFLUENCE Improper influence that deprives the individual freedom of choice or substitutes another's choice for the person's own choice.

■■▬■

Methodist Mission Home of Texas v. N__ A__ B__

Home for unwed mothers (D) v. Unwed mother (P)

Tex. Civ. App., 451 S.W.2d 539 (1970).

NATURE OF CASE: Action to rescind contract.

FACT SUMMARY: Plaintiff sought to recover her child, which she had given up for adoption, by alleging undue influence.

RULE OF LAW
Where the overall facts establish that a party in a physically weakened, emotional situation has been subjected to extensive persuasion, including false statements, undue influence may be found.

FACTS: Plaintiff, an unwed mother, had her baby in the Methodist Mission Home of Texas (Methodist) (D). Plaintiff, after having the child, changed her mind and decided to keep the baby. One of the counselors spent five days with plaintiff attempting to change her mind and to convince her to give it up for adoption. Plaintiff was told she had no right to keep the baby; she was being selfish; her parents were attempting to take advantage of her with their offer to support her and the child. Plaintiff finally consented to give the baby up for adoption. Plaintiff, during this period, was physically weak, emotionally distraught, and quite shy. Plaintiff subsequently sought to revoke her consent to an adoption, alleging that it had been obtained through undue influence. The court, considering the totality of circumstances, agreed, and Methodist (D) appealed.

ISSUE: Will extensive persuasion, false statements, and a physically weakened person who is in an emotional state constitute sufficient grounds to find undue influence?

HOLDING AND DECISION: (Cadena, J.) Yes. No set rule is available to establish what constitutes undue influence in each and every case. Overbearing of a party's will is an ephemeral concept which must be decided on a case-by-case basis based on all of the factors present. We find that the court could reasonably determine that an unwed mother who is in a physically weakened and emotionally distraught state after giving birth can be subjected to undue influence in the form of extensive efforts at persuasion coupled with false or misleading statements. Affirmed.

▶ ANALYSIS

Merely because influence is exerted and is effective, it is not grounds for invalidating a contract. The law does not condemn cajolery, solicitation, importunity, etc. *Robinson v. Stuart*, 73 Texas 267 (1889). It is only when the actor's free will has been so subverted or destroyed that he is really acting on behalf of the person exerting the influence that the law will render the contract voidable. *Rothermel v. Duncan*, 369 S.W.2 917 (1963).

■━■

Quicknotes

UNDUE INFLUENCE Improper influence that deprives the individual freedom of choice or substitutes another's choice for the person's own choice.

■━■

Cousineau v. Walker

Purchaser (P) v. Seller (D)

Alaska Sup. Ct., 613 P.2d 608 (1980).

NATURE OF CASE: Appeal of action seeking to rescind a land sale contract.

FACT SUMMARY: Walker (D) made certain misrepresentations regarding his property, the accuracy of which buyer Cousineau (P) did not investigate.

🏛 RULE OF LAW
A purchaser of land is not obligated to ascertain whether representations made by the vendor are true.

FACTS: Walker (D) owned certain undeveloped land. He listed it for sale. The land was advertised as having 80,000 cubic yards of gravel and certain road access. Cousineau (P), who worked in the gravel business, negotiated to purchase the land. He did not investigate the accuracy of Walker's (D) representations. A sale was made. The land turned out to have only 6,000 cubic yards of gravel and less road access than advertised, although it appeared that Walker's (D) misrepresentations were innocent. Cousineau (P) brought an action for rescission. The trial court found that Cousineau's (P) reliance on the misstatements was not justified and awarded a defense verdict. Cousineau (P) appealed.

ISSUE: Is a purchaser of land obligated to ascertain whether representations made by the vendor are true?

HOLDING AND DECISION: (Boochever, J.) No. A purchaser of land is not obligated to ascertain whether representations made by the vendor are true. At common law, the doctrine of caveat emptor was the rule regarding land sale contracts. In recent times, however, the rule has evolved that a buyer is entitled to rely on assertions made regarding the property, regardless of examination by the buyer. While this most often occurs in instances of fraud, it has also been applied to negligent misrepresentation. The uncontroverted facts demonstrate that all representations and documents prepared in relation to this sale provided for the transfer of gravel rights, and that there was a significant amount of highway frontage with the property. The trial judge's finding that Cousineau (P) did not rely on these false and highly material representations when contemplating the land purchase was clearly erroneous. As noted, the prevailing trend in authority is toward placing a minimal duty on the purchaser to investigate a vendor's fraudulent statements. No reason exists for treating the sale of real property any different from that of commercial goods. As a purchaser of land, Cousineau (P) cannot be barred from recovery unless his actions in discovering the defects were irrational, preposterous, or in bad faith. While Cousineau's (P) acts were lacking in sound business judgment, they cannot be called irrational, preposterous, or in bad faith. Reversed and remanded.

▶ ANALYSIS

Whether reliance was justifiable is one of three elements necessary to rescind a land contract. The threshold question is whether there were false statements. Next, it must be found that the statements were material. Whether there was justifiable reliance is the final issue.

■■■

Quicknotes

MATERIAL FALSE REPRESENTATIONS A statement or conduct by one party to another that constitutes a false representation of a material fact.

MISREPRESENTATION A statement or conduct by one party to another that constitutes a false representation of fact.

■■■

Vokes v. Arthur Murray, Inc.

Dancer (P) v. Dance instructor (D)

Fla. Dist. Ct. App., 212 So. 2d 906 (1968).

NATURE OF CASE: Action for cancellation of contracts.

FACT SUMMARY: Vokes (P) was continually cajoled into purchasing thousands of hours of dancing lessons at Arthur Murray, Inc. (D).

🏛 RULE OF LAW
Where one party has superior knowledge, statements made within the area of such knowledge may be treated as statements of fact.

FACTS: Vokes (P), at age 51, decided she wished to become an accomplished dancer. Over a period of years, by flattery, cajolery, awards, etc., Vokes (P) was convinced to sign up, under a number of contracts, for $31,000 worth of dancing lessons from Arthur Murray, Inc. (D). Vokes (P) was repeatedly informed that she was a promising student who was quickly becoming sufficiently skilled to pursue a career as a professional dancer. Vokes (P) subsequently brought an action to cancel the unused portion of approximately 2,302 hours of lessons to which she had subscribed. Vokes (P) alleged that she had attained little or no skill as a dancer and obviously had no such aptitude. Vokes (P) alleged that Arthur Murray (D) employees had purposefully misrepresented her skills and had taken unconscionable advantage of her. Vokes (P) alleged that she had relied on Arthur Murray (D) employees' superior knowledge as to her ability and the skills necessary to become a professional dancer.

ISSUE: May a party reasonably rely on opinions as assertions of fact when given by a party of superior knowledge on the subject?

HOLDING AND DECISION: (Pierce, J.) Yes. Normally, the party to a contract has no reasonable right to rely on opinions expressed by the other party to the contract. Misrepresentations of opinion are normally not actionable. However, a statement made by a party having superior knowledge may be regarded as a statement of fact even though it would be regarded as opinion if the parties were dealing on the basis of equal knowledge. Where a party undertakes to make representations based on its superior knowledge, it is under a duty to act honestly and to disclose the entire truth. Vokes (P) has stated a valid cause of action. Reversed.

▶ ANALYSIS

Basically, *Vokes* is concerned with reliance and credibility. One has a right to rely on opinions of attorneys, doctors, etc. *Vokes* extends such reasonable reliance to experts or those highly knowledgeable in a field in which plaintiff is generally unfamiliar. *Ramel v. Chasebrook Construction Company*, 135 So. 2d 876 (1961). To be actionable, the misrepresentation must be material and there must be some overreaching in cases such as *Vokes*.

◼◼◼

Quicknotes

MISREPRESENTATION A statement or conduct by one party to another that constitutes a false representation of fact.

◼◼◼

Smith v. Zimbalist

Creditor (P) v. Debtor (D)

Cal. Ct. App., 2 Cal. App. 2d 324, 38 P.2d 170 (1934).

NATURE OF CASE: Appeal of trial court judgment.

FACT SUMMARY: Zimbalist (D) agreed to buy two violins that he and the seller, Smith (P), thought were rare and valuable. They were not, it turned out, and Zimbalist (D) refused to pay the balance owed on the agreement. Smith (P) sued.

🏛 RULE OF LAW
Parties to a proposed contract are not bound where they are honestly mistaken as to the identity of the subject matter of the contract.

FACTS: Zimbalist (D) was a world-class violinist and violin collector. Smith (P) was a collector. Zimbalist (D) offered to buy two violins from Smith's (P) collection, one of which they both thought was made by Josef Guarnerius, the other by Antonius Stradivarius. They agreed on a price of $8,000 for the pair. Zimbalist (D) paid $2,000 up front, and agreed to pay $1,000 per month until the balance was paid. He wrote and signed a memorandum of the sale, and Smith (P) drafted a bill of sale detailing the terms. Later, it was discovered that they were imitations. Smith (P) nevertheless sued to recover the unpaid balance of the agreed upon purchase price. The trial court ruled that the mutual mistake rendered the contract unenforceable.

ISSUE: Parties to a proposed contract are not bound where they are honestly mistaken as to the identity of the subject matter of the contract.

HOLDING AND DECISION: (Houser, J.) No. Parties to a proposed contract are not bound where they are honestly mistaken as to the identity of the subject matter of the contract. The governing principle of law stating is that an article described in a bill of sale amounts to a warranty that such article in fact conforms to its description, and that the seller is bound by the description. The bill of sale in this case stated that the violins were genuine, and Smith (P) therefore gave a warranty that they were in fact genuine. But he was mistaken and, therefore, no enforceable sale has taken place. The rule of caveat emptor may not be applied to the facts of this case. Affirmed.

▶ ANALYSIS

The court takes the warranty as evidence of mistake. But the warranty could have formed the basis of a breach of contract claim by Zimbalist (D). We don't know if Zimbalist (D) received back his $2,000, but he could have sued for it, and under current law, probably would have won. Consider the result of this case in light of *Bentley v. Slavik*, 663 F. Supp. 736 (1987).

■▬■

Quicknotes

CAVEAT EMPTOR Let the buyer beware; doctrine that a buyer purchases at his own risk.

WARRANTY An assurance by one party that another may rely on a certain representation of fact.

■▬■

Bentley v. Slavik

Buyer (P) v. Seller (D)

663 F. Supp. 736 (S.D. Ill. 1987).

NATURE OF CASE: Bench trial in federal district court.

FACT SUMMARY: Karen Bentley (P) bought what she thought was an Auguste Sebastien Philippe Bernardel violin made in 1835. Charles Slavik (D), the seller, said the violin was appraised and valued at between $15,000 and $20,000. But the violin was not a genuine Bernardel. Bentley (P) sued to get her money back.

🏛 RULE OF LAW
Where a warranty is created by a seller, failure to deliver goods that conform to the warranty constitutes a breach of contract.

FACTS: In January 1984, Karen Bentley (P) answered an advertisement placed on a university bulletin board for an Auguste Sebastien Philippe Bernardel violin made in 1835. The ad was placed by Charles Slavik (D), and according to him, the violin was appraised and valued at between $15,000 and $20,000. Bentley (P) went to Slavik's (D) home and inspected the violin for two hours. At the time, Slavik (D) presented Bentley (P) with Certificate No. 5500 from Robert Bernard Tipple, which stated that the violin was authentic. Tipple was a violin maker, authenticator, and appraiser. In reliance on the representation that the violin was authentic, Bentley (P) bought it for $17,500. She paid $15,000 up front and agreed to pay the balance in one month's time. The bill of sale signed by Slavik (D) referred to the sale of "One Bernardel A.S.P. Violin." In a letter accompanying the second check, Bentley (P) expressed pleasure with the purchase. But in April of 1985, Bentley (P) became aware the violin was not a genuine Bernardel. She demanded Slavik (D) return the purchase price and offered to return the violin, but Slavik (D) refused. Despite this, Bentley (P) continued to play the violin, and while she owned it, it required serious repair that was done poorly. Slavik (D) presented evidence that the condition of the violin was poorer than it had been when purchased. At trial, two experts testified the violin was not genuine. There was also evidence that Slavik (D) did not purposefully or willfully misrepresent the maker or value of the violin. He was not an expert, and not in the business of selling violins. The estimated worth of the violin at the time of sale was $2,000.

ISSUE: Where a warranty is created by a seller, does failure to deliver goods that conform to the warranty constitute a breach of contract?

HOLDING AND DECISION: (Stiehl, J.) Yes. Where a warranty is created by a seller, failure to deliver goods that conform to the warranty constitutes a breach of

contract. To determine whether a warranty is created under Illinois law, the intent of the parties as expressed in the bill of sale and in the circumstances surrounding the sale must be examined. Courts use a "basis of the bargain" test that looks to the descriptions or affirmations forming the basic assumption of the bargain between the parties. The description by Slavik (D) of the violin as a Bernardel, the affirmation created by his repeated use of the term "Bernardel," and the presentation of a certificate of authentication support the conclusion that there was a basic assumption that the transaction concerned an 1835 Bernardel violin. Therefore, Uniform Commercial Code (U.C.C.) § 2-313(1)(b) applies, and a warranty under that statute was created by Slavik (D). Since a Bernardel violin was not delivered by Slavik (D), Slavik (D) breached the contract. Bentley's (P) expression of pleasure with her purchase when she mailed her second check was not a ratification, because there was no evidence that at that time, she knew or had reason to know the violin was not a Bernardel. The measure of damages for breach of warranty is the difference at the time and place of acceptance between the value of goods accepted and the value that they would have had if they had been as warranted. The violin had a value of $2,000 when sold, and it was sold for $17,500. So the damages are $15,500. Bentley (P) also alleged in her mistake that the contract was void because of mutual mistake on the part of both parties. Under the Restatement (Second) of Contracts § 152, a mistake by both parties as to "a basic assumption on which the contract was made has a material effect on the agreed exchange of performance, the contract is voidable by the adversely affected party." There was a mistake by both parties here, and the basic assumption that the violin was a Bernardel materially affected the price. Mutual mistakes can make contracts voidable, provided neither party assumed the risk of the mistake. There is no reason to believe that either party exhibited a willingness to bear the risk that the violin was not genuine. So there was a mutual mistake and Bentley (P) is entitled to return of the excess purchase price of $15,500 under this theory as well.

▶ ANALYSIS

As in *Smith v. Zimbalist*, 2 Cal. App. 2d 324, 38 P.2d 170 (1934), there are two legal concepts raised: breach of contract based on warranty, and mutual mistake. Pleading both makes sense where the buyer is the aggrieved party. Where the seller is the aggrieved party, as in *Zimbalist*,

Continued on next page.

neither works for the seller, but both may be raised by the buyer/defendant.

■══■

Quicknotes

BREACH OF CONTRACT Unlawful failure by a party to perform its obligations pursuant to contract.

BREACH OF WARRANTY The breach of a promise made by one party to a contract on which the other party may rely, relieving that party from the obligation of determining whether the fact is true and indemnifying the other party from liability if that fact is shown to be false.

MUTUAL MISTAKE A mistake by both parties to a contract, who are in agreement as to what the contract terms should be, but the agreement as written fails to reflect that common intent; such contracts are voidable or subject to reformation.

■══■

Nelson v. Rice

Seller (P) v. Buyer (D)

Ariz. Ct. App., 198 Ariz. 563, 12 P.3d 238 (2000).

NATURE OF CASE: Appeal from grant of summary judgment to defendants and denial of motion for new trial in contract action.

FACT SUMMARY: Nelson's estate (P) sold two oil paintings at an estate sale to Rice (D) for $60, believing the paintings to be relatively worthless. The paintings later sold for over $1 million at auction. Nelson (P) sued to rescind or reform the sale based on mutual mistake.

🏛 RULE OF LAW
A contract will not be rescinded where one party bears the risk of loss due to conscious ignorance of elemental facts.

FACTS: Martha Nelson died in 1996 and the co-representatives of her estate (the "Estate" (P) hired an appraiser to appraise the Estate's (P) personal property. The appraiser, Judith McKenzie-Larson, informed the Estate (P) that she did not appraise fine art and the Estate (P) assumed she did not find any when she finished appraising the property. At the estate sale, Carl Rice (D), a casual art buyer, purchased two oil paintings for $60. He later discovered the paintings were Magnolia Blossoms on Blue Velvet and Cherokee Roses by Martin Johnson Heade. Christie's auction house sold the paintings at auction for $1,072,000.00 in 1997. The Estate (P) learned of the auction and sued McKenzie-Larson. She had no assets to pay the damages. The Estate (P) then sued Rice (D), arguing mutual mistake and unconscionability. Both parties moved for summary judgment. The trial court granted summary judgment to Rice (D) on grounds that the Estate (P) bore the risk of loss and the sale was not unconscionable because the Estate (P) set the sale price. The court denied the Estate's (P) motion for a new trial, and the Estate (P) appealed.

ISSUE: Will a contract be rescinded where one party bears the risk of loss due to conscious ignorance of core facts?

HOLDING AND DECISION: (Espinosa, C.J.) No. A contract will not be rescinded where one party bears the risk of loss due to conscious ignorance of core facts. The Estate (P) first seeks to rescind the sale based on mutual mistake of the parties as to the worth of the paintings. Both parties must have been mistaken and the mistake undermines the very essence of the contract. Also, the party seeking to rescind cannot bear the risk of loss. Here, the Estate (P) ignored the possibility that the personal property contained fine art. McKenzie-Larson informed the Estate (P) that she did not appraise fine art and the Estate (P) assumed no fine art existed because she did

not tell the Estate (P) to hire a fine art appraiser. That places the risk of loss firmly on the Estate (P). The Estate (P) had plenty of opportunity to ascertain the value of the paintings and deliberately chose not to do so. The Estate (P) next argues that the sale was substantively unconscionable because of the actual terms of the sale. The value of the paintings in hindsight is admittedly significantly higher than the terms of the sale. At the time, however, the terms of the contract were fair because the Estate (P) set the price and Rice (D) paid the price. Affirmed.

▶ ANALYSIS

The "conscious ignorance" doctrine permits the court broad discretion in evaluating a party's knowledge. It is acceptable not to know that Heade is a respected artist, but it is not acceptable to ignore that the oil paintings may have been painted by someone of repute. That is, "ignorance" may be forgiven, but "conscious ignorance" will not be excused. The court has broad discretion to determine where on the spectrum a party's ignorance lies when deciding whether to rescind a contract.

■=■

Quicknotes

MUTUAL MISTAKE A mistake by both parties to a contract, who are in agreement as to what the contract terms should be, but the agreement as written fails to reflect that common intent; such contracts are voidable or subject to reformation.

RESCIND To cancel an agreement and return the parties to their positions prior to the formation of the contract.

SUMMARY JUDGMENT Judgment rendered by a court in response to a motion made by one of the parties, claiming that the lack of a question of material fact in respect to an issue warrants disposition of the issue without consideration by the jury.

UNCONSCIONABILITY A situation in which a contract, or a particular contract term, is unenforceable if the court determines that such terms are unduly oppressive or unfair to one party to the contract.

■=■

Sherwood v. Walker

Cattle purchaser (P) v. Cattle breeder (D)

Mich. Sup. Ct., 66 Mich. 568, 33 N.W. 919 (1887).

NATURE OF CASE: Appeal from judgment for plaintiff in action of replevin for a cow.

FACT SUMMARY: The Walkers (D), having sold a cow to Sherwood (P) in the mistaken belief that it was barren, refused to deliver it.

🏛 RULE OF LAW
Where the parties to a contract for the sale of personal property are mutually mistaken as to a material fact which affects the substance of the whole consideration, the contract is unenforceable and rescindable.

FACTS: The Walkers (D) agreed to sell Sherwood (P) a certain cow, "Rose 2nd of Aberlone," for a price based on live weight of the cow. At the time the contract was entered into, the Walkers (D) indicated their belief that the animal was barren. To this, Sherwood (P) replied that he thought she could be made to breed but that he believed she was not with calf. The cow was not weighed at the time. When the Walkers (D) discovered that the cow was pregnant, and could have been sold for up to $1,000, they refused to deliver it, whereupon Sherwood (P) brought an action of replevin. The trial court held for Sherwood (P), ruling that the contract should have been performed at the agreed-upon price. The state's highest court granted review.

ISSUE: Where the parties to a contract for the sale of personal property are mutually mistaken as to a material fact which affects the substance of the whole consideration, is the contract unenforceable and rescindable?

HOLDING AND DECISION: (Morse, J.) Yes. Where the parties to a contract for the sale of personal property are mutually mistaken as to a material fact which affects the substance of the whole consideration, the contract is unenforceable and rescindable. However, the mutual mistake must not only be as to some material fact but must also affect the substance of the whole consideration. Here, the mistake was as to a crucial, material fact. The parties would not have made the contract if they knew that the cow was capable of breeding. A barren cow is a different creature than a breeding one. The cow was sold for beef, when in fact she had considerable value as a breeder. As a result, there was no contract formed. Reversed and new trial granted.

DISSENT: (Sherwood, J.) There was no "mutual" mistake here since Sherwood (P) believed the cow would breed. Neither party knew the actual quality and condition of the cow at the time of sale. Regardless, no conditions were attached to the sale by either party, and what might have happened to the cow after the sale, formed no element in the contract. And if any mistake was made, it was made by the buyers acting on their own judgment. Because it was their own mistake, they have no remedy.

▶ ANALYSIS

The court's interpretation of the facts in this case suggests the difficulties inherent in ascertaining all the surrounding circumstances in mistaken assumption analysis. As a result, many commentators have suggested an alternative approach. Following the cue of Uniform Commercial Code § 2-615, these commentators have urged that the nondelivery of goods should be excused where, owing to an unexpected occurrence, "the nonoccurrence of which was a basic assumption on which the contract was made," performance has been rendered commercially impracticable.

■══■

Quicknotes

MUTUAL MISTAKE A mistake by both parties to a contract, who are in agreement as to what the contract terms should be, but the agreement as written fails to reflect that common intent; such contracts are voidable or subject to reformation.

REPLEVIN An action to recover personal property wrongfully taken.

■══■

White v. Berenda Mesa Water Dist.

Mistaken bidder (D) v. Bid acceptor (P)

Cal. Ct. App., 7 Cal. App. 3d 894, 87 Cal. Rptr. 338 (1970).

NATURE OF CASE: Appeal in action for breach of contract.

FACT SUMMARY: White (D) made a mixed mistake of fact and judgment in submitting a bid to the Berenda Mesa Water District (P).

🏛 RULE OF LAW
Rescission may be had for a mixed mistake of fact and judgment where it would otherwise be unfair to enforce the contract.

FACTS: Berenda Mesa Water District (District) (P) invited bids on a construction project. White (D), relying on unwarranted soil reports and statements of an engineer, tendered a bid on the assumption that no more than 7 percent of the soil to be excavated was hard rock. In actuality, hard rock composed 50 percent of the soil. Discovering the mistake, White (D) immediately informed the District (P) that he wished to withdraw his bid. The mistake was explained to members of the District's (P) council, but they subsequently accepted White's (D) bid, which was approximately $60,000 lower than the next lowest bid. White (D) refused to perform, and the District (P) brought suit for damages. White (D) alleged that, at most, he was guilty of simple negligence in failing to determine that the reports were not accurate. White (D) further alleged that his mistake was in part factual, and he should be relieved of a significant loss based on such a mixed mistake of fact and judgment since the District (P) had suffered no damage from it.

ISSUE: Should rescission be granted for mixed mistakes of fact and judgment where enforcement would be unfair?

HOLDING AND DECISION: (Coakley, J.) Yes. Normally, rescission will be granted for a material factual mistake but will be denied for a mistake in judgment. One cannot complain of the contract merely because the bargain was bad. Here, the District (P) made the reports, on which White (D) mistakenly relied, available to bidders. This constitutes a factual mistake. White (D) was negligent in failing to properly correlate the reports and to discover the actual soil conditions. Thus, there was a mixed mistake of fact and judgment. Rescission may be had for factual mistakes not the result of a breach of a legal duty. Ordinary, simple negligence does not constitute such a breach of a legal duty. In cases involving mixed mistakes of judgment and fact, where the error is promptly called to the other party's attention, no injury is suffered by the non-mistaken party, and enforcement of the contract would be unfair, rescission is warranted. Judgment reversed.

▶ ANALYSIS

Rescission may be had for mistake of fact if the mistake is material to the contract and is not the result of neglect of a legal duty, if enforcement of the contract as made would be unconscionable, if the other party may be placed in status quo, if there is prompt notice of the mistake and the intent to rescind, and if there is restoration of any value received under the contract. *M. F. Kemper Const. Co. v. City of L.A.*, 37 Cal. 2d 696, 235 P.2d 7 (1951).

■■■

Quicknotes

MATERIAL FACT A fact without the existence of which a contract would not have been entered.

MATERIAL MISTAKE A mistake as to a factual assumption upon which an action or contract is based, and which may be an adequate defense to a criminal prosecution or a cause for voiding or reforming a contract.

MISTAKE OF FACT An unintentional mistake in knowing or recalling a fact without the will to deceive.

■■■

Hoffman v. Chapman

Buyers of lot (D) v. Sellers (P)

Md. Ct. App., 182 Md. 208, 34 A.2d 438 (1943).

NATURE OF CASE: Appeal from reformation of a deed.

FACT SUMMARY: The Hoffmans (D) purchased part of a lot from the Chapmans (P) who accidentally deeded the entire lot.

🏛 RULE OF LAW
If there is clear, convincing and strong evidence of a mutual mistake, the courts will reform an instrument to reflect the true intent of the parties.

FACTS: The Chapmans (P) owned a large lot containing several dwellings. The Chapmans (P) sold a portion of the tract, containing a bungalow, to the Hoffmans (D) who knew they were only purchasing a part of the lot. Through an error, the deed conveyed the entire lot. When the mistake was discovered, the Hoffmans (D) refused to convey the portion of the lot not covered by the original sale to the Chapmans (P). The court reformed the deed. The Hoffmans (D) alleged that the deed description rendered the contract so vague as to evidence that no meeting of the minds as to what was being sold occurred and the transaction was therefore void. The Parol Evidence rule was also raised as barring the admission of evidence to contradict the deed.

ISSUE: May a contract be reformed, where there is strong, unequivocal and convincing evidence of a mutual mistake?

HOLDING AND DECISION: (Delaplaine, J.) Yes. Equity will reform an instrument where there is clear, convincing and strong proof of a mutual mistake. Here, there was the sales contract and a plot clearly showing the portion of the lot which the parties intended to be conveyed. The scrivener who made the mistake worked as an agent for both parties. Under such circumstances, equity would be remiss in not conforming the deed to the intentions of the parties and the Parol Evidence Rule will not bar the introduction of such evidence. The plot and the sales contract clearly describe the property to be conveyed and the contract is not void for vagueness. The negligence herein was minor and resulted in no detriment to the Hoffmans (D), nor were they in any way misled by it. Affirmed.

▶ ANALYSIS

A mistake of law in the making of an agreement or the violation of a positive legal duty of care will normally prevent reformation absent additional factors. *Benesh v. Travelers' Ins. Co.*, 14 N.D. 39, 103 NW 405, and *Boyle v.*

Maryland State Fair 150 Md. 333, 134 A. 124 (1926). A ministerial mistake in drafting, even when by an attorney, may be reformed by equity to reflect the real intent of the parties. *Archer v. McClure*, 166 N.C. 140, 81 S.E. 1081 (1914).

Quicknotes

MUTUAL MISTAKE A mistake by both parties to a contract, who are in agreement as to what the contract terms should be, but the agreement as written fails to reflect that common intent; such contracts are voidable or subject to reformation.

PAROL EVIDENCE RULE Doctrine precluding parties to an agreement from introducing evidence of prior or contemporaneous agreements in order to repudiate or alter the terms of a written contract.

REFORMATION OF CONTRACT An equitable remedy whereby the written terms of an agreement are altered in order to reflect the true intent of the parties; reformation requires a demonstration by clear and convincing evidence of mutual mistake by the parties to the contract.

Williams v. Walker-Thomas Furniture Co.

Buyer (D) v. Seller (P)

350 F.2d 445 (D.C. Cir. 1965).

NATURE OF CASE: Appeal in action in replevin.

FACT SUMMARY: Williams (D) made a series of purchases, on credit, from Walker-Thomas Furniture Co. (P), but defaulted on her payments.

🏛 RULE OF LAW
Where, in light of the general commercial background of a particular case, it appears that gross inequality of bargaining power between the parties has led to the formation of a contract on terms to which one party has had no meaningful choice, a court should refuse to enforce such a contract on the ground that it is unconscionable.

ISSUE: Beginning about 1957, Walker-Thomas Furniture Co. (Walker-Thomas) (P), a retail furniture company, began using a standard form contract for all credit transactions which contained, inter alia, a clause by which the company (P) reserved the right, upon default by a purchaser, to repossess all items contemporaneously being purchased by the buyer at the time of the repossession. This clause was accompanied by one which stated that all credit purchases made from Walker-Thomas (P) were to be handled through one account, with each installment payment spread pro-rata over all items purchased (even where purchased separately and at different times), until all items were paid for. Williams (D) began purchasing items from Walker-Thomas (P) in 1957. In 1962, she bought a stereo set there. When she defaulted on a payment soon thereafter, Walker-Thomas (P) filed this action to replevy (i.e., repossess) all items she had purchased (and was still paying for) since 1957. From judgment for Walker-Thomas (P), this appeal followed.

ISSUE: May a court refuse to enforce an unreasonable contract, even though no evidence of fraud can be produced?

HOLDING AND DECISION: (Wright, J.) Yes. Where, in light of the general commercial background of a particular case, it appears that gross inequality of bargaining power between the parties has led to the formation of a contract on terms to which one party has had no meaningful choice, a court should refuse to enforce such a contract on the ground that it is unconscionable. It is true that the common law, operating by the caveat emptor rationale, refused to look into the essential fairness of a contract absent evidence of out and out fraud. The Uniform Commercial Code (U.C.C.), however, notably § 2-302, as adopted in this jurisdiction, has accepted the rule that courts should seek to prevent overreaching in contracts of adhesion such as the one at bar. Williams

(D) and others come from a socioeconomic class for whom credit is difficult to obtain. To permit Walker-Thomas (P) to exploit this condition with provisions such as those pointed out above is clearly unconscionable. Judgment reversed, and the trial court is ordered to undertake an examination of these provisions in light of this opinion.

DISSENT: (Danaher, J.) The court ignores many policy considerations in its decision today. For one, the high risk of granting credit to the poor for companies like Walker-Thomas (P) is not even addressed. A more cautious approach is warranted.

▌ ANALYSIS

This case points up the major application which the U.C.C. § 2-302 concept of unconscionability has had to date: adhesion (i.e., form) contracts. Note that the general common-law rule regarding such contracts remains the general rule today. That rule is that a person who signs a contract will be held responsible for any clauses or conditions which a reasonable man making a reasonable inspection would have discovered. The U.C.C. rule merely qualifies this to say that, where one party to a form contract has no real choice over whether to accept the terms because of his relative economic position, then the fact he knows of the terms will not be enough to constitute a "meeting of the minds" on his part necessary to form a valid contract.

Quicknotes

ADHESION CONTRACT A contract that is not negotiated by the parties and is usually prepared by the dominant party on a "take it or leave it" basis.

CAVEAT EMPTOR Let the buyer beware; doctrine that a buyer purchases something at his own risk.

FRAUD A false representation of facts with the intent that another will rely on the misrepresentation to his detriment.

REPLEVIN An action to recover personal property wrongfully taken.

UNCONSCIONABLE A situation in which a contract, or a particular contract term, is unenforceable if the court determines that such term(s) are unduly oppressive or unfair to one party to the contract.

In re RealNetworks, Inc., Privacy Litigation

User (P) v. Software provider (D)

2000 WL 631341 (N.D. Ill. 2000).

NATURE OF CASE: Trespass and invasion of privacy suit under federal and common law.

FACT SUMMARY: Lieschke (P) and others brought suit against RealNetworks, Inc. (D) under federal and common law, alleging trespass to property and invasion of privacy. RealNetworks (D) sought dismissal on grounds arbitration was required.

RULE OF LAW
A licensing agreement is not procedurally unconscionable, nor does it fail to provide fair notice of its contents, merely because it is contained as part of a license in a pop-up window on an Internet site.

FACTS: Lieschke (P) and others brought suit against RealNetworks, Inc. (D) under federal and common law, alleging trespass to property and invasion of privacy, claiming that RealNetworks' (D) software products secretly allowed RealNetworks (D) to access and intercept users' electronic communications and stored information without their knowledge or consent. RealNetworks (D), seeking dismissal, argued that before a user can install either of these software packages, they must accept the terms of RealNetworks' (D) license agreement, which appear on the user's screen. Paragraph 10 of the agreement included a clause, providing in part that any and all unresolved disputes arising under the license agreement must be submitted to arbitration in the State of Washington. Defendant cited this clause as binding authority for its assertions that arbitration was required.

ISSUE: Is a licensing agreement procedurally unconscionable, or does it fail to provide fair notice of its contents merely because it is contained as part of a license in a pop-up window on an Internet site?

HOLDING AND DECISION: (Kocoras, J.) No. A licensing agreement is not procedurally unconscionable nor does it fail to provide fair notice of its contents merely because it is contained as part of a license in a pop-up window on an Internet site. Although burying important terms in a "maze of fine print" may contribute to a contract being found unconscionable, the arbitration provision in the instant license agreement is not in fact buried. The agreement here sets out the arbitration provision in the same size font as the rest of the agreement. Moreover, it is not buried in the middle of the entire agreement or located in a footnote or appendix. Rather, it comprises the "attention-getting" final provision of the agreement. The court also rejects the argument that the arbitration provision is substantively unconscionable because it chooses a

geographically distant forum, noting that the designation of any state as a forum is bound to be distant to some potential litigants of a corporation that has a nationwide reach.

ANALYSIS

The *RealNetworks* court noted that the size of the pop-up window, although smaller than the desktop, does not make the license agreement visually difficult to read.

Quicknotes

UNCONSCIONABLE A situation in which a contract, or a particular contract term, is unenforceable if the court determines that such term(s) are unduly oppressive or unfair to one party to the contract.

Conditions, Performance, and Breach

Quick Reference Rules of Law

Audette v. L'Union St. Joseph

Widow claimant (P) v. Decedent's insurer (D)

Mass. Sup. Jud. Ct., 178 Mass. 113, 59 N.E. 668 (1901).

NATURE OF CASE: Appeal from judgment for defendant in action to recover benefits from an insurer.

FACT SUMMARY: Audette (P) could not obtain a sworn statement from her husband's physician to comply with the requirements of the insurer.

🏛 RULE OF LAW
An insurer need not honor a claim unless all of its procedures have been complied with by the claimant.

FACTS: Before his death, Mr. Audette had been insured by L'Union St. Joseph (L'Union) (D). L'Union (D) required a sworn statement from a physician before it would honor any claims. Mr. Audette's doctor refused to issue a sworn certificate because of conscientious scruples. L'Union (D) refused to honor Mrs. Audette's (P) claim, and she sued to collect on the insurance policy.

ISSUE: Must a party comply with all contractual conditions to compel the other party's performance?

HOLDING AND DECISION: (Loring, J.) Yes. An insurer may impose conditions in the nature of claim procedures with which the insured must comply in order to obtain benefits. When one engages for the act of a stranger, he must procure the act to be done, and the refusal of the stranger, without the interference of the other party, is no excuse. Suit herein must be dismissed as premature. Until Mrs. Audette (P) obtains a certificate, L'Union's (D) counterperformance is not yet due. Affirmed.

▶ ANALYSIS

The sworn certificate herein is a condition precedent to L'Union's (D) duty to pay a claim. Until the condition is satisfied, L'Union's (D) duty of performance does not become due. Such conditions are seldom excused by the courts since they often are essential to the bargain between the parties. Each party's performance may be freely conditioned on the happening of some event or performance of some specified act.

■═■

Quicknotes

CONDITION PRECEDENT The happening of an uncertain occurrence which is necessary before a particular right or interest may be obtained or an action performed.

■═■

Inman v. Clyde Hall Drilling Co.

Employee (P) v. Drilling company (D)

Alaska Sup. Ct., 369 P.2d 498 (1962).

NATURE OF CASE: Appeal in action for damages under an employment contract.

FACT SUMMARY: Inman (P) did not give notice within the contractually provided for thirty-day limit that he was claiming damages under his employment contract with Clyde Hall Drilling Co. (D) for being unjustifiably fired.

> ## ⚖ RULE OF LAW
> The court may refuse to recognize and uphold a condition which is contrary to public policy, but it will not act where the facts do not clearly reveal violation of an existent public policy.

FACTS: Under an employment contract signed by Inman (P) and Clyde Hall Drilling Co. (Clyde Hall) (D) on November 16, 1959, thirty-day notice of a claim thereunder was made a condition precedent to any recovery. When his employment was terminated on March 24, 1960, Inman (P), feeling such was without justification, filed suit on April 5, 1960, against Clyde Hall (D) for damages arising out of breach of contract. The complaint was served on Clyde Hall (D) on April 14, 1960, which Inman (P) contended substantially complied with the notice requirements that suit would not be instituted prior to six months after the filing of the written notice of claim. Having denied any breach in its answer, Clyde Hall (D) moved for a summary judgment, asserting the action was barred by Inman's (P) failure to give written notice of his claim. The granting of that motion and the judgment thereon was appealed by Clyde Hall (D).

ISSUE: Is a contractual provision making written notice of a claim under an employment contract a condition precedent to a recovery per se contrary to public policy and, therefore, unenforceable?

HOLDING AND DECISION: (Dimond, J.) No. It is a question of fact requiring evidence whether a particular contractual provision is against public policy and, therefore, will not be recognized or upheld by this court. No evidence of the unfair or unreasonable nature of this provision having been adduced, the court will not imply such. There is no suggestion of any motive—unfair or otherwise—and Inman (P) was fully aware of the provisions of the contract. Nor is there any indication that this limitation on Inman's (P) right of action is offensive to justice. It being our function to act only to prevent such, we are not justified in permitting one party to escape his obligations by refusing to enforce the contract. Since the specific notice requirement was not met, no other manner is sufficient, and the judgment is affirmed.

▶ ANALYSIS

Occasionally, notice provisions will be deemed inequitable as where there is a very short time period in which the accident/claim can be reported. These situations normally occur in insurance claim cases. The notice may normally be required on a company claim form, in writing, and delivered to the company's office or claim center. So long as there is no improper motive and the condition is reasonable, it will normally be upheld, though some courts excuse the condition where no damage has been suffered by the other party.

■=■

Quicknotes

ANTICIPATORY BREACH Breach of a contract subsequent to formation but prior to the time performance is due.

CONDITION PRECEDENT The happening of an uncertain occurrence, which is necessary before a particular right or interest may be obtained or an action performed.

EXPRESS CONDITION A condition that is expressly stated in the terms of a written instrument.

■=■

New York Bronze Powder Co. v. Benjamin Acquisition Corp.

Seller (P) v. Buyer (D)

Md. Ct. App., 351 Md. 8, 716 A.2d 230 (1998).

NATURE OF CASE: Appeal in breach of contract suit.

FACT SUMMARY: New York Bronze Powder Co. (P) brought suit against Benjamin Acquisition Corp. (D) for its failure to pay a $350,000 note for the purchase of the assets of a business.

▥ RULE OF LAW
Absent an express provision stating that a required event in a contract constitutes a condition precedent to performance, the preferred interpretation is that it merely imposes a duty on the obligee to act whose nonperformance gives rise to a remedy for breach.

FACTS: New York Bronze Powder Co. (New York Bronze) (P) entered into an agreement with Benjamin Acquisition Corp. (Benjamin) (D) for the sale by New York Bronze (P) to Benjamin (D) of the assets of a company (Rich) for $4.5 million, together with the assumption of certain of Rich's liabilities. Benjamin (D) expressed concerns regarding the valuation of certain assets and a modification of the purchase agreement was made providing that $350,000 of the purchase price was to be deferred, and Benjamin (D) executed a nonnegotiable note to New York Bronze (P) for $350,000. Under § 3 of the amendment, Benjamin (D) was to have prepared a balance sheet of Rich accompanied by the opinion of a specifically named accounting firm, and promised to use its best efforts to deliver that balance sheet to New York Bronze (P) by June 14, 1990. To the extent that balance sheet reflected a net worth of Rich that was less than $4.5 million, Benjamin (D) was entitled to a dollar-for-dollar credit against the $350,000 deferred purchase price. The accounting firm never completed its audit and Benjamin (D) never made any cash payment on the note. New York Bronze (P) brought suit alleging non-payment of the note and breach of the modified asset purchase agreement. The trial court entered a judgment for $350,000 in favor of New York Bronze (P). Benjamin (D) appealed to the court of special appeals, which held that § 4.2 of the note created a condition precedent, the nonoccurrence of which extinguished Benjamin's (D) obligation to pay the $350,000. New York Bronze (P) petitioned this court for writ of certiorari.

ISSUE: Absent an express provision stating that a required event in a contract constitutes a condition precedent to performance, is the preferred interpretation that it merely imposes a duty on the obligee to act whose nonperformance gives rise to a remedy for breach?

HOLDING AND DECISION: (Smith, J.) Yes. Absent an express provision stating that a required event in a contract constitutes a condition precedent to performance, the preferred interpretation is that it merely imposes a duty on the obligee to act whose nonperformance gives rise to a remedy for breach. The court of special appeals held that New York Bronze (P) was not entitled to the principal amount of the note, or any portion thereof, because it had not surrendered the original note to Benjamin (D). The court reasoned that words in a contract are to be given their ordinary meaning. A "condition precedent" is defined as "an act or event, other than a lapse of time, which, unless the condition is excused, must occur before a duty to perform a promise in the agreement arises." The language in § 4.2 here, requiring the noteholder to surrender the note for cancellation in order to receive payment, fits that definition and qualifies the duty to pay. The issue here is whether the last sentence of § 4.2 is to be construed as a promise on the part of New York Bronze (P) to surrender the note for cancellation, an unsubstantial breach of which Benjamin (D) would not be excused from performance, or whether the last sentence is a condition precedent to enforcement of Benjamin's (D) promise to pay the $350,000. In *Oppenheimer & Co.*, 660 N.E.2d 415 (1995), the Court of Appeals of New York gave guidance for determining whether a contract provision is a condition, requiring courts to "interpret doubtful language as embodying a promise or constructive condition rather than an express condition." This preference is especially strong when a finding of express condition would increase the risk of forfeiture. The court also refers to Restatement (Second) of Contracts § 227(2), which sets forth the preferred interpretation. That section merely imposes a duty on the obligee to perform the act and does not make the doing of the act a condition of the obligor's duty. Thus, the obligee's failure to perform his duty, if material, has the effect of the nonoccurrence of a condition of the obligor's duty. Unless the agreement expressly provides that such act is a condition of the contract, it is a mere promise and the obligor still has a remedy for breach. Here it is doubtful that the parties intended to create a condition. Applying the preferred construction, the last sentence of § 4.2 of the note merely creates a covenant or contractual duty on the part of New York Bronze (P) to surrender the note, and is not a condition precedent to payment on the part of Benjamin (D). Reversed.

Continued on next page.

▌ *ANALYSIS*

The court noted that under New York law, more explicit language than that used here is needed in order to overcome the preference for interpretation of the section as a covenant.

■═■

Quicknotes

CONDITION Requirement; potential future occurrence upon which the existence of a legal obligation is dependent.

CONSIDERATION Value given by one party in exchange for performance, or a promise to perform, by another party.

COVENANT A written promise to do, or to refrain from doing, a particular activity.

■═■

Thos. J. Dyer Co. v. Bishop International Engineering Co.

Subcontractor (P) v. General contractor (D)

303 F.2d 655 (6th Cir. 1962).

NATURE OF CASE: Appeal from grant of summary judgment to plaintiff in action for breach of contract.

FACT SUMMARY: Thos. J. Dyer Co. (P), Bishop International Engineering Co.'s (Bishop's) (D) subcontractor, was to be paid within five days of Bishop (D) being paid.

RULE OF LAW
Where the ground contractor is obligated to pay his subcontractors within a certain time limit after he receives payment, receipt of payment by the general contractor is not a condition precedent to his duty to pay subcontractors.

FACTS: Bishop International Engineering Co. (Bishop) (D), the general contractor, hired Thos. J. Dyer Co. (Dyer) (P) to perform various duties as subcontractors. Bishop (D) was to pay Dyer (P) within five days after Bishop (D) received its payments from the owner of the property. Bishop (D) received only a portion of the money due it by the owner. Bishop (D) then paid Dyer (P) a portion of the money due it. Dyer (P) demanded the balance of the money due it. Bishop (D) alleged that it had no duty to pay Dyer (P) since its receipt of the money due it by the owner was a condition precedent to its duty to pay Dyer (P). Dyer (P) alleged that it was a covenant. The district judge granted Dyer's (P) motion for summary judgment and awarded Dyer (P) money damages and interest. Bishop (D) appealed.

ISSUE: Where the general contractor promises to pay subcontractors after it receives payment from the owner, is the receipt of the money by the general contractor a condition precedent to its duty to pay subcontractors?

HOLDING AND DECISION: (Miller, C.J.) No. In deciding whether a clause creates a condition or a covenant, the intention of the parties is the controlling factor. Bishop (D) undertook the risk that the Owner might be a poor credit risk. Before Bishop (D) can shift that risk to Dyer (P), there must be a clear, unequivocal showing that Dyer (P) agreed to accept this risk, i.e., that this was the intention of the parties. The qualification herein, i.e., "no part of which shall be paid until five (5) days after Owner shall have paid Contractor therefor," is not a clear and unequivocal condition. The most reasonable construction is that Bishop (D) should be given adequate time to pay Dyer (P). It is a covenant to pay the subcontractor the money owed it after a reasonable time. It is immaterial to

Bishop's (D) obligation whether or not it receives payment from the Owner. Judgment affirmed.

ANALYSIS

The court rests the present case squarely on the question: Which party assumed the risk of the owner's nonpayment? Since the intention of the parties on this point is not expressed in the contract, the court establishes a presumption that the general contractor has intended to bear the risk. Bishop (D) has not successfully borne the burden of rebutting the presumption by clear language to the contrary. Only after deciding this allocation-of-risk issue does the court implicitly label as a "covenant" Bishop's (D) promise to pay.

■==■

Quicknotes

CONDITION PRECEDENT The happening of an uncertain occurrence, which is necessary before a particular right or interest may be obtained or an action performed.

COVENANT A written promise to do, or to refrain from doing, a particular activity.

RISK Danger of damage to or loss of property.

■==■

J.J. Shane, Inc. v. Aetna Casualty & Surety Co.

Subcontractor (P) v. Insurance company (D)

Fl. Dist. Ct. App., 723 So. 2d 302 (1998).

NATURE OF CASE: Appeal in breach of contract action.

FACT SUMMARY: J.J. Shane, Inc. (P), a subcontractor, brought suit against general contractor, Recchi (D), for failure to make complete payment on a construction project.

🏛 RULE OF LAW
Subcontract agreements may contain valid payment provisions which shift the risk of payment failure by the owner from the general contractor to the subcontractor if they expressly state such intention.

FACTS: J.J. Shane, Inc. (Shane) (P) was a subcontractor to general contractor, Recchi (D), during the construction of the Omni extension in downtown Miami. The construction project was owned by Dade County. Recchi (D) failed to make complete payment for Shane's (P) work on the project and Shane (P) brought suit. Recchi (D) maintained that under the contract payment to Shane (P) was conditioned upon receipt of payment from the county/owner. The jury entered a verdict in favor of Recchi (D) and Shane (P) appealed.

ISSUE: May subcontract agreements contain valid payment provisions which shift the risk of payment failure by the owner from the general contractor to the subcontractor if they expressly state such intention?

HOLDING AND DECISION: (Green, J.) Yes. Subcontract agreements may contain valid payment provisions which shift the risk of payment failure by the owner from the general contractor to the subcontractor if they expressly state such intention. Recchi (D) contended that since it had not yet been paid, and was in fact in litigation for such payment, Recchi's (D) contractual obligation to pay Shane (P) had not yet arisen. In most subcontract agreements, payment by the owner to the contractor is not ordinarily a condition precedent to the contractor's duty to pay the subcontractor. However, subcontractor agreements may contain valid payment provisions shifting the risk of payment failure by the owner from the general contractor to the subcontractor. In order to make such a shift, the contract must unambiguously express that intention. Here the subject payment provision plainly and unambiguously provided for such a shift. Thus, if the owner's nonpayment to the general contractor is undisputed, the cause for payment by the subcontractor was prematurely filed. Reversed and remanded with instructions that the case be dismissed without prejudice.

▶ ANALYSIS

This case sets forth the general rule stated in *Peacock Constr. Co., Inc. v. Modern Air Conditioning, Inc.*, 353 So.2d 840, 842 (Fla. 1977). That court's rationale that payment to the subcontractor was presumed not contingent on the owner's payment since small subcontractors must receive payment for their work in order to remain viable, and thus cannot be presumed to have assumed to risk of the owner's failure to provide payment to the general contractor.

■══■

Quicknotes

BREACH OF CONTRACT Unlawful failure by a party to perform its obligations pursuant to contract.

■══■

Thompson v. Lithia Chrysler Jeep Dodge of Great Falls

Buyer (P) v. Seller (D)

Mont. Sup. Ct., 343 Mont. 392, 185 P.3d 332 (2008).

NATURE OF CASE: Appeal from trial court judgment granting a motion to compel arbitration.

FACT SUMMARY: Corey and Kimber Thompson (P) agreed to buy a Dodge truck at a particular rate of interest from Lithia Chrysler Jeep Dodge of Great Falls (Lithia) (D), but changed their minds when they were told their interest rate would be higher than that agreed to in the contract. Lithia (D) moved to compel arbitration, and the trial court granted the motion. The Thompsons (P) appealed, arguing the arbitration clause was invalid since a valid contract was never formed.

🏛 RULE OF LAW
When a party challenges a contract containing an arbitration clause on the ground that the parties never entered a contract, the court is the appropriate forum to determine whether a contract exists, prior to compelling arbitration.

FACTS: Corey and Kimber Thompson (P) signed a contract to buy a Dodge truck from Lithia Chrysler Jeep Dodge of Great Falls (Lithia) (D) in January 2005. The contract listed the annual percentage rate of 3.9 percent, contained an arbitration provision, and stated that the contract was not binding until financing was completed on the basis of the agreed upon rate. The Thompsons (P) drove the truck home and used it for a little over a week. In February 2005, Lithia (D) contacted them and told them that they would need to sign new finance papers with a higher annual percentage rate of 4.9 percent. They refused, and Lithia (D) told them they would have to return the truck. The Thompsons (P) say they brought the truck back on that same day and attempted to get back their trade-in vehicle, but were told it had been sold. Lithia (D) also refused to return their $2,000 down payment, and refused, the Thompsons (P) claim, to take back the truck. The Thompsons (P) left it at the dealership anyway. The Thompsons (P) then contacted the financing company to ensure that the contract and order were not enforced, since they had returned the truck. They claim that they were told there was no record of a loan. Later, Lithia (D) submitted financing papers to the financing company, which accepted the loan, and in January 2006, the Thompsons' (P) lawyer received a letter from Lithia's (D) lawyer stating that Lithia (D) decided to execute a "rate buy down concession" instead of rescinding the transaction. According to the letter, the "rate buy down concession" occurred when the dealership paid money towards the loan on the Thompsons' (P) behalf, so that the interest rate reflected on the original contract could be maintained. The Thompsons (P)

filed suit against Lithia (D) in March 2006. Lithia (D) filed motions to stay the proceedings and compel arbitration, among others. The district court granted the motions, concluding that because the Thompsons (P) were challenging the contract as a whole, and not just the arbitration clause, the matter had to be heard by an arbitrator.

ISSUE: When a party challenges a contract containing an arbitration clause on the ground that the parties never entered a contract, is the court the appropriate forum to determine whether a contract exists, prior to compelling arbitration?

HOLDING AND DECISION: (Rice, J.) Yes. When a party challenges a contract containing an arbitration clause on the ground that the parties never entered a contract, the court is the appropriate forum to determine whether a contract exists, prior to compelling arbitration. If the parties never formed a contract, they never agreed to arbitrate and arbitration would be inappropriate. This is a narrow exception to the rule established in *Buckeye Check Cashing, Inc. v. Cardegna*, 546 U.S. 440 (2006), which held that a challenge to the validity of the contract as a whole, and not specifically to the arbitration clause, must go to the arbitrator. The reason for the distinction is that there is a difference between the validity of a contract and a question as to whether a contract had been formed. The Thompsons (P) argue that no contract had been formed because of the failure to get financing at the agreed upon interest rate, which they argue was a condition precedent to the formation of the contract. A review of the contract's terms suggests that the Thompsons (P) agreed to purchase the Dodge for a specific price that was premised on 3.9 percent financing, and that no contract would have been formed unless financing under those terms was approved. If a condition precedent to formation is not fulfilled, there is no agreement and the contract is not binding. Since the court is the proper forum for determining whether a contract was entered into, the district court erred in granting the motion to compel arbitration. Therefore, this was a condition precedent to the contract's formation. Whether the condition precedent was met is a question of disputed fact that warrants a trial. The district court therefore erred by granting the Lithia's (D) motion to compel arbitration and stay the proceedings. Reversed and remanded.

▶ ANALYSIS

The court points out that a condition precedent to formation is different from a condition precedent to performance

Continued on next page.

of a contract obligation. The condition is a condition precedent to formation where the contract specifically states that it will not be binding unless some condition is met. If a contract is not binding, it is not a contract. Careful scrutiny of the language of the contract usually will indicate what type of condition is at play.

■≡■

Quicknotes

CONDITION PRECEDENT The happening of an uncertain occurrence which is necessary before a particular right or interest may be obtained or an action performed.

■≡■

Stewart v. Newbury

Excavator (P) v. Client (D)

N.Y. Ct. App., 220 N.Y. 379, 115 N.E. 984 (1917).

NATURE OF CASE: Appeal from judgment for plaintiff in action for damages for breach of a construction contract.

FACT SUMMARY: Stewart (P), who was contracted to do excavating for Newbury (D), alleged that he was to be paid in the "usual manner," i.e., 85 percent every 30 days, 15 percent being retained until work was completed, even though this was not written into the contract. When Newbury (D) failed to pay, Stewart (P) stopped work.

🏛 RULE OF LAW
Where a contract is made to perform work and no agreement is made as to payment, the work must be substantially performed before payment can be demanded.

FACTS: Stewart (P) was contracted by Newbury (D) to do excavating work and claimed that over the telephone Newbury (D) promised to pay in the "usual manner." That is to say, 85 percent each 30 days or end of the month, 15 percent being retained until completion of the work. Newbury (D) denied so promising. Excavation began in July and continued until the end of September, when Newbury (D) refused to pay the first bill. Stewart (P) claimed that Newbury (D) would not permit him to continue work because there were alleged variations from specifications. The trial judge charged the jury that if no agreement for payment was made, the builder could expect payment at reasonable intervals, if it were not understood that payments were due monthly, and if payments were not made, the builder could abandon the work. The trial court found for Stewart (P) and awarded damages. Newbury (D) appealed and the appeals court affirmed. Newbury (D) appealed to this court on objections to the trial court's jury charge.

ISSUE: Must the work be substantially performed before payment can be demanded where a contract is made to perform work and no agreement is made as to payment?

HOLDING AND DECISION: (Crane, J.) Yes. Where a contract is made to perform work and no agreement is made as to payment, the work must be substantially performed before payment can be demanded. At trial, the judge charged the jury that payment should be made at reasonable times if the payment term was not express and the parties had no understanding. Newbury (D) requested the judge instruct the jury that payment at the end of the project was appropriate in the absence of an express agreement or understanding, but the judge refused. The judge effectively told the jury that the plaintiff could abandon the work and demand payment due if he believed he was entitled to partial payments at reasonable times even in the absence of an express agreement. This is not the law. The judgment must be reversed and a new trial ordered.

▶ ANALYSIS

It is not unusual in a bilateral contract that the parties will neglect to state in what order their promises will be performed. First, a party must perform before he is entitled to payment. That is to say, performance is a constructive condition precedent to payment. Periodic payments, as herein illustrated, are not implied. If periodic payments are agreed to, performance is a constructive condition precedent to first payment, which is a constructive condition precedent to the next stage of performance, etc. These rules are ordinary business practice and have been said to be the "practice of centuries."

Quicknotes

SUBSTANTIAL PERFORMANCE Performance of all the essential obligations pursuant to an agreement.

Monroe Street Properties, Inc. v. Carpenter

Mortgage seller (P) v. Mortgage purchaser trustee (D)

407 F.2d 379 (9th Cir. 1969).

NATURE OF CASE: Appeal from judgment for defendant in action for breach of contract.

FACT SUMMARY: Monroe Street Properties, Inc. (P) could not tender 10 first mortgages until Western Equities (D) had tendered its stock.

RULE OF LAW
No counterperformance is due until the other party has tendered his performance where concurrent performance is required.

FACTS: Western Equities (Western) (D), through Carpenter (D), its trustee, offered to purchase 10 first mortgages from Monroe Street Properties, Inc. (Monroe) (P) in exchange for shares of Western (D) stock. Western (D) was to have its stock qualified by the SEC and placed on the American Stock Exchange. At that time, Monroe (P) was to place the first mortgages in escrow and obtain title insurance policies. Western (D) had its stock listed, but Monroe (P) could not obtain title policies because the properties were already subject to prior encumbrances. Monroe (P) could not pay off these encumbrances until Western (D) performed, and its stock could be pledged as collateral for a loan to pay off the mortgage encumbrances. Monroe (P) sued for breach of contract when Western (D) failed to place its stock in escrow. Western (D) moved for summary judgment, alleging that its performance was not due until Monroe (P) placed the mortgages with title policies in escrow. The court granted Western's (D) motion and Monroe (P) appealed.

ISSUE: Must both parties tender their performance at the same time where concurrent performance is required?

HOLDING AND DECISION: (Hufstedler, J.) Yes. Where concurrent performance by both parties is required under the contract, both are obligated to tender their performance at the same time. If one party cannot tender his performance, the other party's duty to perform is excused. Here, Monroe (P) was obligated to tender 10 first mortgages with title insurance. Unless and until it can perform, Western's (D) counterperformance is not due. Since Monroe (P) never tendered the policies and insurance, the summary judgment grant was appropriate. Affirmed.

▶ ANALYSIS

Concurrent conditions normally relate to contemporaneous performance, i.e., I will give you this magazine if you will give me $1. No duty to perform arises unless both parties are able to tender their respective performance at the same time. The law normally does not require instantaneous counterperformance, merely constructive contemporaneous performance. Thus, clear title may not be obtained until the vendor receives a check and can then turn it over to their mortgagor.

■=■

Quicknotes

ESCROW A written contract held by a third party until the conditions therein are satisfied, at which time it is delivered to the obligee.

SUMMARY JUDGMENT Judgment rendered by a court in response to a motion by one of the parties, claiming that the lack of a question of material fact in respect to an issue warrants disposition of the issue without consideration by the jury.

TITLE POLICY A policy insuring against loss incurred as the result of a defective title.

■=■

Jacob & Youngs, Inc. v. Kent

Homebuilder (P) v. Buyer (D)

N.Y. Ct. App., 230 N.Y. 239, 129 N.E. 889 (1921).

NATURE OF CASE: Appeal from reversal of judgment for defendant in action for damages for breach of a construction contract.

FACT SUMMARY: Jacob & Youngs, Inc. (P) was hired to build a $77,000 country home for Kent (D). When the dwelling was completed, it was discovered that through an oversight, pipe not of Reading manufacture (though of comparable quality and price), which had been specified in the contract, was used. Kent (D) refused to make final payment of $3,483.46 upon learning of this.

RULE OF LAW
An omission, both trivial and innocent, will sometimes be atoned for by allowance of the resulting damage and will not always be the breach of a condition to be followed by forfeiture. For damages in construction contracts, the owner is entitled merely to the difference between the value of the structure if built to specifications and the value it has as constructed.

FACTS: Jacob & Youngs (P) built a country residence for Kent (D) for $77,000. A balance of $3,483.46 remained unpaid. Kent (D) took up residence in June 1914 when the work was finished. The construction contract specified that only "well galvanized, lap welded pipe of the grade known as standard pipe of Reading manufacture" was to be used for the plumbing work. In March 1915, Kent (D) learned that some of the pipe used was made by factories other than Reading. Jacob & Youngs (P) were told to do the work again. Most of the plumbing was encased in the walls. Replacing the pipes would have meant demolishing substantial parts of the completed residence. Jacob & Youngs (P) left the work untouched and requested certification that final payment was due. When the certificate was refused, Jacob & Youngs (P) filed suit. The evidence showed that the mistake made was due to an oversight by the subcontractor. The only difference found between Reading pipe and the others used was the name stamped on the pipe. Jacob & Youngs's (P) evidence showing that the pipe used was the same in quality, value, cost, and appearance as that of Reading pipe were excluded at trial. The trial court directed a verdict in favor of Kent (D). The appellate division reversed and granted a new trial. Kent (D) appealed.

ISSUE: Was the omission by Jacob & Youngs (P) so trivial and innocent so as not to be a breach of the condition?

HOLDING AND DECISION: (Cardozo, J.) Yes. Where the significance of the default or omission is grievously out of proportion to the oppression of the forfeiture, the breach is considered to be trivial and innocent. A change will not be tolerated if it is so dominant and pervasive so as to frustrate the purpose of the contract. The contractor cannot install anything he believes to be just as good. It is a matter of degree judged by the purpose to be served, the desire to be gratified, the excuse for deviation from the letter, and the cruelty of enforced adherence. Under the circumstances, the measure of damages should not be the cost of replacing the pipe, which would be great. Instead, the difference in value between the dwelling as specified and the dwelling as constructed should be the measure, even though it may be nominal or nothing. Usually, the owner is entitled to the cost of completion but not where it is grossly unfair and out of proportion to the good to be obtained. This simply is a rule to promote justice when there is substantial performance with trivial deviation. Affirmed.

DISSENT: (McLaughlin, J.) Jacob & Youngs (P) failed to perform as specified. It makes no difference why Kent (D) wanted a particular kind of pipe. Failure to use the kind of pipe specified was either intentional or due to gross neglect, which amounted to the same thing.

▶ ANALYSIS

Substantial performance cannot occur where the breach is intentional as it is the antithesis of material breach. The part unperformed must not destroy the purpose or value of the contract. Because here there is a dissatisfied landowner who stands to retain the defective structure built on his land, there arises the problem of unjust enrichment. Usually, it would appear that the owner would pocket the damages he collected rather than remedying the defect by tearing out the wrong pipe and replacing it with the specified pipe. The owner would have a home substantially in compliance and a sum of money greatly in excess of the harm suffered by him. Note that under the doctrine of de minimis not curat lex, that is, that the law is not concerned with trifles, trivial defects, even if willful, will be ignored. The party which claims substantial performance has still breached the contract and is liable for damages but in a lesser amount than for a willful breach. The court denied a motion for reargument (230 N.Y. 656, 130 N.E. 933) stating that it did not overlook the specification in the contract

Continued on next page.

that the defective work was to be replaced. This promise is a collateral covenant, and replacement was only warranted when a defect was trivial. This collateral agreement was not nullified but rather the remedy was restricted to damages from the breach.

■══■

Quicknotes

CONDITION Requirement; potential future occurrence upon which the existence of a legal obligation is dependent.

FRUSTRATION OF PURPOSE A doctrine relieving the parties to a contract from liability for nonperformance of their duties thereunder when the purpose of the agreement ceases to exist due to circumstances not subject to either party's control.

SUBSTANTIAL PERFORMANCE Performance of all the essential obligations pursuant to an agreement.

■══■

Jacob & Youngs, Inc. v. Kent

Homebuilder (P) v. Buyer (D)

N.Y. Ct. App., 230 N.Y. 656, 130 N.E. 933 (1921).

NATURE OF CASE: Motion to reargue.

FACT SUMMARY: [Jacob & Youngs, Inc. (P) was hired to build a $77,000 country home for Kent (D). When the dwelling was completed, it was discovered that through an oversight, pipe not of Reading manufacture (though of comparable quality and price), which had been specified in the contract, was used. Kent (D) refused to make final payment of $3,483.46 upon learning of this.]

 RULE OF LAW
[Rule of law not stated in casebook excerpt.]

FACTS: [Jacob & Youngs (P) built a country residence for Kent (D) for $77,000. A balance of $3,483.46 remained unpaid. Kent (D) took up residence in June 1914 when the work was finished. The construction contract specified that only "well galvanized, lap welded pipe of the grade known as standard pipe of Reading manufacture" was to be used for the plumbing work. In March 1915, Kent (D) learned that some of the pipe used was made by factories other than Reading. Jacob & Youngs (P) were told to do the work again. Most of the plumbing was encased in the walls. Replacing the pipes would have meant demolishing substantial parts of the completed residence. Jacob & Youngs (P) left the work untouched and requested certification that final payment was due. When the certificate was refused, Jacob & Youngs (P) filed suit. The evidence showed that the mistake made was due to an oversight by the subcontractor. The only difference found between Reading pipe and the others used was the name stamped on the pipe. Jacob & Youngs's (P) evidence showing that the pipe used was the same in quality, value, cost, and appearance as that of Reading pipe were excluded at trial. The trial court directed a verdict in favor of Kent (D). The appellate division reversed and granted a new trial. Kent (D) appealed.]

ISSUE: [Issue not stated in casebook excerpt.]

HOLDING AND DECISION: (Per curiam) The promise to replace defective work was not a condition of the agreement, but was independent of and collateral to the agreement when the defect is trivial. The remedy is restricted to damages. The court did not overlook the promise to remedy in its decision. Motion denied.

▎ *ANALYSIS*

The issue is whether the defect was insignificant or constituted a material breach. If trivial, then substantial performance was achieved and the promise to replace does not take precedence. If Jacob & Youngs (P) had complied with the architect's request, it could be argued that they were admitting to a material breach.

■=■

Quicknotes

MATERIAL BREACH Breach of a contract's terms by one party that is so substantial as to relieve the other party from its obligations pursuant thereto.

■=■

VRT, Inc. v. Dutton-Lainson

Invention owner (P) v. Manufacturer (D)

Neb. Sup. Ct., 247 Neb. 845, 530 N.W.2d 619 (1995).

NATURE OF CASE: Breach of contract suit.

FACT SUMMARY: VRT, Inc. (P) sought payment of past-due and future royalty payments it claimed it was owed pursuant to an agreement with Dutton-Lainson (D).

RULE OF LAW
To bring a breach of contract action, a plaintiff must first show that the plaintiff substantially performed its obligations under the contract and any deviations from the contract must be relatively minor and unimportant.

FACTS: VRT, Inc. (P), formerly Sanitas (P), was formed to manufacture, market, and distribute Vanderheiden's invention. After hiring an attorney to file a patent application on the patient care equipment, VRT (P) sought a manufacturer. After having been told that such patent was filed by its attorney, VRT (P) entered into a contract with Dutton-Lainson (D) whereby VRT (P) sold Dutton-Lainson (D) those assets relating to such equipment. VRT (P) also delivered documents purporting to assign to Dutton-Lainson (D) the patent application and VRT's (P) interest in the invention. VRT's (P) attorney had in fact not filed the patent application as represented. VRT (P) filed suit for professional negligence against the attorney and sought recovery from its attorney for loss of royalties beyond the 10th year. The suit was settled. VRT (P) brought suit against Dutton-Lainson (D) claiming that it was in breach of contract by failing to pay VRT (P) royalties due under the parties' agreement. The district court ruled that Dutton-Lainson (D) was obligated to pay both past-due and future royalties. Dutton-Lainson (D) appealed.

ISSUE: To bring a breach of contract action, must a plaintiff first show that the plaintiff substantially performed its obligations under the contract and must any deviations from the contract be relatively minor and unimportant?

HOLDING AND DECISION: (Caporale, J.) Yes. To bring a breach of contract action, a plaintiff must first show that the plaintiff substantially performed its obligations under the contract and any deviations from the contract must be relatively minor and unimportant. If substantial performance is shown, a contract action may be maintained, but without prejudice to any showing of damage on the part of the defendant for failure to receive full and complete performance. Since the attorney-client relationship is one of agency, general agency rules apply. The omissions and acts of an attorney are to be regarded as the acts of the client, and the attorney's neglect is equivalent to the client's neglect. VRT's (P) failure to deliver and assign a filed patent application was not a minor and unimportant deviation from its obligation under the contract. Thus substantial performance was not established and VRT (P) was precluded from bringing suit. Reversed and remanded.

ANALYSIS

The attorney-client relationship is governed by the law of agency. If a principal holds out an agent as having the authority to represent the principal, this is the equivalent of an assertion that trust and confidence may be reposed in the agent and that the principal may be bound by the agent's acts within the scope of the agent's employment. Where the agent acts fraudulently, the principal is liable.

■■■■

Quicknotes

SUBSTANTIAL PERFORMANCE Performance of all the essential obligations pursuant to an agreement.

■■■■

Walker & Co. v. Harrison

Neon sign company (P) v. Sign renter (D)

Mich. Sup. Ct., 347 Mich. 630, 81 N.W.2d 352 (1957).

NATURE OF CASE: Appeal from judgment for plaintiff in action to recover damages for breach of contract.

FACT SUMMARY: Harrison (D) rented a neon sign and sought to repudiate the rental agreement when Walker & Co. (P) delayed in repairing the sign.

🏛 RULE OF LAW
A party attempting to repudiate a contract must convince the court that the other party has materially breached the contract.

FACTS: Walker & Co. (P) contracted to rent a neon sign to Harrison (D). The rental agreement included repair service "as deemed necessary by [Walker (P)] to keep sign in first class advertising condition." Shortly after the sign was installed, someone hit it with a tomato. Rust was allegedly visible on the chrome and cobwebs had collected in the corners. Harrison (D) made several calls to Walker (P) complaining of the sign's condition, but maintenance was not forthcoming. Harrison (D) repudiated the contract and Walker (P) sued for the rent. [Walker (P) subsequently repaired the sign.] The trial court found for Walker (P) and Harrison (D) appealed.

ISSUE: Must a party attempting to repudiate a contract convince the court that the other party has materially breached the contract?

HOLDING AND DECISION: (Smith, J.) Yes. A party attempting to repudiate a contract must convince the court that the other party has materially breached the contract. It is essential to one party's repudiation of a contract that he demonstrates a "material breach" by the other party. As to the criterion for "materiality," there is no single touchstone. Here, Harrison (D) claims that Walker's (P) repeated failures to repair or maintain the sign constituted material breach. Although Walker's (P) delay in rendering service was certainly irritating, it cannot be said as a matter of law that the delay was a material breach. Harrison (D) himself breached the contract when he ceased payments. It is dangerous for a party to determine unilaterally that the other party has committed a material breach. Affirmed.

▮ *ANALYSIS*

The primary advantage in alleging "material breach" is that the alleging party, if successful, may rescind the whole contract. If a breach is not material, the breachee may recover damages flowing therefrom but may not cancel the contract. In the present case, for example, it would not be surprising to find that Harrison (D) wanted out of his contract for reasons other than the breach and alleged "materiality" as a means to that end. As the court indicates, there is no simple test for materiality (which is unfortunate since so much can hinge on the characterization). Among the factors often considered are: (1) to what extent has the contract been performed prior to the breach; (2) was the breach willful; (3) was the breach "quantitatively serious;" and (4) what will be the consequences of the determination (e.g., will it work extreme hardship on one of the parties). Some of the above factors should undoubtedly be given more weight than others and arguably, some of them overlap. Perhaps the most important factor is the last one which openly acknowledges "materiality" as a conclusory label to be applied insofar as a sense of "justice" requires it.

■▬■

Quicknotes

MATERIAL BREACH Breach of a contract's terms by one party that is so substantial as to relieve the other party from its obligations pursuant thereto.

REPUDIATION The actions or statements of a party to a contract that evidence his intent not to perform, or to continue performance, of his duties or obligations thereunder.

■▬■

K & G Construction Co. v. Harris

General contractor (P) v. Subcontractor (D)

Md. Ct. App., 223 Md. 305, 164 A.2d 451 (1960).

NATURE OF CASE: Appeal in action for breach of contract.

FACT SUMMARY: After Harris (D) allegedly negligently injured K & G Construction Co.'s (K & G's) (P) property, K & G (P) refused to make progress payments due to Harris (D).

🏛 RULE OF LAW
Where there is a breach of a mutually dependent clause, the nonbreaching party may suspend his performance, and the breaching party remains under a duty to continue to perform.

FACTS: K & G Construction Co. (K & G) (P) hired Harris and Brooks (Harris) (D) to perform subcontract work. Progress payments were to be made for work performed by Harris (D). All work was to be performed in a workmanlike manner, in accordance with best practices. Harris (D) was required to obtain liability insurance to cover any damage caused by them. One of Harris's (D) employees allegedly was negligent in operating a bulldozer, which caused the collapse of a wall. The claim was submitted to Harris's (D) insurer, but Harris (D) disclaimed all liability. The damage was estimated at $3,400. K & G (P) refused to make the progress payment due Harris (D) of $1,484.50. Harris (D) continued work for one more month, and then stopped performing for nonpayment. K & G (P) sued for damages for breach of contract and for damages done to the house (the insurer had denied the claim). Harris (D) cross-complained for the money due for services rendered. The court granted judgment for Harris (D), finding that while his employee was negligent, this did not excuse K & G's (P) duty to make the progress payments. K & G (P) appealed, alleging that this constituted a substantial breach of the contract, and this excused its duty to make the progress payments since they were dependent on Harris's (D) duty to perform in a workmanlike manner.

ISSUE: Where performance is found to be mutually dependent, does a breach by one party excuse performance by the other party while still leaving the breaching party obligated to perform?

HOLDING AND DECISION: (Prescott, J.) Yes. Today, covenants are almost universally construed as creating dependent duties. If one party breaches his duty, the other party is relieved of his obligation to perform. The breaching party remains obligated to continue his performance, even though the nonbreaching party has ceased to perform. Here, Harris's (D) duty was to perform in a workmanlike manner. This was one of the central parts of the agreement. The damage caused by the negligence of Harris's (D) employee was substantial. This excused K & G's (P) duty to make the progress payments, and Harris (D) remained obligated to perform. When Harris (D) ceased performance, this constituted a second breach; merely submitting the claim to the insurer while disclaiming liability was not an attempt to cure the breach. Reversed.

▶ ANALYSIS

If the breach is not material, the nonbreaching party may not suspend his performance and may seek only damages. If the work/performance is divisible, breach during one part of the contract will normally not excuse suspension of performance during other segments of the contract. A material breach prevents a finding of substantial performance by the breaching party.

━━━

Quicknotes

ADEQUATE ASSURANCES Refers to a situation in which one party is excused from performance of his obligations under a contract if the other party to the contract indicates that he does not intend to perform when the time for performance thereunder arrives; the nonbreaching party in that case is excused from further performance, unless he receives adequate assurances that performance will be rendered.

ANTICIPATORY REPUDIATION Breach of a contract subsequent to formation but prior to the time performance is due.

SUBSTANTIAL PERFORMANCE Performance of all the essential obligations pursuant to an agreement.

━━━

Bartus v. Riccardi

Hearing aid seller (P) v. Buyer (D)

Utica, N.Y. City Ct., 55 Misc. 2d 3, 284 N.Y.S.2d 222 (1967).

NATURE OF CASE: Action for breach of contract.

FACT SUMMARY: Bartus (P) gave Riccardi (D) an Acousticon hearing aid, Model A-665, which was supposedly the improved model of the A-660 hearing aid ordered by Riccardi (D).

🏛 RULE OF LAW
A seller may offer to cure a nonconforming tender even though the buyer has previously revoked his acceptance and it is beyond the contract time if there are reasonable grounds to believe that the nonconforming goods would be accepted and there is reasonable notice of intent to cure.

FACTS: Riccardi (D) was informed by a hearing clinic that he needed a hearing aid. The Model A-660 Acousticon was recommended for his needs. Riccardi (D) was informed by Bartus (P), who sold hearing aids, that the A-660 had been improved, and Riccardi (D) purchased the improved model, the A-665. After using the model for several days, Riccardi (D) returned it. Bartus (P) subsequently informed Riccardi (D) that he would get him the A-660 or any other model he wished. Riccardi (D) refused to accept a replacement, and Bartus (P) brought suit on the unpaid balance of the contract price of the A-665. Bartus (P) alleged that he had the right to cure even after the rejection of the model as nonconforming.

ISSUE: Does the failure to tender strict performance and the subsequent rejection and revocation by the buyer prevent the seller from attempting a cure?

HOLDING AND DECISION: (Hymes, J.) No. Under Uniform Commercial Code (U.C.C.) § 2-508, the Uniform Commercial Code has altered the concept of strict performance. A seller is permitted to cure a nonconforming delivery before the expiration of the contract time by notifying the buyer of his intention and by delivery before the contract has expired. U.C.C. § 2-508(2) would allow a cure beyond the contract time even if acceptance has been revoked if the seller had reasonable grounds to believe the nonconforming goods would be accepted and he reasonably notifies the buyer of his intent to promptly deliver conforming goods. Bartus (P) had reason to believe that the A-665 would be accepted, and he reasonably notified Riccardi (D) of his offer to cure. Riccardi (D) had not altered his position at that time by purchasing a hearing aid elsewhere. Judgment for Bartus (P).

▶ ANALYSIS

If the buyer, after rejecting the nonconforming goods, alters his position before notice of an attempted cure, and this was commercially reasonable under the circumstances, the buyer will not be liable where the seller subsequently attempts to cure. Whether the action is commercially reasonable depends on whether the contract has expired; the buyer's needs for prompt delivery; the seller's apparent ability to perform; prior conduct of the parties; etc.

━━■

Quicknotes

CURE In a commercial transaction, the seller has a right to correct a delivery of defective goods within the time originally provided for performance as specified in the contract.

MATERIAL BREACH Breach of a contract's terms by one party that is so substantial as to relieve the other party from its obligations pursuant thereto.

SUBSTANTIAL PERFORMANCE Performance of all the essential obligations pursuant to an agreement.

━━■

A.B. Parker v. Bell Ford, Inc.

Truck purchaser (P) v. Truck seller (D)

Ala. Sup. Ct., 425 So. 2d 1101 (1983).

NATURE OF CASE: Appeal from directed verdict denying damages for breach of warranty.

FACT SUMMARY: A.B. Parker (Parker) (P) contended Bell Ford, Inc. (D) breached its warranty on a truck it sold to Parker (P) and that he could recover therefor.

🏛 RULE OF LAW
Notification of breach of warranty to the seller is a condition precedent to eligibility for recovery for such breach.

FACTS: A.B. Parker (Parker) (P) purchased an automobile from Bell Ford, Inc. (Bell) (D), which was manufactured by Ford Motor Company (Ford) (D). The tires began to wear down immediately, and Parker (P) complained to Bell (D). Bell (D) took steps to remedy the problem, yet it persisted. Parker (P), without further consultation with Bell (D) or Ford (D), sued both parties for breach of warranty. A directed verdict was entered for Bell (D) and Ford (D) on the basis that notification of the breach was a condition precedent to recovery, and no notice was given. Parker (P) appealed.

ISSUE: Is notification of breach of warranty to the seller a condition precedent to recovery?

HOLDING AND DECISION: (Embry, J.) Yes. Notification of breach of warranty to the seller is a condition precedent to recovery. Proper notice as required by Uniform Commercial Code (U.C.C.) § 7-2-607 fulfills two purposes. First, it opens settlement negotiations. Second, it allows the seller the opportunity to cure the breach or inspect the nonconforming goods. Because no notice of breach was given following the initial repairs, no recovery could result. Affirmed.

▶ *ANALYSIS*

Because this case involved the sale of goods, the U.C.C applied. If it had not, common law principles would have governed, and recovery might have been allowed.

■═■

Quicknotes

BREACH OF WARRANTY The breach of a promise made by one party to a contract that the other party may rely on a fact, relieving that party from the obligation of determining whether the fact is true and indemnifying the other party from liability if that fact is shown to be false.

CONDITION PRECEDENT The happening of an uncertain occurrence, which is necessary before a particular right or interest may be obtained or an action performed.

DIRECTED VERDICT A verdict ordered by the court in a jury trial.

■═■

Emanuel Law Outlines, Inc. v. Multi-State Legal Studies, Inc.

Publisher (P) v. Bar review course (D)

899 F. Supp. 1081 (S.D.N.Y. 1995).

NATURE OF CASE: An action for breach of an installment contract.

FACT SUMMARY: Emanuel Law Outlines, Inc. (ELO) (P) brought suit against Multistate Legal Studies, Inc. (Multi-State) (D) alleging breach of an installment contract and Multi-State (D) countersued alleging it was ELO (P) that breached the agreement.

> ## 🏛 RULE OF LAW
> If a contract contains express terms as to its termination, those terms will not be supplemented or subsumed by the Uniform Commercial Code.

FACTS: Emanuel Law Outlines, Inc. (ELO) (P), a publisher of legal study aids, contracted with Multistate Legal Studies, Inc. (Multi-State) (D), a provider of bar review preparation courses, to provide capsule summaries of nine subjects for students enrolled in Multi-State's (D) California bar review course. The contract spanned three years, and one provision called for a supplement for the Criminal Procedure text outline. All portions of the course work were provided timely and the installment payments were made timely except for the final supplement for Criminal Procedure. The Supplement was due no later than May 1, 1993. In January of 1993, ELO (P) notified Multi-State (D) by phone that its writer/editor would be having heart bypass surgery and that the Supplement would potentially be delayed. A second call was placed in April and the subject matter of this conversation between ELO (P) and Multi-State (D) is in dispute. ELO (P) claims that Multi-State (D) agreed to a delay in delivery of the Supplement until early June, while Multi-State (D) denies that the May 1st deadline was changed. The Supplement was delivered on June 3, 1993, but Multi-State (D) refused to make the installment payment claiming ELO (P) had breached the agreement. Multi-State (D) claims that it sent written notification on April 27th reminding ELO (P) of the May 1st deadline and that failure to meet the deadline would be considered a material breach of the contract. Multi-State (D) also claims it sent a second letter dated May 7th purportedly cancelling Multi-State's (D) obligations under the contract. ELO (P) claims it did not receive the letters Multi-State (D) claims to have mailed and Multi-State (D) failed to obtain any form of delivery verification. ELO (P) consequently sued for breach because of Multi-State's (D) refusal to pay. Multi-State (D) countersued alleging ELO (P) breached and that the late delivery damaged their reputation with their students.

ISSUE: If a contract contains express terms as to its termination, will those terms be supplemented or subsumed by the Uniform Commercial Code?

HOLDING AND DECISION: (Newman, J.) No. If a contract contains express terms as to its termination, those terms will not be supplemented or subsumed by the Uniform Commercial Code (U.C.C.). The express terms of this contract prevent its termination unless the breaching party receives written notice of the breach and the breach is not cured more than 30 days after the receipt of the notice. The requirement of notification by writing includes a requirement that the alleged breaching party receive the notice. This implies that the party sending notice must prove that it has been received. Multi-State (D) failed to prove that the two letters it claims to have sent ELO (P) informing it of the breach were ever received. Multi-State (D) argues that under the U.C.C. § 20607 no notice of the breach is required, but the U.C.C. will not be used to replace express terms in a contract. Because ELO (P) received no notice of a breach prior to its performance, then ELO (P) cured the breach within the terms of the contract and it is Multi-State (D) who is in breach for refusal to make the installment payment. Moreover, Multi-State (D) failed to prove its claim of damage to its reputation because it had no written complaint from any of its students, and did not establish that it had to refund tuition to any of its students related to the late delivery of the Supplement. Judgment for ELO (P) and Multi-State (D) counterclaim is dismissed.

▶ ANALYSIS

The U.C.C. serves as a gap-filler for contracts, but it will not be used to supplement contracts where no supplementation is required. Sophisticated business entities contracting at arm's length and crafting express terms into their agreements cannot look to the U.C.C to assert breach when the parties have not deviated from the express terms of the contract.

■■■

Quicknotes

BREACH The violation of an obligation imposed pursuant to contract or law, by acting or failing to act.

■■■

Scavenger, Inc. v. GT Interactive Software, Inc.

Game developer (P) v. Game distributor (D)

N.Y. Sup. Ct., App. Div., 273 A.D.2d 60, 708 N.Y.S.2d 405 (2000).

NATURE OF CASE: Appeal of decision to grant partial summary judgment on a breach of contract claim.

FACT SUMMARY: Scavenger, Inc. (P) brought a claim against GT Interactive Software, Inc. (GT) (D) after GT (D) failed to make scheduled payments on contracted for CD-ROM games.

🏛 RULE OF LAW

A breach of one part of a divisible contract does not impair enforcement of any of the remaining parts.

FACTS: Scavenger, Inc. (Scavenger) (P) had contracted with GT Interactive Software, Inc. (GT) (D) to produce four CD-ROM games. While encompassed within the four corners of one document, the production and payment schedule for each game was separate. Scavenger (P) brought suit after GT (D) failed to pay on the first two games delivered. GT (D) argued that Scavenger (P) breached when failing to deliver the two final games and that the scheduled payments could not be enforced. The trial court granted summary partial judgment in favor of Scavenger (P) requiring GT (D) to pay $2,411,114 for the two games delivered. GT (D) appealed.

ISSUE: Does a breach of one part of a divisible contract impair enforcement of any of the remaining parts?

HOLDING AND DECISION: (Memorandum Decision) No. A breach of one part of a divisible contract does not impair enforcement of any of the remaining parts. In this instance, the contract is divisible with a separate payment and production schedule for each of the four games. Consequently, the trial court was correct in granting summary judgment for Scavenger (P) and requiring GT (D) to pay for the two games delivered.

⟩ ANALYSIS

A severable or divisible contract is one in which independent agreements about different subjects are made in the same document at the same time. The question of whether or not a contract is divisible is mainly a question of the intent of the parties as determined by the language and subject matter of the agreements. A contract is entire if the performance of one party is dependent upon the performance of the other, but is divisible if the contract embraces separate distinct promises that admit to separate execution. Here, each game had a production schedule and payment schedule that could be completed discretely without any inter-relation to the other games. Each game represented a separate contract and each of

the four parts of this contract could be enforced separately. Separate payment schedules are a tip-off that the contract may be divisible.

■══■

Quicknotes

SEVERABLE CONTRACT A contract divisible so that the performance of one of its promises is not dependent upon the other and failure to perform one promise does not result in a breach of the total contract.

SUMMARY JUDGMENT Judgment rendered by a court in response to a motion by one of the parties claiming, that the lack of a question of material fact in respect to an issue warrants disposition of the issue without consideration by the jury.

■══■

Cantrell-Waind & Associates, Inc. v. Guillaume Motorsports, Inc.

Real estate broker (P) v. Seller (D)

Ark. Ct. App., 62 Ark. App. 66, 968 S.W.2d 72 (1998).

NATURE OF CASE: Appeal in breach of contract action.

FACT SUMMARY: Cantrell-Waind & Associates, Inc. (P) sued Guillaume Motorsports, Inc. (D) for its failure to pay them a real estate broker's commission pursuant to a land sale contract.

RULE OF LAW
A party to a contract has an implied obligation not to do anything that would prevent, hinder, or delay performance of the contract.

FACTS: Guillaume Motorsports, Inc. (Guillaume) (D) agreed to lease real property to the Bowers. The lease agreement contained an option to purchase and provided for the payment of commission to Cantrell-Waind & Associates, Inc. (Cantrell-Waind) (P). The Bowers' attorney notified Guillaume (D) that they chose to exercise the option. Guillaume (D) then approached Mr. Bower and offered to credit him with half Cantrell-Waind's (P) commission if he agreed to delay the closing date, which he declined to do. The closing took place and Cantrell-Waind (P) was not paid its commission. Cantrell-Waind (P) filed suit against Guillaume (D) for breach of contract. Guillaume (D) moved for summary judgment on the basis that it was not obligated to close the transaction before the August 1 date specified in the contract. The court granted summary judgment in favor of Guillaume (D) and Cantrell-Waind (P) appealed.

ISSUE: Does a party to a contract have an implied obligation not to do anything that would prevent, hinder, or delay performance of the contract?

HOLDING AND DECISION: (Bird, J.) Yes. A party to a contract has an implied obligation not to do anything that would prevent, hinder, or delay performance of the contract. The term of the contract providing that a commission was due only if closing occurred before August 1 is a condition precedent. When a contract term leaves a decision to the discretion of one party, that decision is unreviewable by a court unless it is charged with bad faith. A party has an implied obligation not to do anything that would prevent, hinder, or delay performance of a contract. The nonoccurrence of such condition is excused only when the condition need no longer occur in order for the performance of the duty to become due. Every contract imposes on the parties a duty of good faith and fair dealing. The circuit court erred in failing to recognize such duty existed and thus Guillaume (D) was obligated not to deliberately avoid closing. This holding presents a genuine issue of material fact as to whether Guillaume's (D) actions prevented or hindered the occurrence of the condition precedent. Reversed and remanded.

▌ANALYSIS

The Restatement (Second) of Contracts (1981) excuses nonperformance of a condition precedent where its prevention or hindrance is caused through breach of the duty of good faith and fair dealing.

Quicknotes

CONDITION PRECEDENT The happening of an uncertain occurrence which is necessary before a particular right or interest may be obtained or an action performed.

IMPLIED COVENANT OF GOOD FAITH AND FAIR DEALING An implied warranty that the parties will deal honestly in the satisfaction of their obligations and without an intent to defraud.

Locke v. Warner Bros. Inc.

Actress (P) v. Film studio (D)

Cal. Ct. App., 57 Cal. App. 4th 354, 66 Cal. Rptr. 2d 921 (1997).

NATURE OF CASE: Appeal of grant of summary judgment to defendant in breach of contract action.

FACT SUMMARY: Locke (P) had a development deal with Warner Bros. Inc. (Warner) (D), but none of her projects were ever picked up and Warner (D) never hired her as a director. Locke claimed breach of contract on the grounds that Warner (D) frustrated the purpose of the development deal.

🏛 RULE OF LAW
Contracts contain an implied covenant of good faith and fair dealing such that one party cannot frustrate the other party's right to receive the benefit of the bargain.

FACTS: Sondra Locke (P) appeared with Clint Eastwood in a 1975 film. The two began a relationship that lasted over a decade. When the relationship ended, Locke (P) sued Eastwood on various grounds and the two reached a settlement. Part of the settlement included a development deal for Locke (P) with a film studio, Warner Brothers, Inc. (D). Warner (D) would pay $1.5 million to Locke (P) over three years in exchange for a first look at her potential film projects and consideration of Locke (P) as a director. This deal was a so-called "pay or play" deal. Locke (P) was unaware that Eastwood promised to reimburse Warner (D) for payments to Locke (P) if Warner (D) did not develop any of Locke's projects. Locke (P) had an office on Warner's (D) lot and proposed multiple projects to Warner (D), but Warner (D) rejected all of them and did not hire Locke (P) to direct any film. Locke (P) sued Warner (D) on a breach of contract action based on Warner's (D) alleged frustration of Locke (P) receiving the benefit of the Locke-Warner agreement. Testimony showed that Warner (D) never intended to develop any of Locke's (P) projects and that the agreement was "Clint's deal." Warner (D) moved for summary judgment, which the court granted finding Warner (D) did consider the projects and did not breach the contract by failing to produce any of Locke's (P) projects. The trial court's order specifically held that judicial review cannot apply to "subjective artistic and business decisions" such as deciding what projects to produce. Locke (P) appealed.

ISSUE: Do contracts contain an implied covenant of good faith and fair dealing such that one party cannot frustrate the other party's right to receive the benefit of the bargain?

HOLDING AND DECISION: (Klein, J.) Yes. Contracts contain an implied covenant of good faith and fair dealing such that one party cannot frustrate the other party's right to receive the benefit of the bargain. The trial court erred in holding that it could not review Warner's (D) decision not to produce any of Locke's (P) projects. Warner (D) had the right to refuse the projects, but the refusals must be in good faith. All contracts have the implied covenant of good faith and fair dealing. An issue of material fact exists as to whether Warner (D) had the good faith intention of developing a Locke project when appropriate or if Warner (D), in bad faith, struck down all Locke projects across the board. Locke (P) presented testimony which is sufficient to raise an issue of material fact. Warner (D) argues that Locke (P) is seeking to ignore Warner's (D) discretionary power to reject her projects, but that is not the case. Warner (D) retains the power to reject her projects, but the rejection must be in good faith. Categorically refusing to work with Locke (P) raises a question of fact. Reversed in part; affirmed in part.

▶ ANALYSIS

Warner (D) could determine that all of Locke's (P) proposals were terrible and did not deserve development and the courts would not second guess such subjective judgment. The triable issue is whether Warner (D) actually viewed Locke's (P) proposals as terrible or simply ignored all of her proposals. The court also noted Warner (D) had multiple agreements with other producers and directors that amounted to nothing, but the theory that Warner (D) entered the agreement with Locke (P) just to pacify Eastwood taints Warner's (D) claim that it gave considered thought to Locke's proposals. Warner's (D) purposes for entering the contract could not prevent it from living up to its spirit.

━━━

Quicknotes

BREACH OF CONTRACT Unlawful failure by a party to perform its obligations pursuant to contract.

IMPLIED COVENANT OF GOOD FAITH AND FAIR DEALING An implied warranty that the parties will deal honestly in the satisfaction of their obligations and without an intent to defraud.

ISSUE OF MATERIAL FACT A fact that is disputed between two or more parties to litigation that is essential to proving an element of the cause of action or a defense asserted, or which would otherwise affect the outcome of the proceeding.

Continued on next page.

SUMMARY JUDGMENT Judgment rendered by a court in response to a motion made by one of the parties, claiming that the lack of a question of material fact in respect to an issue warrants disposition of the issue without consideration by the jury.

∎▬∎

Swartz v. War Memorial Commission of Rochester

Exclusive concessionaire (P) v. Contracting memorial commission (D)

N.Y. Sup. Ct., App. Div., 25 A.D. 2d 90, 267 N.Y.S.2d 253 (1966).

NATURE OF CASE: Appeal from dismissal in declaratory judgment action.

FACT SUMMARY: The War Memorial Commission of Rochester (D) threatened to remove Swartz (P) as its exclusive concessionaire unless he obtained a license to sell beer.

🏛 RULE OF LAW
A party must use reasonable efforts and diligence to render his best performance.

FACTS: Swartz (P) was appointed the exclusive concessionaire for food and refreshments for the Rochester War Memorial Building by the War Memorial Commission of Rochester (Commission) (D). The contract required Swartz (P) to furnish all concession goods. A clause provided that the sale of liquor or beer was prohibited. However, if the prohibition was lifted by the Commission (D), the exclusive rights granted to Swartz (P) would be extended to cover beer and/or liquor. Swartz (P) was obligated to obtain all required licenses. The Commission (D) lifted its prohibition on beer, but Swartz (P) refused to obtain a license for its sale. The Commission (D) threatened to cancel the contract, and Swartz (P) sought a declaration of his rights under the contract, alleging that he was not obligated to sell beer. The Commission (D) alleged that the contract impliedly obligated Swartz (P) to use his best efforts and diligence to sell all authorized goods for the benefit of both parties.

ISSUE: Is a party obligated to use his best efforts and diligence to perform all acts allowed under the contract for the benefit of both parties?

HOLDING AND DECISION: (Per curiam) Yes. Swartz (P) was granted the exclusive right to sell all concessions in the War Memorial Building. Since the Commission (D) was to receive a percentage of the revenues, it was an implied contractual condition that Swartz (P) would use his best efforts and diligence to perform his duties in the manner most profitable to both parties. This was the intention of both parties, and it included the sale of any goods, e.g., beer, which was subsequently allowed for sale by the Commission (D). Failure to use such diligence and efforts amounts to breach of contract. Affirmed as modified.

▶ ANALYSIS

Noncooperation is a breach of an implied duty to use best efforts in such contracts. While a party may not impose new duties or obligations on the other party, the sale of beer and other alcoholic beverages was contemplated when the contract was executed. Thus, there was no material alteration of Swartz's (P) contractual duties when the Commission (D) finally gave its approval to offer beer for sale under the concessions contract.

■▬■

Quicknotes

DECLARATORY JUDGMENT A judgment of the court establishing the rights of the parties.

■▬■

Stop & Shop, Inc. v. Ganem

Market (P) v. Lessor (D)

Mass. Sup. Jud. Ct., 347 Mass. 697, 200 N.E.2d 248 (1964).

NATURE OF CASE: Appeal from judgment for plaintiff in bill for declaratory relief by lessees under percentage lease.

FACT SUMMARY: Lessee, operator of a supermarket, who had entered into a percentage lease agreement, contemplated going out of business. The lessee sought a declaration of its rights under the lease.

🏛 RULE OF LAW
In a commercial lease agreement wherein the lessee agrees to pay a fixed rental plus a percentage of his profits, an implied covenant that the lessee will not go out of business will be found only when there is a marked disparity between fixed rent and fair rental value.

FACTS: Stop & Shop, Inc. (P), operator of a supermarket, leased a lot from Ganem (D) for a period of 13 years. The minimum rent was $22,000 a year plus 1¼ percent of all gross sales above $1,269,230.60 made each year. The percentage rent was to be paid only if sales exceeded $3,000,000 a year. On only two occasions was any percentage rent paid. Stop & Shop (P), wanting to discontinue its supermarket on the premises but intending to continue paying the fixed rent until the lease had run, sought a declaratory judgment that it could go out of business. The trial court found for Stop & Shop (P) and Ganem (D) appealed.

ISSUE: In a commercial lease agreement wherein the lessee agrees to pay a fixed rental plus a percentage of his profits, will an implied covenant that the lessee will not go out of business be found automatically?

HOLDING AND DECISION: (Whittemore, J.) No. In a commercial lease agreement wherein the lessee agrees to pay a fixed rental plus a percentage of his profits, an implied covenant that the lessee will not go out of business will be found only when there is a marked disparity between fixed rent and fair rental value. A covenant to continue business under a percentage lease need not be express; it may be implied that the lessee will not go out of business so as to avoid paying part of its profits to the lessor while the lease runs. However, generally only where the minimum rent is not substantial will a court conclude that the parties contemplated continued operation. Here, the minimum rent is substantial. Any suggestion that the figure of $22,000 a year does not reflect the fair rental value is offset by the fact that percentage rent was paid for only two years. Thus, Ganem (D) has failed to sustain his burden of showing a marked disparity between fixed rent and fair rental value. Thus, there is no implied covenant in which Stop & Shop (P) is obligated to continue operation. Affirmed.

▶ ANALYSIS

Conditions which are implied in fact usually relate to conditions of good faith and cooperation, in other words, those conditions which the parties assumed were so necessary to the fulfillment of the agreement that they were assumed to be controlling. The test is whether a reasonable man would have believed that the parties had bargained with the assumption that a set of facts existed and would continue to exist.

■■■

Quicknotes

DECLARATORY RELIEF A judgment of the court establishing the rights of the parties.

(IMPLIED) COVENANT OF GOOD FAITH (AND FAIR DEALING) An implied warranty that the parties will deal honestly in the satisfaction of their obligations and without an intent to defraud.

LEASE An agreement or contract which creates a relationship between a landlord and tenant (real property) or lessor and lessee (real or personal property).

■■■

Market Street Associates Limited Partnership v. Frey

Lessee assignee (P) v. [Party not identified] (D)

941 F.2d 588 (7th Cir. 1991).

NATURE OF CASE: Appeal from summary judgment dismissing action seeking specific performance.

FACT SUMMARY: A principal of Market Street Associates Limited Partnership (P) allegedly deliberately failed to notify General Electric Pension Trust (General Electric) (D) of an obscure clause that could result in forfeiture of General Electric's (D) property.

🏛 RULE OF LAW
A party to a contract may not intentionally exploit the other party's oversight of an important fact.

FACTS: J.C. Penney entered into a sale-leaseback arrangement with General Electric Pension Trust (General Electric) (D) on a property. A clause in the lease provided that if General Electric (D) failed to negotiate with the lessee regarding future financing, the property could be purchased at less than market value. Years later, Market Street Associates Limited Partnership (Market Street) (P), J.C. Penney's assignee, attempted to negotiate financing with General Electric (D). General Electric (D), no longer being aware of the clause, refused to negotiate. Market Street (P) then sought to exercise its option and sued for specific performance. At his deposition, the principal of Market Street (P) primarily responsible for the property testified that his counterpart at General Electric (D) might not be aware of the clause and that he had realized it during negotiations. Based on this, the district court entered summary judgment dismissing the action, holding Market Street (P) to have acted in bad faith. Market Street (P) appealed.

ISSUE: May a party to a contract intentionally exploit the other party's oversight of an important fact?

HOLDING AND DECISION: (Posner, J.) No. A party to a contract may not intentionally exploit the other party's oversight of an important fact. That parties to a contract must act in good faith does not mean, as some courts seem to believe, that the parties must act in an altruistic or fiduciary manner toward each other; they need not do so. Furthermore, it is quite legitimate for a party to use his superior knowledge to drive an advantageous bargain. However, it is one thing to have superior knowledge, but it is quite another to know that the other party is unaware of a crucial fact and take advantage of this ignorance. This constitutes sharp practice, which departs from good faith. Here, the district court held that Market Street's (P) principal had engaged in such conduct. This may be true, but it is a factual issue, addressable only at trial, not at the summary judgment level. Reversed and remanded.

▌ *ANALYSIS*

A mutual mistake is grounds for nullifying a contract or a term thereof. Unilateral mistake may or may not be. As the court stated here, unilateral mistake combined with an opponent's overreaching may be grounds for rescission.

Quicknotes

GOOD FAITH An honest intention to abstain from any unconscientious advantage of another.

MUTUAL MISTAKE A mistake by both parties to a contract, who are in agreement as to what the contract terms should be, but the agreement as written fails to reflect that common intent; such contracts are voidable or subject to reformation.

SPECIFIC PERFORMANCE An equitable remedy whereby the court requires the parties to perform their obligations pursuant to a contract.

SUMMARY JUDGMENT Judgment rendered by a court in response to a motion by one of the parties, claiming that the lack of a question of material fact in respect to an issue warrants disposition of the issue without consideration by the jury.

UNILATERAL MISTAKE A mistake or misunderstanding as to the terms of a contract made by one party which is generally not a basis for relief by rescission or reformation.

Clark v. West

Author (P) v. Publisher (D)

N.Y. Ct. App., 193 N.Y. 349, 86 N.E. 1 (1908).

NATURE OF CASE: Appeal from affirmance of demurrer in action for breach of contract and an accounting.

FACT SUMMARY: West (D) paid Clark (P) only $2 per page for writing a legal treatise, and Clark (P) demanded the $6 per page he had been promised if he quit drinking, alleging that West (D) had not objected when he continued to drink.

RULE OF LAW

Waiver of a contract condition is not implied by mere acceptance of the proffered performance.

FACTS: West (D) entered into a contract with Clark (P) whereby Clark (P) was to write a multivolume treatise on corporations for West (D). The contract price was $6 per page if Clark (P) totally abstained from liquor during the contract or $2 per page if he drank. West (D) became aware that Clark (P) was drinking moderately during the term of the contract but made no objection. West (D) accepted Clark's (P) work and paid him $2 per page. Clark (P) sued for the difference, claiming that he was owed $6 per page. West (D) demurred, and both the trial court and the court of appeals sustained the demurrer. Clark (P) appealed, claiming that West (D) had waived the abstinence requirement and that the waiver was effective since abstinence was a mere condition precedent to West's (D) obligation to pay $6 per page.

ISSUE: Is waiver of a contract condition implied by mere acceptance of the proffered performance?

HOLDING AND DECISION: (Werner, J.) No. Waiver of a contract condition is not implied by mere acceptance of the proffered performance. A condition to a contract may be waived, but mere acceptance of performance does not constitute a waiver. While it is West's (D) contention that Clark's (P) abstinence was the consideration for the payment of $6 rather than $2, a careful analysis of the contract shows that it was the writing of the treatise, rather than abstinence, which was the bargained-for consideration. Since abstinence was not the consideration for the contract, it was a condition which could be waived without a new agreement based upon a good consideration. No formal agreement or additional consideration is required to waive a condition precedent to performance. West (D) received and accepted the bargained-for consideration, i.e., the treatise. If the condition was waived, then West (D) is liable for the $6 contract price, but mere silence and acceptance of performance will not be deemed a waiver of the condition. However, since Clark (P) alleges an express waiver of the condition, he should be allowed to prove this at trial. The demurrer is therefore overruled and the case remanded for trial.

ANALYSIS

Frequently, as in *Clark v. West,* it is difficult to determine whether one is dealing with a promise or a condition. Modification of a promise typically requires a new consideration, while the waiver of a condition does not. A condition may be described as qualifying a contractual duty by providing either that performance is not called for unless a stated event occurs or fails to occur or that performance may be suspended or terminated if a stated event occurs or fails to occur. Stated more simply, the condition is outside of and modifies the promised performance called for under the contract.

Quicknotes

BREACH OF CONTRACT Unlawful failure by a party to perform its obligations pursuant to contract.

DEMURRER The assertion that the opposing party's pleadings are insufficient and that the demurring party should not be made to answer.

Schenectady Steel Co., Inc. v. Bruno Trimpoli General Const. Co., Inc.

Vendor (P) v. Contractor (D)

N.Y. Sup. Ct., App. Div., 43 A.D.2d 234, 350 N.Y.S.2d 920 (1974).

NATURE OF CASE: Appeal to the appellate division from trial court judgment and award of damages.

FACT SUMMARY: A contractor (D) hired a steel supplier (P) to supply structural steel for a bridge that had to be built on a deadline. The supplier (P) failed to supply the steel on time and was fired. The supplier then sued to recover the reasonable value of the services it provided.

🏛 RULE OF LAW

The waiver of a "time of the essence" provision in a contract converts the contract into one in which performance must take place within a reasonable period of time.

FACTS: [Parties not identified in casebook excerpt.] A contractor (Contractor) (D) was hired by the State of New York on May 8, 1968, to build a bridge by December 31, 1969. Contractor (D) contracted with a steel supplier (Steel Supplier) (P) to provide the steel necessary for the bridge. The contract provided that "time is of the essence" and that the "work will be completed in 1968." Steel Supplier (P) had a series of setbacks: it failed to be able to procure the steel beams in one piece from its supplier, and had to weld smaller pieces together instead; those welds then failed to pass engineering tests; and weather suspended operations for a time. Meanwhile, Contractor (D) began in January 1969 to pressure Steel Supplier (P) to complete its obligations, and by letters dated January 29, 1969, and February 11, 1969, demanded that Steel Supplier (P) provide a schedule as to how it would complete its obligations. Steel Supplier (P) failed to provide the schedule but made vague assurances it would proceed "with all possible speed." Contractor (D) visited Steel Supplier's (P) shop on March 1, 1969, and was so dissatisfied at the progress, that as of March 5, 1969, Contractor (D) cancelled the contract and contracted for the steel elsewhere. On March 11, 1969, Steel Supplier (P) proposed a definite completion date, but that didn't change Contractor's (D) decision to move on. Steel Supplier (P) brought this action to recover the value of the services it provided, and Contractor (D) counterclaimed for failure to perform. The trial court applied the Uniform Commercial Code (U.C.C.) to the case and dismissed Steel Supplier's (P) claim and entered judgment for Contractor (D) in the amount of $8,628.08.

ISSUE: Does the waiver of a "time of the essence" provision in a contract convert the contract into one in which performance must take place within a reasonable period of time?

HOLDING AND DECISION: (Reynolds, J.) Yes. The waiver of a "time of the essence" provision in a contract converts the contract into one in which performance must take place within a reasonable period of time. First, the U.C.C. was not applicable here. The Code applies to transactions of goods, not to service or construction contracts. Contractor (D) was not contracting for the steel beams only, but for their erection and installation with the transfer of title to the steel incidental to the overall transaction. Second, timeliness was the pivotal issue here. The contract required that the work be completed in 1968 and provided that "time is of the essence." Contractor (D) could have cancelled the contract on December 31, 1968, since Steel Supplier (P) did not complete the work on time, but by not electing to do so, Contractor (D) waived its right to cancel for untimely performance and converted the contract into one requiring completion within a reasonable time. But even following this waiver, Contractor (D) could re-impose time as an essential element, and this was accomplished through Contractor's letters of January 29 and February 11. Steel Suppliers' (P) failure to give assurances asked for, beyond that it would proceed "with all possible speed," and the state of progress viewed by Contractor (D) during its visit to Steel Supplier's (P) shop, justified Contractor's (D) termination of the contract.

CONCURRENCE: (Greenblott, J.) The result was correct, but the U.C.C. was correctly applied by the trial court.

CONCURRENCE AND DISSENT: (Cooke, J.) The U.C.C. does not apply, as the majority ruled, since service predominates. And time was clearly of the essence in the original contract. But compliance with that provision was waived by Contractor's failure to cancel the contract on Steel Suppliers' (P) non-performance with the time limits. The contract at that point converted into one under which performance within a reasonable time was all that was required. Clearly, by the date of cancellation—March 5, 1969—a reasonable time had not yet expired. Contractor's (D) letters of January 29 and February 11 may have re-imposed time as an essential element in the contract, but Contractor (D) again waived compliance with that provision by failing to cancel the contract after Steel Supplier's (P) refusal to set a completion date. Because Contractor's (D) cancellation of the contract on March 5, 1969, came when time was once again not of the essence,

Continued on next page.

and termination, without providing a reasonable time for completion, was improper, judgment should be reversed.

▶ *ANALYSIS*

The threshold issue in this case is whether the U.C.C. applies to the facts. The reason it is an issue is because the sale of the steel itself is considered by the court to be incidental to the service provided by the vendor, namely, the erection and installation of the steel girders. It raises an important point that is applicable to all jurisdictions: The construction industry is well known for lacking a definitive body of contract law. Currently, contract law related to the industry is a blend of common law and Article 2 of the U.C.C., and there is no way to predict which will apply, or whether both will apply, to a particular situation. Many scholars argue that applying the U.C.C. to construction contracts could clarify the law.

■▬■

Quicknotes

TIME IS OF THE ESSENCE Contract provision specifying that the time period in which performance is rendered constitutes an essential term of the agreement.

■▬■

Schenectady Steel Co., Inc. v. Bruno Trimpoli General Const. Co., Inc. (Schenectady II)

Vendor (P) v. Contractor (D)

N.Y. Ct. App., 34 N.Y.2d 939, 359 N.Y.S.2d 560, 316 N.E.2d 875 (1974).

NATURE OF CASE: Appeal from appellate division to appeals court.

FACT SUMMARY: [A contractor (D) hired a steel supplier (P) to supply structural steel for a bridge that had to be built on a deadline. The supplier (P) failed to supply the steel on time and was fired. The supplier (P) then sued to recover the reasonable value of the services it provided.]

🏛 RULE OF LAW
The waiver of a "time of the essence" provision in a contract converts the contract into one in which performance must take place within a reasonable period of time.

FACTS: [Parties not identified in casebook excerpt.] [A contractor (Contractor) (D) was hired by the State of New York on May 8, 1968, to build a bridge by December 31, 1969. Contractor (D) contracted with a steel supplier (Steel Supplier) (P) to provide the steel necessary for the bridge. The contract provided that "time is of the essence" and that the "work will be completed in 1968." Steel Supplier (P) had a series of setbacks: it failed to be able to procure the steel beams in one piece from its supplier, and had to weld smaller pieces together instead; those welds then failed to pass engineering tests; and weather suspended operations for a time. Meanwhile, Contractor (D) began in January 1969 to pressure Steel Supplier (P) to complete its obligations, and by letters dated January 29, 1969, and February 11, 1969, demanded that Steel Supplier (P) provide a schedule as to how it would complete its obligations. Steel Supplier (P) failed to provide the schedule but made vague assurances it would proceed "with all possible speed." Contractor (D) visited Steel Supplier's (P) shop on March 1, 1969, and was so dissatisfied at the progress, that as of March 5, 1969, Contractor (D) cancelled the contract and contracted for the steel elsewhere. On March 11, 1969, Steel Supplier (P) proposed a definite completion date, but that didn't change Contractor's (D) decision to move on. Steel Supplier (P) brought this action to recover the value of the services it provided, and Contractor (D) counterclaimed for failure to perform. The trial court applied the Uniform Commercial Code (U.C.C.) to the case and dismissed Steel Supplier's (P) claim and entered judgment for Contractor (D) in the amount of $8,628.08.]

ISSUE: Does the waiver of a "time of the essence" provision in a contract convert the contract into one in which performance must take place within a reasonable period of time?

HOLDING AND DECISION: [Judge not stated in casebook excerpt.] Yes. The waiver of a "time of the essence" provision in a contract converts the contract into one in which performance must take place within a reasonable period of time. The majority was incorrect in finding that the "time of the essence" element was re-imposed, but even under the lesser standard of reasonable time, Steel Suppliers (P) failed to comply. In addition, whether the U.C.C. applies to this case is immaterial.

▶ ANALYSIS

This ruling illustrates exactly why the application of the U.C.C. is not immaterial. It reaches the same result as the appeals division majority, but under a different standard—the reasonable time standard—as opposed the majority's time of the essence standard. Where two different panels of judges can reach the same result using different standards, a reassessment of the standards is warranted.

Quicknotes

TIME IS OF THE ESSENCE Contract provision specifying that the time period in which performance is rendered constitutes an essential term of the agreement.

[handwritten annotations:]

time of essence was an express condition.

Case about waiver

✓ how you may a constructive condition an express condition

Bruno didn't complain that it wasn't finished → "waiver" that time frame cannot be reinstated

Bruno went somewhere else to get contract done b/c schenetady couldn't

Burger King Corp. v. Family Dining, Inc.

Licensor (P) v. Licensee (D)

426 F. Supp. 485 (E.D. Pa.), *aff'd mem.* 566 F.2d 1168 (3d Cir. 1977).

NATURE OF CASE: Motion to dismiss action seeking declaratory judgment voiding a contract.

FACT SUMMARY: Burger King Corp. (P), after years of not requiring strict compliance with a contractual term, sought to void the contract for violation thereof.

RULE OF LAW
A party to a contract may, by its actions, excuse the other from compliance with a contractual condition.

FACTS: Burger King Corp. (P) granted Family Dining, Inc. (D) an exclusive territorial license to operate Burger King restaurants. The contract called for Family Dining (D) to open one additional restaurant every year for 10 years and then to operate at least 10 for the remainder of the duration of the contract. Family Dining (D) did not always strictly comply with this term, although Burger King Corp. (P) did not make an issue of it. Toward the tenth year of the contract, Family Dining (D) was operating only eight restaurants, although it was getting ready to open two others. Burger King Corp. (P) brought an action seeking to terminate the contract for failure to comply with the term mandating the number of restaurants. After trial, Family Dining (D) moved to dismiss.

ISSUE: May a party to a contract, by its actions, excuse the other from compliance with a contractual condition?

HOLDING AND DECISION: (Hannum, J.) Yes. A party to a contract may, by its actions, excuse the other from compliance with a contractual condition. As a general rule, a condition may be excused without other reason if its requirement will involve extreme forfeiture or penalty, and its existence or occurrence forms no essential part of the exchange for the promisor's performance. When a party indicates, by its actions, that it does not consider strict compliance with a condition important, it demonstrates that the condition does not form an essential part of the contract. Here, Burger King (P) for several years did not demand strict compliance, indicating that strict compliance was not essential. Since Family Dining (D) has invested substantial time and capital into the contract, to void the contract would constitute extreme penalty. This being so, the elements for excusing compliance with the term at issue are present. Motion granted.

▶ ANALYSIS

This was an action for declaratory relief. Strictly speaking, declaratory relief actions are not equitable in nature. Nevertheless, the court, in deciding upon whether to grant relief, can seek reference to equitable principles. This is essentially what the court did here.

■=■

Quicknotes

DECLARATORY JUDGMENT An adjudication by the courts which grants not relief but is binding over the legal status of the parties involved in the dispute.

■=■

[handwritten margin notes:]

exclusive contract to open 1 per year for 10 years.

they waived compliance w/ original schedule

waiver = they waived that condition that you open up a burger king in that year.

Burger king sold to Pilsbury cancel contract b/c late on #9 + 10 restaurants (but really wanting to franchise out rather than be stuck w/ your agreement w/ family dining

court said Family dining should not have to forfeit the contract so we're not going to allow you to reinstate the waiver at this pnt

R & R of Connecticut, Inc. v. Stiegler

[Parties not identified.]

Conn. App. Ct., 4 Conn. App. 240, 493 A.2d 293 (1985).

NATURE OF CASE: Equitable action to enjoin land-lord from terminating a lease agreement.

FACT SUMMARY: Tenant (P) sought to enjoin landlord (D) from terminating its lease agreement due to the tenant's (P) failure to timely exercise its option to renew its lease on equitable grounds.

> 🏛 **RULE OF LAW**
> A tenant's late notice of an intention to renew a lease of commercial property may be excused on equitable grounds.

FACTS: The plaintiff was a tenant of the subject premises where it operated a supermarket. The defendant leased the premises to Ortiz who assigned the lease to the plaintiff for a term of five years and six months. The lease contained an option to renew for an additional five-year period, which could only be exercised by written notice 12 months prior to expiration of the lease. Defendant notified plaintiff that the lease would terminate on its expiration date because of the tenant's failure to exercise the option. Plaintiff's attorney sent a letter indicating its desire to renew the lease, but defendant had already entered into an agreement to sell the property to McDonald's Corporation. The trial court concluded that the death of plaintiff's attorney, the large monetary loss to be suffered by the plaintiff, the speculative loss that the landlord might incur, and the customer loss from the community justified equitable relief for the plaintiff. Defendant appealed.

ISSUE: May a tenant's late notice of an intention to renew a lease of commercial property be excused on equitable grounds?

HOLDING AND DECISION: (Hull, J.) Yes. A tenant's late notice of an intention to renew a lease of commercial property may be excused on equitable grounds. The law in this jurisdiction is well settled. In *F.B. Fountain Co. v. Stein*, 118 A. 47 (1922), the court held that in the case of mere neglect in fulfilling a condition precedent of a lease, "equity will relieve when the delay has been slight, the loss to the lessor small, and when not to grant relief would result in such hardship to the tenant as to make it unconscionable to enforce literally the condition precedent of the lease." Defendant argued that this rule is limited to three types of cases, including those: (1) in which the forfeiture of the buildings and improvements would unjustly enrich the landlord; (2) where the delay was slight; and (3) where the landlord misrepresented that it would record the lease. The plaintiff claims that the facts of this case bring it within these circumstances. Under *F.B.*

Fountain Co., the following criteria must be met before equity will grant relief in cases such as this: (1) whether failure to give notice was mere neglect or gross or willful negligence; (2) whether or not the delay was slight; and (3) whether the loss to the lessor was small. Here there is no evidence regarding the degree of the tenant's negligence in failing to give notice. Reversed and remanded.

▶ **ANALYSIS**

The general rule is that a party will not be granted relief against a mistake incurred by its own negligence; however, relief may be granted nonetheless if the other party has not been prejudiced. Here the court only stated that the tenant (P) may have been negligent in giving notice and held that the tenant's (P) attorney's death warranted equitable relief. Thus, the record failed to show whether the tenant's (P) failure to give notice was either willful or amounted to gross negligence, which would preclude equitable relief.

■═■

Quicknotes

CONDITION PRECEDENT The happening of an uncertain occurrence, which is necessary before a particular right or interest may be obtained or an action performed.

EQUITABLE ACTION (ACTION IN EQUITY) Lawsuit in which a plaintiff seeks equitable remedies.

■═■

C & J Fertilizer, Inc. v. Allied Mutual Ins. Co.

Insured company (P) v. Insurer (D)

Iowa Sup. Ct., 227 N.W.2d 169 (1975).

NATURE OF CASE: Appeal from judgment for defendant on action to recover for burglary loss.

FACT SUMMARY: C & J Fertilizer, Inc. (P) had an insurance policy with Allied Mutual Ins. Co. (Allied) (D) covering it for burglary loss. A burglary occurred, but Allied (D) refused to pay because there were no visible marks or physical damage to the building exterior at the place of entry, as required under the policy.

🏛 RULE OF LAW
Insurance policies contain an implied warranty of fitness for their intended purpose, and the reasonable expectations of the policyholder will be honored, with unconscionable clauses disallowed.

FACTS: C & J Fertilizer, Inc. (C & J) (P) had an insurance policy with Allied Mutual Ins. Co. (Allied) (D) covering burglary loss at its fertilizer plant. A burglary occurred, but Allied (D) refused to pay on the grounds that there were no visible marks or physical damage on the building exterior at the place of entry of the burglar. This requirement was included in the insurance policy under its definition of burglary. Its purpose was to prevent fraud and payments on "inside jobs." An interior door had been damaged when the burglar entered a separate room and stole chemicals. The lower court held for Allied (D), stating that the definition of burglary under the policy was unambiguous and not met in this case. C & J (P) relied on the theories of reasonable expectation, implied warranty of fitness for intended purpose, and unconscionability of the burglary definition. The trial court found that there had been no discussion of policy provisions between the parties at the time the policy was secured, and there was no evidence that C & J (P) knew the policy definition of burglary.

ISSUE: Do insurance policies contain an implied warranty of fitness for their intended purpose, and will the reasonable expectations of the policyholder be honored, with unconscionable clauses dishonored?

HOLDING AND DECISION: (Reynoldson, J.) Yes. Insurance policies contain an implied warranty of fitness for their intended purpose, and the reasonable expectations of the policyholder will be honored, with unconscionable clauses disallowed. Insurance policies, such as the one here, are mass-produced, standardized adhesion policies. The policyholder should not be bound to unknown terms which are beyond the range of reasonable expectation. Here, nothing led C & J (P) to reasonably anticipate that it would have no coverage unless the exterior of the premises was marked or damaged. Further, Allied (D) breached an implied warranty that the policy would be reasonably fit for its intended purpose. There is no reason why this doctrine should not apply to insurance policies as well as the sale of tangible goods, as it now does. Finally, C & J (P) should prevail because the liability-avoiding provision in the definition of burglary is, in these circumstances, unconscionable, based on the standardized nature of the contract, the unequal bargaining positions, and the unreasonably favorable terms of the definition to Allied (D). Reversed and remanded.

DISSENT: (LeGrand, J.) The definition of burglary as contained in the policy was unambiguous, and its purpose was to omit coverage for "inside jobs." The court should not disturb contracts which clearly state their meaning simply because the meaning is disliked.

▶ ANALYSIS

There is a definite trend in recent cases to disallow unconscionable terms in adhesion contracts, especially insurance contracts. The courts will either deny enforcement of the contract as a whole or as to the unconscionable terms only. The term unconscionable is derived from the Uniform Commercial Code, § 2-302, and refers to terms in a contract that are so manifestly unfair as to be oppressive.

Quicknotes

ADHESION CONTRACT A contract that is not negotiated by the parties and is usually prepared by the dominant party on a "take it or leave it" basis.

BOILERPLATE Standard language commonly appearing in documents having a definite meaning in the same context without variation.

UNCONSCIONABILITY Rule of law whereby a court may excuse performance of a contract, or of a particular contract term, if it determines that such term(s) are unduly oppressive or unfair to one party to the contract.

Western Hills, Oregon, Ltd. v. Pfau

Vendor (P) v. Vendees (D)

Or. Sup. Ct., 265 Or. 137, 508 P.2d 201 (1973).

NATURE OF CASE: Appeal from an action seeking specific performance.

FACT SUMMARY: Western Hills, Oregon, Ltd. (P), the vendor, brought this suit against Pfau (D) and others, the vendees, seeking to compel specific performance of an agreement to purchase real property.

🏛 **RULE OF LAW**
When a contract makes a party's duty to perform conditional on his personal satisfaction, the promisor is the sole judge of the quality of the work.

FACTS: Western Hills, Oregon, Ltd. (Western Hills) (P), the owner of a tract of land, contracted with Pfau (D) and others to purchase the property. The contract contained a clause which provided that "closing of transaction is subject to the ability of the purchasers to negotiate with the City of McMinnville as to planned development satisfactory to both first and second parties." Pfau (D) made preliminary proposals for a planned development to the McMinnville Planning Commission, but, although the commission's reaction to these proposals was favorable, Pfau (D) abandoned the attempts to secure approval of a development plan. Pfau (D) then notified Western Hills (P) that the defendants did not wish to go through with the purchase. Western Hills (P) refused to release Pfau (D) and the others from the agreement and brought this action for specific performance. Pfau (D) contended that the obligation to purchase never became absolute because the condition quoted above was never fulfilled. The evidence showed that Pfau (D) did not proceed with the approval application with the Planning Commission because the unavailability of city sewers would make the development too expensive. However, Pfau (D) knew of this at the time of the agreement. The trial court granted specific performance, and Pfau (D) appealed.

ISSUE: When a contract makes a party's duty to perform conditional on his personal satisfaction, is the promisor the sole judge of the quality of the work?

HOLDING AND DECISION: (McAllister, J.) Yes. When a contract makes a party's duty to perform conditional on his personal satisfaction, the promisor is the sole judge of the quality of the work, and his right to reject, if in good faith, is absolute and may not be reviewed by court or jury. The condition in the contract in the present case requires the exercise of the parties' personal judgment. However, dissatisfaction must be bona fide and in good faith. It is inherent in this requirement of dissatisfaction that the promisor not be allowed to base a claim of

dissatisfaction on circumstances which were known or anticipated by the parties at the time of contracting. In the present case, Pfau (D) and the others entered the agreement with full knowledge that the city sewer service would not be available and will not be allowed to justify abandoning their attempts to secure city approval simply because of the additional expense of providing a sewer system. Not having performed their duty to use reasonable diligence to obtain city approval, the defendants may not rely on the nonoccurrence of the condition. The decree of the trial court is affirmed.

▶ **ANALYSIS**

In *Anaheim Co. v. Holcombe*, 246 Or. 541 (1967) the Oregon Supreme Court considered an earnest money agreement which contained a provision making the purchaser's offer contingent on obtaining a loan of $25,000. The court held that when an agreement contains such a term, it imposes upon the vendee an implied condition that he make a reasonable effort to procure the loan. Thus, in the present case, the defendants had a similar duty, arising by implication, to make a reasonable effort to secure the city's approval.

▪══▪

Quicknotes

BONA FIDE True, honest, or genuine. May refer to a person's legal position based on good faith or lacking notice of fraud (such as a bona fide purchaser for value) or to the authenticity of a particular document (such as a bona fide last will and testament).

GOOD FAITH An honest intention to abstain from any unconscientious advantage of another.

SPECIFIC PERFORMANCE An equitable remedy whereby the court requires the parties to perform their obligations pursuant to a contract.

▪══▪

Indoe v. Dwyer

Seller (P) v. Buyer (D)

N.J. Super. Ct., 176 N.J. Super. 594, 424 A.2d 456 (1980).

NATURE OF CASE: Cross-motions for summary judgment in breach of contract.

FACT SUMMARY: Plaintiffs sought to enforce a contract for sale of their home to the Dwyers (D), whose attorney refused to approve the contract.

🏛 RULE OF LAW
An attorney approval clause in a contract for the purchase of real estate is valid and such approval may be denied for any reason, absent bad faith or capriciousness.

FACTS: Dwyer (D) submitted an offer on plaintiff's property. Later that day a realtor's printed form contract was prepared and presented to Dwyer (D) for signature. As she believed the document to be merely a bid, she signed the agreement. The plaintiffs executed the contract. When a copy of the fully executed contract was returned to her she was informed that the contract did not include the wall-to-wall carpeting in the sale. Defendants' attorney notified plaintiffs he was withholding his approval of the contract and that defendants would not proceed with the transaction. Plaintiffs brought suit and both parties moved for summary judgment.

ISSUE: Is an attorney approval clause in a contract for the purchase of real estate valid?

HOLDING AND DECISION: (Gaynor, J.) Yes. An attorney approval clause in a contract for the purchase of real estate is valid and such approval may be denied for any reason, absent bad faith or capriciousness. The plaintiffs contended that defendants breached the contract by their failure to consummate the purchase in accordance with the agreement, and that the attorney approval clause in the contract did not permit disapproval for unspecified reasons or for any of the reasons disclosed by defendants. Defendants argued that there was no breach as the clause rendered its efficacy contingent on the approval of either attorney and there was no showing of bad faith. While a clause providing for approval in a contract within a specified time by the attorney for either party has not been construed or applied, a similar issue has been presented with respect to contractual provisions requiring that title be satisfactory to the purchaser's attorney. Those cases apply an objective standard of whether the title is marketable. Applying such principles here, parties to a real estate transaction are entitled to the benefit of the judgment of a counselor and the applicable standard here is good faith. This compels the conclusion that the defendants' attorney's

disapproval of the contract terminated the transaction. Defendants' motion granted and plaintiff's motion denied.

▶ ANALYSIS

The court notes that the purpose of an attorney's approval clause is to allow the party to obtain the advice of counsel before entering into a binding contractual agreement. The exercise of the attorney's judgment is not thereafter subject to review and, absent a showing of bad faith or capriciousness on the part of the party or its attorney, such disapproval must be upheld.

■━■

Quicknotes

BAD FAITH Conduct that is intentionally misleading or deceptive.

GOOD FAITH An honest intention to abstain from any unconscientious advantage of another.

■━■

Hochster v. De La Tour

Employee (P) v. Employer (D)

Q.B., 2 Ellis & Bl. 678, 118 Eng. Rep. 922 (1853).

NATURE OF CASE: Action to recover damages for breach of contract.

FACT SUMMARY: Before Hochster (P) was due to perform his contract of employment for De La Tour (D), De La Tour (D) announced his intention to repudiate the contract, whereupon Hochster (P) immediately commenced an action for breach of contract.

🏛 RULE OF LAW
A party to a contract who renounces his intention to perform may not complain if the other party, instead of waiting until performance is due, elects to sue immediately for breach of contract.

FACTS: In April, Hochster (P) contracted to serve as De La Tour's (D) employee beginning on June 1. On May 11, De La Tour (D) wrote to Hochster (P) that he had changed his mind and declined Hochster's (P) services. On May 22, Hochster (P) brought this action for breach of contract.

ISSUE: When the time for performance has not arrived, but one party nevertheless indicates his intention not to perform, must the other party wait until the performance should have occurred before bringing action for breach of contract?

HOLDING AND DECISION: (Lord Campbell, C.J.) No. The man who wrongfully renounces a contract into which he has deliberately entered cannot complain if he is immediately sued for damages by the injured party; allowing the injured party, either to sue immediately, or wait till the time when the act was to be done. If Hochster (P) had to wait until June 1 to sue, he would not be able to enter any employment which would interfere with his promise to begin work at that time. And, after renunciation by De La Tour (D), Hochster (P) should be at liberty to consider himself absolved from any future performance, being free to seek other employment in mitigation of damages. Judgment for Hochster (P).

▶ ANALYSIS

This is the leading case on the so-called doctrine of anticipatory breach. The court's reasoning is erroneous insofar as it felt that Hochster (P) would otherwise be caught in a dilemma: to remain idle and hope for a favorable future judgment or to obtain other employment and thereby forfeit his rights against De La Tour (D). The court overlooked the rule that where a party manifests prospective unwillingness to perform, the other party may suspend his performance and change his position without surrendering

his right to sue after the breach occurs. In other words, the court could have considered the repudiation as (1) a defense to an action brought by De La Tour (D) and (2) an excuse of the constructive condition that Hochster (P) be ready, willing, and able to perform on June 1.

■═■

Quicknotes

ANTICIPATORY REPUDIATION Breach of a contract subsequent to formation but prior to the time performance is due.

■═■

Drake v. Wickwire

Client (P) v. Attorney (D)

Alaska Sup. Ct., 795 P.2d 195 (1990).

NATURE OF CASE: Malpractice suit.

FACT SUMMARY: Drake (P) sued his attorney, Wickwire (D), for allegedly inducing him to break an earnest money sales agreement.

RULE OF LAW
When an obligor repudiates a duty before he has committed a breach by nonperformance and before he has received all of the agreed consideration for it, the repudiation alone gives rise to a claim for damages for total breach.

FACTS: Drake (P) signed an exclusive listing agreement with Hosley, authorizing Hosley to act as Drake's (P) agent to sell some land, and providing for the payment of a 10 percent commission if, during the period of the listing agreement, Hosley located a buyer willing and able to purchase at Drake's (P) terms, or if Drake (P) entered into a binding sale. Hosley found a group of buyers and the parties signed an "earnest money receipt" for the sale of the property. Hosley received the title report listing a judgment in favor of Drake's (P) ex-wife as the sole encumbrance on the title. Hosley called Drake's (P) attorney, Wickwire (D), who stated that the judgment would be paid with the cash received at the closing. Wickwire (D) subsequently sent a letter to Hosley stating that Drake's (P) offer to sell had been withdrawn. Drake (P) sold the property through a different broker to other buyers. Hosley sued Drake (P) for the real estate commission, which was awarded to Hosley. Drake (P) brought a malpractice action against Wickwire (D) for allegedly inducing Drake (P) to break the earnest money sales agreement.

ISSUE: When an obligor repudiates a duty before he has committed a breach by nonperformance and before he has received all of the agreed consideration for it, does the repudiation alone give rise to a claim for damages for total breach?

HOLDING AND DECISION: (Matthews, C.J.) Yes. When an obligor repudiates a duty before he has committed a breach by nonperformance and before he has received all of the agreed consideration for it, the repudiation alone gives rise to a claim for damages for total breach. In order to constitute repudiation, the party's language must be sufficiently positive to be reasonably interpreted to mean that the party either cannot or will not perform. In addition, language that amounts to a statement of intent not to perform except under conditions that go beyond the contract also constitutes repudiation. Here Wickwire (D) did not act reasonably in treating Hosley's statement as a repudiation. The statement was ambiguous and insufficient to indicate the buyers would repudiate the contract. Reversed and remanded.

DISSENT: (Rabinowitz, J.) The majority incorrectly finds Wickwire guilty of malpractice.

ANALYSIS

In addition, Wickwire (D) could have sought adequate assurances of performance under Restatement (Second) of Contracts § 251. That section provides that if reasonable grounds arise to suspect that the obligor will commit a breach of contract by nonperformance that would give rise to a claim for total breach, "the obligee may demand adequate assurance of due performance and may, if reasonable, suspend any performance for which he has not already received the agreed exchange until he receives such assurance." If the obligor fails to provide such assurance within a reasonable time, then the obligee may treat such failure as a repudiation.

Quicknotes

DUTY An obligation owed by one individual to another.

MALPRACTICE A failure to perform one's professional duties during the course of a client relationship, either intentionally or negligently, or the poor or improper discharge of one's professional obligations.

NONPERFORMANCE Failure to perform a duty.

Cohen v. Kranz

Home buyer (P) v. Seller (D)

N.Y. Ct. App., 12 N.Y.2d 242, 238 N.Y.S.2d 928, 189 N.E.2d 473 (1963).

NATURE OF CASE: Action for return of deposit for realty purchase.

FACT SUMMARY: Having contracted to buy Kranz's (D) home, Cohen (P) obtained an adjournment of the original November 15, 1959, closing date until December 15, 1959.

🏛 RULE OF LAW
While a vendor of real estate with incurable title defects is automatically in default, a vendor with curable title must be put in default by the vendee's tender of performance and demand for a good title deed.

FACTS: Cohen (P) agreed to purchase Kranz's (D) house. Cohen (P) gave Kranz (D) a $4,000 down payment and the escrow was to close on November 15. Cohen (P) requested and was granted a 30-day extension of the closing date (December 15). On November 30, Cohen (P) informed Kranz (D) that he did not want the house because of defects in it which rendered title allegedly unmarketable. A demand was made for a return of the down payment on November 30 and again on December 15. Kranz (D) refused and suit was brought. The court found that a protective covenant existed, a fence extended over the property line, and the swimming pool lacked a proper certificate of occupancy. Judgment was rendered for Cohen (P). Kranz (D) appealed alleging that no tender had been offered at closing and he had never been informed of the nature of the defects so that he could attempt to cure them prior to closing. The Appellate Division, Second Division, reversed on the law and facts and directed judgment on the counterclaim for $1,500. Cohen appealed.

ISSUE: Can a real estate vendor be in default because of curable title defects absent vendee's tender of performance and demand for good title deed?

HOLDING AND DECISION: (Burke, J.) No. Unlike a real estate vendor whose title has incurable defects, a vendor with curable title defects is not automatically in default. Rather, he must be placed in default by the vendee's tender of performance and demand for a good title deed. The defects herein being curable and Cohen (P) having made no tender, the appellate court's decision was correct. Failure to specify the objections to title and an unjustified attempt to cancel the contract by Cohen (P) not only made attempts to cure the minor defects before closing unnecessary and wasteful, it rendered them impossible. Judgment is affirmed.

▶ ANALYSIS

The nature of curable defects must be disclosed by the vendee. If they can be cured, the vendor is given a reasonable time to do so even if it extends a short time past the specified closing date. A vendee may not take unfair advantage of minor defects to escape his contractual duties. Equity will prevent such unfair surprise. Specific performance with a reduction in price due to minor curable or even incurable defects may be awarded by some courts if deemed equitable to do so.

Quicknotes

CONDITION Requirement; potential future occurrence upon which the existence of a legal obligation is dependent.

SPECIFIC PERFORMANCE An equitable remedy whereby the court requires the parties to perform their obligations pursuant to a contract.

CHAPTER 9

Impossibility, Impracticability, and Frustration

Quick Reference Rules of Law

Paradine v. Jane

Landlord (P) v. Tenant (D)

K.B., Aleyn 26, 82 Eng. Rep. 897 (1647).

NATURE OF CASE: Action on a lease for rent past due.

FACT SUMMARY: Jane (D) argued that he should not have to pay rent owing on land he leased from Paradine (P) because he had been deprived of the land's use when it was occupied by the invading army of German Prince Rupert.

RULE OF LAW
When a party by his own contract creates a charge or duty upon himself, he is bound to make it good notwithstanding any frustration because he might have provided against it in the contract.

FACTS: Paradine (P) brought suit upon a lease for years, declaring that Jane (D) had failed to pay rent for three years on the lands held under the lease. Jane (D) answered that the lands had been occupied by the invading army of Prince Rupert of Germany and that, as a result, Jane (D) had been unable to take the profits from the land. Jane (D) argued that he was frustrated in the performance of his duties under the lease.

ISSUE: When a party by his own contract creates a charge or duty upon himself, is he bound to make good notwithstanding any frustration?

HOLDING AND DECISION: [No judge stated in casebook excerpt.] Yes. When a party by his own contract creates a charge or duty upon himself, he is bound to make it good notwithstanding any frustration because he might have provided against it in the contract. The lessee claimed he should not have to pay because the invading enemies threw him off his leased land. Jane (D), however, could have bargained for such an occurrence in the lease and chose not to do so. Jane's rent to Paradine (P) remained due and owing despite the occupation of the leased land by an invading army. Judgment for Paradine (P).

ANALYSIS

Another report of this same case said that the decision was placed principally on the ground, "If the tenant for years covenant to pay rent, though the lands let him be surrounded with water, yet he is chargeable with the rent, much more here." Style 47, 82 Eng. Rep. 519 (1647). This case is cited as the leading case in support of the strict 17th century English Rule that impossibility will not be recognized as an excuse for the promisee's nonperformance of his duty. Corbin writes that Jane (D) had no covenant of quiet enjoyment. "The agreed equivalent for the defendant's promise to pay rent was the conveyance of the leasehold property interest and delivery of possession. There was merely a frustration of the tenant's purpose of enjoying the profits of use and occupation." 6 Corbin, § 1322.

Quicknotes

IMPOSSIBILITY A doctrine relieving the parties to a contract from liability for nonperformance of their duties thereunder, if the subject matter of the contract ceases to exist, a person essential to the performance of the contract is deceased, or the service or goods contracted for has become illegal.

Taylor v. Caldwell

Event promoter (P) v. Hall (D)

K.B., 3 B. & S. 826, 122 Eng. Rep. 309 (1863).

NATURE OF CASE: Action for damages for breach of a contract for letting of premises.

FACT SUMMARY: Taylor (P) contracted to let Caldwell's (D) hall and gardens for four fetes and concerts, for four days, for 100 pounds per day. Taylor (P) expended money in preparation and for advertising, but Caldwell (D) could not perform when the hall burned down without his fault.

🏛 RULE OF LAW
In contracts in which the performance depends on the continued existence of a given person or thing, a condition is implied that the impossibility of performance arising from the perishing of the person or thing shall excuse the performance.

FACTS: By written agreement Caldwell (D) agreed to let the Surrey Gardens and Musical Hall at Newington, Surrey for four days for giving four Grand Concerts and Day and Night Fetes. Taylor (P) was to pay 100 pounds at the end of each day. Before any concerts were held, the hall was completely destroyed by fire without any fault of either of the parties. Taylor (P) alleged that the fire and destruction of the hall was a breach and that it resulted in his losing large sums in preparation and advertising for the concerts and fetes.

ISSUE: Was Caldwell (D) excused from performance by the accidental destruction of the hall and gardens which had made his performance impossible?

HOLDING AND DECISION: (Blackburn, J.) Yes. Caldwell (D) was excused from performance. First, the agreement was not a lease but a contract to "let." The entertainments that were planned could not be made without the existence of the hall. Ordinarily, when there is a positive contract to do something that is not unlawful, the contractor must perform or pay damages for not doing it even if an unforeseen accident makes performance unduly burdensome or even impossible. This is so when the contract is absolute and positive and not subject to either express or implied conditions, and that if it appears that the parties must have known from the beginning that the contract could not be fulfilled unless a particular, specified thing continued to exist and there is no express or implied warranty that the thing shall exist, the contract is not positive and absolute. It is subject to the implied condition that the parties shall be excused in case, before breach, performance becomes impossible from the perishing of the thing without fault of the contractor. This appears to be within the intention of the parties when they enter into

a contract. The excuse from the contract's performance is implied in law because from the nature of the contract it is apparent it was made on the basis of the continued existence of the particular, specified thing. Verdict for defendants made absolute.

▶ ANALYSIS

It was important for Judge Blackburn not to find the agreement to be a lease, otherwise the decision would come within direct conflict of *Paradine v. Jane*, K. B., 1647, 82 Eng. Rep. 897 (1647), which held that a lease must be performed to the letter despite unforeseen hardship or good fortune. Next, performance is excused only if the destruction of the specified thing is without fault. Had Caldwell been shown to be guilty of arson in the destruction of the hall, he would not have been excused. If there is impossibility of performance due to no one's fault, the one seeking to enforce performance takes the risk. It might be said that the court was actually apportioning the loss if the contract was, in effect, a joint venture with Taylor paying Caldwell 100 pounds out of each day's admission fees to the concerts (Caldwell was supplying the band). The view of this case is found in Uniform Commercial Code § 2-613 where for total destruction of the specified thing, the contract is avoided, or if the specified thing is goods which have so deteriorated as to no longer conform, the contract can be avoided or the goods can be accepted with an allowance for their lesser value. Note that there is not a satisfactory distinction between a contract to let and a lease.

Quicknotes

CONDITION Requirement; potential future occurrence upon which the existence of a legal obligation is dependent.

IMPOSSIBILITY A doctrine relieving the parties to a contract from liability for nonperformance of their duties thereunder, if the subject matter of the contract ceases to exist, a person essential to the performance of the contract is deceased, or the service or goods contracted for has become illegal.

WARRANTY An assurance by one party that another may rely on a certain representation of fact.

CNA International Reinsurance Co., Ltd. v. Phoenix

Insurance company (P) v. Estate (D)

Fla. Dist. Ct. App., 678 So. 2d 378 (1996).

NATURE OF CASE: Appeal from granting of insured's motion to dismiss subrogation claims against deceased actor's estate.

FACT SUMMARY: CNA International Reinsurance Co., Ltd. and American Casualty (P), insurers, having paid policyholders for claims under entertainment package policies after movie productions they were involved with were delayed or abandoned due to the key actor's apparently drug-related death, brought subrogation claims against Phoenix (D), the actor's estate, for breach of contract and fraud.

🏛 RULE OF LAW
The defense of impossibility of performance due to death applies even when the death is the fault of the person obligated to perform the personal services contract.

FACTS: This case arises from the death of the actor River Phoenix, apparently due to an overdose of illegal drugs, before completion of two films in which he had contracted to appear. As a result of the death, one film project was totally abandoned and the other completed with another actor replacing Phoenix. CNA International Reinsurance Insurance Co., Ltd. and American Casualty (P), insurers, having paid the policyholders for claims under entertainment package policies after the movie productions they were involved with were delayed or abandoned due to the key actor's death, brought subrogation claims against Phoenix (D), the actor's estate, for breach of contract and fraud. The trial court granted the estate's (D) motion to dismiss with prejudice, and the insurers (P) appealed.

ISSUE: Does the defense of impossibility of performance due to death apply even when the death is the fault of the person obligated to perform the personal services contract?

HOLDING AND DECISION: (Joanos, J.) Yes. The defense of impossibility of performance due to death applies even when the death is the fault of the person obligated to perform the personal services contract. Personal services contracts contain an implied condition that death shall dissolve the contract. The insurers' (P) contention that the defense of impossibility of performance does not apply in this case is rejected because that doctrine requires that the impossibility be fortuitous and unavoidable, and that it occur through no fault of either party. The insurers (P) argue that because the actor's death occurred from an intentional, massive overdose of illegal drugs, that this is not a situation in which neither party was at fault. At oral argument of this case, however, it became apparent that any attempt to discern fault in a death case such as this one, or in a similar case, perhaps involving the use of tobacco or alcohol, would create another case-by-case and hard-to-interpret rule of law. Being mindful that there are already too many of these in existence, we are not persuaded by the facts or the arguments presented to depart from the clear and unambiguous rule that death renders a personal services contract impossible to perform. In such contracts, there is an implied condition that death shall dissolve the contract. Affirmed.

▶ ANALYSIS

The *CNA* court noted that the parties to the agreements in this case could have provided specifically for the contingency of loss due to the use of illegal drugs, as they provided for other hazardous or life-threatening contingencies.

■=■

Quicknotes

IMPLIED CONDITION A condition that is not expressly stated in the terms of an agreement, but which is inferred from the parties' conduct or the type of dealings involved.

■=■

Clark v. Wallace County Cooperative Equity Exchange

Farmer (P) v. Grain elevator (D)

Kan. Ct. App., 26 Kan. App. 2d 463, 986 P.2d 391 (1999).

NATURE OF CASE: Appeal from trial court judgment.

FACT SUMMARY: Ray C. Clark (P), a farmer, agreed to sell the Wallace County Cooperative Equity Exchange (D) 4,000 bushels of corn to be delivered after the crop was harvested. A freeze damaged the crop, and Clark (P) failed to deliver the full amount. He (P) argued he was excused from performance.

🏛 RULE OF LAW
A seller under contract to supply goods is not excused from performance when the goods perish if the goods are not identified when the contract is made.

FACTS: In January 1995, Ray C. Clark (P), a farmer, agreed to sell the Wallace County Cooperative Equity Exchange (Coop) (D) 4,000 bushels of corn to be delivered after the crop was harvested. In September 1995, there was a freeze in the area that damaged the crop, and Clark (P) raised only around 2,200 bushels of corn, which he delivered to Coop (D). Clark (P) argued he was excused from delivering the remaining 1,400 bushels because of the freeze. Coop (D) argued Clark (P) was not excused and held the cost of the shortage out of the grain sale. Clark (P) filed a lawsuit to recover the money withheld.

ISSUE: Is a seller under contract to supply goods excused from performance when the goods perish if the goods are not identified when the contract is made?

HOLDING AND DECISION: (Lewis, J.) No. A seller under contract to supply goods is not excused from performance when the goods perish if the goods are not identified when the contract is made. Identification of corn yet to be grown is accomplished by identification of the land on which it will be grown. Kansas adopted the Uniform Commercial Code (U.C.C.), and § 2-613 excuses performance of a seller of goods if the goods are identified when the contract is made and the goods suffer casualty without fault of either party before risk of loss passes to the buyer. But the unambiguous terms of the contract in this case did not expressly require Clark (P) to grow the corn himself or to grow it in any particular location, only to deliver it to Coop (D). So § 2-613 does not help Clark (P) in this case. U.C.C. § 2-615 also does not help Clark (P). That section provides that a seller is not in breach of his obligations under a contract for sale if performance as agreed has been made impracticable by the occurrence of a contingency, the nonoccurrence of which was a basic assumption on which the contract was made. There is a

difference between subjective and objective impracticability; the first has to do with whether the seller cannot do the thing, the latter, with whether the thing cannot be done by anyone. Only objective impracticability relieves a party of his or her contractual obligation, and in this case, there was no objective impracticability because the corn was not identified to be from specific land. Clark (P) could have delivered the 4,000 bushels if he had purchased it from another farm. Because he had the ability to deliver the grain, he is not excused from the contract. Affirmed.

▶ ANALYSIS

The way in which commodities are identified varies among jurisdictions. Clearly, in farming states, to allow a farmer to be excused from performance of a contract because of a freeze would put all of the risk of loss on the purchasers, which would hinder the way business is conducted in that context. Also note the court's distinction between subjective and objective impracticability. Subjective practicability indicates that a person or persons are unable to do something, but it does not contemplate that the thing cannot be done under any circumstances. In this case, the grain could have been delivered to Coop (D); it's just that Clark (P) could not grow the grain that could have been delivered.

■■■

Quicknotes

IMPRACTICABILITY A doctrine relieving the parties to a contract from liability for nonperformance of their duties thereunder, if the subject matter of the contract ceases to exist.

■■■

Transatlantic Financing Corp. v. United States

Wheat exporter (P) v. Federal government (D)

363 F.2d 312 (D.C. Cir. 1966).

NATURE OF CASE: Appeal from dismissal of action for unforeseen costs in execution of a contract for carriage.

FACT SUMMARY: Transatlantic Financing Corp. (Transatlantic) (P), under charter of the United States (D), contracted to ship a full cargo of wheat from Galveston, Texas, to Iran. Shipment was contemplated on Transatlantic's (P) SS CHRISTOS through the Suez Canal, but war broke out between Egypt and Israel, forcing the closure of the canal. The SS CHRISTOS had to steam an extra 3,000 miles around the Cape of Good Hope.

RULE OF LAW
A thing is legally impossible when it can only be done at an excessive and unreasonable cost.

FACTS: Transatlantic Financing Corp. (Transatlantic) (P), under charter to the United States (D), contracted to carry a full cargo of wheat on its SS CHRISTOS from Galveston, Texas, to a safe port in Iran. On July 26, 1956, Egypt nationalized the Suez Canal. During the international crisis resulting from this, the parties contracted on October 2, 1956, for Transatlantic (P) to ship the wheat as described. The charter stated the termini of the voyage but not the route. The SS CHRISTOS sailed October 27, 1956, on a planned route through the Suez Canal. On October 29, 1956, war between Egypt and Israel broke out. On October 31, 1956, Great Britain and France invaded the Suez Canal Zone. On November 2, 1956, Egypt obstructed the canal with sunken vessels, closing it to traffic. Transatlantic (P) sought an agreement for additional compensation for a voyage around the Cape of Good Hope from a concededly unauthorized department of agriculture employee who advised Transatlantic (P) that it had to perform the charter according to its terms but could always file a claim. The SS CHRISTOS changed course for the Cape of Good Hope, arriving in Bandar Shapur, Iran, on December 30, 1956. The planned 10,000-mile voyage was increased by 3,000 miles. Transatlantic (P) sought the added expense of $43,972 over the $305,842 contract price. The district court dismissed the libel (an action in admiralty).

ISSUE: Is a thing legally impossible when it can only be done at an excessive and unreasonable cost?

HOLDING AND DECISION: (Wright, J.) Yes. A thing is legally impossible when it can only be done at an excessive and unreasonable cost. When impossibility of performance is raised as an argument to excuse performance of a contractual obligation, three things must be considered: (1) a contingency—something unexpected—must have occurred; (2) the risk of the unexpected occurrence must not have been allocated by agreement or custom; and (3) occurrence of the contingency must have rendered performance impracticable. Unless all three requirements are satisfied, the argument of impossibility must fail. The first requirement was met. It was reasonable to assume that when no route was mentioned in the charter, the usual and customary route (through the Suez Canal) would be taken. As to the second requirement, circumstances seemed to indicate that risk may have been allocated to Transatlantic (P), as the parties knew or should have known of the crisis. Freight rates were most likely affected by the increased risk of voyage in the Suez area. While one might not have foreseen that nationalization of the canal would have brought about a subsequent closure, the circumstances did indicate Transatlantic's (P) willingness to assume abnormal risks. Finally, the occurrence of the contingency did not render performance commercially impracticable under the circumstances, since the goods shipped out were not subject to harm from the longer, less temperate Southern route. The ship and crew were fit for the longer voyage, and Transatlantic (P) was no less able than the Government (D) to purchase insurance. In fact, the ship's operator would be more reasonably expected to cover the hazards of war. To justify relief there must be more of a variation between expected cost and the cost of performing by alternative means than was present here as the promisor can be presumed to have accepted greater than normal risk and impracticability is argued on the basis of expense alone. Affirmed.

ANALYSIS

In determining impossibility, the court will look first to see which party assumed the risk of unforeseen circumstances. If that cannot be determined, then it looks to see whether performance was legally impossible. Legally impossible means impracticable, that is, at excessive and unreasonable cost. Knowledge of the crisis would tend to show assumption of the risk. The court, with respect to unreasonable cost, examined Transatlantic's (P) theory of relief. If the contract was impossible, it was a nullity from the start. Transatlantic (P) asked for quantum meruit not for the total performance as it should have. The court believed that Transatlantic (P) wanted to avoid losing any of what appeared to be an advantageous contract price. The court would not place a burden on one party to

Continued on next page.

preserve the other's profit. Note that when the court discussed foreseeability of the risk, that foreseeability is as much a fiction as implied conditions, and the parties might honestly have not foreseen the canal closure. Foreseeability is used as a tool in considering where the risk was to be allocated.

■■■■

Quicknotes

CHANGE OF CONDITIONS A defense to a claim of ameliorative waste, based on the theory that a change in the surrounding area warranted the alterations to the property.

IMPOSSIBILITY A doctrine relieving the parties to a contract from liability for nonperformance of their duties thereunder, if the subject matter of the contract ceases to exist, a person essential to the performance of the contract is deceased, or the service or goods contracted for has become illegal.

■■■■

Eastern Air Lines, Inc. v. McDonnell Douglas Corp.

Jet purchaser (P) v. Jet supplier (D)

532 F.2d 957 (5th Cir. 1976).

NATURE OF CASE: Appeal from judgment awarding damages for breach of contract.

FACT SUMMARY: Pursuant to contract, McDonnell Douglas Corp. (McDonnell) (D) was to deliver jets to Eastern Air Lines, Inc. (P). Delivery was late due to McDonnell (D) subordinating civilian production to military production at the request of the government.

RULE OF LAW
Acts of government, whether formal or informal, which prevent performance under a contract constitute an excuse for breach.

FACTS: Pursuant to written contract, McDonnell Douglas Corp. (McDonnell) (D) was to deliver jets to Eastern Air Lines, Inc. (Eastern) (P). After the contracts were executed, there was an escalation of production of military aircraft. Under the Defense Production Act, the government could issue orders to manufacturers to give priority to military production. Instead, the government employed "jawboning" telephone calls to businesses requesting priority on an informal basis with an implied threat that formal directives would follow if the informal requests were ignored. An "excusable delay" clause in the contract provided an excuse for breach in case of causes beyond McDonnell's (D) control, including, but not limited to, any act of government, governmental priorities, etc. The trial court ruled that evidence of "jawboning" was inadmissible because it was immaterial and ruled for Eastern (P), saying McDonnell's (D) late delivery was a breach.

ISSUE: Do informal acts of government calling for military production priority excuse late performance under a contract?

HOLDING AND DECISION: (Ainsworth, J.) Yes. Fundamentally coercive acts of government, whether formal or informal, constitute an excuse for breach. The governmental priority program was beyond McDonnell's (D) control, and its good-faith compliance was proximately caused by the governmental program. The "excusable delay" clause in the contract did not limit McDonnell's (D) rights. This clause excused delays due to act of government, and this is what we had here, whether a formal or informal act. When the promisor had anticipated a particular event by specifically providing for it in a contract, he should be relieved of liability for the occurrence of such an event regardless of whether or not it was foreseeable. Reversed and remanded for a new trial.

ANALYSIS

The doctrine of commercial impracticability is set forth in Restatement of Contracts, § 454. The doctrine provides that where the contract is proceeding so differently from what the parties had anticipated, involving unanticipated and "extreme" difficulty or expense in performing, it may be discharged even without objective impossibility of performance. The unexpected difficulty and expense resulting must be extreme. Uniform Commercial Code § 2-615 applies this doctrine to contracts for the sale of goods.

━━■

Quicknotes

GOOD-FAITH COMPLIANCE A sincere or unequivocal intention to fulfill an obligation or to comply with specifically requested conduct.

━━■

Albre Marble and Tile Co., Inc. v. John Bowen Co., Inc.

Tile subcontractor (P) v. General construction contractor (D)

Mass. Sup. Jud. Ct., 338 Mass. 394, 155 N.E.2d 437 (1959).

NATURE OF CASE: Action to recover the value of work and labor furnished.

FACT SUMMARY: Albre Marble and Tile Co., Inc. (P) sought to recover the value of the expenses it incurred in preparing to undertake the work that had been subcontracted out to it by John Bowen Co., Inc. (D), the general contractor, but which never got under way because the general contract was itself declared invalid.

RULE OF LAW
A party may recover those expenditures made in reliance on a contract or in preparation to perform it when made pursuant to the specific request of the other party as set forth in the contract.

FACTS: As general contractor on a construction project, John Bowen Co., Inc. (Bowen) (D) subcontracted some of the work out to Albre Marble and Tile Co., Inc. (Albre) (P). The subcontracts called for Albre (P) to furnish and submit all necessary or required samples, shop drawings, tests, affidavits, etc., for approval, all as ordered or specified. Albre (P) incurred expenses in preparing such samples, drawings, etc. When the general contract was held invalid in a court case, Albre (P) brought suit against Bowen (D) to recover the fair value of work and labor furnished prior to the termination of the general contract and for the aforementioned expenses incurred in preparation for performance of the subcontracted work. Bowen (D) asserted that recovery for expenses incurred in preparation for performance of contractual obligations was improper, and the court agreed. Albre (P) appealed.

ISSUE: May a party recover those expenditures made in reliance on a contract or in preparation to perform it when made pursuant to the specific request of the other party as set forth in the contract?

HOLDING AND DECISION: (Spalding, J.) Yes. A party may recover those expenditures made in reliance on a contract or in preparation to perform it when made pursuant to the specific request of the other party as set forth in the contract. The facts here are that Bowen's (D) actions directly led to its general contract being invalid and thus it had the primary involvement in creating the impossibility that rendered further performance of the subcontracts impossible. Thus, as between the two parties, Bowen (D) should suffer whatever loss was thereby sustained by Albre (P). The damages to be assessed are limited solely to the fair value of the acts Albre (P) did pursuant to the specific request of Bowen (D) as contained in the subcontracts. Plaintiff's exceptions overruled in part and sustained in part, and the case remanded.

ANALYSIS

There is case law which denies recovery even when preparatory expenses were incurred in meeting a request made by the other party to the contract. However, in those cases the supervening act rendering further performance of the contract impossible was not caused by the fault of either party, and that is a most significant difference.

Quicknotes

IMPOSSIBILITY A doctrine relieving the parties to a contract from liability for nonperformance of their duties thereunder, if the subject matter of the contract ceases to exist, a person essential to the performance of the contract is deceased, or the service or goods contracted for has become illegal.

QUASI-CONTRACT An implied contract created by law to prevent unjust enrichment.

SUPERVENING CAUSE An independent cause, which is the proximate cause of an act.

UNJUST ENRICHMENT The unlawful acquisition of money or property of another for which both law and equity require restitution to be made.

Krell v. Henry

Apartment owner (P) v. Coronation viewer (D)

C.A., 2 K.B. 740 (1903).

NATURE OF CASE: Appeal in action for damages for breach of a contract for a license for use.

FACT SUMMARY: Henry (D) paid a deposit of £25 to Krell (P) for the use of his apartment in Pall Mall, London, for the purpose of a viewing sight for King Edward VII's coronation procession. The King became ill causing a delay of the coronation upon which Henry (D) refused to pay a £50 balance for which Krell (P) sued.

RULE OF LAW

Where the object of one of the parties is the basis upon which both parties contract, the duties of performance are constructively conditioned upon the attainment of that object.

FACTS: In two letters of June 20, 1902, Henry (D) contracted through Krell's (P) agent, Bisgood, to use Krell's (P) flat in Pall Mall, London, to view the coronation procession of King Edward VII which had been advertised to pass along Pall Mall. The contract made no mention of this purpose. The period of use of the flat was the daytime only of June 26 and 27, 1902 for £75, £25 paid in deposit with the £50 remainder due on June 24, 1902. Henry (D) became aware of the availability of Krell's (P) flat as an announcement to that effect had been made which was reiterated by Krell's (P) housekeeper who showed Henry (D) the rooms. When the King became very ill, the coronation was delayed and Henry (D) refused to pay the £50 balance, for which Krell (P) brought suit.

ISSUE: Was the defeat of the basis upon which Henry (D) contracted a defeat of the contract?

HOLDING AND DECISION: (Williams, L.J.) Yes. It can be inferred from the surrounding circumstances that the rooms were taken for the purpose of viewing the processions and that was the foundation of the contract. It was not a lease of the rooms—they could not be used at night—but a license for use for a particular purpose. With the defeat of the purpose of the contract, the performance is excused.

ANALYSIS

This case is an extension of *Taylor v. Caldwell*, K.B., 3 B. & S. 826, 122 Eng. Rep. 309 (1863), and, as in that case, it was necessary to remove the roadblock of a lease in order to avoid a conflict with *Paradine v. Jane*, K.B., 1647, 82 Eng. Rep. 897 (1647). The rule explained here is "frustration of purpose" or "commercial frustration." It has not been made clear whether this doctrine rests upon the failure of consideration or the allocation of the risks. While there is a

frustration, performance is not impossible. No constructive condition of performance has failed as Krell (P) made no promise that the condition would occur. Rather, a constructive condition based upon the attainment of the purpose or object has arisen. Note that the frustration should be total or nearly total though that is a matter of degree.

■≡■

Quicknotes

CONDITION Requirement; potential future occurrence upon which the existence of a legal obligation is dependent.

CONSIDERATION Value given by one party in exchange for performance, or a promise to perform, by another party.

FRUSTRATION OF PURPOSE A doctrine relieving the parties to a contract from liability for nonperformance of their duties thereunder when the purpose of the agreement ceases to exist due to circumstances not subject to either party's control.

IMPOSSIBILITY A doctrine relieving the parties to a contract from liability for nonperformance of their duties thereunder, if the subject matter of the contract ceases to exist, a person essential to the performance of the contract is deceased, or the service or goods contracted for has become illegal.

■≡■

Western Properties v. Southern Utah Aviation, Inc.

Sublessor (P) v. Sublessee (D)

Utah Ct. App., 776 P.2d 656 (1989).

NATURE OF CASE: Appeal of dismissal and cross-appeal summary judgment in breach of contract action.

FACT SUMMARY: Western Properties (P) sued Southern Utah Aviation, Inc. (Southern) (D) for unpaid rent due when Southern (D) abandoned the leasehold after the city denied its plan to develop the property.

🏛 RULE OF LAW
Under the defense of impossibility, a contractual obligation is discharged if an unforeseen event occurs after formation and without fault on the part of the obligated party, which makes performance of the obligation impossible or highly impracticable.

FACTS: Western Properties (Western) (P) leased vacant land from Cedar City, which it subleased to Southern Utah Aviation, Inc. (Southern) (D) for a 15-year term, with a covenant that Southern (D) was to construct a maintenance building on the premises. The building was to become property of Western (P) upon termination of the sublease. Southern (D) applied to the city for site plan approval, which was denied. Southern (D) defaulted in its lease payments and abandoned the property without constructing the building. Western (P) sued for unpaid rent and the value of the maintenance building. The trial court granted partial summary judgment and awarded rent accrued to the date of abandonment. Western's (P) claims for further rent and the value of the maintenance building were dismissed. Western (P) appealed the dismissal. Southern (D) cross-appealed from the earlier summary judgment.

ISSUE: Under the defense of impossibility, is a contractual obligation discharged if an unforeseen event occurs after formation and without fault on the part of the obligated party, which makes performance of the obligation impossible or highly impracticable?

HOLDING AND DECISION: (Conder, J.) Yes. Under the defense of impossibility, a contractual obligation is discharged if an unforeseen event occurs after formation and without fault on the part of the obligated party, which makes performance of the obligation impossible or highly impracticable. The rationale is based on the fact that parties make certain assumptions in forming their agreement, and enforcement is prevented where such assumptions are erroneous. Here the parties assumed the city would approve the development of the leased land. Such failure was sufficiently unforeseen to apply the impossibility defense. The other facts required for application of the defense have been established. The court found that Southern (D)

could not build the maintenance building without city approval and that there was no factual basis for implicating Southern (D) in the city's failure to approve the development. Southern (D) seems to have made every effort that could reasonably be required to induce the city to give its approval. Thus the obligation to construct the maintenance building was discharged from the time the performance of the obligation was deemed impossible. Affirmed.

▶ ANALYSIS

The court notes that while construction of the building was impossible, occupancy of the land was not. The court concluded, however, that the purpose of the leasehold was effectively frustrated by the defendant's inability to develop the land. Frustration of purpose is a defense to performance based on the fact that the purpose of the contract becomes pointless. Since there was no purpose in leasing the land once development became impossible, the obligation to pay rent was discharged as well.

■═■

Quicknotes

IMPOSSIBILITY A doctrine relieving the parties to a contract from liability for nonperformance of their duties thereunder, if the subject matter of the contract ceases to exist, a person essential to the performance of the contract is deceased, or the service or goods contracted for has become illegal.

■═■

Enforcement Remedies

Quick Reference Rules of Law

Protectors Insurance Service, Inc. v. United States Fidelity & Guaranty Company

Insurance agent (P) v. Insurance company (D)

132 F.3d 612 (10th Cir. 1998).

NATURE OF CASE: Breach of contract suit.

FACT SUMMARY: Protectors Insurance Service, Inc. (P) sued United States Fidelity & Guaranty Company (D) for breach of its contract, and received both lost profits damages and reduction in market value damages.

🏛 **RULE OF LAW**
In a breach of contract action where the loss of business is alleged to be caused by the wrongful acts of another, damages are to be measured by either the value of the going concern or lost future profits.

FACTS: Protectors Insurance Service, Inc. (Protectors) (P) was an agent of United States Fidelity & Guaranty Company (USF&G) (D) and had a written contract authorizing it to solicit and submit applications for USF&G (D) insurance. Over 80 percent of Protectors' (P) business was derived from USF&G (D). USF&G (D) notified Protectors (P) that it was going to terminate its personal lines contract with Protectors (P) in 180 days if the goals of its rehabilitation program were not met by the end of 1992. USF&G (D) then sent a letter notifying Protectors (P) that it would not accept any new personal lines business nor renew the current business. Protectors (P) brought suit alleging USF&G breached its contract by not making a good-faith effort at rehabilitation to avoid termination of the agreement. The jury returned a verdict of $844,650. USF&G (D) appealed, arguing that the lost profits award portion of the recovery should be vacated because it represents an impermissible double recovery.

ISSUE: In a breach of contract action where the loss of business is alleged to be caused by the wrongful acts of another, are damages to be measured by either the value of the going concern or lost future profits?

HOLDING AND DECISION: (Brown, J.) Yes. In a breach of contract action where the loss of business is alleged to be caused by the wrongful acts of another, damages are to be measured by either the value of the going concern or lost future profits. USF&G (D) argued that the lost profits award portion of the recovery should be vacated because it represents an impermissible double recovery. This court agrees. In a breach of contract action, the objective is to place the injured party in the same position it would have enjoyed but for the breach. A double recovery for the same injury is invalid. Protectors (P) argued that there was no double recovery in this case since there was no factual basis in the record for finding that the damages for the decreased sales price of the

company were based upon, or included, future lost profits. Many jurisdictions follow the view that when the loss of business is alleged to be caused by the wrongful acts of another, damages are to be measured by either the value of the going concern or lost future profits. The "going concern value" is the price a willing buyer would pay, and a willing seller would accept, in a free marketplace for the particular business. Damages are measured by awarding the difference between the going concern value and the price actually received by the plaintiff upon sale of the business. Here the record supports the jury's award of $35,000. The award of lost profit damages in addition to this amount, however, was an impermissible double recovery. The $809,650 lost profit damage award is vacated, and the $35,000 diminution in market value award affirmed. Remanded.

▶ **ANALYSIS**

Note that generally the "going concern" and "lost profit" measures are considered alternative remedies; however, the court here concluded that the lost profit award was to be vacated due to clear proof in the record of the value of Protectors' (P) business as a going concern, which must necessarily take into account its future profit-earning potential. Lost future profits, on the other hand, may only be utilized where there is no other means available of valuating the business. A plaintiff is not entitled to receive both the fair market value of his business plus the profits the business may have earned.

■══■

Quicknotes

LOST PROFITS The potential value of income earned or goods which are the subject of the contract; may be used in calculating damages where the contract has been breached.

■══■

Hadley v. Baxendale

Mill operator (P) v. Carrier (D)

Ex., 9 Ex. 341, 156 Eng. Rep. 145 (1854).

NATURE OF CASE: Action for damages for breach of a carrier contract.

FACT SUMMARY: Hadley (P), a mill operator in Gloucester, arranged to have Baxendale's (D) company, a carrier, ship his broken mill shaft to the engineer in Greenwich for a copy to be made. Hadley (P) suffered a £300 loss when Baxendale (D) unreasonably delayed shipping the mill shaft causing the mill to be shut down longer than anticipated.

🏛 RULE OF LAW
The injured party may recover either those damages as may reasonably be considered arising naturally from the breach itself or may recover those damages as may reasonably be supposed to have been in contemplation of the parties, at the time they made the contract, as the probable result of a breach of it.

FACTS: Hadley (P), a mill operator in Gloucester, arranged to have Baxendale's (D) shipping company return his broken mill shaft to the engineer in Greenwich who was to make a duplicate. Hadley (P) delivered the broken shaft to Baxendale (D) who in consideration for his fee promised to deliver the shaft to Greenwich in a reasonable time. Baxendale (D) did not know that the mill was shut down while awaiting the new shaft. Baxendale (D) was negligent in delivering the shaft within a reasonable time. Reopening of the mill was delayed five days costing Hadley (P) lost profits and paid out wages of £300. Hadley (P) had paid Baxendale (D) £25 to ship the mill shaft. Baxendale (D) paid into court £25 in satisfaction of Hadley's (P) claim. The jury awarded an additional £25 for a total £50 award. [Note: The headnote taken from the English reporter and reprinted in the casebook is in error when it states that Hadley's (P) servant told Baxendale (D) the mill was stopped and the shaft must be sent immediately.]

ISSUE: Shall damages to be awarded be left to the discretion of the jury?

HOLDING AND DECISION: (Alderson, B.) No. The jury requires a rule for its guidance in awarding damages justly. When a party breaches his contract, the damages he pays ought to be those arising naturally from the breach itself, and, in addition, those as may reasonably be supposed to have been in contemplation of the parties, at the time they made the contract, as the probable result of the breach of it. Therefore, if the special circumstances under which the contract was made were known to both parties, the resulting damages upon breach would be those reasonably contemplated as arising under those communicated and known circumstances. But if the special circumstances were unknown then damages can only be those expected to arise generally from the breach. Hadley's (P) telling Baxendale (D) that he ran a mill and his mill shaft which he wanted shipped was broken did not notify Baxendale (D) that the mill was shut down. Baxendale (D) could have believed reasonably that Hadley (P) had a spare shaft or that the shaft to be shipped was not the only defective machinery at the mill. Here, it does not follow that a loss of profits could fairly or reasonably have been contemplated by both parties in case of breach. Such a loss would not have flowed naturally from the breach without the special circumstances having been communicated to Baxendale (D). Remanded for new trial with instructions to calculate damages without considering lost profits. Rule absolute.

▌ ANALYSIS

This case lays down two rules guiding damages. First, only those damages as may fairly and reasonably be considered arising from the breach itself may be awarded. Alternatively, those damages which may reasonably be supposed to have been in contemplation of the parties at the time they made the contract as the probable result of a breach of it may be awarded. The second is distinguished from the first because with the latter, both parties are aware of the special circumstances under which the contract is made. Usually those special circumstances are communicated by the plaintiff to the defendant before the making of the contract. But that is not an absolute condition. If the consequences of the breach are foreseeable, the party who breaches will be liable for the lost profits or expectation damages. Foreseeability and assumption of the risk are ways of describing the bargain. If there is an assumption of the risk, the seller or carrier must necessarily be aware of the consequences. A later English case held that there would be a lesser foreseeability for a common carrier than for a seller as a seller would tend to know the purpose and use of the item sold while the common carrier probably would not know the use of all items it carried. If all loss went on to the seller, this would obviously be an incentive not to enter into contracts. Courts balance what has become a "seller beware" attitude by placing limitations on full recovery. The loss must be foreseeable when the contract is entered into. It cannot be overly speculative. The seller's breach must be judged by willingness, negligence, bad faith, and availability of replacement items. Restatement (First), § 331(2) would allow recovery in the situation

Continued on next page.

in this case under an alternative theory. If the breach were one preventing the use and operation of property from which profits would have been made, damages can be measured by the rental value of the property or by interest on the value of the property. Uniform Commercial Code § 2-715(2) allows the buyer consequential damages for any loss which results from general or particular needs of which the seller had reason to know.

■══■

Quicknotes

CONSEQUENTIAL DAMAGES Monetary compensation that may be recovered in order to compensate for injuries or losses sustained as a result of damages that are not the direct or foreseeable result of the act of a party, but that nevertheless are the consequence of such act and which must be specifically pled and demonstrated.

EXPECTANCY The expectation or contingency of obtaining possession of a right or interest in the future.

LOST PROFITS The potential value of income earned or goods which are the subject of the contract; may be used in calculating damages where the contract has been breached.

■══■

Mader v. Stephenson

Damage recoverers (P) v. Contract breacher (D)

Wy. Sup. Ct., 552 P.2d 1114 (1976).

NATURE OF CASE: Appeal in an action for contractual damages.

FACT SUMMARY: Having been awarded actual damages caused by breach of contract, plus interest, the Maders (P) appealed the court's denial of attorney fees and the overall costs of bringing the suit.

> 🏛 **RULE OF LAW**
> Absent statutory authority or contractual agreement, attorney fees and other costs of bringing a lawsuit are not recoverable.

FACTS: The Maders (P) recovered $1,000 damages plus interest as the actual damages in their breach of contract action against Stephenson (D). However, they appealed the trial court's denying them additional damages of: (1) $500 for attorney fees; (2) $212 for airfare to and from the trial; and (3) $500 for their travel time, telephone calls, and expenses in "pursuit of justice." Stephenson (D) claimed that, absent statutory authority, such fees were not recoverable and that no statute existed that entitled the Maders (P) to recovery of such costs, nor had there been a contractual agreement.

ISSUE: Absent statutory authority or contractual agreement, are attorney fees and other costs of bringing a lawsuit recoverable?

HOLDING AND DECISION: (Per curiam) No. Absent statutory authority or contractual agreement, attorney fees and other costs of bringing a lawsuit are not recoverable as damages. The Maders (P) make an unsupported claim on appeal for costs incurred. If the appeal is not reasonably brought, costs are assessed to the appellee. Here, nothing justifies the appeal, so attorney's fees and costs are taxed to the Maders (P). Affirmed.

▶ *ANALYSIS*

An award of damages in the United States does not ordinarily include reimbursement of the successful party's attorney fees. The rationale is that a contrary rule would discourage impecunious plaintiffs from prosecuting meritorious claims. See Note, "Attorney's Fees: Where Shall the Ultimate Burden Lie?" 20 *Vand. L. Rev.* 1216 (1967). However, the majority of jurisdictions do uphold agreements in leases, notes, and credit contracts that if collection of payments creates legal fees, such reasonable attorney fees will be payable.

■■■

Quicknotes

ACTUAL DAMAGES Measure of damages necessary to compensate victim for actual injuries suffered.

■■■

Rockingham County v. Luten Bridge Co.

Municipality (P) v. Bridge construction company (D)

35 F.2d 301 (4th Cir. 1929).

NATURE OF CASE: Appeal in action for damages for breach of a construction contract.

FACT SUMMARY: Rockingham County (D) contracted with Luten Bridge Co. (Luten) (P) to construct a bridge. While work was in progress Rockingham County (D) wrongfully notified Luten (P) to cease work. However, Luten (P) continued construction for another month.

🏛 RULE OF LAW
When an aggrieved party receives notice of a major breach by the opposing contracting party then the aggrieved party acquires an immediate duty to mitigate damages reasonably.

FACTS: Rockingham County (D) contracted with the Luten Bridge Co. (Luten) (P) to construct a bridge. While construction was in progress on the bridge the Commissioners of Rockingham County (D) voted to have the remainder of the bridge completed by another construction firm. Rockingham County (D) then notified Luten (P) to cease work. This order was in breach of the contract between the parties. Luten (P) temporarily ignored the order and continued construction on the bridge for another month. Luten (P) then brought suit for breach of contract. The trial court found that Rockingham County (D) was in breach and awarded Luten (P) costs incurred to the date of the notice of the breach, and its lost profit on the contract but refused to award Luten (P) its costs incurred for the one month's construction after Luten (P) had received notice to cease construction.

ISSUE: Does an aggrieved party have a duty to mitigate damages reasonably once the party receives notice of a major breach by the opposing contracting party?

HOLDING AND DECISION: (Parker, J.) Yes. When an aggrieved party receives notice of a major breach by the opposing contracting party then the aggrieved party acquires an immediate duty to mitigate damages reasonably. An aggrieved party acquires a responsibility not to cause any unnecessary waste. In this case when Rockingham County (D) notified Luten (P) to cease work, Luten (D) had a duty to cease work even though such notice was wrongful. Any construction work that was done after the notice is considered waste and was done at Luten's (P) own peril. We conclude that Luten (P) is entitled to recover all costs incurred except for the last month's work of construction and may recover its lost profit. Reversed and remanded.

▶ ANALYSIS

The principal case demonstrates the black letter rule that an aggrieved party has a duty to mitigate damages. This rule has sometimes been called the rule of avoidable consequences. When a party fails to mitigate his damages as in the principal case then the party is precluded from recovering that which was wasted. The principal case is also noteworthy for demonstrating the majority view on damages for an aggrieved contractor which is the recovery of all costs incurred to date plus lost profit.

■═■

Quicknotes

CONSEQUENTIAL DAMAGES Monetary compensation that may be recovered in order to compensate for injuries or losses sustained as a result of damages that are not the direct or foreseeable result of the act of a party, but that nevertheless are the consequence of such act and which must be specifically pled and demonstrated.

LOST PROFITS The potential value of income earned or goods which are the subject of the contract; may be used in calculating damages where the contract has been breached.

MITIGATION OF DAMAGES A plaintiff's implied obligation to reduce the damages incurred by taking reasonable steps to prevent additional injury.

■═■

Gruber v. S-M News Co.

Card designer (P) v. Consignment seller (D)

126 F. Supp. 442 (S.D.N.Y. 1954).

NATURE OF CASE: Action for damages for breach of contract.

FACT SUMMARY: Gruber (P) claimed that S-M News (S-M) (D) had failed to exercise good faith in distributing the specially manufactured Christmas cards which Gruber (P) had sent S-M (D) on consignment.

> 🏛 **RULE OF LAW**
> If full performance by a defendant would have resulted in a loss to a plaintiff, then this loss must be deducted from any damages awarded to the plaintiff for his out-of-pocket expenses made in reliance on the defendant's promises of performance.

FACTS: Gruber (P) completely performed his contract to manufacture 90,000 sets of Christmas cards, which the S-M News Co. (S-M) (D) obliged itself to exercise reasonable diligence in selling through its 700 wholesalers at $0.84 a box payment to Gruber (P). Credit was to be allowed by Gruber (P) for all unsold sets. However, when S-M (D) distributed the cards to only four wholesalers, Gruber (P) sought $101,800 damages for expected profits. When this court held that Gruber (P) failed to bear the burden of proof as to a means of computing his expected profits, Gruber (P) sought recovery only of his out-of-pocket expenses made in reliance on S-M's (D) promises. S-M (D) countered that there could be no recovery since, even had S-M (D) fully performed, there would have been a loss to Gruber (P).

ISSUE: If full performance by a defendant would have resulted in a loss to a plaintiff, then must this loss be deducted from damages awarded to the plaintiff for his out-of-pocket expenses made in reliance on the defendant's promises?

HOLDING AND DECISION: (Murphy, J.) Yes. According to the Restatement, if full performance by a defendant would have resulted in a loss to a plaintiff, then this loss must be deducted from damages awarded to the plaintiff for his out-of-pocket expenses made in reliance on the defendant's promises of performance. However, S-M (D) did not carry its burden of establishing the probability of such a loss. While it is true that, when the cards were sold in 1949 by Gruber (P), he realized only $0.06 per box rather than the promised $0.84 planned in the 1945 sale, this was possibly due to their 1945 theme, which was the newly formed United Nations, which by 1949 had lost some of its glamour. Accordingly, Gruber (P) was awarded any expenses made in reliance on S-M's (D) contractual promises minus the net amount Gruber (P) received from the sale of cards distributed by S-M (D). Judgment accordingly.

▶ ANALYSIS

When the plaintiff cannot establish his loss of profits with sufficient certainty, he is still permitted to recover his expenses of preparation and part performance as well as other foreseeable expenses incurred in reliance upon the contract. This relief is awarded "on the assumption that the value of the contract would have at least covered the outlay." McCormick, *Damages*, 586. For example, a farmer who purchases and plants defective seed may or may not be able to prove the value of the crop but is allowed to recover the cost of the seed, rental value of the land, and the cost of sowing the seed.

■■■■

Quicknotes

LOST PROFITS The potential value of income earned or goods which are the subject of the contract; may be used in calculating damages where the contract has been breached.

■■■■

Anglia Television Ltd. v. Reed

Television company (P) v. Performer (D)

H.L., 3 All. E.R. 690 (1971).

NATURE OF CASE: Appeal from award of damages for breach of contract.

FACT SUMMARY: Reed (D) contended that Anglia Television Ltd. (Anglia) (P) could not ask for damages for wasted expenditures incurred before the contract was concluded with Reed (D) because these expenditures were for Anglia's (P) benefit at a time when it was uncertain whether there would be any contract or not.

🏛 RULE OF LAW
In a breach of contract action, wasted expenditure can be recovered when it is wasted by reason of the defendant's breach of contract.

FACTS: Anglia Television Ltd. (Anglia) (P) entered into a contract with Reed (D) whereby Reed (D) would perform in a play for television. Because of a booking error, Reed (D) repudiated the contract. Anglia (P) tried to find a substitute for Reed (D), could not, and then accepted Reed's (D) repudiation. Anglia (P) abandoned the proposed project and sued Reed (D) for damages. Anglia (P) did not claim their loss of profits as damages, but instead claimed wasted expenditures. They had incurred director's, designer's and manager's fees and claimed that money had been wasted because Reed (D) did not perform his contract. Reed (D) did not dispute his liability, but contended that Anglia (P) could not ask for damages for wasted expenditures incurred before the contract was concluded with Reed (D) because the expenditures were for Anglia's (P) benefit at a time when it was uncertain whether there would be any contract or not. The court allowed Anglia (P) to recover for expenditures incurred both before and after the contract was concluded, if such expenditure was reasonably in contemplation of the parties as likely to be wasted if the contract was broken. Reed (D) appealed.

ISSUE: In a breach of contract action, can wasted expenditure be recovered when it is wasted by reason of the defendant's breach of contract?

HOLDING AND DECISION: (Lord Denning, J.) Yes. In a breach of contract action, wasted expenditure can be recovered when it is wasted by reason of the defendant's breach of contract. A plaintiff in a breach of contract case has an election as far as damages are concerned. He can claim for his loss of profits; or for his wasted expenditure. He must elect between them. He cannot claim both. He can also claim expenditures which happened both before and after the contract was concluded, provided the expenditures were such as would reasonably be in the contemplation of the parties as likely to be wasted if the contract was broken. Applying that principle here, it is plain that, when Mr. Reed (D) entered into this contract, he must have known perfectly well that a large amount of expenditures had already been incurred and that if he broke the contract, all those expenditures would be wasted. He must pay damages for all the expenditures so wasted. The appeal should be dismissed.

▶ ANALYSIS

In a contract situation, the promisee may have changed his position in reliance on the contract, either incurring expenses in preparing to perform or foregoing opportunities to make other contracts. In such a case, the court may recognize a claim based on reliance rather than on the promisee's expectation. It does this by attempting to put him back in the same position as he would have been in had the contract not been made.

■■■

Quicknotes

DETRIMENTAL RELIANCE Action by one party resulting in loss that is based on the conduct or promises of another.

ELECTION OF DAMAGES The choosing from alternative measures of damages that are inconsistent, after such choice the elector is bound to his selection.

REPUDIATION The actions or statements of a party to a contract that evidence his intent not to perform, or to continue performance, of his duties or obligations thereunder.

■■■

Hessler v. Crystal Lake Chrysler-Plymouth, Inc.

Car dealership (D) v. Car buyer (P)

Ill. App. Ct., 338 Ill. App. 3d 1010, 273 Ill. Dec. 96, 788 N.E.2d 405 (2003).

NATURE OF CASE: Appeal of judgment by the trial court.

FACT SUMMARY: Donald R. Hessler (P) sued Crystal Lake Chrysler-Plymouth, Inc. (Crystal Lake) (D) for breach of contract when the dealership failed to deliver a car he contracted to buy. The court awarded him $29,853 in damages, representing the difference between what he contracted to pay Crystal Lake (D) and what he paid to another dealer to buy a similar car.

RULE OF LAW
Under the Uniform Commercial Code, the correct formula to calculate damages in the case where one party repudiates and the aggrieved party covers is the difference between the cost of cover and the contract price.

FACTS: Donald R. Hessler (P) signed an agreement in February 1997 to purchase a 1997 Plymouth Prowler from Crystal Lake Chrysler-Plymouth, Inc. (Crystal Lake) (D) through a co-owner of the dealership, Gary Rosenberg. The car was not yet produced when Hessler (P) signed the agreement, and the manufacturer's list price was supposed to be $39,000. The terms of the contract provided that Hessler (P) would pay $5,000 over list price by the manufacturer, and that the car would be delivered "ASAP." Rosenberg testified at trial that Hessler (P) was the first person to place an order for a Prowler. In May 1997, Salvatore Palandri entered into a contract with Crystal Lake (D) to purchase a 1997 Prowler for $50,000 with $10,000 down, and his contract stipulated that Palandri would receive the first car delivered to the dealership. In September 1997, Hessler (P) obtained a list of dealers due to receive Prowlers from a Chrysler representative and called Rosenberg to tell him that his dealership was among those due to receive Prowlers. Rosenberg told Hessler (P) that he would not sell Hessler (P) a car because he had gone behind Rosenberg's back, and that contracting Chrysler would cause Rosenberg problems. He also stated that Hessler (P) was not the first person with whom he contracted to sell a Prowler, and that the first car the dealership received was already "committed." Hessler (P) then began calling around to other dealerships to find a Prowler, but did not obtain one after calling a total of 38. He eventually found one and bought it on Oct. 24, 1997, for $77,706. On Oct. 27, 1997, Crystal Lake (D) sold the only one it received to Palandri for $54,859. Hessler (P) indicated that he was willing to purchase another one from Crystal Lake (D), but none was available. He also continued to research prices for Prowlers, and by Jan. 1998, the lowest price was $77,706. He then sued Crystal Lake (D) for breach of contract. The court awarded him $29,853 in damages, representing the difference between what he contracted to pay Crystal Lake (D) and what he paid to another dealer to buy a similar car.

ISSUE: Under the Uniform Commercial Code, is the correct formula to calculate damages in the case where one party repudiates and the aggrieved party covers the difference between the cost of cover and the contract price?

HOLDING AND DECISION: (Callum, J.) Yes. Under the Uniform Commercial Code (U.C.C.), the correct formula to calculate damages in the case where one party repudiates and the aggrieved party covers is the difference between the cost of cover and the contract price. Because this transaction involves the sale of goods, it is governed by the U.C.C. The contract stated that Crystal Lake (D) would deliver a Prowler to Hessler (P) "ASAP," and the trial court did not err in finding under the U.C.C. that Rosenberg's subsequent statements to Hessler (P) that he would not sell Hessler (P) a car reasonably indicated to Hessler (P) that Crystal Lake (D) would not deliver to him a Prowler under their agreement, and that Crystal Lake (D) thereby repudiated the contract. The trial court also did not err in finding that Chrystal Lake (D) breached the contract when it sold its first Prowler to Palandri, or in finding that the cover price $77,706 was a proper cover price, since it was the best price available at the time. Because Hessler (P) covered after Crystal Lake's (D) breach by purchasing a Prowler elsewhere, Section 2-712(2) of the U.C.C. as adopted by Illinois provides the correct measure of damages, which is the difference between the cost of cover and the contract price. The amount of damages was therefore correct. Affirmed.

ANALYSIS

This case illustrates a judicial interpretation of U.C.C. rules regarding the relationship between anticipatory repudiation, cover, and damages, which are appropriate to this section of the casebook. But the interesting part of decision—most of which was edited out of the casebook—has to do with the interpretation of "ASAP." The court first ruled that the contract was completely integrated, but then still admitted parol evidence to clarify the meaning of "ASAP." The court stated that application of the Parol Evidence Rule determines only which terms are contained in the parties' final agreement. It does not preclude the admission of extrinsic evidence to interpret those terms.

Continued on next page.

Where a contract term is ambiguous, a court may consider extrinsic evidence to interpret the term, the court held, and based on these principles, there was no error in relying on the owner's testimony about the meaning of "ASAP"—and no error in ruling that the defendant agreed to sell its first Prowler to Hessler (P).

■■■■

Quicknotes

PAROL EVIDENCE Evidence given verbally; extraneous evidence.

■■■■

National Controls, Inc. v. Commodore Business Machines, Inc.

Seller (P) v. Buyer (D)

Cal. Ct. App., 163 Cal. App. 3d 688, 209 Cal. Rptr. 636 (1985).

NATURE OF CASE: Appeal judgment for plaintiff in breach of contract action.

FACT SUMMARY: National Controls, Inc. (P) brought a breach of contract action against Commodore Business Machines, Inc. (Commodore) (D) as a result of Commodore's (D) declining to accept and pay for 850 units of merchandise that it had previously ordered.

RULE OF LAW

An award of lost profits may be given to a "lost volume seller" if the seller proves that had the breaching buyer performed, it would have realized the profits from both the original sale and the resale of the goods.

FACTS: Commodore Business Machines, Inc. (Commodore) (D) placed a phone order with National Controls, Inc. (NCI) (P), a manufacturer of electronic weighing and measuring device, for 900 scales to be delivered in installments of 50, 150, 300 and 400. After receiving the initial 50 scales, it did not accept the additional 850. Those units were resold to National Semiconductor. The trial court concluded that NCI (P) was a "lost volume seller" who was entitled to recover the loss of profit it would have made on the sale of the 850 units to Commodore (D), notwithstanding their subsequent sale. NCI (P) was awarded $280,000 in damages at trial and Commodore (D) appealed.

ISSUE: May an award of lost profits be given to a "lost volume seller?"

HOLDING AND DECISION: (Scott, J.) Yes. An award of lost profits may be given to a "lost volume seller" if the seller proves that had the breaching buyer performed, it would have realized the profits from both the original sale and the resale of the goods. Commodore (D) contended that the trial court erred in awarding NCI (P) lost profit damages, and that even if lost profits were the appropriate measure of damages, it was entitled to credit for the proceeds of NCI's resale of those units. Damages caused by a buyer's breach or repudiation of a sales contract are generally measured by the difference between the resale price and the contract price of the goods. When this measure of damages is inappropriate, "the seller's measure of damages is the difference between the market and the contract prices as provided in Uniform Commercial Code (U.C.C.) § 2-708." An award of lost profits may be given to a seller who demonstrates that he is a "lost volume seller," i.e., even though the seller resold the goods, that sale would have been made regardless of the buyer's breach. The "lost volume seller" must prove that had the breaching buyer performed, the seller would have realized the profits from both sales. The record demonstrates that both sales to National Semiconductor and Commodore (D) were within the capacity of NCI's (P) manufacturing plant and, thus, had there been no breach it would have enjoyed the profits from both. Affirmed.

ANALYSIS

The applicable code provision here is U.C.C. § 2-708(2), which provides that "[i]f the measure of damages provided in subdivision (1) is inadequate to put the seller in as good a position as performance would have done, then the measure of damages is the profit (including reasonable overhead) which the seller would have made from full performance by the buyer, together with . . . due credit for payments or proceeds of resale." While Commodore (D) argued that it should have received credit for the resale of the units to National Semiconductor, the court followed the majority view that the set-off requirement does not apply to "lost volume sellers."

Quicknotes

LOST PROFITS The potential value of income earned or goods which are the subject of the contract; may be used in calculating damages where the contract has been breached.

LOST-VOLUME SELLER A seller who can accommodate more than one buyer and for whom a buyer's breach does not release the goods for sale to another customer; in such a case, the appropriate measure of damages is the net profit the seller would have earned pursuant to the sale.

Horton v. O'Rourke

Real estate seller (D) v. Real estate buyer (P)

Fla. 2d Dist. Ct. App., 321 So. 2d 612 (1975).

NATURE OF CASE: Appeal of judgment after a bench trial.

FACT SUMMARY: Howard P. Horton (D) appealed a judgment awarding four purchasers (P) compensatory damages for breach of four real estate contracts due to unmarketable title.

🏛 RULE OF LAW
The standard measure of contract damages giving purchasers in a land sale contract the benefit of their bargain is erroneous unless it can be shown that the seller acted in bad faith.

FACTS: Four purchasers (P) entered contracts with H & H Construction Company (H & H) (D), which was owned by Howard P. Horton (D), to purchase homes under construction on land owned by Overlord Investments, Inc. (D). When construction finished, the purchasers (P) took possession without closing under rental agreements. Closing was conditioned on clearance of title defects. Once they took possession, the purchasers (P) received notice of a federal tax lien on the property. They were assured the lien would be cleared, and they proceeded to make improvements to their rented homes. Twenty-two months later, H & H (D) informed them that the title defect could not be cleared. H & H (D) agreed to either return deposits or to enter into new rental agreements at a higher rate. About a month later, Overlord Investments (D), which was the record title holder of the land, brought suit to oust each purchaser. The purchasers (P) then filed individual suits for specific performance against Overlord Investments (D) and H & H (D), alleging a principal-agent relationship. After a bench trial, the court denied specific performance, exonerated Overlord Investments (D), and awarded the purchasers (P) pecuniary damages against H & H (D) equal to the difference between the value of the land when it should have been conveyed less the contract price that has not yet been paid.

ISSUE: Is the standard measure of contract damages giving purchasers in a land sale contract the benefit of their bargain erroneous unless it can be shown that the seller acted in bad faith?

HOLDING AND DECISION: (McNulty, C.J.) Yes. The standard measure of contract damages giving purchasers in a land sale contract the benefit of their bargain is erroneous unless it can be shown that the seller acted in bad faith. In Florida, in the absence of bad faith, the damages recoverable for breach by the seller of a contract to convey title to real estate are the purchase money paid by the purchaser, with interest and expenses from the investigation of title. In this case, damages should also include the cost of improvements made by the purchasers (P) in contemplation of the conveyance. There is no suggestion of bad faith on H & H's (D) part. The judgment is reversed.

ANALYSIS

Damages are measured to put the buyer in the position he or she would have been in had there been no contract—not the position they would have been in had there been no breach. The reason for that is (1) the sale is contingent on clearance of title, under the contract, and (2) if the seller cannot clear title, through no fault of his or her own, he or she should not be held accountable for the problem. If the seller decides not to pay to clear title, there would be evidence of bad faith, and a different measure of damages would be applied.

━━■

Quicknotes

BAD FAITH Conduct that is intentionally misleading or deceptive.

━━■

Parker v. Twentieth Century-Fox Film Corp.

Actress (P) v. Movie company (D)

Cal. Sup. Ct., 3 Cal. 3d 176, 474 P.2d 689, en banc (1970).

NATURE OF CASE: Action for damages for breach of a contract for employment.

FACT SUMMARY: MacLaine (P), an actress, was to have the lead role in the motion picture, "Bloomer Girl," to be produced by Twentieth Century-Fox Film Corp. (Fox) (D) and she was to receive $750,000 in salary. Fox (D) decided not to make the movie and offered the leading role in a film, "Big Country, Big Man," instead, which MacLaine (P) refused.

🏛 RULE OF LAW
The general measure of recovery by a wrongfully discharged employee is the amount of salary agreed upon for the period of service, less the amount which the employer affirmatively proves the employee has earned or with reasonable effort might have earned from other employment.

FACTS: Shirley MacLaine (P) was hired for the lead role in the film, "Bloomer Girl," to be produced by Twentieth Century-Fox Film Corp. (Fox) (D). She was to receive a salary of $750,000 for 14 weeks. Under the contract, MacLaine (P) was to have approval over the director or any substitute, the dance director, and the screenplay. Twentieth Century-Fox Film Corp. (Fox) (D) decided not to make the film and offered MacLaine (P) the lead in "Big Country, Big Man," which, unlike the other film, was not a musical, but a western. Also, Fox (D) did not offer MacLaine (P) approval of the director or screenplay (and there was no need for a dance director). "Bloomer Girl" was to have been filmed in Los Angeles; "Big Country, Big Man" was to be made in Australia. MacLaine (P) rejected the second film offer and sued for her salary and resulting damages.

ISSUE: Is the general measure of recovery by a wrongfully discharged employee the amount of salary agreed upon for the period of service, less the amount which the employer affirmatively proves the employee has earned or with reasonable effort might have earned from other employment?

HOLDING AND DECISION: (Burke, J.) Yes. The general measure of recovery by a wrongfully discharged employee is the amount of salary agreed upon for the period of service, less the amount which the employer affirmatively proves the employee has earned or with reasonable effort might have earned from other employment. Fox (D), in claiming that MacLaine (P) unreasonably refused the second film offer, must show that the other employment was comparable to the first, or, at least, substantially similar to that which their employee has been deprived. The employee's rejection of or failure to seek other available employment of a different or inferior kind may not be used to mitigate damages. If the western film offer were found different or inferior to the musical film offer, it makes no difference whether MacLaine (P) reasonably or unreasonably refused the second offer. The western was a different and inferior film where MacLaine (P) could not use her singing and dancing talents as in the musical. The western required travel to Australia for extensive outdoor filming rather than the use of sound stages in Los Angeles. The "Big Country" offer impaired or eliminated several rights of approval. Accordingly, as the second offer was different and inferior to the first, MacLaine (P) was awarded $750,000. Affirmed.

DISSENT: (Sullivan, C.J.) Employment which is different in kind should not be required to be accepted by the employee, but the mere existence of differences between two jobs in the same field should not be sufficient to release the employee and would effectively eliminate any obligation to attempt to minimize damage arising from a wrongful discharge.

▶ ANALYSIS

The court points out that if the other offer of employment is of a different or inferior kind, it does not matter whether the employee acts reasonably or unreasonably in rejecting the offer. The person with the duty to mitigate need not expose himself to undue risk, expense, or humiliation. It may be possible, considering the fact that MacLaine (P) made no westerns in the past, that in the management of an actress's career, such a film may have been considered a risk or, even possibly, a humiliation. Also, many cases have held that the employee is not required to accept employment unreasonably distant from the original location. The court apparently thought that Australia was unreasonably distant when MacLaine (P) was regularly working in Los Angeles and had intended to work on "Bloomer Girl" there. Note that in mitigating, the employee also does not have to accept a position of lesser rank or at a lower salary. Also, MacLaine (P) asked for damages in addition to her salary but such special damages are rarely awarded in cases of wrongful discharge. Damages for injury to the reputation of the employee are considered to be too remote and not within the contemplation of the parties. There is authority for damages when the denied employment would have enhanced the employee's

Continued on next page.

reputation such as a motion picture credit, but this has only been applied once in the United States, but is common in England. The dissent would apparently foist an unacceptable film role upon an actress. Due to the nature of the industry and its regularly accepted business practices, the majority probably kept in mind the actor's need "to feel right" about a role and script before accepting it.

■══■

Quicknotes

MITIGATION OF DAMAGES Doctrine requiring the non-breaching party to a contract to exercise ordinary care in attempting to minimize the damages incurred as a result of the breach.

■══■

In re WorldCom, Inc.

Athlete (P) v. Debtor (D)

361 B.R. 675 (Bankr. S.D.N.Y. 2007).

NATURE OF CASE: Motion for summary judgment in bankruptcy court.

FACT SUMMARY: Professional athlete Michael Jordon (P) sued to recover money owed to him under an endorsement contract with WorldCom, Inc. (MCI) (D) after MCI (D) filed for bankruptcy.

RULE OF LAW
A non-breaching party in a service contract who is not a lost volume seller has a duty to mitigate damages by reasonable effort and without substantial loss or injury.

FACTS: Professional athlete Michael Jordon (P) entered into an endorsement agreement with WorldCom, Inc. (MCI) (D) in July 1995. Under the agreement, MCI had a ten-year license to use Jordan's (P) name and likeness to advertise MCI's products and services. The agreement required a total of 16 hours of work per contract year from Jordan (P), and it did not prevent Jordan (P) from endorsing other products. For this he was to be paid a $5 million signing bonus and an annual base compensation of $2 million. In July 2002, MCI filed for bankruptcy under chapter 11, and rejected the agreement as of July 2003, under the Bankruptcy Code. Jordan (P) filed a claim in the amount of $8 million, representing $2 million for each of the payments that were due in years 2002–2005. MCI (D) argued that the claim should be reduced to $4 million because Jordan (P) had an obligation to mitigate damages and failed to do so, and that the company was under no obligation to pay Jordan for contract years 2004 and 2005, the years following MCI's (D) rejection of the agreement due to bankruptcy. Jordan (P) argued that MCI's (D) objection should be dismissed because (1) Jordan was a "lost volume seller" and therefore, had no duty to mitigate damages; (2) there was no evidence that Jordan (P) could have entered into a "substantially similar" endorsement agreement; and (3) Jordan (P) acted reasonably when he decided not to pursue other endorsements after MCI's (D) rejection of the agreement.

ISSUE: Does a non-breaching party in a service contract who is not a lost volume seller have a duty to mitigate damages by reasonable effort and without substantial loss or injury?

HOLDING AND DECISION: (Gonzalez, J.) Yes. A non-breaching party in a service contract who is not a lost volume seller has a duty to mitigate damages by reasonable effort and without substantial loss or injury. The duty to mitigate damages, or the doctrine of avoidable

consequences, bars recovery for losses suffered by a non-breaching party that could have been avoided by reasonable effort and without substantial loss or injury. First, Jordan (P) is not a "lost volume seller," and therefore had a duty to mitigate. A lost volume seller is one who has the capacity to perform the contract that was breached in addition to other potential contracts due to unlimited resources or production capacity. But to qualify as a lost volume seller, he must prove (1) that he had the capability to perform both contracts simultaneously; (2) that the second contract would have been profitable; and (3) that he would have entered into the second contract if the first contract had not been terminated. A key aspect of the lost volume seller theory is that the original contract and the second contract are independent events, because the lost volume seller's intent to enter into new contracts is the same before and after a purchaser's breach. Jordan (P) focuses on the first element, arguing he is a lost volume seller because he could have entered into endorsement contracts that ran concurrently with his MCI (D) agreement, and therefore, additional endorsement contracts would not have been substitutes for the MCI (D) agreement and would not have mitigated damages. But he failed to show that he *would have* entered into subsequent transactions. The evidence showed that he did not have the subjective intent to take on additional endorsements, regardless of the breach of contract with MCI (D), because he did not want to dilute his image. Because the evidence shows that Jordan (P) would not have entered into subsequent agreements, he failed to establish that he is a lost volume seller, and he is therefore not relieved from the duty to mitigate damages. Second, Jordan (P) failed to make reasonable efforts to avoid consequences or minimize his damages. He admitted that he implemented a business strategy of not accepting new endorsements in order to avoid diluting his image. Third, Jordan's (P) beliefs that another endorsement would dilute his impact as an endorser or harm his reputation were not reasonable justifications for not mitigating damages. And his argument that he acted reasonably by focusing solely on his efforts to become an NBA team owner is not support for an argument that he was relieved of his obligation to mitigate damages. Jordan (P) failed to mitigate damages, which was his duty, but a new hearing is necessary to determine what Jordan (P) could have received if he had made reasonable efforts to mitigate.

Continued on next page.

▶ *ANALYSIS*

The lost volume seller theory is based on the idea that some sellers are in the business of constantly offering a particular service or product, so that finding a substitute for a lost opportunity due to breach by another party is impossible. For example, Disneyworld has a virtually unlimited capacity for attracting guests to the park. If one customer breaches a contract to attend, her spot will likely be filled by another guest, but that second guest would have been admitted at some point anyway. So Disney cannot make up for the breach.

■▬■

Quicknotes

LOST VOLUME SELLER A seller who can accommodate more than one buyer and for whom a buyer's breach does not release the goods for sale to another customer; in such a case, the appropriate measure of damages is the net profit the seller would have earned pursuant to the sale.

MITIGATION OF DAMAGES Doctrine requiring the non-breaching party to a contract to exercise ordinary care in attempting to minimize the damages incurred as a result of the breach.

■▬■

Peevyhouse v. Garland Coal Mining Co.

Farm owner (P) v. Coal mining lessee (D)

Okla. Sup. Ct., 382 P.2d 109 (1962), *cert. denied*, 375 U.S. 906 (1963).

NATURE OF CASE: Cross-appeals from award of damages for breach of contract.

FACT SUMMARY: Garland Coal Mining Co. (D) promised it would perform restorative and remedial work on the Peevyhouses' (P) farm at the end of the lease period, but then argued that the cost of the repair work would far exceed the total value of the farm.

RULE OF LAW
Where a contract provision breached is merely incidental to the main purpose, and where the economic benefit which would result to lessor by full performance of the work is grossly disproportionate to the cost of performance, the damages which lessor may recover are limited to the diminution in value resulting to the premises because of the nonperformance.

FACTS: The Peevyhouses (P) owned a farm with coal deposits on it. This land was leased in November 1954 to Garland Coal Mining Co. (Garland) (D) for five years for coal mining purposes. Garland (D) also agreed to perform restorative and remedial work at the end of the lease period at a cost estimated at about $29,000. After Garland (D) failed to restore the land, the Peevyhouses (P) sued for $25,000. Garland (D) introduced testimony at trial as to the diminution of value of the farm due to Garland's (D) failure to perform under the contract. The jury awarded the Peevyhouses (P) $5,000, which was more than the total value of the farm even after the remedial work was done, but only a fraction of the cost of performance. The Peevyhouses (P) appealed, arguing that damages should be the cost to obtain performance of the work not done due to Garland's (D) default.

ISSUE: Where a contract provision breached was merely incidental to the main purpose, and where the economic benefit which would result to lessor by full performance of the work is grossly disproportionate to the cost of performance, are the damages which lessor may recover limited to the diminution in value resulting to the premises because of the nonperformance?

HOLDING AND DECISION: (Jackson, J.) Yes. Where a contract provision breached was merely incidental to the main purpose, and where the economic benefit which would result to lessor by full performance of the work is grossly disproportionate to the cost of performance, the damages which lessor may recover are limited to the diminution in value resulting to the premises because of the nonperformance. The damages recoverable are

to be a reasonable amount that is not contrary to substantial justice and that prevents the Peevyhouses (P) from recovering a greater amount for breach of an obligation than would have been gained by full performance. The judgment was excessive and should be reduced to $300. Affirmed.

DISSENT: (Irwin, J.) Garland (D) knew that the cost of performance would be disproportionate to the value or benefits received by the Peevyhouses (P) when it entered into the contract. The function of a court is to enforce a contract as it is written. The Peevyhouses (P) were entitled to specific performance, or failing that, the cost of that performance.

ANALYSIS

The Restatement (Second) of Contracts, § 348 reflects this court's decision. Section 348(2)(a) states that "if a breach results in defective or unfinished construction and the loss in value to the injured party is not proved with sufficient certainty, he may recover damages based on the diminution in the market price of the property caused by the breach." Under § 348 (2)(b), he may, in the alternative, recover damages based on "the reasonable cost of completing performance or of remedying the defects if that cost is not clearly disproportionate to the probable loss of value."

Quicknotes

BREACH OF CONTRACT Unlawful failure by a party to perform its obligations pursuant to contract.

NONPERFORMANCE Failure to perform a duty.

Patton v. Mid-Continent Systems, Inc.

Truck stop operator (P) v. Credit card supplier (D)

841 F.2d 742 (7th Cir. 1988).

NATURE OF CASE: Appeal from award of punitive damages for breach of contract.

FACT SUMMARY: Patton (P) contended he was entitled to punitive damages for breach of contract.

🏛 RULE OF LAW
Punitive damages are recoverable for breach of contract only where the breach includes elements of fraud, malice, oppression, or gross negligence.

FACTS: Patton (P), an operator of truck stops, agreed to honor Mid-Continent Systems, Inc.'s (Mid-Continent) (D) credit cards in return for an agreement that they would have an exclusive on the acceptance in a specified territory. Mid-Continent (D) allowed other truck stops the ability to accept the card in the same territory, and Patton (P) sued for breach. The jury returned a verdict awarding Patton (P) both compensatory and punitive damages. Mid-Continent (D) appealed on the basis it was error to award punitive damages for breach of contract.

ISSUE: Are punitive damages recoverable for breach of contract in the absence of fraud, malice, oppression, or gross negligence?

HOLDING AND DECISION: (Posner, J.) No. Punitive damages are not recoverable for breach of contract in the absence of fraud, malice, oppression, or gross negligence. The facts in this case do not establish any type of intentional conduct in the commission of the breach. As a result, punitive damages were improperly awarded, and the order must be vacated and the case remanded.

▌ *ANALYSIS*

Breach of contract is a strict liability concept. Regardless of fault, if the contractual obligations are not fulfilled, a breach occurs. Punitive damages aimed at punishing certain acts can only be appropriate where the conduct is intentional. In the area of breach of conduct, such conduct must also include an ill will toward the plaintiff.

■══■

Quicknotes

PUNITIVE DAMAGES Damages exceeding the actual injury suffered for the purposes of punishment, deterrence and comfort to plaintiff.

■══■

Wassenaar v. Panos

Employee (P) v. Employer (D)

Wisc. Sup. Ct., 111 Wis. 2d 518, 331 N.W.2d 357 (1983).

NATURE OF CASE: Appeal in breach of employment contract suit.

FACT SUMMARY: Wassenaar (P) brought suit against his former employer, Panos (D), for breach of an employment contract.

🏛 RULE OF LAW
The standard measure of damages in wrongful discharge cases is the salary the employee would have earned during the unexpired term of the contract plus the expenses of securing other employment reduced by the income the employee has earned, will earn, or with reasonable diligence could earn, during that term.

FACTS: Panos (D) terminated Wassenaar's (P) employment 21 months prior to the contract's expiration date. Wassenaar (P) was unemployed for two and a half months before obtaining other employment. The trial court found that Panos (D) terminated the employment without just cause. The jury awarded $24,640 in damages, which was the sum the employee had calculated as his damages on the basis of the stipulated damages clause of the contract, and which represented his salary for 21 months, the unexpired term of the contract. The court of appeals reversed, holding the stipulated damages clause unenforceable as a penalty and remanding the case to the circuit court for a new trial on the issue of damages.

ISSUE: Is the standard measure of damages in wrongful discharge cases the salary the employee would have earned during the unexpired term of the contract plus the expenses of securing other employment reduced by the income the employee has earned, will earn, or with reasonable diligence could earn, during that term?

HOLDING AND DECISION: (Abrahamson, J.) Yes. The standard measure of damages in wrongful discharge cases are the salary the employee would have earned during the unexpired term of the contract plus the expenses of securing other employment reduced by the income the employee has earned, will earn, or with reasonable diligence could earn, during that term. While this court agrees with the appeals court that the validity of a stipulated damages clause is a question of law for the trial judge and not a mixed question of law and fact for the jury, this does not automatically relieve the trial court of its duty to consider evidence or give the appellate court free discretion to review the trial court's decision. In deciding whether the stipulated damages clause is valid, the trial court should examine the relevant circumstances. The test

of validity to be applied in determining whether a stipulated damages clause is valid is whether the clause was reasonable under the totality of the circumstances. The reasonableness test strikes a balance between the two competing policies in favor and against enforcement of these clauses by ensuring that the court respects the parties' bargain but prevents abuse. In determining whether a clause is reasonable, relevant factors include: (1) whether the parties intended to provide for damages or a penalty; (2) whether the injury was caused by the breach or is incapable of accurate estimate at the time of contract; and (3) whether the stipulated damages were a reasonable forecast of the harm caused by the breach. The first factor, the subjective intent of the parties, has little bearing on whether the clause is objectively reasonable. The second factor, or the "difficulty of ascertainment test," provides that the greater the difficulty of estimating or proving damages, the more likely the stipulated damages will be reasonable. The third factor measures the reasonableness of the parties' forecast by looking at the clause from the time of contracting and the time of breach. Here Panos (D) argued that the stipulated damages clause was void as a penalty because the harm was capable of estimation at the time of contract formation and relatively easy to prove at trial. Panos (D) also argued that calculating damages based on the entire wage for the unexpired term results in a windfall to the employee (P). The standard measure of damages in wrongful discharge cases are the salary the employee would have earned during the unexpired term of the contract plus the expenses of securing other employment reduced by the income the employee has earned, will earn, or with reasonable diligence could earn, during that term. Such damages are generally ascertainable at the time of trial. When calculating damages for wrongful discharge, the court rarely awards consequential damages. However, the arguments against consequential damages fail when the parties foresee the possibility of damages not usually awarded by law and agree on an estimated amount. Here the parties' estimate of anticipated damages was reasonable when consequential damages are taken into account. The contract formula of full salary for the period after the breach is a fair measure of damages. The judgment of the trial court is affirmed.

▶ ANALYSIS

Consequential damages may be awarded in breach of employment cases where the actual harm suffered and damages that would be awarded are not the same. However, where, such as here, the parties have contracted in

Continued on next page.

anticipation of such damages, and the stipulated damages clause is a reasonable reflection of the harm actually incurred, then the clause is valid and enforceable. Here Panos (D) did not meet its burden in showing that the clause was unreasonable.

■▬■

Quicknotes

CONSEQUENTIAL DAMAGES Monetary compensation that may be recovered in order to compensate for injuries or losses sustained as a result of damages that are not the direct or foreseeable result of the act of a party, but that nevertheless are the consequence of such act and which must be specifically pled and demonstrated.

WRONGFUL DISCHARGE Unlawful termination of an individual's employment.

■▬■

Kvassay v. Murray

Seller (P) v. Buyer (D)

Kan. Ct. App., 15 Kan. App. 2d 426, 808 P.2d 896 (1991).

NATURE OF CASE: Appeal from a decision nullifying a liquidated damages clause.

FACT SUMMARY: Kvassay (P) brought suit seeking liquidated damages from Murray (D) for breaching a contract for the sale of baklava.

RULE OF LAW
A stipulation for damages upon a future breach of contract can comprise a valid liquidated damages clause if the set amount is determined to be reasonable and the damages are difficult to ascertain.

FACTS: Kvassay (P) contracted to sell 24,000 cases of baklava [a Greek pastry] to Murray (D) at a unit cost of $19.00 per case. The sales were to span a year's duration and the contract included a clause stating that if Murray (D) refused delivery that Kvassay (P) would be entitled to damages in the amount of $5.00 per case. After accepting delivery of some 3,000 cases of baklava and encountering difficulty making payments, Murray (D) refused to purchase any more baklava. Kvassay (P) brought suit for breach to enforce the liquidated damages clause, but the trial court ruled that the clause was invalid and unenforceable because the damage amount was unreasonably high. Kvassay (P) sought review with the court of appeals.

ISSUE: Can a stipulation for damages upon a future breach of contract comprise a valid liquidated damages clause if the set amount is determined to be reasonable and the damages are difficult to ascertain?

HOLDING AND DECISION: (Walker, J.) Yes. A stipulation for damages upon a future breach of contract can comprise a valid liquidated damages clause if the set amount is determined to be reasonable and the damages are difficult to ascertain. Liquidated damages clauses in sales contracts are governed by Uniform Commercial Code (U.C.C.) § 2-718, as adopted by the Kansas legislature. This section provides three criteria for determining if the clause is reasonable: (1) the anticipated or actual harm caused by the breach; (2) the difficulty of proving loss; and (3) the difficulty of obtaining an adequate remedy. The trial court compared Kvassay's (P) prior income to what he would receive under the liquidated damages cause, which was an inappropriate measure. When a buyer breaches a sales contract, damages are typically designed to place the seller in the same position as if the contract had been fulfilled. Consequently, the proper measure to evaluate if the liquidated damages clause is reasonable is to compare it to the actual lost profits from the breach. Evidence of lost profits was excluded from the jury at trial, and this amount provides the appropriate measurement under § 2-718. This court reverses and remands with the instruction for the trial court to employ the appropriate measure when evaluating if the liquidated damages clause is reasonable.

ANALYSIS

The court of appeals did review the evidence that was admitted at trial concerning "pre-contract" profit estimates that Kvassay (P) had calculated when setting his price for the baklava. This evidence appeared to show that the liquidated damages set in the contract were unreasonably high, but without an evaluation of "actual" lost profits, it is impossible to properly apply the three-part measure outlined in the U.C.C. Typically contracting parties are allowed to set their own terms, and if the parties agreed on a set amount of damages it would seem inappropriate for a court to intervene. However, while courts are not supposed to infringe on the freedom to contract, the courts will intervene in instances where terms are unconscionable. Setting liquidated damages higher than the expected profit from fulfilling the contract is one example of when unconscionable terms will be invalidated.

■=■

Quicknotes

LIQUIDATED DAMAGES An amount of money specified in a contract representing the damages owed in the event of breach.

■=■

Wedner v. Fidelity Security Systems, Inc.

Alarm service leaser (P) v. Alarm service provider (D)

Pa. Super. Ct., 228 Pa. Super. 67, 307 A.2d 429 (1973).

NATURE OF CASE: Appeal from judgment for plaintiff in action for breach of contract.

FACT SUMMARY: Fidelity Security Systems, Inc. (D) had a limitation on liability provision in its contract with Wedner (P).

🏛 RULE OF LAW
Unless public policy is offended, private parties may contractually limit their liability for breach or negligence.

FACTS: Wedner (P) leased Fidelity Security Systems, Inc.'s (Fidelity) (D) alarm service. The contract provided that Fidelity's (D) liability would be limited to the cost of one year's service for its negligence or breach of contract. Wedner (P) suffered a $46,180 loss as the result of a robbery due to the failure of the alarm system. Wedner (P) sued Fidelity (D) for this amount, and it defended on the ground that the contract limited its liability to $312. Wedner (P) alleged that this was an unenforceable liquidated damage provision unrelated to any losses actually sustained. The first trial ended in a nonsuit and grant of a new trial. The second trial resulted in an award to Wedner (P) of only liquidated damages of $312. The court en banc dismissed filed exceptions and Wedner (P) appealed.

ISSUE: May parties to a private contract limit their liability for breach or negligence if public policy is not offended?

HOLDING AND DECISION: (Watkins, J.) Yes. Unless public policy is offended, private parties may contractually limit their liability for breach or negligence. The provision herein is not a penalty or liquidated damage provision. Rather, it is a contractual limitation on liability for loss associated with negligence or breach of contract. The parties occupied an equal bargaining position, and the limitation does not violate public policy. We find that parties to a private contract may contractually limit their liability absent a statute to the contrary or a finding that the provision offends public policy. Affirmed.

DISSENT: (Cercone, J.) The same rule to a limitation on liability provision should be applied to a liquidated damages provision. If the limitation is unreasonable or not related to the probable loss, it would be unenforceable. A contract must provide for at least a minimally adequate remedy. The clause herein is unreasonable.

▶ ANALYSIS

Consequential damages may be limited or excluded unless the limitation or exclusion is unconscionable. Limitations on consequential damages for injury to the person in the case of consumer goods is prima facie unconscionable but limitations on damages where the loss is commercial is not. Restatement of Contracts §§ 574, 575 and Uniform Commercial Code § 2-719 (3).

United States v. Algernon Blair, Inc.

Federal government (P) v. Contractor (D)

479 F.2d 638 (4th Cir. 1973).

NATURE OF CASE: Action to recover in quantum meruit the value of labor and equipment furnished.

FACT SUMMARY: Coastal Steel Erectors, a subcontractor, brought suit in the name of the United States (P) against Algernon Blair, Inc. (D), the prime contractor on a government project, to recover in quantum meruit the value of the labor and materials it had furnished up to the point at which it justifiably ceased work.

RULE OF LAW
A promisee is allowed to recover in quantum meruit the value of services he gave to a defendant who breached their contract irrespective of whether he would have lost money had the contract been fully performed and would thus be precluded from recovering in a suit on the contract.

FACTS: Algernon Blair, Inc. (Algernon) (D) was the prime contractor on a government project. Coastal Steel Erectors (Coastal), a subcontractor on the project, furnished materials and labor up to the point that Algernon (D) breached its contract with Coastal. At that point, Coastal ceased work and brought an action under the Miller Act, in the name of the United States (P), to recover in quantum meruit the value of the equipment and labor it had theretofore supplied. The district court found Algernon (D) had breached the contract, but held that Coastal would have lost money on the contract had it been fully performed. For this reason, it denied recovery, and Coastal appealed.

ISSUE: Is a promisee allowed to recover in quantum meruit the value of services he gave to a defendant who breached their contract irrespective of whether he would have lost money had the contract been fully performed and would thus be precluded from recovering in a suit on the contract?

HOLDING AND DECISION: (Craven, J.) Yes. A promisee is allowed to recover in quantum meruit the value of services he gave to a defendant who breached their contract irrespective of whether he would have lost money had the contract been fully performed and would thus be precluded from recovering in a suit on the contract. Regardless of whether or not the promisee would have lost money had he completed the contract, he can recover in quantum meruit the value of the services he gave to a defendant who breached the contract. It is an accepted principle of contract law, often applied in the case of construction contracts, that the promisee upon breach has the option to forgo any suit on the contract and claim only the reasonable value of his performance. Thus,

Coastal can recover for the equipment and labor it supplied despite the fact that it would have lost money on the contract and would thus have been unable to recover in a suit on the contract. Recovery in quantum meruit is measured by the reasonable value of the performance and is undiminished by any loss which would have been incurred by complete performance. Reversed and remanded for findings as to the reasonable value of the equipment and labor supplied by Coastal.

ANALYSIS

The applicable standard in determining the "reasonable value" of services rendered is the amount for which such services could have been purchased from one in the plaintiff's position at the time and place the services were rendered. Some courts have held that the contract price is not only evidence of the reasonable value but is a ceiling on recovery, but others disagree. The rationale is that one should not recover more for part performance than he would have upon full performance.

Quicknotes

QUANTUM MERUIT Equitable doctrine allowing recovery for labor and materials provided by one party, even though no contract was entered into, in order to avoid unjust enrichment by the benefited party.

Oliver v. Campbell

Discharged attorney (P) v. Client (D)

Cal. Sup. Ct., 43 Cal. 2d 298, 273 P.2d 15, en banc (1954).

NATURE OF CASE: Appeal in action in quantum meruit.

FACT SUMMARY: Oliver (P), an attorney, sued for the reasonable value of his services ($10,000) after being discharged after partially performing on a contract which would have paid him $750 if fully performed.

> ## 🏛 RULE OF LAW
> Where an employment contract has been fully performed so that all that remains is the payment of a liquidated amount, a wrongfully discharged employee can only sue for the contract price.

FACTS: Oliver (P), an attorney, agreed to represent Campbell (D) in a suit for separate maintenance and in a cross-complaint for divorce. Oliver's (P) fee was fixed at $750. The trial became incredibly complicated and lasted 29 days. At the end of trial, but before the judge had rendered a verdict, Campbell (D) discharged Oliver (P) and refused to pay him the balance due on the contract. Campbell (D) died shortly thereafter and Oliver (P) submitted a bill for $10,000, as the reasonable value of his services, to the estate. After the claim was rejected, Oliver (P) brought suit in quantum meruit for the reasonable value of his services alleging that he had been wrongfully discharged. The court denied relief alleging that Oliver (P) could only sue for the contract price since it was set by the contract.

ISSUE: May a wrongfully discharged employee who has only partially performed the contract bring a suit in quantum meruit for the reasonable value of his services?

HOLDING AND DECISION: (Carter, J.) Yes. If the employee is wrongfully discharged before fully completing the contract, he may treat it as rescinded and sue for the reasonable value of his services in quantum meruit. Since the contract has been rescinded, the price fixed in the contract does not apply and the employee may recover the reasonable value of his services previously performed even though they exceed the entire contract price. If the employee has fully performed, he may only bring suit for the contract price. If the contract has been fully performed and the only duty remaining is the payment of a liquidated amount to the employee, the action should be on the contract, not in quantum meruit. This is the case herein. The trial was over and no further duties remained except signing any final orders. In such cases, the aggrieved employee may only bring suit on the contract. Judgment for

the balance due on the contract should have been awarded to Oliver (P). Reversed and remanded.

DISSENT: (Schauer, J.) The contract did not limit Oliver's (P) duties to the trial, but to a final judgment on the case (i.e., appeals). The court found that the reasonable value of his services was $5,000 and Oliver (P) should receive that amount or a new trial.

▶ ANALYSIS

The same rationale and measure of damages applies in agency cases. Restatement of Contracts, § 347. Normally restitution (quantum meruit in cases involving personal services since the services cannot be returned) and an action on the contract are mutually exclusive remedies. The plaintiff must elect to pursue either one or the other since one is founded on the existence of a contract while the other treats it as repudiated. The court in *Oliver* avoids this problem by finding that since Oliver (P) had fully performed and the value of his services was fixed at $750, the contract price.

■=■

Quicknotes

QUANTUM MERUIT Equitable doctrine allowing recovery for labor and materials provided by one party, even though no contract was entered into, in order to avoid unjust enrichment by the benefited party.

WRONGFUL DISCHARGE Unlawful termination of an individual's employment.

■=■

Martin v. Schoenberger

[Parties not identified.]

Pa. Sup. Ct., 8 W. & c. S. 367 (1845).

NATURE OF CASE: Action for breach of contract.

FACT SUMMARY: [Facts not stated in casebook excerpt.]

🏛 RULE OF LAW
A party may not recover the contract price where he has only partially performed or has not performed at all.

FACTS: [Facts not stated in casebook excerpt.]

ISSUE: May a party who has not performed or who has only tendered partial performance recover the contract price in a breach of contract action?

HOLDING AND DECISION: [Judge not stated in casebook excerpt.] No. A party who has not performed or who has only tendered part performance cannot recover the contract price in a breach of contract action. To allow such a recovery would destroy confidence between men and in contract law. It would allow a party to only partially perform to his convenience or cupidity.

▶ *ANALYSIS*

Generally, in such situations, where plaintiff is not in breach, he may recover lost profits or the reasonable value of his services in quantum meruit. These remedies take into account the fact that no or only partial performance has been rendered. They allow recovery for what the non-breaching party has actually lost or the value of what has actually been given to the other party, thus providing adequate relief for the breach.

■═■

Quicknotes

QUANTUM MERUIT Equitable doctrine allowing recovery for labor and materials provided by one party, even though no contract was entered into, in order to avoid unjust enrichment by the benefited party.

■═■

Lancellotti v. Thomas

Purchaser of business (P) v. Business owner (D)

Pa. Super. Ct., 341 Pa. Super. 1, 491 A.2d 117 (1985).

NATURE OF CASE: Appeal of award of damages for breach of contract.

FACT SUMMARY: Lancellotti (P) backed out of an agreement to purchase a business from Thomas (D) who had been paid $25,000.

🏛 RULE OF LAW
A party breaching a contract may be entitled to restitution to prevent forfeiture.

FACTS: Lancellotti (P) contracted to buy Thomas's (D) business. Pursuant to this, Lancellotti (P) paid $25,000. A dispute subsequently arose regarding certain improvements called for in the contract, and Lancellotti (P) eventually abandoned the business. Lancellotti (P) sued for a return of the $25,000. Thomas (D) counterclaimed for $6,665 in rent, which had been deferred under the contract. The trial court instructed the jury that a breaching party was not entitled to restitution. The jury awarded Thomas (D) $6,665. Lancellotti (P) appealed.

ISSUE: May a party breaching a contract be entitled to restitution to prevent forfeiture?

HOLDING AND DECISION: (Spaeth, J.) Yes. A party breaching a contract may be entitled to restitution to prevent forfeiture. The common law rule held that a breaching party was not so entitled, on the premise that a wrongdoer should not profit from his wrongdoing. However, the common law rule has been slowly eroded. Recognizing that the purpose of contract law is not to punish, courts have increasingly permitted breaching parties to recover if forfeiture would otherwise occur and prejudice to the nonbreaching party will not occur. This is the position of the Restatement. Here, the trial court instructed the jury that a breaching party could not recover, so once the jury found that Lancellotti (P) had breached, his recourse was foreclosed. The matter must be remanded for a determination of whether restitution would prejudice Thomas (D).

DISSENT: (Tamilia, J.) Any departure from the common law rule must come from the Pennsylvania Supreme Court, which as yet has not seen fit to change the common law rule in this jurisdiction.

▶ ANALYSIS

The acceptance of the rule stated here has been slow in coming. While the law of contracts is not criminal law, a breaching party does appear to have "done wrong." For this reason, the law has been reluctant to help the breaching party. The rule has evolved as contract law has come to focus more on economics and less on morality.

Quicknotes

FORFEITURE The loss of a right or interest as a penalty for failing to fulfill an obligation.

RESTITUTION The return or restoration of what the defendant has gained in a transaction to prevent the unjust enrichment of the defendant.

Centex Homes Corp. v. Boag

Condominium builders (P) v. Apartment purchasers (D)

N.J. Super. Ct., 128 N.J. Super. 385, 320 A.2d 194 (1974).

NATURE OF CASE: Action for breach of contract and specific performance.

FACT SUMMARY: Boag (D) backed out of a contract to purchase a new condominium apartment, stopping payment on a $6,870 check issued to Centex Homes Corp. (P).

🏛 RULE OF LAW
Specific performance should not be granted except where the vendor of real property will suffer an economic injury for which damages at law will not be adequate or equitable considerations warrant a granting of the decree.

FACTS: Boag (D) agreed to purchase a new condominium apartment from a development owned by Centex Homes Corp. (Centex) (P). A contract was signed, and Boag (D) gave Centex checks for $525 and $6,870. Boag (D) subsequently learned that he would have to leave town because of his job, and he stopped payment on the $6,870 check, informing Centex (P) that he would not perform. Centex (P) brought suit for specific performance. Boag (D) defended, alleging that damages would adequately compensate Centex (P) for the breach, and specific performance should be denied.

ISSUE: Should specific performance be granted only where the remedy at law is inadequate or equitable factors mandate such an award?

HOLDING AND DECISION: (Gelman, J.) Yes. Specific performance should not automatically be granted to the vendor of real property. We adopt a rule that specific performance should be granted the vendor of real property only where he will suffer an economic injury when damages at law will not be adequate or other equitable factors (e.g., change in situation) mandate such a result. Since land is deemed unique, specific performance is always available to vendees. However, the doctrine of mutuality of remedies no longer requires that the exact same remedies be offered to all parties to the contract. It is enough that the injured party has sufficient remedies available to adequately compensate him for a breach. Condominiums in a large development are not unique; prices at which they are offered to the public are fixed; variances in price can be calculated. Centex (P) can, therefore, determine its actual damages. Damages under the liquidated damage provision are limited to funds in Centex's (P) possession, $525. Count for damage relief dismissed.

ANALYSIS

Centex is a marked departure from the normal rule that land is unique and specific performance should be routinely granted. While *Centex* is somewhat limited to the sale of condominiums, the court clearly indicates that it should be applied to other forms of real estate where money damages are adequate. In *Silverman v. Alcoa Plaza Associates*, 37 A.D. 2d 166 (1971), the court found that shares of stock plus a proprietary lease constituted a sale of personalty.

Quicknotes

INADEQUACY OF REMEDY AT LAW Requirement for a suit to be brought in equity that the available legal remedy be unsatisfactory for the desired relief.

SPECIFIC PERFORMANCE An equitable remedy whereby the court requires the parties to perform their obligations pursuant to a contract.

Laclede Gas Co. v. Amoco Oil Co.

Residential gas distributor (P) v. Propane gas supplier (D)

522 F.2d 33 (8th Cir. 1975).

NATURE OF CASE: Appeal in action for injunctive relief or damages for breach of contract.

FACT SUMMARY: Laclede Gas Co. (P) agreed to purchase all the propane used by it from Amoco Oil (D).

🏛 **RULE OF LAW**
A requirements contract may be specifically enforced.

FACTS: Laclede Gas Co. (Laclede) (P) agreed to purchase all of the propane used by it from Amoco Oil (D). Amoco Oil (D) refused to supply propane, and Laclede (P) sought a mandatory injunction prohibiting the continuing breach. The court found that no valid contract existed since it lacked mutuality. Laclede (P) appealed, alleging that this was a requirements contract which could be specifically enforced by way of an injunction.

ISSUE: May a requirements contract be specifically enforced?

HOLDING AND DECISION: (Ross, J.) Yes. A requirements contract is valid and binding. Mutuality exists, and both parties must act in good faith. Mutuality of remedy is not required to specifically enforce the contract. Laclede (P) has a right to specifically enforce its requirements contract by way of a mandatory injunction. The court may resolve any ambiguities. As for the amount which must be supplied, this is based on Laclede's (P) reasonable needs. The remedy at law herein is not adequate. To be adequate, it must be as certain, prompt, complete, and efficient to attain the ends of justice as specific performance. This was a long-term contract, and there is no guarantee that present supplies will be available in the future. Damages would be difficult to predict. For these reasons, specific performance should be granted. Reversed and remanded.

▶ **ANALYSIS**

As provided by § 370 of the Restatement of Contracts (1932), specific enforcement will not be decreed unless the terms of the contract are so expressed that the court can determine with reasonable certainty what is the duty of each party and the conditions under which performance is due. In *Boeving v. Vandover*, 240 Mo. App. 117 (1949), specific performance of a contract to sell an automobile was granted because of the extreme shortage of new cars.

■══■

Quicknotes

BILATERAL CONTRACT An agreement pursuant to which each party promises to undertake an obligation, or to forbear from acting, at some time in the future.

ILLUSORY PROMISE A promise that is not legally enforceable because performance of the obligation by the promisor is completely within his discretion.

REQUIREMENTS CONTRACT An agreement pursuant to which one party agrees to purchase all his required goods or services from the other party exclusively for a specified time period.

■══■

Karpinski v. Ingrasci

Oral surgeon employer (P) v. Oral surgeon employee (D)

N.Y. Ct. App., 28 N.Y.2d 45, 268 N.E.2d 751 (1971).

NATURE OF CASE: Appeal from reversal of grant of injunctive relief and damages for breach of a restrictive covenant against competition.

FACT SUMMARY: Karpinski (P), an oral surgeon, hired Ingrasci (D), an oral surgeon, in order to open a second office on terms where Ingrasci (D), should he decide to terminate his employment with Karpinski (P), would not be able to compete in a five-county regional area with Karpinski (P). Violation of the restrictive covenant against competition would make Ingrasci (D) liable for $40,000 damages to Karpinski (P).

RULE OF LAW
A member of one of the learned professions, upon becoming an assistant to another member thereof, may, upon a sufficient consideration, bind himself not to engage in the practice of his profession upon the termination of his employment contract, and relief for violation of these contracts will not be denied merely because the agreement is unlimited as to time, where the area of restraint is limited and reasonable.

FACTS: Karpinski (P), an oral surgeon in Cayuga County, New York, desired to expand his practice. His business was nearly all by referral from dentists. Upon being told it was difficult for many patients to travel to his office, Karpinski (P) decided to open a second, more centrally located office and hired Ingrasci (D), a new oral surgeon, to man it. The employment agreement contained a restrictive covenant that Ingrasci (D) agreed to never practice dentistry and/or oral surgery in Cayuga, Cortland, Seneca, Tompkins, or Ontario except in association with Karpinski (P) or if Karpinski (P) terminated the agreement and hired another oral surgeon. In consideration, Ingrasci (D) executed a $40,000 promissory note to Karpinski (P) to become payable if Ingrasci (D) left Karpinski (P) and practiced dentistry and/or oral surgery in any of the five stated counties. When the contract expired after three years, the parties were unable to reach a new accord, and Ingrasci (D) opened his own practice a week later, with 90 percent of his patients being referrals in the five-county area. Karpinski (P) had to close his second office. Karpinski (P) sought an injunction and money damages. The trial court granted the injunction, but the appellate court reversed. Karpinski (P) appealed.

ISSUE: Is the restrictive covenant covering a geographic area reasonable and enforceable? Can monetary damages be awarded in addition to the equitable relief of injunction?

HOLDING AND DECISION: (Fuld, C.J.) Yes, to both questions. First, while there are strong considerations of public policy militating against approving the loss of one's livelihood, if the covenant is reasonable it will be upheld. A reasonable territorial limitation is determined upon the facts of each case. Here, the five counties, being small and rural, were the areas from which Karpinski (P) obtained his patients. Because the covenant covers only the area over which his practice extended, the territorial limitation is reasonable. As long as the territorial limit is reasonable, the covenant will not be struck down because it is unlimited in time. Because Ingrasci (D) opened his practice after only a week, it is clear that his patients were derived from his association with Karpinski (P). However, because the covenant restricts Ingrasci (D) from the practice of dentistry and oral surgery, it is unreasonable to the extent that Ingrasci (D) cannot practice dentistry while Karpinski (P) only practices oral surgery. The court, in balancing the equities, can sever the restrictions down to an appropriate size. The court, in granting injunctive relief, will only prohibit Ingrasci (D) from practicing oral surgery in the five-county area but not prevent his practice of dentistry. Protection will only be granted in the direct area of competition. As for damages, money damages can be granted with injunctive relief where it appears from the whole of the contract and circumstances that performance of the covenant was intended and not merely payment of damages in case of breach. Because the injunction will halt further damages, it would be grossly unfair to award the total amount of the promissory note. Instead, it should be determined what the amount of actual damages suffered by Karpinski (P) is and award that amount. Reversed and remanded.

ANALYSIS

The ancient test of a geographic restriction was whether it covered the entire state (illegal) or part of it (legal). Today, it is a question of reasonableness. Usually, it is illegal if it is shown to be a restriction greater than the goodwill of the enterprise, but this pertains more to cases where the seller of the business agrees not to compete with the purchaser. Here, reasonableness is found by examining the extent of territorial limitation, which here was acceptable because it did not go beyond the region served by the practice. It must also be determined that the former employee will not suffer an undue hardship by not being allowed to compete. There is a natural desire by the court not to restrain trade.

Continued on next page.

The court, therefore, used its power to sever the agreement and limit Ingrasci (D) to not practicing oral surgery and allowing his practice of dentistry.

■━━■

Quicknotes

RESTRICTIVE COVENANT A promise contained in a deed to limit the uses to which the property will be made.

■━━■

Howard Schultz & Associates v. Broniec

Contracting employer (P) v. Auditor employee (D)

Ga. Sup. Ct., 239 Ga. 181, 236 S.E.2d 265 (1977).

NATURE OF CASE: Appeal in action for injunctive relief.

FACT SUMMARY: Broniec (D) agreed not to compete or disclose any information learned from his audit of Howard Schultz & Associates (P).

🏛 RULE OF LAW
A court will not rewrite an unenforceable restrictive covenant so that it is valid.

FACTS: Howard Schultz & Associates (Schultz) (P) hired Broniec (D) to audit accounts. As part of the employment agreement, Broniec (D) agreed to not engage, directly or indirectly, as principal, agent, employer, or employee, in any capacity, in a business which would be in competition with Schultz (P). The restrictive covenant was to last for two years and would apply to any territory in which Schultz (P) operated. The covenant also applied to the disclosure of any information obtained from Schultz's (P) business or the solicitation of its customers. Broniec (D) subsequently terminated his employment. Schultz (P) brought an action to enforce the covenant by injunction, alleging that Broniec's (D) conduct had violated it. Schultz's (P) suit was dismissed on the ground that the clause was unenforceable since it was overbroad. Schultz (P) appealed, alleging that the court should rewrite the clause to constitute a valid restriction.

ISSUE: May an unenforceable restrictive covenant be rewritten by the court so that it will be valid?

HOLDING AND DECISION: (Hill, J.) No. If a restrictive covenant is overbroad and is rendered unenforceable, the courts will not engage in rewriting it in a narrower scope to render it valid. Employers who impose restrictions which are greater than necessary hope to deter their employees from competing. If the clause is deemed invalid, that is the price the employer must pay for its overreaching tactics. Here, the clause prevents Broniec (D) from competing in any capacity, and this is too vague and overbroad. Moreover, the territorial restrictions which cover several states are overbroad. Such clauses must normally be limited to the territory in which the employee was working. Finally, there is no showing that Schultz's (P) business required such protections or that the capacity in which Broniec (D) was employed would involve any injury to Schultz (P). With respect to covenants of nondisclosure,

these can be enforced separately from the covenant not to compete. Affirmed.

▶ ANALYSIS

Where there are two separate and distinct restrictive covenants, only one of which is valid, the invalid one may be struck and the other enforced. Thus, in *Aladdin v. Kransoff*, 214 Ga. 519 (1958), the court upheld a covenant not to compete in a janitorial supply business in Atlanta for two years. The covenant not to disclose all past, present, and potential customers was deemed overbroad since plaintiff had a right only to restrict disclosure of current customers. This clause was deemed unenforceable.

Quicknotes

RESTRICTIVE COVENANT   A promise contained in a deed to limit the uses to which the property will be made.

Third Party Beneficiaries

Quick Reference Rules of Law

Lawrence v. Fox

Lender (P) v. Third-party borrower (D)

N.Y. Ct. App., 20 N.Y. 268 (1859).

NATURE OF CASE: Appeal from judgment for plaintiff in action by a third party to recover damages for breach of contract.

FACT SUMMARY: Fox (D) promised Holly, for consideration, that he would pay Holly's debt to Lawrence (P).

RULE OF LAW
A third party is not precluded for want of privity of contract from maintaining an action on a contract made for his benefit.

FACTS: Holly owed Lawrence (P) $300. Holly loaned $300 to Fox (D) in consideration of Fox's (D) promise to pay the same amount to Lawrence (P), thereby erasing Holly's debts to Lawrence (P). Fox (D) did not pay Lawrence (P), and Lawrence (P) brought an action for breach of Fox's (D) promise to Holly. The jury returned a verdict in Lawrence's (P) favor. Fox (D) appealed and the appellate court affirmed the verdict. Fox (D) appealed to this court.

ISSUE: Is a third party precluded for want of privity of contract from maintaining an action on a contract made for his benefit?

HOLDING AND DECISION: (Gray, J.) No. A third party is not precluded for want of privity of contract from maintaining an action on a contract made for his benefit. In this case, Holly received ample consideration for the money to be paid to Lawrence (P) so the promise becomes as if Fox (D) promised Lawrence (P) directly. This principle of third party beneficiaries, which has been long applied in trust cases, is in fact a general principle of law. Affirmed.

CONCURRENCE: (Johnson, C.J.) The situation is one of agent and principal where the principal could ratify the actions of the agent once he learned of them.

DISSENT: (Comstock, J.) In general, there must be privity of contract. Here Lawrence (P) had nothing to do with the promise on which he brought the action. "It was not made to him, nor did the consideration proceed from him. If [Lawrence (P)] can maintain the suit, it is because an anomaly has found its way into the law on this subject."

▶ ANALYSIS

This is the leading case which started the general doctrine of "third party beneficiaries." In the parlance of the original Restatement of Contracts, Lawrence (P) was a "creditor" beneficiary. Restatement (Second) § 133 has eliminated the creditor/donee distinction which the original Restatement fostered and has lumped both under the label of "intended" beneficiary. Although the court in the present case went to some effort to discuss trusts and agency, ultimately the court allowed Lawrence (P) to recover because it was manifestly "just" that he should recover. Such has been the creation of many a new legal doctrine. The dissenting justices were primarily worried about freedom of contract and the continuing ability of promisor and promisee to rescind or modify their contract. As the doctrine has developed, various rules have arisen to handle these situations.

■■■■

Quicknotes

CREDITOR BENEFICIARY A creditor who receives the benefits of a contract between a debtor and another party, pursuant to which the other party is obligated to tender payment to the creditor.

PRIVITY OF CONTRACT A relationship, between the parties to a contract, which is required in order to bring an action for breach.

THIRD-PARTY BENEFICIARY A party who benefits from a promise made pursuant to a contract although he is not a party to the agreement.

■■■■

Seaver v. Ransom

Niece (P) v. Will beneficiary (D)

N.Y. Ct. App., 224 N.Y. 233, 120 N.E. 639 (1918).

NATURE OF CASE: Appeal from judgment for plaintiff in action by a third party to recover damages for breach of a contract.

FACT SUMMARY: Beman made a promise to his wife for the benefit of their niece, Seaver (P), who sued Beman's executor (D) for breach of that promise.

🏛 RULE OF LAW
A third party for whose benefit a promise was made may successfully bring an action for breach of that promise.

FACTS: One Mrs. Beman, on her deathbed, wished to leave some property to her niece, Seaver (P). Her husband induced his dying wife to sign a will leaving all property to him by promising that he would leave a certain amount in his own will to Seaver (P). Mr. Beman died without making such a provision for Seaver (P). Seaver (P) brought suit against Ransom (D), as executor of Beman's estate, for Beman's breach of his promise to his dying wife. The trial court awarded damages to Seaver (P) and the appellate court affirmed. Ransom (D) appealed.

ISSUE: May a third party for whose benefit a promise was made successfully bring an action for breach of that promise?

HOLDING AND DECISION: (Pound, J.) Yes. A third party for whose benefit a promise was made may successfully bring an action for breach of that promise. Although a general rule requires privity between a plaintiff and a defendant as necessary to the maintenance of an action on the contract, one of several exceptions to the rule is the case where a contract is made for the benefit of another member of the family. Here, Mrs. Beman was childless, and Seaver (P) was a beloved niece. The blood relationship, or lack thereof, does not determine the enforcement of the promise. The reason for this "family" exception (and other exceptions) to the rule is that it is just and practical to permit the person for whose benefit a contract is made to enforce it against one whose duty it is to pay. Finally, in this particular case, the Seaver (P) could prevail if it was an action for damages or an action for specific performance wherein Ransom (D) becomes a trustee for Seaver's (P) benefit Affirmed.

▶ ANALYSIS

In this case, the court (as does the original Restatement of Contracts) uses the term "donee beneficiary" to describe Seaver (P). The Restatement (Second) erases the creditor/donee distinction and labels both types of beneficiaries as "intended." Although the court here is very insistent on the close family relationship, subsequent New York cases have erased that requirement for donee beneficiaries as the doctrine governing third-party beneficiaries has expanded. These subsequent cases represent the now-prevailing view in the country.

■■■

Quicknotes

DONEE BENEFICIARY A third party, not a party to a contract, but for whose benefit the contract is entered with the intention that the benefits derived therefrom be bestowed upon the person as a gift.

INTENDED BENEFICIARY A third party who is the recipient of the benefit of a transaction undertaken by another.

THIRD-PARTY BENEFICIARY A party who benefits from a promise made pursuant to a contract although he is not a party to the agreement.

■■■

H.R. Moch Co., Inc. v. Rensselaer Water Co.

Building owner (P) v. Utility company (D)

N.Y. Ct. App., 247 N.Y. 160, 159 N.E. 896 (1928).

NATURE OF CASE: Appeal from dismissal in action by a third party to recover damages for breach of contract.

FACT SUMMARY: Rensselaer Water Co.'s (D) breach of its contract with the city caused damage to H.R. Moch Co. (P), a citizen of the city.

🏛 RULE OF LAW
A third-party beneficiary may not maintain an action on a contract which merely benefited him in an "incidental" or "secondary" manner.

FACTS: Rensselaer Water Co. (D) contracted with the city of Rensselaer to supply water at fire hydrants. The service was at the rate of $42.50 per year for each hydrant. While this contract was in force, citizen H.R. Moch Co.'s (Moch) (P) warehouse burned down because of Rensselaer Water's (D) failure to fulfill the terms of its contract with the city. Rennselaer Water (D) moved to dismiss Moch's (P) complaint and the trial court denied the motion. On appeal, the appellate court reversed the denial. Moch (P) appealed.

ISSUE: May a third-party beneficiary maintain an action on a contract which merely benefited him in an "incidental" or "secondary" manner?

HOLDING AND DECISION: (Cardozo, C.J.) No. A third-party beneficiary may not maintain an action on a contract which merely benefited him in an "incidental" or "secondary" manner. Moch (P) is merely an incidental beneficiary of Rensselaer Water's (D) contract and as such may not recover on the contract. No legal duty rests upon the city of Rensselaer to supply its citizens with fire protection, nor does any express intention appear in Rensselaer Water's (D) contract that Rensselaer Water Co. (D) should be liable for breach to individual members of the public as well as to the city. Rensselaer Water (D) could not justifiably be found to owe a contractual duty to every individual member because the burden would be crushing. Moch (P) also cannot recover on tort theory or under breach of statutory duty. Affirmed.

▶ ANALYSIS

Justice Cardozo is primarily worried, in this well-known opinion, about the excessive and unpredictable burdens which a contrary decision would put on water companies (e.g., the whole city might be laid low by fire). Cardozo's comment that the city has no legal obligation to its citizens has confused many subsequent courts and probably should not be relevant. (Indeed, Restatement (Second) § 133 erases the creditor/donee distinction in

the original Restatement of Contracts.) What courts should be concerned with in distinguishing between "intended" and "incidental" beneficiaries is the information which the promisor [here Rensselaer Water Co. (D)] has in order that he might properly monetize his risk of incurring liability to many third parties. Of course, a promisor should bear the burdens of those risks which he has been paid to take. Although there are some decisions contrary to the present case, it still remains the prevailing view. (Cf., Restatement (Second) § 145(2), which responds to Justice Cardozo's worry.)

Quicknotes

INCIDENTAL BENEFICIARY A third-party beneficiary who receives benefits from the performance of a contract without the intentions of the contracting parties to do so.

INTENDED BENEFICIARY A third party who is the recipient of the benefit of a transaction undertaken by another.

THIRD-PARTY BENEFICIARY A party who benefits from a promise made pursuant to a contract although he is not a party to the agreement.

Western Waterproofing Co. v. Springfield Housing Authority

Subcontractor (P) v. Client (D)

669 F. Supp. 901 (C.D. Ill. 1987).

NATURE OF CASE: Cross-motions for summary judgment in action for damages for failure to secure a bond.

FACT SUMMARY: Western Waterproofing Co. (P) contended that the Springfield Housing Authority (D) improperly failed to require its contractor to obtain a payment bond.

RULE OF LAW
A third-party beneficiary action may be asserted by an unpaid subcontractor against a public entity where that entity has failed to procure a payment bond from a general contractor.

FACTS: The Springfield Housing Authority (SHA) (D) hired general contractor Bildoc, Inc., pursuant to a public housing waterproofing project. Under Illinois law, the SHA (D) was to require Bildoc to obtain a payment bond. However, the contract only required a performance bond, although the section containing this requirement was entitled "performance and payment bond." Bildoc subcontracted with Western Waterproofing Co. (Western) (P), which performed certain work. Bildoc did not pay Western (P). When Bildoc proved to be judgment-proof, Western (P) sued the SHA (D) for failing to ensure that Bildoc obtain a payment bond. The parties filed cross-motions for summary judgment.

ISSUE: May a third-party beneficiary action be asserted by an unpaid subcontractor against a public entity where that entity has failed to procure a payment bond from a general contractor?

HOLDING AND DECISION: (Mills, J.) Yes. A third-party beneficiary action may be asserted by an unpaid subcontractor against a public entity where that entity has failed to procure a payment bond from a general contractor. State law mandates that a public entity entering into public works contracts require a payment bond. Statutory provisions applicable to a contract are deemed part of that contract. Further, although the language of the contract calls for only a performance bond, the contract section is entitled "performance and payment bond." This raised an ambiguity as to whether the contract called for a payment bond, and this ambiguity must be construed against the SHA (D), the drafter of the contract. Since Western (P) was to be directly benefited by the contract in question, it was an intended third-party beneficiary thereof and may properly sue upon it. Summary judgment granted to Western (P).

ANALYSIS

Two different types of bonds were at issue here, serving different functions. A performance bond is posted to ensure that if work is not completed, funds will exist to complete the work; it benefits the owner-developer. A payment bond benefits the subcontractors/materialmen by ensuring payment if the general becomes insolvent.

Quicknotes

THIRD-PARTY BENEFICIARY A party who benefits from a promise made pursuant to a contract although he is not a party to the agreement.

Lucas v. Hamm

Will legatee (P) v. Drafting attorney (D)

Cal. Sup. Ct., 56 Cal. 2d 583, 364 P.2d 685, en banc (1961), *cert. denied* 368 U.S. 987 (1962).

NATURE OF CASE: Appeal in suit seeking damages for negligence and breach of contract.

FACT SUMMARY: Hamm (D) carelessly drafted a will for Emmick. As a result, Lucas (P) and others (P) were deprived of the right to receive a substantial bequest.

> ## RULE OF LAW
> The intended legatees of a will may recover against an attorney for negligence and for breach of his contract with the testator if he mistakenly drafts an invalid instrument or provision.

FACTS: Hamm (D), an attorney, agreed to draft a will for Emmick. Lucas (P) and others (P) were designated as legatees of a substantial portion of Emmick's estate. Because Hamm (D) paid insufficient attention to the rule against restraints on alienation and the rule against perpetuities, the provisions purporting to bequeath much of Emmick's property to Lucas (P) and the others (P) were not valid. As a result, they were forced to reach a settlement with Emmick's blood relatives and were thereby deprived of about $75,000 of the money they would have received. They then brought suit against Hamm (D), alleging that he had been negligent and that he had breached his contract with Emmick. Hamm's (D) demurrer was sustained, however, and the complaint was dismissed. Lucas (P) and the others (P) then appealed.

ISSUE: May the intended legatees of a negligently drafted will recover against the attorney who prepared the instrument?

HOLDING AND DECISION: (Gibson, C.J.) Yes. The intended legatees of a will may recover against an attorney for negligence and for breach of his contract with the testator if he mistakenly drafts an invalid instrument or provision. This rule is mandated by that public policy which seeks to discourage negligence by permitting recoveries against parties whose conduct is deemed to, in fact, be negligent. No unfairness results from the rule since the intended legatees of a will are clearly to be viewed as beneficiaries of a contract to draft that instrument. Moreover, any damage to these legatees which would result from negligent draftsmanship would be entirely foreseeable. In this particular case, however, it would be unjust to allow recovery against Hamm (D) because the complex and unsettled quality of the law relating to restraints against alienation and to the rule against perpetuities makes Hamm's (D) errors completely excusable. Affirmed.

▶ ANALYSIS

The rule of *Lucas v. Hamm* has been followed by the California Supreme Court. That court has observed, however, that *Lucas v. Hamm* was resolved on the basis of tort liability and that the case has few implications in terms of third-party beneficiary contracts. This assertion is not without merit since, in the absence of negligence or some other tort, no action for breach of contract could have been maintained by Lucas (P).

Quicknotes

NEGLIGENCE Conduct falling below the standard of care that a reasonable person would demonstrate under similar conditions.

Erickson v. Grande Ronde Lumber Co.

Creditor (P) v. Debtor (D)

Or. Sup. Ct., 162 Or. 556, 94 P.2d 139 (1939).

NATURE OF CASE: Appeal in action on a note against the debtor and the guarantor.

FACT SUMMARY: Erickson (P) sued both Grande Ronde Lumber Co. (D), the debtor, and its guarantor, the Stoddard Co. (D).

RULE OF LAW
Where one promises to pay the debts of another, upon a default, the creditor may sue both parties to recover the amount due.

FACTS: Stoddard Co. (D) agreed to pay the debts of Grande Ronde Lumber Co. (Grande) (D). Erickson (P), a creditor of Grande (D), brought suit against both Grande (D) and Stoddard (D) on a past-due obligation. After a joint and several judgment was rendered against Stoddard (D) and Grande (D), they appealed, alleging that only one of them could be liable for the debt. Erickson (P), according to the allegation, had to rely on a novation, i.e., a substitution of Stoddard (D) for Grande (D), or reject the proffered guaranty offer and sue only Grande (D).

ISSUE: Where one promises to pay the debts of another, upon a default, may the creditor sue both parties to recover the amount due?

HOLDING AND DECISION: (Rossman, J.) Yes. Where one promises to pay the debts of another, upon a default, the creditor may sue both parties to recover the amount due. An offer by a third party to pay the debts of another does not constitute a novation which would release the original debtor from his obligation if accepted by the creditor. Rather, it is a promise to pay which creates an enforceable contract against the promisor, while the original debtor remains liable under the original obligation. Upon a default, the creditor may bring suit against either or both parties and can obtain a joint and several judgment against them. Judgment affirmed.

▶ ANALYSIS

Under the English rule, a donee beneficiary may not sue to enforce the contract unless he has formally accepted the gift. Under the American rule, acceptance is presumed based on the bringing of the suit by the donee. *Wood v. Moriarty*, 15 R.I. 518, 9 A. 427 (1887). Payments by promisor on a debt do not toll the running of the statute of limitations, since the original debtor is liable for his own promise to pay. *Verrill v. Weinstein*, 135 Me. 126, 190 A. 634 (1937).

Quicknotes

DONEE BENEFICIARY A third party, not a party to a contract, but for whose benefit the contract is entered with the intention that the benefits derived therefrom be bestowed upon the person as a gift.

Detroit Bank and Trust Co. v. Chicago Flame Hardening Co.

Widow's guardian (P) v. Stipend holder (D)

541 F. Supp. 1278 (N.D. Ind. 1982).

NATURE OF CASE: Action for breach of contract.

FACT SUMMARY: Detroit Bank and Trust Co. (P), as guardian of Scott, contended that Chicago Flame Hardening Co. (D) breached its contract of which Scott was a third-party beneficiary.

🏛 RULE OF LAW
A third-party beneficiary contract may be modified if the contract does not forbid it and the beneficiary has not reasonably relied upon it.

FACTS: Scott's husband entered into an agreement with other partners in Chicago Flame Hardening Co. (Chicago Flame) (D) that their surviving spouses would receive a stipend. The principals subsequently rescinded the agreement. Scott's husband died, and thereafter she sued to recover the stipend. Her guardian, Detroit Bank and Trust Co. (P), argued that no modification or rescission could occur without her consent because she was a third-party beneficiary. Chicago Flame (D) contended the contract did not preclude modification, and Scott had not changed her position in reliance on it.

ISSUE: May a third-party beneficiary contract be modified if the contract does not forbid it and the beneficiary has not reasonably relied upon it?

HOLDING AND DECISION: (Lee, J.) Yes. A third-party beneficiary contract may be modified if the contract does not forbid it and the beneficiary has not reasonably relied upon it. In this case, the contract included no clause limiting or precluding rescission. Further, Scott did not rely on the agreement to in any way change her position. Thus, it was validly changed, and she is not entitled to any payment. Judgment for Chicago Flame (D).

▶ ANALYSIS

This case illustrates the modern view of analysis involving third-party beneficiary contracts. The old rule, codified in the Restatement (First) of Contracts, was that the parties could not change the contract unless that power was specifically reserved.

■━■

Quicknotes

THIRD-PARTY BENEFICIARY A party who benefits from a promise made pursuant to a contract although he is not a party to the agreement.

■━■

Rouse v. United States

Purchaser of house (D) v. Federal government (P)

215 F.2d 872 (D.C. Cir. 1954).

NATURE OF CASE: Appeal in action by a third party to recover damages for breach of contract.

FACT SUMMARY: Rouse (D) promised to pay Bessie, Winston's creditor, but refused to do so after discovering flaws in his own contract with Bessie and in Bessie's contract with her creditor.

> 🏛 **RULE OF LAW**
> A third-party beneficiary's rights against the promisor rise no higher than those of the promisee; however, its rights may rise higher against the promisor than they could against the promisee.

FACTS: The Government's (P) assignor sold a heating plant to Bessie, who gave her a promissory note for $1,008.37 payable in monthly installments of $28.01. Bessie later sold her house to Rouse (D), who agreed in the contract of sale "to assume payment of $850 for the heating plant payable $28 per Mo." Bessie defaulted on her note, and the Government (P) sued Rouse (D) as a third-party beneficiary of Rouse's (D) contract with Bessie. Rouse (D) defended by alleging (1) that Bessie fraudulently misrepresented the condition of the heating plant and (2) that the Government's (P) assignor didn't install the heater properly in the first place.

ISSUE:
(1) May a promisor assert against a third-party beneficiary a defense which he would have against the promisee?
(2) May a promisor assert against a third-party beneficiary a defense which the promisee would have against the beneficiary?

HOLDING AND DECISION: (Edgerton, J.)
(1) Yes. The rights of the third-party beneficiary rise no higher than those of the promisee; or, in other words, one who promises to make a payment to the promisee's creditor can assert against the creditor any defense that the promisor could assert against the promisee. Thus, Rouse's (D) defense of fraud, which he would certainly have been entitled to show against Bessie, is equally effective against the beneficiary or any valid assignee of the original beneficiary.
(2) No. Here, Rouse's (D) promise was to pay a specified sum of money to the beneficiary (P), and it is irrelevant whether or not the promisee (Bessie) was actually indebted in that amount. "Where the promise is to pay a specific debt . . . this interpretation will generally be the true one." 12 Williston, § 399. The result would be different if Rouse (D) had merely promised to discharge whatever liability the promisee was under. In that case,

the promisor must certainly be allowed to show that the promisee was under no enforceable liability. Reversed and remanded.

▶ **ANALYSIS**

This well-known case is a law student's dream insofar as it clearly lays out what defenses are, and are not, available to a promisor in an action by a third party beneficiary. While the promisor usually may assert against the beneficiary any defense which he could assert against the promisee, he usually may not assert defenses which the promisee might have raised against the beneficiary. In support of its denial of Rouse's (D) second defense, the court rests on Williston's presumption as to the nature of the promisor's promise. Unless it is clearly indicated that a promisor is only undertaking to pay "the debt" of the promisee (whatever it may turn out to be), it will be presumed that the promise is to pay the specific amount, regardless of whether it is actually owed. [Whether this "presumption" necessarily effects a "just" result in all (or even most) ambiguous cases is open to some question.]

◼▬◼

Quicknotes

CREDITOR BENEFICIARY A creditor who receives the benefits of a contract between a debtor and another party, pursuant to which the other party is obligated to tender payment to the creditor.

THIRD-PARTY BENEFICIARY A party who benefits from a promise made pursuant to a contract although he is not a party to the agreement.

◼▬◼

CHAPTER 12

Assignment and Delegation

Quick Reference Rules of Law

Herzog v. Irace

Physician (P) v. Attorneys (D)

Me. Sup. Jud. Ct., 594 A.2d 1106 (1991).

NATURE OF CASE: Appeal of an award of damages for breach of assignment.

FACT SUMMARY: Although Jones assigned a personal injury claim to Herzog (P) and so notified his attorneys, Irace (D) and Lowry (D), they failed to pay the settlement to Herzog (P).

🏛 RULE OF LAW
An assignment is binding upon the obligor when the obligor is notified of the intent of the assignor to relinquish the right to the assignee.

FACTS: Jones, who was injured in a motorcycle accident, hired attorneys Irace (D) and Lowry (D) to represent him in a personal injury action. Jones required surgery for his injuries, which was performed by Herzog (P), a physician. Since Jones was unable to pay for this treatment, he signed a letter stating that he requested "that payment be made directly . . . to John Herzog [P]" of money received in settlement for his claim. Herzog (P) notified Irace (D) and Lowry (D) of the assignment in 1988. The following year, Jones received a $20,000 settlement for his claim. Jones instructed Irace (D) and Lowry (D) to pay the money to him rather than to Herzog (P). Irace (D) and Lowry (D) followed this instruction, and Jones failed to pay Herzog (P) for the medical treatment. Herzog (P) brought a breach of assignment action against Irace (D) and Lowry (D), and the trial court ruled in favor of Herzog (P). The appellate court affirmed, and Irace (D) and Lowry (D) appealed to the Maine Supreme Judicial Court.

ISSUE: Is an assignment binding upon the obligor when the obligor is notified of the intent of the assignor to relinquish the right to the assignee?

HOLDING AND DECISION: (Brody, J.) Yes. An assignment is binding upon the obligor when the obligor is notified of the intent of the assignor to relinquish the right to the assignee. The letter directing payment to be made directly to Herzog (P) clearly and unequivocally showed Jones's intent to relinquish his control over any money received for his personal injury claim. Irace (D) and Lowry (D) were duly notified of this assignment, and therefore the settlement money should have been paid to Herzog (P). Although the assignment interfered with the ethical obligations that Irace (D) and Lowry (D) owed to Jones, the rules of professional conduct do not override the client's right to assign the proceeds of a lawsuit to a third party. Affirmed.

▶ ANALYSIS

Limitations on the right of assignment exist in many situations. Most states have a statute which restricts the assignment of wages. Also, public policy considerations protect assignors who attempt to assign future rights. The Restatement (Second) of Contracts § 317(2) does not allow assignment where the duty to the obligor would be materially changed.

∎═∎

Quicknotes

ASSIGNMENT A transaction in which a party conveys his or her entire interest in property to another.

ASSIGNOR A party who assigns his interest or rights to another.

OBLIGOR Promisor; a party who has promised or is obligated to perform.

∎═∎

Macke Co. v. Pizza of Gaithersburg, Inc.

Coffee company purchaser (P) v. Pizza company (D)

Md. Ct. App., 259 Md. 479, 270 A.2d 645 (1970).

NATURE OF CASE: Appeal in an action for damages for breach of contract.

FACT SUMMARY: The Pizza Shops (D), claiming that their contracts with Virginia Coffee Services were for personal services, refused to honor the contracts' assignment to the Macke Co. (P).

🏛 RULE OF LAW
Unless otherwise agreed, contractual duties can be delegated unless they require such unique personal service that this would materially change the nature of performance.

FACTS: Pizza of Gaithersburg, Inc., Pizzeria, Inc., the Pizza Pie Corp., Inc., and Pizza Oven (Pizza Shops) (D) were commonly owned by three individuals as partners or proprietors. Pizza Shops (D) contracted to have Virginia Coffee Service (Virginia Coffee) install and service its vending machines. The contract contained no clause excluding an assignment. Accordingly, when the Macke Co. (P) purchased Virginia Coffee, Macke (P) received an assignment of the Pizza Shops (D) contract. When Pizza Shops (D) attempted to terminate the contract, Macke (P) sought damages for breach. Pizza Shops (D) argued that the contractual duties were not delegable because these were personal service contracts, entered into only because Pizza Shops (D) relied on Virginia's skill, judgment, and reputation. Macke (P) replied that servicing vending machines required no special skill such that a delegation would materially change the performance due under the contracts. Macke (P) appealed the trial court's ruling for Pizza Shops (D).

ISSUE: Are contractual duties delegable when they do not require such unique personal service that a delegation would materially change the nature of performance?

HOLDING AND DECISION: (Singley, J.) Yes. Unless otherwise agreed, contractual duties can be delegated when they do not require such unique personal services that a delegation would materially change the nature of performance. But we do not regard these agreements as personal service contracts. They were either a license or a concession entitling Virginia to lease of portion of Pizza Shops' (D) premises and pay Pizza Shops (D) a percentage of the vending machine sales. This did not require rare genius or extraordinary skill. Our holding accords with the Restatement of Contracts § 160(3) allowing delegation unless "performance by the person delegated varies . . . materially from performance by the person named in the

contract as the one to perform, and there has been no . . . assent to the delegation." Reversed and remanded.

▶ ANALYSIS

Assignment questions should be analyzed separately in terms of assignment of rights, delegation of duties, or both. It is necessary to keep in mind the distinction between assignment of rights and delegation of duties. An assignment is a transfer of rights. A delegation is a transfer of duties of performance. Often, an assignment would also involve a delegation without the contract explicitly stating that fact.

■══■

Quicknotes

ASSIGNMENT A transaction in which a party conveys his or her entire interest in property to another.

DELEGATION The authorization of one person to act on another's behalf.

■══■

Sally Beauty Co. v. Nexxus Products Co.

Distribution company (P) v. Cosmetic manufacturer (D)

801 F.2d 1001 (7th Cir. 1986).

NATURE OF CASE: Appeal from a summary judgment dismissing breach of contract action.

FACT SUMMARY: Nexxus Products Co. (Nexxus) (D) was sued for canceling its exclusive distribution contract with Best Barber & Beauty Supply Company, Inc. (Best) after Sally Beauty Co. (P), the wholly owned subsidiary of a Nexxus (D) competitor, merged with Best.

🏛 RULE OF LAW
Before the duty of performance under an exclusive distribution contract may be delegated to a competitor, or the wholly owned subsidiary of a competitor, the obligee must consent.

FACTS: Nexxus Products Co. (Nexxus) (D) entered into a contract with Best Barber & Beauty Supply Company, Inc. (Best), under which Best would be the exclusive Texas distributor for Nexxus (D) hair care products. When Best was acquired by and merged into Sally Beauty Co. (Sally) (P), Nexxus (D) canceled the agreement. Sally (P) sued, claiming Nexxus (D) breached the contract by canceling. Nexxus (D) defended by asserting the contract was not assignable, or in the alternative, not assignable to Sally Beauty (P). After a series of motions and hearings, the district court granted Nexxus's (D) motion for summary judgment, ruling that the contract was for personal services and therefore unassignable. Sally (P) appealed.

ISSUE: Must the obligee consent before the duty to perform under an exclusive distribution contract may be delegated to a competitor or the wholly owned subsidiary of a competitor?

HOLDING AND DECISION: (Cudahy, J.) Yes. Before the duty of performance under an exclusive distribution contract may be delegated to a competitor or the wholly owned subsidiary of a competitor, the obligee must consent. Summary judgment in this case cannot be affirmed on the basis set forth by the lower court, but it can be affirmed if another ground has support in the record. Contracts for the sale or distribution of goods are governed by the Uniform Commercial Code (U.C.C.) The U.C.C. recognizes that in some cases an obligor will find it convenient or necessary to relieve himself of his contractual performance duties. Hence, the U.C.C. permits an obligor to delegate and perform his duty through a delegate, unless the contract states otherwise or the obligee has a substantial interest in having the original obligor perform the acts required by the contract. In this case, it defies common sense to require a manufacturer to leave the distribution of its products to a distributor under the control of a

competitor or potential competitor. Sally (P), unlike Best, is a subsidiary of one of Nexxus's (D) direct competitors. This raises a serious question regarding Sally's (P) ability to perform the distribution agreement in the same manner as Best. Nexxus (D) should not be forced to accept performance of the distributorship agreement by Sally (P). Affirmed.

DISSENT: (Posner, J.) The general rule does not allow the change of corporate form, including a merger, in and of itself to affect contractual rights and obligations. Instead the law requires that a change in business form be likely to impair performance of the contract. As such, the judgment should be remanded for a trial to decide whether the merger altered the condition of performance such that Nexxus (D) is entitled to declare the contract broken.

▶ ANALYSIS

As outlined in *Sally Beauty*, a contractual duty is delegable unless delegation would materially change performance of the duty or violate a contract provision or legal prohibition. Duties that fall within those categories are classified as non-delegable. When an obligor attempts to delegate a non-delegable duty, the obligee may refuse the delegate's performance and sue the original obligor. Other remedies allow the obligee to recover damages from the original obligor for any defective performance of the delegate or withhold performance until the obligee receives adequate assurances of the delegate's performance.

Quicknotes

ADEQUATE ASSURANCES Refers to a situation in which one party is excused from performance of his obligations under a contract if the other party to the contract indicates that he does not intend to perform when the time for performance thereunder arrives; the nonbreaching party in that case is excused from further performance, unless he receives adequate assurances that performance will be rendered.

DELEGATION The authorization of one person to act on another's behalf.

OBLIGEE Promisee; a party who is the recipient of a promise or obligation to perform.

In re Kaufman

Creditor (P) v. Debtor (D)

Okla. Sup. Ct., 37 P.3d 845 (2001).

NATURE OF CASE: Certified questions to the state supreme court from the U.S. Bankruptcy Court.

FACT SUMMARY: John A. Kaufman (D) settled a wrongful death claim. The settlement agreement prohibited the assignment of his monthly payments under the structured settlement. He sold them anyway. When he later filed for bankruptcy, he tried to enforce the anti-assignment clause against the company to which he assigned the payments.

🏛️ **RULE OF LAW**

(1) Where an anti-assignment provision is clear and unambiguous in its limitation of the power of the annuitant to sell, mortgage, encumber, or anticipate future payments, by assignment or otherwise, the restriction on alienability is valid.

(2) Although an anti-assignment provision is valid, well-settled principles of Oklahoma law prevent an assignor from enforcing the clause against its assignee.

FACTS: John A. Kaufman (D) settled a wrongful death claim with Love's Country Stores, Inc. and U.S. Fidelity & Guaranty Company. As part of the settlement, Kaufman (D) signed a settlement agreement providing that he would get a lump-sum payment as well as periodic monthly payments of around $2,000, and that he had no "power to sell, mortgage, encumber, or anticipate the future payments by assignment or otherwise." The insurer then hired a company to make Kaufman's (D) periodic payments, and the company purchased an annuity to ensure the payments. Kaufman (D) then saw a television commercial by J.G. Wentworth S.S.C. (Wentworth) (P) advertising the purchase of structured settlements. Kaufman (D) signed an agreement with Wentworth (P) under which he sold his right to receive 60 monthly annuity payments of around $2,000 with a total value of around $120,500, to Wentworth (P) for a lump sum payment of $80,500. Kaufman (D) used the money to start a business that later failed, and he filed for bankruptcy. In the bankruptcy petition, Kaufman (D) listed the agreement with Wentworth (P) as an unsecured claim and proposed that the annuity payments be used to fund his Chapter 13 plan. Wentworth (P) filed a motion for relief from the automatic stay requesting permission to seize the contracted-for annuity payments. Kaufman (D) argued that the agreement with Wentworth (P) was invalid because of the anti-assignment language in the settlement agreement. The bankruptcy court then certified two questions to the state supreme court.

ISSUES:

(1) Where an anti-assignment provision is clear and unambiguous in its limitation of the power of the annuitant to sell, mortgage, encumber, or anticipate future payments, by assignment or otherwise, is the restriction on alienability valid?

(2) Although an anti-assignment provision is valid, do well-settled principles of Oklahoma law prevent an assignor from enforcing the clause against its assignee?

HOLDING AND DECISION: (Kauger, J.)

(1) Yes. Where an anti-assignment provision is clear and unambiguous in its limitation of the power of the annuitant to sell, mortgage, encumber, or anticipate future payments, by assignment or otherwise, the restriction on alienability is valid. In Oklahoma, the default rule is to support free alienability, but that policy is not absolute, and it must yield to contract provisions that clearly and unambiguously prohibit assignment. In determining whether contractual rights may be alienated, the parties' intent as shown in the agreement's language must be considered. The settlement agreement in this case specifically provides that Kaufman (D) has no "power to sell, mortgage, encumber, or anticipate the future payments by assignment or otherwise." The language is clear and definite in its intent to prohibit Kaufman (D) from alienating the annuity payments.

(2) Yes. Although an anti-assignment provision is valid, well-settled principles of Oklahoma law prevent an assignor from enforcing the clause against its assignee. To allow Kaufman (D) as assignor to enforce the clause against Wentworth, his assignee, would yield an inequitable result.

▶ *ANALYSIS*

The court in this case touches on a widely accepted principles regarding contract law: judicial respect for the freedom to contract. Where the parties' intent is clear and unambiguous, courts will most often go out of their way to uphold the contract, even when the provision in the contract inhibits one party's right to contract with others.

■—■

Quicknotes

ASSIGNEE A party to whom another party assigns his interest or rights.

Continued on next page.

ASSIGNMENT   A transaction in which a party conveys his or her entire interest in property to another.

FREEDOM OF CONTRACT   A basic freedom guaranteed by Article I, Sec. 10, Cl. 1, of the U.S. Constitution and which may not be denied by the state.

■━━■

Seale v. Bates

Dance student (P) v. Dance studio owners (D)

Colo. Sup. Ct., 145 Colo. 430, 359 P.2d 356 (1961).

NATURE OF CASE: Appeal in an action for contract rescission.

FACT SUMMARY: The Seales (P) and Hanscome (P) failed to timely object when their dance-lesson contract was assigned to a different dance studio.

🏛 RULE OF LAW
The failure to timely object to the assignment of a non-assignable personal service contract amounts to a waiver of the breach and consent to the assignment.

FACTS: The Seales (P) and Hanscome (P) were students at the Bates Dance Studio (Bates) (D). However, they continued their lessons at the Dale Studio when Bates (D) assigned their fully paid contracts to Dale. Later, due to dissatisfaction with the Dale Studio's size, the instructors' sex, etc., they sought rescission for breach of contract and restitution of their money, despite the fact that Dale stood ready to perform. They argued that their contract was for Bates's (D) personal services and therefore that the assignment was a breach of contract. The trial court dismissed the complaints on the ground that the parties' (P) conduct by continuing the lessons with Dale and failing to timely object to the non-assignable personal service contract's assignment amounted to a waiver of the breach and consent to the assignment.

ISSUE: Does the failure to timely object to the assignment of a non-assignable personal service contract amount to a waiver of the breach and consent to the assignment?

HOLDING AND DECISION: (Doyle, J.) Yes. The failure to timely object to the assignment of a non-assignable personal service contract amounts to a waiver of the breach and consent to the assignment. While it is true that this was a personal service contract and non-assignable without the consent of the Seales (P) and Hanscome (P), nevertheless, they failed to rescind when the assignment was brought to their attention. Although this is the only substantial breach we find, the fact that the parties (P) continued their lessons under the assignment with Dale justified the trial court's finding a waiver and consent. Affirmed.

▶ ANALYSIS

The obligee is not legally bound to accept performance by the delegatee where the contract calls for or is founded upon personal confidence, skill, or service. Ordinarily, such a relationship is not presumed in construction contracts or service contracts which are not unique. For example, a teacher employed to teach in a town's school could not assign this right to another teacher, thereby imposing upon the town the obligation to accept the substitute's services, nor could a scholarship award be assigned by the winner to another.

■■■

Quicknotes

ASSIGNMENT A transaction in which a party conveys his or her entire interest in property to another.

■■■

Western Oil Sales Corp. v. Bliss & Wetherbee

Oil contract assignor (D) v. Leaseholders (P)

Texas Comm. of App., 299 S.W. 637 (1927).

NATURE OF CASE: Appeal in an action for damages for breach of contract.

FACT SUMMARY: Western Oil Sales Corp. (D) assigned to American Oil Co. its contract to buy oil and claimed that it was thereby released from all future contractual liability.

🏛 RULE OF LAW
Although an obligor under a contract may delegate his duties to another, he nevertheless remains liable for the performance obligations unless the obligee consents to this release.

FACTS: Western Oil Sales Corp. (Western) (D) assigned to the American Oil Co. its contract to buy oil produced from leaseholds owned by McCamey, Shearin & Dumas. Western (D) also notified these sellers that it would no longer be liable for payment for any future deliveries made under the contract. Therefore, the sellers: (1) treated the contract as terminated; (2) conveyed the leaseholds to Bliss & Wetherbee (P); and (3) assigned to them all rights and claims against Western (D). The trial court ruled for Bliss & Wetherbee (P) in their suit against Western (D) for damages for breach of contract. The court of civil appeals affirmed. Western (D) appealed, arguing that its assignment of the contract and notice thereof to the sellers thereby released Western (D) from further contractual obligations.

ISSUE: Does an obligor who delegates his contractual duties to another nevertheless remain liable for performance unless the obligee consents to his release?

HOLDING AND DECISION: (Harvey, J.) Yes. Although an obligor under a contract may delegate his duties to another, he nevertheless remains liable for the performance obligations unless the obligee consents to his release. The mere fact that a contract is assignable does not mean that either party, by assigning, can release himself from liability, unless the other party consents. However, as soon as Western (D) repudiated all liability, the sellers were justified as treating this as an anticipatory breach and terminating the contract. Affirmed.

▍ ANALYSIS

Professor Conway remarked that despite a delegation of his duties based on contract, the original obligor (assignor-delegator) remains liable to his obligee if the assignee-delegatee does not render satisfactory performance. That is to say, the obligor is essentially a surety for the performance by the assignee-delegatee. The exception would be when there has been a novation which explicitly releases the original obligor and substitutes a new obligor in his place.

━■━

Quicknotes

OBLIGEE Promisee; a party who is the recipient of a promise or obligation to perform.

OBLIGOR Promisor; a party who has promised or is obligated to perform.

━■━

Associates Loan Co. v. Walker

Assignee (P) v. Buyer (D)

N.M. Sup. Ct., 76 N.M. 520, 416 P.2d 529 (1966).

NATURE OF CASE: Appeal from a judgment invalidating an installment contract.

FACT SUMMARY: Associates Loan Co. (P) sought to enforce a contract it acquired as an assignee for the sale of a water softener to Walker (D).

🏛 RULE OF LAW
An assignee of a right to bring a legal action acquires only the rights the assignor had, and all equities and defenses that could be raised by the debtor against the assignor are available to the debtor against the assignee.

FACTS: Walker (D) owned and operated a dairy farm. He purchased a water softener from Daniel Partin by virtue of an installment contract. Partin had represented to Walker (D) that the improvements to the drinking water from the water softener would improve his cattle's milk production. Based upon this representation, the parties agreed orally that Walker (D) could use the device on a trial basis and if milk production increased, then Walker (D) would complete the purchase. Walker (D) executed the written installment contract in conjunction with this oral agreement. Subsequently, Partin assigned the written contract to Associates Loan Co. (Associates) (P). The device did not improve milk production as promised and Walker (D) made no payments to Associates (P), although Partin had made a couple of initial payments to Associates (P) during the trial period. Ultimately Stirman Rivers, who had acquired Partin's business, removed the water softener from Walker's (D) property. Associates (P) sued Walker (D) to enforce the written installment contract. Walker's (D) defense was that the oral condition precedent to the written contract had not been satisfied and so the written contract did not come into existence. The trial court agreed and Associates (P) appealed.

ISSUE: Does an assignee of a right to bring a legal action acquire only the rights the assignor had, and are all equities and defenses that could be raised by the debtor against the assignor available to the debtor against the assignee?

HOLDING AND DECISION: (Spiess, J.) Yes. An assignee of a right to bring a legal action acquires only the rights the assignor had, and all equities and defenses that could be raised by the debtor against the assignor are available to the debtor against the assignee. Associates (P) claims that § 50A-9-318(1) of the Uniform Commercial Code (U.C.C.), as adopted by New Mexico, applies and that Walker's (D) defense is not recognized. This section provides that unless an account debtor has made an enforceable agreement not to assert defenses or claims arising from the sale that the rights of the assignee are subject to the terms of the contract between the assignor and debtor and any defense of the debtor which arises prior to the notification of the assignment. Essentially Associates (P) is arguing that by virtue of the U.C.C. Walker (D) is bound by the terms of the installment contract and the condition precedent defense, having not accrued prior to the assignment, is without merit. Associates (P) fails to recognize that the U.C.C. does not usurp other well-established law in the field of contracts. An assignee can only acquire all of the rights the assignor had to assign. In this instance, a valid condition precedent was not met and the terms of the installment contract as to Walker (D) never came into existence and cannot now be enforced. The judgment of the trial court is affirmed.

▶ ANALYSIS

Associates (P) failed to raise the Parol Evidence Rule in an attempt to invalidate the contemporaneous oral agreement with the trial court, and, consequently, waived this point on appeal. It is also unclear if Associates (P) would have an action against Stirman River, the successors of Partin, with regard to their contractual terms for the rights assigned under the installment contract. What this case clearly illustrates is that while the U.C.C. is a gap-filler for contracts, it does not usurp or totally replace existing common law as to contracts. The U.C.C. only serves its purpose as a gap-filler when there are gaps to fill.

■━■

Quicknotes

ASSIGNMENT A transaction in which a party conveys his or her entire interest in property to another.

■━■

The Statute of Frauds

Quick Reference Rules of Law

C.R. Klewin, Inc. v. Flagship Properties, Inc.

Construction manager (P) v. Contractor (D)

Conn. Sup. Ct., 220 Conn. 569, 600 A.2d 772 (1991).

NATURE OF CASE: Certified appeal in action for breach of contract.

FACT SUMMARY: Flagship Properties, Inc. (D) orally agreed to use C.R. Klewin, Inc. (Klewin) (P) as a construction manager on a project likely to take more than one year to complete, but contracted with another contractor after becoming dissatisfied with Klewin's (P) work.

> ## 🏛 RULE OF LAW
> The Statute of Frauds, requiring a writing for an agreement that is not to be performed within one year from the making thereof, will not render unenforceable an oral contract that fails to specify explicitly the time for performance, even when performance will likely take more than one year.

FACTS: Flagship Properties, Inc. (Flagship) (D) representatives held a dinner with C.R. Klewin, Inc. (Klewin) (P) representatives. During the meeting, Klewin (P) suggested what fee it would require to serve as a construction manager. At the end of the meeting, the Flagship (D) agent said that they had a deal and the agents from both parties shook hands. No other terms or conditions were conclusively established. The agreement was publicized and a press conference was held. Construction began on May 4, 1987, on the first phase of the project. In March 1988, Flagship (D) retained another contractor for the next phase. Klewin (P) filed suit in district court for breach of an oral contract. Flagship's (D) motion for summary judgment was granted. Klewin (P) appealed. The Second Circuit Court of Appeals certified questions to the Connecticut Supreme Court on issues not addressed in Connecticut case law.

ISSUE: Will the Statute of Frauds, requiring a writing for an agreement that is not to be performed within one year from the making thereof, render unenforceable an oral contract that fails to specify explicitly the time for performance when performance of that contract within one year of its making is very unlikely?

HOLDING AND DECISION: (Peters, C.J.) No. The Statute of Frauds, requiring a writing for an agreement that is not to be performed within one year from the making thereof, will not render unenforceable an oral contract that fails to specify explicitly the time for performance, even when performance will likely take more than one year. The Statute of Frauds excludes contracts except those whose performance cannot possibly be completed within one year. Connecticut case law has narrowly construed the Statute of Frauds in this area. In this case, the oral agreement did not specify a time for completion. When an oral contract does not expressly dictate that performance will last beyond one year, the contract will be construed as a matter of law to be a contract of indefinite duration for purposes of the Statute of Frauds. Given this narrow interpretation of the Statute of Frauds, it is enough that the agreement left open the possibility of completion within one year. The contract is enforceable.

▶ *ANALYSIS*

Historians are unclear as to the reason for including the one-year category in the Statute of Frauds. Commentators, however, agree in that the Statute does not accomplish any of its possible purposes very well. Most jurisdictions construe the one-year provision as narrowly as possible to minimize the number of contracts voided by its operation.

■▬■

Quicknotes

STATUTE OF FRAUDS A statute that requires specified types of contracts to be in writing in order to be binding.

■▬■

Erhlich v. Diggs

Manager (P) v. Client (D)

169 F. Supp. 2d 124 (E.D.N.Y. 2001).

NATURE OF CASE: Motion for summary judgment on an action to enforce an oral contract.

FACT SUMMARY: Erhlich (P), the manager for the music group Gravediggaz, brought suit to enforce an oral Management Agreement which he claims entitled him to commissions earned on the solo work of rap musician Diggs (D).

> 🏛 **RULE OF LAW**
> An agreement that, by its terms, requires greater than one year for performance is not enforceable unless it is memorialized in writing.

FACTS: Erhlich (P), a manager of musical groups, alleged that he entered into an oral Management Agreement with the rap group Gravediggaz. The terms of the Agreement allegedly included compensation for Erhlich (P) in the form of commissions in the amount of fifteen percent of the gross earnings of the group, and each of its members, for all entertainment-related employment. Erhlich (P) contends that it is standard in the industry for the commissions to extend to the earnings of each individual member of the group, whether or not those earnings were generated individually or from performances as a group member. The contract could be terminated at will by either party, or any member of the group, at any time. This contract was executed in California and was not terminated by either party. Some three years later, Diggs (D), a former member of the group had established a solo career and had become a member of a new music group in New York. Erhlich (P) brought suit to enforce the Management Agreement against Diggs's (D) current earnings. Prior to trial, Diggs (D) filed a motion for summary judgment raising the Statute of Frauds as an affirmative defense.

ISSUE: Is an agreement that, by its terms, requires greater than one year for performance enforceable if it is not memorialized in writing?

HOLDING AND DECISION: (Dearie, J.) No. An agreement that, by its terms, requires greater than one year for performance is not enforceable unless it is memorialized in writing. The Statute of Frauds requires a written agreement for contracts when performance will span a year or more in duration. However, different jurisdictions have interpreted the application of this legal principle differently when at-will termination is a part of the contract and the court is presented with a conflict of laws issue as to which forum's law controls, California or New York. Under California law, if the contract can be terminated within one year, then the contract is deemed to be enforceable because

performance can occur in less than a year's time. California law would eliminate the Statute of Frauds defense in this instance simply by virtue of the fact that Diggs (D) had the power to terminate the agreement at will within one year. New York law, on the other hand, requires all legal obligations to be extinguished in under a year's duration. Because earnings from the group Gravediggaz may continue indefinitely into the future, even though the group has disbanded, then under New York law performance on the contract could not be completed within one year's duration and the Statute of Frauds would apply. In this instance, California law applies because the "center of gravity" of the transaction occurred in California and California had the greatest interest in the litigation. Consequently, the Statute of Frauds defense does not apply and Diggs's (D) motion for summary judgment is denied.

📌 **ANALYSIS**

When applying the Statute of Frauds, the duration of performance, and what legally constitutes performance, of the contract is key. As illustrated here, different jurisdictions interpret performance differently. California examines whether or not a contract is "capable" of performance within one year while New York examines the time necessary to complete all of the legal obligations generated by the contract. Arguably, New York's interpretation better satisfies the purpose of the defense, which is to prevent fraud in long term or costly business arrangements. The terms of complex contracts should be memorialized in writing to protect the parties and prevent swearing matches in court. The Statute of Frauds defense is supposed to serve as a bright line rule, but as seen in this instance, the application of it is still murky depending on the jurisdiction in which the contract was executed.

■═■

Quicknotes

STATUTE OF FRAUDS A statute that requires specified types of contracts to be in writing in order to be binding.

■═■

Crabtree v. Elizabeth Arden Sales Corp.

Potential employee (P) v. Cosmetics company (D)

N.Y. Ct. App., 305 N.Y. 48, 110 N.E.2d 551 (1953).

NATURE OF CASE: Appeal in action for damages for breach of an employment contract.

FACT SUMMARY: Crabtree (P) was hired by Elizabeth Arden Sales Corp. (D) to be the latter's sales manager. No formal contract was signed but separate writings pieced together showed Crabtree (P) to have been hired for a two-year term with pay raises after the first and second six months. When he did not receive his second pay raise, Crabtree (P) sued for damages for breach.

🏛 RULE OF LAW

The Statute of Frauds does not require the memorandum expressing the contract to be in one document. It may be pieced together out of separate writings, connected with one another either expressly or by the internal evidence of subject matter and occasion.

FACTS: In September 1947, Crabtree (P) began negotiating with Elizabeth Arden Sales Corp. (Arden) (D) for the position of the latter's sales manager. Being unfamiliar with the cosmetics business and giving up a well-paying, secure job, Crabtree (P) insisted upon an agreement for a definite term. He asked for three years at $25,000 per year. But Arden (D) offered two years, with $20,000 per year the first six months, $25,000 per year the second six months, and $30,000 per year the second year. This was written down by Arden's (D) personal secretary with the notation "2 years to make good." A few days later, Crabtree (P) telephoned Johns, Arden's (D) executive vice-president, to accept the offer. Crabtree (P) received a "welcome" wire from Arden (D). When he reported for work, a "payroll change" card was made up and initialed by Johns showing the above pay arrangement with a salary increase noted "as per contractual agreement." Crabtree (P) received his first pay raise as scheduled, but not his second one. Arden (D) allegedly refused to approve the second increase, denying Crabtree (P) had been hired for any specific period. The trial court found in favor of Crabtree and awarded him damages, and the appellate division affirmed.

ISSUE: May the memorandum expressing the contract be pieced together out of separate writings, connected with one another either expressly or by the internal evidence of subject matter and occasion and still satisfy the Statute of Frauds?

HOLDING AND DECISION: (Fuld, J.) Yes. The Statute of Frauds does not require the memorandum expressing the contract to be in one document. It may be pieced together out of separate writings, connected with

one another either expressly or by the internal evidence of subject matter and occasion. First, as it is alleged that the contract is for a period of two years, there must be written evidence of its terms to be enforceable as the two-year performance places it within the Statute of Frauds. The payroll cards, one initialed by Arden's (D) executive vice-president and the other by its comptroller, unquestionably constituted a memorandum under the Statute. It is enough that they were signed with the intent to authenticate the information contained therein and that such information evidences the terms of the contract. The cards had all essential terms except for duration. But as the memorandum can be pieced together from more than one document, all that is required between the papers is a connection established simply by reference to the same subject matter or transaction. Parol evidence is permissible in order to establish the connection. As the note prepared by Arden's (D) personal secretary shows, it was made in Miss Arden's (D) presence as well as that of Johns and of Crabtree (P); hence, the dangers of parol evidence were at a minimum. All of the terms must be set out in writing and cannot be shown by parol. That memo, the paper signed by Johns, and the paper signed by the comptroller all refer on their face to the Crabtree (P) transaction. The comptroller's paper shows that it was prepared for the purpose of a "salary increase per contractual arrangements with Miss Arden" (D). That is a reference to more than comprehensive evidence and parol evidence can explain. "[Two] years to make good" probably had no other purpose than to denote the duration of the arrangement and parol evidence may explain its meaning. Affirmed.

▷ ANALYSIS

When there is more than one writing and all are signed by the party to be charged, and it is clear by their contents that they relate to the same transaction, there is little problem. When not all the documents are signed, difficulties obviously crop up. It becomes difficult to say the memorandum has been authenticated to the party to be charged. When the unsigned document is physically attached to the signed writing, the Statute of Frauds is satisfied. And, as illustrated by this case, this is true when the signed document by its terms expressly refers to the unsigned document. The cases conflict where the papers are not attached or fail to refer to the other. The minority holds that is a failure to show sufficient authentication. The better view is that if the signed document does not expressly refer to the unsigned, it is sufficient if internal

Continued on next page.

evidence refers to the same subject matter or transaction. If so, extrinsic evidence is admissible to help show the connection between the documents.

∎═∎

Quicknotes

PAROL EVIDENCE RULE Doctrine precluding parties to an agreement from introducing evidence of prior or contemporaneous agreements in order to repudiate or alter the terms of a written contract.

STATUTE OF FRAUDS A statute that requires specified types of contracts to be in writing in order to be binding.

∎═∎

McIntosh v. Murphy

Assistant manager (P) v. Employer (D)

Hawaii Sup. Ct., 52 Haw. 29, 469 P.2d 177 (1970).

NATURE OF CASE: Appeal in breach of an alleged one-year employment contract.

FACT SUMMARY: Murphy (D) fired McIntosh (P), a California resident, after orally contracting with him for a job in Honolulu, which technically was one weekend short of being performable within one year.

🏛 RULE OF LAW
The Statute of Frauds notwithstanding, an oral contract is nevertheless enforceable when it is based on a promise which the promisor should reasonably expect would induce either action or forbearance on the part of the promises and when injustice can be avoided only by enforcing the contract.

FACTS: In reliance on an oral employment contract to be sales manager of Murphy's (D) Honolulu car dealership, McIntosh (P), a Los Angeles resident, moved to Honolulu at substantial expense. McIntosh (P) had telegrammed Murphy (D) that he would arrive in Honolulu on Sunday, April 26, 1964. On Saturday, April 25, 1964, Murphy (D) telephoned McIntosh (P) that he could begin working as "assistant manager" on Monday, April 27, 1964. Although Murphy (D) later claimed the employment contract was for one year, Murphy (D) discharged McIntosh (P) on July 16, 1964. When McIntosh (P) then sued for damages, Murphy (D) claimed that the contract violated the Statute of Frauds provision requiring "any agreement that is not to be performed within one year from the making thereof" to be in writing to be enforceable. Murphy's (D) claim was that the contract was made on the weekend of the 25th, but the year's employment did not begin to run until Monday, the 27th. However, the trial court ruled that such an interpretation would be an unjust and mechanical application and that, as a matter of law, the contract was outside the statute. Murphy (D) appealed a jury verdict for McIntosh (P).

ISSUE: Are some oral contracts enforceable even though their provisions violate the Statute of Frauds?

HOLDING AND DECISION: (Levinson, J.) Yes. Notwithstanding the Statute of Frauds, an oral contract is nevertheless enforceable when it is based on a promise which the promisor should reasonably expect would induce either action or forbearance on the part of the promises and when injustice can be avoided only by enforcing the contract. This is the rule of Restatement of Contracts § 217A [now § 139]. It is in accord with the court's equity powers, which it has traditionally used to mitigate harsh, mechanical applications of the law. Ordinarily, the courts utilize the concepts of "part performance" or "equitable estoppel" to avoid the unconscionable injury which would otherwise occur should the statute be applied in these cases. We hold that such equitable factors apply here since no other remedy would correct this injustice. Affirmed.

DISSENT: (Abe, J.) By this holding, the judiciary is usurping the power of the legislature, whose sole function it is to amend or repeal the statute if it brings about undue hardship.

▶ ANALYSIS

This case points up a major new approach in the courts now relying upon the doctrine of promissory estoppel as a basis of taking a case out of the statute. See also *Alaska Airlines, Inc. v. Stephenson* (217 F.2d 295, 1954), wherein the plaintiff gave up a secure position as a pilot for Western Airlines to become general manager of Alaska Airlines. Based on an oral contract, he moved his family from California to Alaska and abandoned his tenure rights with Western Airlines. Alaska Airlines discharged him shortly thereafter. In ruling for the plaintiff, the court utilized promissory estoppel, suggesting that this approach "will generally be followed throughout the country."

▬▬◼

Quicknotes

AMELIORATE Improve.

EQUITABLE ESTOPPEL A doctrine that precludes a person from asserting a right to which he or she was entitled due to his or her action, conduct or failing to act, causing another party to justifiably rely on such conduct to his or her detriment.

PART PERFORMANCE Exception to the Statute of Frauds rendering a contract enforceable if one party commenced performance in reliance on the existence of a contract and there is no other explanation for the party's conduct.

STATUTE OF FRAUDS A statute that requires specified types of contracts to be in writing in order to be binding.

▬▬◼

Azevedo v. Minister

Hay purchaser (D) v. Hay seller (P)

Nev. Sup. Ct., 86 Nev. 576, 471 P.2d 661 (1970).

NATURE OF CASE: Appeal in an action to enforce an oral contract.

FACT SUMMARY: Azevedo (D) claimed that his oral contract to purchase a quantity of hay from Minister (P) was barred by the Statute of Frauds.

🏛 RULE OF LAW
Periodic written accountings of an oral agreement between merchants can satisfy the Statute of Frauds requirement of a confirming memorandum.

FACTS: Azevedo (D) orally agreed to buy hay from Minister (P). This agreement required Azevedo (D) to deposit in advance in an escrow account the money to be paid for the hay. Then, as Azevedo (D) hauled away the loads on various dates, Minister (P) provided him with two periodic written accounting statements showing the dates of delivery, the truckers' names, bale counts, the amount remaining in the escrow account, and the amount of hay remaining to be hauled. This agreement continued for about three months, until Minister (P) loaded only two of the four trucks sent by Azevedo (D) since the funds remaining on deposit in escrow were inadequate. Azevedo (D) then refused to buy any more hay. Minister (P), alleging that the contract required Azevedo (D) to purchase a full 1,500 tons, sued. Azevedo (D): (1) denied that the contract specified a quantity; (2) argued that the oral agreement was barred by the Statute of Frauds provision requiring a written confirming memorandum of an oral agreement between merchants; and (3) claimed that—even given Minister's (P) argument that the accountings constituted such a memorandum—they were not sent within a reasonable time. Azevedo (D) appealed the trial court's ruling for Minister (P).

ISSUE: May periodic written accountings of an oral agreement between merchants satisfy the Statute of Frauds requirement of a confirming memorandum?

HOLDING AND DECISION: (Mowbray, J.) Yes. Periodic written accountings of an oral agreement between merchants can satisfy the Statute of Frauds requirement of a confirming memorandum. According to the official Comment of the Uniform Commercial Code (U.C.C.), § 2-201, only three requirements must be contained in the memorandum: (1) evidence of a contract for the sale of goods; (2) authentication identifying the parties to be charged; and (3) the quantity. But an examination of the two accountings contains all three, none of which was challenged by Azevedo (D) upon their receipt. Finally, as to the "reasonable time" factor: these accountings were sent

after 10 weeks. It was up to the trier of fact to decide whether—given the circumstances—that was within a reasonable time. Affirmed.

▶ ANALYSIS

When merchants conclude an oral contract, it is common for one to send the other a letter of confirmation or possibly a printed form of the contract. Of course, this confirmation will serve as a memorandum and will be signed only by the party sending it, thus leaving one party at the mercy of the other. The U.C.C. remedies this by allowing the receiver 10 days to reply after he has reason to know of the memorandum's contents.

■━■

Quicknotes

STATUTE OF FRAUDS A statute that requires specified types of contracts to be in writing in order to be binding.

■━■

Cohn v. Fisher

Sailboat owner (P) v. Offeror (D)

N.J. Super. Ct., 118 N.J. Super. 286, 287 A.2d 222 (1972).

NATURE OF CASE: Motion for summary judgment in alleged breach of oral contract.

FACT SUMMARY: After making partial payment for Cohn's (P) boat, Fisher (D) canceled his check, arguing that their oral contract was unenforceable under the Statute of Frauds.

> ## 🏛 RULE OF LAW
> The Statute of Frauds requirement of a written memorandum of an oral contract can be satisfied by a check made in payment for the goods ordered and properly annotated.

FACTS: Cohn (P) accepted Fisher's (D) telephoned offer of $4,650 for his sailboat. They met the following day, and Fisher (D) gave Cohn (P) a check for $2,325 on which he wrote: "Deposit on aux, sloop, D'Arc Wind, full amount $4,650." However, Fisher (D) later notified Cohn (P) that he would not be able to close the deal by the agreed-upon date. Cohn (P) refused to accept the delay. Therefore, Fisher (D) stopped payment on the check. Cohn (P) then sold the boat to another party for $3,000 and sought damages of $1,679.50. Cohn (D) admitted the oral contract but moved for summary judgment based on the Uniform Commercial Code (U.C.C.) requirement that a contract for the sale of goods for the price of $500 or more must comply with the Statute of Frauds requirement of a written memorandum to be enforceable. Cohn (P) claimed that the notations on the check constituted a sufficient memorandum.

ISSUE: Can the Statute of Frauds requirement of a written memorandum of an oral contract be satisfied by a check made in payment for the goods ordered and properly annotated?

HOLDING AND DECISION: (Rosenberg, J.) Yes. The Statute of Frauds requirement of a written memorandum of an oral contract can be satisfied by a check made in payment for the goods orally ordered and properly annotated. The check must: (1) indicate a contract for sale; (2) be signed by the party to be charged; and (3) expressly state the quantity term. But all three of these elements are to be found on the check. In fact, the contract could also be held enforceable by two alternate theories: (1) Fisher's (D) testimony in depositions and his answers to demands for admission may constitute an admission of the contract or (2) payment and acceptance of the check may constitute partial performance. Motion for summary judgment is denied.

▶ ANALYSIS

Under U.C.C. § 2-201 satisfaction of the Statute of Frauds is required to make a sales contract enforceable only if the sales contract has a "price" of $500 or more. Note that the price of goods and the value of the same goods need not be equivalent or even related. U.C.C. § 2-201 specifies four ways in which the statute may be satisfied: (1) proper writing; (2) the party charged admits in his pleadings, testimony, or otherwise in court that a contract was made; (3) partial performance; (4) a signed letter of confirmation between merchants.

■■■

Quicknotes

STATUTE OF FRAUDS A statute that requires specified types of contracts to be in writing in order to be binding.

■■■

Potter v. Hatter Farms, Inc.

Turkey seller (P) v. Potential turkey buyer

Or. Ct. App., 56 Or. App. 254, 641 P.2d 628 (1982).

NATURE OF CASE: Appeal of award of damages for breach of contract.

FACT SUMMARY: Potter (P) argued that Hatter Farms, Inc. (D) was estopped to raise the Statute of Frauds defense in a breach of contract action.

▥ RULE OF LAW
Promissory estoppel may be allowed as an exception to the Uniform Commercial Code (U.C.C.) Statute of Frauds.

FACTS: Potter (P) orally agreed with Hatter Farms, Inc. (D) that the latter would purchase a quantity of young turkeys from him. All the terms of the agreement other than transportation were agreed upon. Relying on the agreement, Potter (P) turned down another offer. When the parties could not agree on transportation, Hatter (D) reneged. Potter (P) sued for breach. Hatter Farms (D) raised the U.C.C. Statute of Frauds as a defense, which Potter (P) claimed was barred by promissory estoppel. Hatter Farms' (D) motion for summary judgment was denied, and Potter (P) subsequently was awarded damages. Hatter Farms (D) appealed.

ISSUE: May promissory estoppel be allowed as an exception to the U.C.C. Statute of Frauds?

HOLDING AND DECISION: (Gillette, J.) Yes. Promissory estoppel may be allowed as an exception to the U.C.C. Statute of Frauds. U.C.C. § 1-103 permits promissory estoppel to apply to any of its substantive sections, unless the provision in question displaces the doctrine. The U.C.C. Statute of Frauds is silent as to displacement. This court does not believe that displacement should be inferred. U.C.C. § 1 203 provides that all contracts involve an obligation of good faith, and to permit promissory estoppel in any section silent on its application is consistent with this duty. While it is true that permitting an estoppel exception theoretically weakens the statute, this court does not believe it likely that would-be wrongdoers would set up a fraudulent scheme in violation of the statute on the slender hope of prevailing through estoppel. This being so, promissory estoppel was properly permitted to be raised by Potter (P). Affirmed.

▶ ANALYSIS

Promissory estoppel is a useful equitable doctrine which is used to plug various gaps caused by mechanical application of rules of contract law. When a party detrimentally relies on a promise, the promisor may be estopped to assert a legal rule which might otherwise excuse

performance. The most common application of promissory estoppel is in the area of contract formation.

━━▪

Quicknotes

PROMISOR Party who promises to render an obligation to another in the future.

PROMISSORY ESTOPPEL A promise that is enforceable if the promisor should reasonably expect that it will induce action or forbearance on the part of the promisee, and does in fact cause such action or forbearance, and it is the only means of avoiding injustice.

STATUTE OF FRAUDS A statute that requires specified types of contracts to be in writing in order to be binding.

SUMMARY JUDGMENT Judgment rendered by a court in response to a motion made by one of the parties, claiming that the lack of a question of material fact in respect to an issue warrants disposition of the issue without consideration by the jury.

━━▪

Costco Wholesale Corp. v. Worldwide Licensing Corp.

Retailer (P) v. Wholesale supplier (D)

78 Was. App. 637, 898 P.2d 347 (1995).

NATURE OF CASE: Appeal of summary judgment.

FACT SUMMARY: Costco Wholesale Corp. (P) entered into a contract to purchase jewelry with Worldwide Licensing Corp. (D). Each party subsequently made modifications to the original agreement, and each claimed that the Statute of Frauds precluded the other's modification.

🏛 RULE OF LAW

(1) Where a contract satisfies the Statue of Frauds under the Uniform Commercial Code (U.C.C.), the original satisfaction passes through to the contract as modified, thereby requiring no new memorandum of the modification to that satisfactory original contract.
(2) An oral modification as to quantity in a contract for the sale of goods is not enforceable under the pass-through power.
(3) If the Statute of Frauds bars an oral modification, the modification nevertheless can be used as evidence that no other modification to the contract existed.

FACTS: Costco Wholesale Corp. (Costco) (P) entered into a contract with Worldwide Licensing Corp. (Worldwide) (D) to purchase five pallets of jewelry for sale in Costco's (P) stores. Loren Coleman, an independent sales representative for Worldwide (D), Ed Dose, a Worldwide (D) division president, and Megghan Harruff, a Costco (P) manager, participated in the negotiations. Harruff expressed that she thought the merchandise would sell quickly, and Coleman then urged Dose, outside of Harruff's hearing, that Dose should produce more than the five pallets ordered. Dose reluctantly agreed. Over time, the jewelry failed to sell very well, and Costco (P) expressed displeasure with the packaging. Worldwide (D) became concerned about selling the already manufactured three additional pallets and told Coleman to offer Costco (P) an $8 dollar per box adjustment in price on the amount they still were trying to sell, provided they agreed to purchase the remaining three pallets at the adjusted price. Dose testified that Coleman indicated that Costco (P) agreed to the order. Coleman testified that he did not say that Costco (P) agreed to the order, that Dose authorized an $8 dollar per unite rebate, and that Dose did not make it contingent on the additional order. Costco (P) agreed to the rebate, sent the rebate form to Coleman, who then faxed it to Worldwide (D), and Worldwide (D) processed it, pending Dose's approval. But Costco refused the three

additional pallets, and Worldwide (D) refused to pay the rebate. Coleman's commission was based on the rebated sales price. Costco (P) sued Worldwide (D), seeking the rebate. Worldwide (D) denied the rebate agreement and alleged the Statute of Frauds as an affirmative defense. The trial court entered summary judgment in favor of Costco (P).

ISSUE:
(1) Where a contract satisfies the statue of frauds under the Uniform Commercial Code, does the original satisfaction pass through to the contract as modified, thereby requiring no new memorandum of the modification to that satisfactory original contract?
(2) Is an oral modification as to quantity in a contract for the sale of goods enforceable under the pass-through power?
(3) If the Statute of Frauds bars an oral modification, can the modification nevertheless be used as evidence that no other modification to the contract existed?

HOLDING AND DECISION: (Webster, J.)
(1) Yes. Where a contract satisfies the statue of frauds under the Uniform Commercial Code, the original satisfaction passes through to the contract as modified, thereby requiring no new memorandum of the modification to that satisfactory original contract. In this case, the original contract was for the sale of goods for more than $500, and therefore falls within the Statute of Frauds under the U.C.C. The contract was in writing and therefore satisfied the Statute of Frauds. So assuming the modifications to the contract in this case include (1) the rebate, and (2) the additional purchase, the pass-through power of the original contract's satisfaction makes the contract as modified enforceable.
(2) No. An oral modification as to quantity in a contract for the sale of goods is not enforceable under the pass-through power. The Statute of Frauds explicitly stipulates that the contract as modified can only be enforced up to the quantity shown in the writing. The rebate did not require an additional writing and is therefore enforceable, because it only concerns price, but the contract is only enforceable up to the original five-pallet order. So the contract, as modified to include a rebate, has satisfied the Statute of Frauds, but the alleged promise to purchase additional jewelry is barred. Summary judgment was proper to strike Worldwide's (D) affirmative Statute of Frauds defense.
(3) Yes. If the Statute of Frauds bars an oral modification, the modification nevertheless can be used as evidence

Continued on next page.

that no other modification to the contract existed. Even though Worldwide (D) had no Statute of Frauds defense, Costco (P) still had to prove the terms of the contract, that Worldwide (D) breached it, and damages. Worldwide (D) can use evidence of the three-pallet additional order to prove that no valid modification to the price existed without offending the Statute of Frauds proscription on enforcement. The Statue of Frauds only forbids judicial enforcement of an alleged promise; it does not forbid using the alleged promise as evidence that no modification to the contract actually exists. So there is an issue of material fact concerning the existence of the modification because Worldwide (D) is only bound if Coleman had actual or apparent authority to enter into a deal on Worldwide's (D) behalf, and summary judgment was inappropriate on that point. Reversed and remanded on that point.

▶ ANALYSIS

This is a tricky case, because it seems implicitly contradictory as written. The bottom line is that the U.C.C. recognizes a pass-through power of an original contract that satisfies the Statute of Frauds, but the power is limited and does not apply to quantities of goods. And even if a particular modification is found to be unenforceable because it concerns quantities, the modification can be used as evidence to undercut a claim of a modification that is inter-related to the quantities modification.

■══■

Quicknotes

MODIFICATION A change to the terms of a contract without altering its general purpose.

STATUTE OF FRAUDS A statute that requires specified types of contracts to be in writing in order to be binding.

SUMMARY JUDGMENT Judgment rendered by a court in response to a motion made by one of the parties, claiming that the lack of a question of material fact in respect to an issue warrants disposition of the issue without consideration by the jury.

■══■

Lawrence v. Anderson

Rescuer physician (P) v. Victim's daughter (D)

Vt. Sup. Ct., 108 Vt. 176, 184 A. 689 (1936).

NATURE OF CASE: Appeal from judgment for defendant in collection action.

FACT SUMMARY: After unsuccessfully attempting to collect medical bills from the estate of Anderson's (D) deceased father, Lawrence (P) attempted to recover from Anderson (D) as surety for the debt.

🏛 **RULE OF LAW**
An oral promise to pay the debt of another is enforceable under the Statute of Frauds when the promisor assumes direct and original liability therefor.

FACTS: Lawrence (P), a physician, gave roadside emergency treatment to Anderson's (D) father. At that time, Anderson (D) allegedly told him that she would pay for the father's medical care. Lawrence (P) treated the father in a hospital until being dismissed from the case after one day. The father soon died, and for a year and a half, Lawrence (P) unsuccessfully tried to collect from the estate. He then brought this action to collect from Anderson (D) as a surety for the debt. Anderson (D) argued that the oral promise was unenforceable under the Statute of Frauds as a promise made for the purpose of discharging the primary obligation of a third party since the services were not legally beneficial to her. Lawrence (P) claimed that Anderson's (D) direct promise to pay made her primarily liable as a promisor and that, as such, the oral promise was outside the statute. Lawrence (P) appealed the trial court's ruling for Anderson (D).

ISSUE: Is an oral promise to pay the debt of another enforceable under the Statute of Frauds when the promisor assumes direct and original liability?

HOLDING AND DECISION: (Powers, C.J.) Yes. An oral promise to pay the debt of another is enforceable under the Statute of Frauds when the promisor assumes direct and original liability therefor. Ordinarily, Anderson (D) would not be liable under these circumstances since the services sued for were not legally beneficial to her. However, here she made an original and direct promise to pay. Therefore, the Statute of Frauds does not apply since this is not a promise to pay the debt of another but rather a promise to pay the debt of the promisor. However, Lawrence (P) cannot turn Anderson's (D) sole obligation into a joint obligation of her and the father without her consent. Furthermore, a strong rebuttable presumption arises that, by making his original charges against the father, Lawrence (P) regarded him to be the original debtor and Anderson's (D) promise to be secondary. Since Lawrence (P) did not rebut this presumption, it must prevail, and we must hold that Anderson's (D) statement amounted to an oral promise to act as surety for the debt of a third party, which must be written. Affirmed.

▶ **ANALYSIS**

In addition to the above-mentioned rule regarding original, rather than collateral, promises being outside the Statute of Frauds, there is a similar and often-used doctrine called the main purpose rule. That rule holds that if the promisor's primary purpose in making a contract to answer for the debt, default, or miscarriage of another is to serve his own interests rather than to serve as guarantor or surety to the promisee for the debt of the third party, the promise is not within the statute.

■■■

Quicknotes

STATUTE OF FRAUDS A statute that requires specified types of contracts to be in writing in order to be binding.

■■■

Yarbro v. Neil B. McGinnis Equipment Co.

Farm equipment company (P) v. Purchaser (D)

Ariz. Sup. Ct., 101 Ariz. 378, 420 P.2d 163, en banc (1966).

NATURE OF CASE: Appeal of award of damages pursuant to breach of suretyship agreement.

FACT SUMMARY: Yarbro (D) orally agreed to make payments on farm equipment to Neil B. McGinnis Equipment Co. (P) on behalf of Russell (D), as Yarbro (D) used the equipment himself.

🏛 RULE OF LAW
One orally guaranteeing to make payments on equipment on behalf of another may not raise a Statute of Frauds defense if the primary purpose of the guaranty is personal benefit.

FACTS: Russell (D) purchased certain farm equipment from Neil B. McGinnis Equipment Co. (McGinnis) (P). The equipment was often used by Yarbro (D), an acquaintance of Russell (D). Russell (D) was chronically in arrears in installment payments, and several times McGinnis (P) threatened to repossess. On four separate occasions, Yarbro (D) orally promised to pay off delinquent installments, although he never did. After an attempted repossession was physically resisted, McGinnis (P) filed a collection action. Yarbro (D) was held liable for the entire amount owed, and he appealed.

ISSUE: May one orally guaranteeing to make payments on equipment on behalf of another raise a Statute of Frauds defense if the primary purpose of the guaranty is personal benefit?

HOLDING AND DECISION: (Bernstein, Vice C.J.) No. One orally guaranteeing to make payments on equipment on behalf of another may not raise a Statute of Frauds defense if the primary purpose of the guaranty is personal benefit. The Statute of Frauds applies to suretyship agreements. However, a well-recognized exception occurs when the guarantor's primary purpose in guaranteeing was to secure a pecuniary advantage for himself, and so, in effect, answer for his debt. In other words, he must be the primary beneficiary of the guarantee. Here, it appears from the record that Yarbro (D) was using the equipment on a regular basis and that he therefore had a personal interest in not seeing the equipment repossessed. This being so, the benefit to him was sufficiently personal to bring into operation the personal benefit exception to the Statute of Frauds. Affirmed as modified.

▶ ANALYSIS

Yarbro (D) also argued that, irrespective of the statute, his promises were void for want of consideration. The court disagreed. The same personal benefit that permitted the

Statute of Frauds exception, said the court, constituted consideration. Also, McGinnis (P) had relied on Yarbro's (D) promises to pay, creating an estoppel.

■=■

Quicknotes

JOINT AND SEVERAL LIABILITY Liability amongst tortfeasors allowing the injured party to bring suit against any of the defendants, individually or collectively, and to recover from each up to the total amount of damages awarded.

STATUTE OF FRAUDS A statute that requires specified types of contracts to be in writing in order to be binding.

SURETYSHIP A situation in which one party guarantees payment of the debt of another party to a creditor.

■=■

Dienst v. Dienst

Wealthy wife (P) v. Penniless husband (D)

Mich. Sup. Ct., 175 Mich. 724, 141 N.W. 591 (1913).

NATURE OF CASE: Appeal in an action to enforce an alleged antenuptial contract.

FACT SUMMARY: In response to Mrs. Dienst's (P) divorce action, Mr. Dienst (D) sought to enforce her alleged oral promise to make a will naming him sole beneficiary.

🏛 RULE OF LAW
Contracts that charge any person upon any agreement made upon consideration of marriage, other than mutual promises to marry, must be in writing to be enforceable.

FACTS: Following a period of written correspondence, Mr. (D) and Mrs. (P) Dienst married. He was 66; she was 62. Her estate was worth $70,000; he was penniless. Soon thereafter, Mrs. Dienst (P) brought this action for a divorce. Mr. Dienst (D) filed a cross-bill wherein he set up a verbal antenuptial agreement whereby Mrs. Dienst (P) had allegedly agreed to execute a will leaving him all of her property should he survive her. Mrs. Dienst (P) argued that the antenuptial contract was within the Statute of Frauds as an agreement made in consideration of marriage, which, to be enforceable, must be in writing. However, Mr. Dienst (D) denied this, claiming that the consideration consisted of his giving up his home, employment, and political preference and leaving Kansas to reside with Mrs. Dienst (P) in Michigan. The trial court sustained Mrs. Dienst's (P) demurrer. Mr. Dienst (D) appealed.

ISSUE: Must contracts which charge any person upon any agreement made upon consideration of marriage, other than mutual promises to marry, be in writing to be enforceable?

HOLDING AND DECISION: (McAlvay, J.) Yes. Contracts that charge any person upon any agreement made upon consideration of marriage, other than mutual promises to marry, must be in writing to be enforceable. But it is clear to us from Mr. Dienst's (D) averment that the claimed agreement and undertaking was made in consideration of marriage since immediately upon Mrs. Dienst's (P) making this commitment, Mr. Dienst (P) proposed marriage, which Mrs. Dienst (P) accepted. Affirmed and remanded.

▶ ANALYSIS

What constitutes a sufficient writing or memorandum? A memorandum is sufficient if it states with reasonable certainty: (1) the identity of the parties; (2) the subject matter of the contract; (3) the essential terms and conditions of all promises and by whom and to whom made; and (4) the signature—or even initials—of the charged party.

Quicknotes

STATUTE OF FRAUDS A statute that requires specified types of contracts to be in writing in order to be binding.

Shaughnessy v. Eidsmo

Lessees (P) v. Lessor (D)

Minn. Sup. Ct., 222 Minn. 141, 23 N.W.2d 362 (1946).

NATURE OF CASE: Appeal from an order denying a motion for a new trial.

FACT SUMMARY: The Shaughnessys (P) leased Eidsmo's (D) property in reliance on his oral agreement to give them an option to purchase it.

🏛 RULE OF LAW
Under the doctrine of part performance, the taking possession of property under an oral contract, in reliance upon and with unequivocal reference to the vendor-vendee relationship, without having to prove irreparable injury through fraud, is sufficient to avoid the Statute of Frauds.

FACTS: The Shaughnessys (P) orally leased a house and lot from Eidsmo (D) for one year with an option to purchase the property at lease expiration and with credit on the purchase price for the rent already paid. Eidsmo (D) also agreed to sell them a stove on the property. However, when the lease expired, Eidsmo (D) failed to deliver the deed despite the Shaughnessys' (P) frequent demands. Eidsmo (D) claimed to be too busy, but he gave assurances that he would draw up the contract and, in fact, showed the Shaughnessys (P) a rough draft thereof. Accordingly, the Shaughnessys (P) continued in possession, paying an additional $570 on the property. Also, when the agreement was originally made, the premises were subject to a $4,200 mortgage of which the Shaughnessys (P) were unaware and did not assume. When the Shaughnessys (P) sought specific performance, Eidsmo (D) pled the oral contract's unenforceability under the Statute of Frauds. The Shaughnessys (P) answered that, under the doctrine of part performance, their taking possession of the real property pursuant to the oral contract, coupled with partial payment, in reliance upon and with reference to the vendor-vendee relationship, removed the contract from the statute. Eidsmo (D) argued that this exception was inapplicable unless a plaintiff showed irreparable injury through fraud. The trial court ruled for the Shaughnessys (P) and denied Eidsmo's (D) motion for a new trial. Eidsmo (D) appealed.

ISSUE: Under the doctrine of part performance, is it essential for the plaintiff to prove irreparable injury through fraud in order to remove an oral contract from the Statute of Frauds?

HOLDING AND DECISION: (Matson, J.) No. Under the doctrine of part performance, the taking of possession of property under an oral contract, in reliance upon and with unequivocal reference to the vendor-vendee relationship, without having to prove irreparable injury

through fraud, is sufficient to avoid the Statute of Frauds. This is the Restatement view, which we now adopt. We now overrule those decisions requiring proof of injury or great hardship in addition to part performance. In fact, there exist two means of avoiding the statute in these cases: either by proving irreparable injury or by proving partial payment or taking of possession in reliance on the vendor-vendee relationship. According to Williston, the latter alternative suffices since: (1) the statute is a rule of evidence, and, thus, any acts clearly referable to the existence of the contract satisfy in equity the purposes of the statute and (2) it would be unconscionable for equity to allow a vendor to rely on the statute in such cases. Affirmed.

▶ ANALYSIS

A court sitting in equity may also take a contract outside the statute when the party seeking to avoid enforcement has promised to either put the contract in writing or not to raise the statute as a defense. This applies if the enforcing party justifiably relied on this promise to his detriment. A minority of jurisdictions will estop a party from defending on the basis of the statute whenever the statute's application would cause fraud or unjust enrichment.

■≡■

Quicknotes

STATUTE OF FRAUDS A statute that requires specified types of contracts to be in writing in order to be binding.

■≡■

CHAPTER 1

Discharge of Contracts

Quick Reference Rules of Law

Goldbard v. Empire State Mutual Life Ins. Co.

Disabled barber (P) v. Insurer (D)

N.Y. Sup. Ct., App. Div., 5 A.D.2d 230, 171 N.Y.S.2d 194 (1958).

NATURE OF CASE: Suit to recover pursuant to a policy of insurance.

FACT SUMMARY: Goldbard (P) filed an insurance claim with Empire State Mutual Life Ins. Co. (Empire) (D). Empire (D) then offered to settle with Goldbard (P) for part of the amount of his claim.

🏛 RULE OF LAW
Whether or not a subsequent agreement supersedes an existing contract must be determined by reference to the objectively manifested intentions of the parties.

FACTS: Goldbard (P), a barber, sued Empire State Mutual Life Insurance Company (Empire) (D) for monthly benefits when he suffered a hand infection which allegedly prevented him from working. He sought $2,800, but Empire (D) wanted to pay only $800. Goldbard (P) complained to the State Insurance Department, through whose representative Empire (D) offered Goldbard (P) $800 provided he would not renew his policy. After initially rejecting this offer, Goldbard (P) telephoned his acceptance through the Department's representative. But when Empire (D) sent Goldbard (P) a release form, he ignored it and sued for $2,800. Empire (D) claimed that a settlement and compromise had been reached, limiting its liability to $800. The trial court awarded $2,800 to Goldbard (P), but the appellate tribunal reduced the judgment to $800.

ISSUE: May an existing contract be superseded by a subsequent agreement?

HOLDING AND DECISION: (Breitel, J.) Yes. Whether or not a subsequent agreement supersedes an existing contract must be determined by reference to the objectively manifested intentions of the parties. In this case, there is no evidence from which it may be inferred that the parties agreed to the $800 figure. Any settlement which occurred was, at best, an executory accord, and such an agreement would be enforceable under state law only if it had been reduced to writing. Therefore, Goldbard (P) is entitled to recover in full without reference to the subsequent agreement, if any. But the amount of his judgment must be reduced to $2,600 because of certain concessions made during trial. As modified, affirmed.

not be enforced. This analysis is consistent with the approach adopted by the *Goldbard* case because consideration is itself a manifestation of intent.

■=■

▌ ANALYSIS

In determining the validity of a modification agreement, the inquiry of most courts focuses upon the question of whether or not consideration has been given. Unless the new agreement is supported by a new consideration, it will

First American Commerce Co. v. Washington Mutual Savings Bank

Borrower (P) v. Lender (D)

Utah Sup. Ct., 743 P.2d 1193 (1987).

NATURE OF CASE: Appeal of summary judgment dismissing action to collect monies owed.

FACT SUMMARY: First Security Realty (D) contended its contractual obligation to make loan disbursements to First American Commerce Co. (P) followed the assignment of collection rights.

🏛 RULE OF LAW
When a lender assigns repayment rights, any duty to make outstanding loan disbursements remains with the lender.

FACTS: First Security Realty Services (First Security) (D) agreed to loan certain sums to First American Commerce Co. (First American) (P). Certain amounts were to be withheld pending performance of specified conditions. First Security (D) then assigned its rights to Washington Mutual Savings Bank (Washington Mutual) (D). When First American (P) had performed the conditions, it requested disbursement of the outstanding loan amount. First Security (D) refused, contending that the duty followed the assignment, a proposition with which Washington Mutual (D) did not agree. First American (P) sued both. First Security (D) obtained summary judgment, and First American (P) appealed.

ISSUE: When a lender assigns repayment rights, does any duty to make outstanding loan disbursements remain with the lender?

HOLDING AND DECISION: (Durham, J.) Yes. When a lender assigns repayment rights, any duty to make outstanding loan disbursements remains with the lender. An assignment constitutes a transfer of rights. A transfer of duties, on the other hand, is known as a delegation. Unlike an assignment, a delegation requires the assent of the party to whom the duty is owed to be transferred. Reversed and remanded to determine the parties' intent and other factual issues.

▶ ANALYSIS

The legal term for what First Security (D) argued was created by its assignment is "novation." Novation is a subsequent agreement modifying a contract. The court here merely pointed out that a novation requires the assent of both contracting parties, something that did not occur here.

Quicknotes

ASSIGNMENT A transaction in which a party conveys his or her entire interest in property to another.

NOVATION The substitution of one party for another in a contract with the approval of the remaining party and discharging the obligations of the released party.

CHAPTER 15

Bargains That Are Illegal or Against Public Policy

Quick Reference Rules of Law

T.F. v. B.L.

Child's biological mother (P) v. Mother's former partner (D)

Mass. Sup. Jud. Ct., 442 Mass. 522, 813 N.E.2d 1244 (2004).

NATURE OF CASE: Action for order of child support.

FACT SUMMARY: T.F. (P) sought child support from B.L. (D) who had agreed to co-parent a child conceived by T.F. (P) by artificial insemination while the two were a couple.

🏛 RULE OF LAW
An implied agreement to co-parent a child is unenforceable as against public policy because parenthood by contract is not the law of Massachusetts.

FACTS: While living together as a same sex couple, T.F. (P) and B.L. (D) agreed that B.L. (D) would take on the responsibilities of a parent and T.F. (P) would conceive by artificial insemination and deliver a child. After T.F. (P) became pregnant, the couple separated. T.F. (P) delivered the child and B.L. (D) refused to provide support. T.F. (P) sought an order requiring child support and the trial court posed the question of whether parenthood by contract was the law of Massachusetts to the court of appeals.

ISSUE: Is an implied agreement to co-parent a child unenforceable as against public policy because parenthood by contract is not the law of Massachusetts?

HOLDING AND DECISION: (Cowin J.) Yes. An implied agreement to co-parent a child is unenforceable as against public policy because parenthood by contract is not the law in Massachusetts. There was sufficient evidence for the trial court to find that B.L. (D) agreed to take on parental responsibilities in that she expressed a desire to adopt the child, referred to herself as a separated parent, visited the mother and child in the hospital, promised to support the child and promised to change her work hours to help raise the child. In order to protect freedom of personal choice, however, agreements to enter into parenthood should not be enforced against persons who subsequently reconsider. Remanded to lower court for further proceedings consistent with this opinion.

CONCURRENCE AND DISSENT: (Greaney, J.) Parenthood by contract is not the law of Massachusetts, but the equitable authority of the Probate and Family court extends to protect the best interest of the child such that the agreement should be enforced. The fact that B.L. (D) is not a parent and there is no statutory remedy should not preclude an order requiring child support. The American Law Institute's analysis recommends that B.L's (D) prior conduct equitably estops her from denying a support obligation to the child.

ANALYSIS

By phrasing the issue in terms of whether one can become a parent by operation of contract rather than as a function of conduct, the court here took the opposite approach from that taken in *Elisa B. v. Superior Court*, 37 Cal. 4th 108, 117 P.3d 660, 33 Cal. Rptr. 3d 46 (2005). In *Elisa B.*, the court reasoned from the premise that a de facto parenthood relationship existed and can exist between a person and the child of their same sex partner.

Quicknotes

BEST INTERESTS OF CHILD Standard used by courts when rendering decisions which involve a child or children.

CHILD SUPPORT Payments made by one parent to another in satisfaction of the non-custodial parent's legal obligation to provide for the sustenance of the child.

ESTOPPEL An equitable doctrine precluding a party from asserting a right to the detriment of another whom justifiably relied on the conduct.

PUBLIC POLICY Policy administered by the state with respect to the health, safety and morals of its people in accordance with common notions of fairness and decency.

Troutman v. Southern Railway Co.

Lobbyist (P) v. Benefiting-client (D)

441 F.2d 586 (5th Cir. 1977), *cert denied*, 404 U.S. 871 (1971).

NATURE OF CASE: Appeal of award of damages for breach of contract.

FACT SUMMARY: Troutman (P) used his access to high government officials to present Southern Railway's (D) case in a dispute it was having with the Interstate Commerce Commission (ICC).

🏛 **RULE OF LAW**
A contract to use one's access to present another's case to high officials is not unenforceable as contrary to policy.

FACTS: Southern Railway Co. (D) stood to lose a good deal of revenue due to a regulatory decision by the ICC. Southern Railway (D) approached Troutman (P), whom it knew to have personal relationships with several high Kennedy Administration officials, including the President himself. Troutman (P) agreed to present the merits of Southern Railway's (D) case to the Administration in hope that the Administration would side with Southern Railway (D). Troutman (P) did this, and the Administration did in fact side with Southern Railway (D), which prevailed against the ICC. Troutman (P) was not paid an agreed-upon fee by Southern Railway (D), and he sued. A jury awarded Troutman (P) $175,000, and Southern Railway (D) appealed, contending that a contract to influence government officials is unenforceable as against public policy.

ISSUE: Is a contract to use one's access to present another's case to high officials unenforceable as contrary to policy?

HOLDING AND DECISION: (Wisdom, J.) No. A contract to use one's access to present another's case to high officials is not unenforceable as contrary to policy. Such a contract is unenforceable only when it contemplates an individual using personal or political access to an official in an attempt to influence that official's decision based on the influence alone. When, however, the merits of the case are presented and the decision is based on these merits, nothing improper has occurred. All citizens have a constitutional right to petition the government, and the use of lobbyists is an integral part of the process. Here, Troutman (P) merely used his access to present the merits of Southern Railway's (D) case. Affirmed.

▶ *ANALYSIS*

The line between improper influence and legitimate lobbying can be a thin one. Which side of the fence any particular case may fall on will almost always be a factual one. This being so, the validity of contracts for such services is generally a question for the jury.

■■■

Quicknotes

PUBLIC POLICY Policy administered by the state with respect to the health, safety and morals of its people in accordance with common notions of fairness and decency.

■■■

Northern Indiana Public Service Co. v. Carbon County Coal Co.

Coal purchaser (P) v. Coal provider (D)

799 F.2d 265 (7th Cir. 1986).

NATURE OF CASE: Appeal in action seeking declaratory judgment nullifying a contract.

FACT SUMMARY: Northern Indiana Public Service Co. (P) brought an action against Carbon County Coal Co. (D) seeking to void a supply contract.

🏛 RULE OF LAW
A contract not inherently illegal but in breach of a law will not be voided if the equities favor enforcement.

FACTS: Northern Indiana Public Service Co. (Northern Indiana) (P) signed a long-term contract to purchase coal from Carbon County Coal Co. (Carbon County) (D). Changes in the economy which depressed the price of coal made the contract onerous for Northern Indiana (P). Northern Indiana (P) brought an action seeking to void the contract on the basis of, among other things, illegality. A 1920 federal statute prohibited a company operating a railroad from mining or leasing coal operations on federal land. Carbon County (D) was half-owned by a subsidiary of a subsidiary of a railroad company. The district court refused to declare the contract void, and a jury awarded damages to Carbon Country (D) on its counterclaim. Northern Indiana (P) appealed.

ISSUE: Will a contract not inherently illegal but in breach of a law be voided if the equities favor enforcement?

HOLDING AND DECISION: (Posner, J.) No. A contract not inherently illegal but in breach of a law will not be voided if the equities favor enforcement. When a contract covers an illegal subject, such as a contract to commit a crime, the doctrine of illegality will usually make the contract unenforceable. The illegality doctrine does not automatically come into play just because one party commits unlawful acts to carry out his part of the bargain. In this instance, a court may weigh the factors favoring enforcement against the factors militating against doing so. Here, an old and seldom-noticed federal statute is being violated in a much attenuated manner. On the other hand, public policy favors enforcing contracts. The court's view is that this policy outweighs the minor detriments to be found by a minor violation of an obscure law, and, therefore, the illegality doctrine will not be invoked. Affirmed.

▶ ANALYSIS

The level of strictness with which the doctrine will be applied varies among the circuits. The Fifth Circuit has shown a reluctance to apply it. The Seventh Circuit, originally apt to strictly apply it, appears to have relaxed a bit with this decision.

■=■

Quicknotes

IN PARI DELICTO Doctrine that a court will not enforce an illegal contract in an action for losses incurred as a result of the breach of that contract.

■=■

Cochran v. Dellfava

Investor (P) v. Recruiter (D)

Rochester, N.Y. City Ct., Small Claims, 136 Misc. 2d 38, 517 N.Y.S.2d 854 (1987).

NATURE OF CASE: Action seeking rescission of agreement to participate in an illegal investment enterprise.

FACT SUMMARY: Cochran (P), a losing investor in a "chain scheme," sued for recovery of her investment.

🏛 RULE OF LAW
A participant in a "chain scheme" may not sue for recovery of invested monies.

FACTS: Cochran (P) was recruited by Dellfava (D) to invest $2,200 in a variation on the classic "chain" or "pyramid" scheme. As is always the case with such enterprises, the latecomers tended to lose their investments, which was the case with Cochran (P). She sued for recovery of her monies.

ISSUE: May a participant in a "chain scheme," sue for recovery of invested monies?

HOLDING AND DECISION: (Schwartz, J.) No. A participant in a "chain scheme" may not sue for recovery of invested monies. It is the general rule that parties enter into illegal contracts at their own risk, for the law will not extend its aid to either party but will leave them where their own acts have left them. The law does recognize an exception to this. Where the plaintiff's conduct was malum prohibitum only, and the plaintiff's conduct was less culpable than the defendant's, the plaintiff may recover. Here, while Cochran's (P) conduct was most likely malum prohibitum, her conduct was equally culpable as that of Dellfava (D). They both entered into a scheme they knew was illegal. The fact that Cochran (P) lost was due not to any virtue on her part but simple fortuity. This does not make her conduct less culpable and will not bring her within the exception to the general rule. Plaintiff's claim dismissed.

▶ ANALYSIS

Whether a plaintiff's conduct was less culpable than the defendant's usually goes not to the acts themselves but to the parties' respective mental states. Duress or undue influence will often take away a defendant's in pari delicto defense. Another such situation is when a plaintiff acts out of charitable motives. Neither was the case here.

■═■

Quicknotes

IN PARI DELICTO Doctrine that a court will not enforce an illegal contract in an action for losses incurred as a result of the breach of that contract.

MALUM PROHIBITUM An action that is not inherently wrong, but which is prohibited by law.

■═■

Maizitis v. TUV America, Inc.

Employee (P) v. Employer (D)

2007 WL 582391 (N.D. Ohio 2007).

NATURE OF CASE: Motion for summary judgment.

FACT SUMMARY: Maizitis (P) signed an employment contract that he believed was unenforceable because it violated Ohio public policy. Neither party breached the contract. Maizitis (P) sued TUV America, Inc. (D) for compelling him to sign it.

RULE OF LAW
The laws of Ohio and Massachusetts do not recognize a cause of action for the non-breach of a contract that allegedly violates public policy.

FACTS: TUV America, Inc. (TUV) (D) was Maizitis's (P) employer. When TUV (D) promoted Maizitis (P), the company asked him to assign a new employment agreement that included, among other things, a non-solicitation clause prohibiting him from inducing other employees, vendors, or customers away from TUV (D). Neither party breached the contract, but when his position was eliminated and his employment terminated, Maizitis (P) sued TUV (D), arguing that the contract violated state public policy and that TUV (D) should pay damages for compelling him to sign it. He argued the contract violated Ohio's public policy, and that Ohio law governed the contract. TUV (D) argued that Massachusetts law governed, but the court found the point to be irrelevant.

ISSUE: Do the laws of Ohio and Massachusetts recognize a cause of action for the non-breach of a contract that allegedly violates public policy?

HOLDING AND DECISION: (O'Malley, J.) No. The laws of Ohio and Massachusetts do not recognize a cause of action for the non-breach of a contract that allegedly violates public policy. Maizitis (P) did not state a claim for breach of contract, and has not alleged a breach of the agreement by TUV (D). Instead, he argued that TUV (D) compelled him to enter into and be bound by a contract that violated public policy in the state of Ohio, and in the alternative, that his mistaken belief that his agreement was valid led him to leave his job with another employer. Assuming the contract violates public policy his arguments do not describe a breach of contract or provide a basis for any other cause of action related to the agreement. He believes that the court should give him a remedy under the circumstances because he could or should have breached his agreement with TUV (D) but failed to do so. But no case law supports his argument that a party is entitled to receive additional compensation—additional in that he was paid during his employment—for performing obligations under a contract because he could

have invalidated the agreement. TUV's (D) motion for summary judgment is granted.

ANALYSIS

This case illustrates the point that non-breach of a contract—whether it violates public policy or is void for another reason—is not grounds for a civil action. Entrance into an illegal contract can result in criminal action, however.

Quicknotes

PUBLIC POLICY Policy administered by the state with respect to the health, safety and morals of its people in accordance with common notions of fairness and decency.

Glossary

Common Latin Words and Phrases Encountered in the Law

A FORTIORI: Because one fact exists or has been proven, therefore a second fact that is related to the first fact must also exist.

A PRIORI: From the cause to the effect. A term of logic used to denote that when one generally accepted truth is shown to be a cause, another particular effect must necessarily follow.

AB INITIO: From the beginning; a condition which has existed throughout, as in a marriage which was void ab initio.

ACTUS REUS: The wrongful act; in criminal law, such action sufficient to trigger criminal liability.

AD VALOREM: According to value; an ad valorem tax is imposed upon an item located within the taxing jurisdiction calculated by the value of such item.

AMICUS CURIAE: Friend of the court. Its most common usage takes the form of an amicus curiae brief, filed by a person who is not a party to an action but is nonetheless allowed to offer an argument supporting his legal interests.

ARGUENDO: In arguing. A statement, possibly hypothetical, made for the purpose of argument, is one made arguendo.

BILL QUIA TIMET: A bill to quiet title (establish ownership) to real property.

BONA FIDE: True, honest, or genuine. May refer to a person's legal position based on good faith or lacking notice of fraud (such as a bona fide purchaser for value) or to the authenticity of a particular document (such as a bona fide last will and testament).

CAUSA MORTIS: With approaching death in mind. A gift causa mortis is a gift given by a party who feels certain that death is imminent.

CAVEAT EMPTOR: Let the buyer beware. This maxim is reflected in the rule of law that a buyer purchases at his own risk because it is his responsibility to examine, judge, test, and otherwise inspect what he is buying.

CERTIORARI: A writ of review. Petitions for review of a case by the United States Supreme Court are most often done by means of a writ of certiorari.

CONTRA: On the other hand. Opposite. Contrary to.

CORAM NOBIS: Before us; writs of error directed to the court that originally rendered the judgment.

CORAM VOBIS: Before you; writs of error directed by an appellate court to a lower court to correct a factual error.

CORPUS DELICTI: The body of the crime; the requisite elements of a crime amounting to objective proof that a crime has been committed.

CUM TESTAMENTO ANNEXO, ADMINISTRATOR (ADMINISTRATOR C.T.A.): With will annexed; an administrator c.t.a. settles an estate pursuant to a will in which he is not appointed.

DE BONIS NON, ADMINISTRATOR (ADMINISTRATOR D.B.N.): Of goods not administered; an administrator d.b.n. settles a partially settled estate.

DE FACTO: In fact; in reality; actually. Existing in fact but not officially approved or engendered.

DE JURE: By right; lawful. Describes a condition that is legitimate "as a matter of law," in contrast to the term "de facto," which connotes something existing in fact but not legally sanctioned or authorized. For example, de facto segregation refers to segregation brought about by housing patterns, etc., whereas de jure segregation refers to segregation created by law.

DE MINIMIS: Of minimal importance; insignificant; a trifle; not worth bothering about.

DE NOVO: Anew; a second time; afresh. A trial de novo is a new trial held at the appellate level as if the case originated there and the trial at a lower level had not taken place.

DICTA: Generally used as an abbreviated form of obiter dicta, a term describing those portions of a judicial opinion incidental or not necessary to resolution of the specific question before the court. Such nonessential statements and remarks are not considered to be binding precedent.

DUCES TECUM: Refers to a particular type of writ or subpoena requesting a party or organization to produce certain documents in their possession.

EN BANC: Full bench. Where a court sits with all justices present rather than the usual quorum.

EX PARTE: For one side or one party only. An ex parte proceeding is one undertaken for the benefit of only one party, without notice to, or an appearance by, an adverse party.

EX POST FACTO: After the fact. An ex post facto law is a law that retroactively changes the consequences of a prior act.

EX REL.: Abbreviated form of the term "ex relatione," meaning upon relation or information. When the state brings an action in which it has no interest against an individual at the instigation of one who has a private interest in the matter.

FORUM NON CONVENIENS: Inconvenient forum. Although a court may have jurisdiction over the case, the action should be tried in a more conveniently located court, one to which parties and witnesses may more easily travel, for example.

GUARDIAN AD LITEM: A guardian of an infant as to litigation, appointed to represent the infant and pursue his/her rights.

HABEAS CORPUS: You have the body. The modern writ of habeas corpus is a writ directing that a person (body) being detained (such as a prisoner) be brought before the court so that the legality of his detention can be judicially ascertained.

IN CAMERA: In private, in chambers. When a hearing is held before a judge in his chambers or when all spectators are excluded from the courtroom.

IN FORMA PAUPERIS: In the manner of a pauper. A party who proceeds in forma pauperis because of his poverty is one who is allowed to bring suit without liability for costs.

INFRA: Below, under. A word referring the reader to a later part of a book. (The opposite of supra.)

IN LOCO PARENTIS: In the place of a parent.

IN PARI DELICTO: Equally wrong; a court of equity will not grant requested relief to an applicant who is in pari delicto, or as much at fault in the transactions giving rise to the controversy as is the opponent of the applicant.

IN PARI MATERIA: On like subject matter or upon the same matter. Statutes relating to the same person or things are said to be in pari materia. It is a general rule of statutory construction that such statutes should be construed together, i.e., looked at as if they together constituted one law.

IN PERSONAM: Against the person. Jurisdiction over the person of an individual.

IN RE: In the matter of. Used to designate a proceeding involving an estate or other property.

IN REM: A term that signifies an action against the res, or thing. An action in rem is basically one that is taken directly against property, as distinguished from an action in personam, i.e., against the person.

INTER ALIA: Among other things. Used to show that the whole of a statement, pleading, list, statute, etc., has not been set forth in its entirety.

INTER PARTES: Between the parties. May refer to contracts, conveyances or other transactions having legal significance.

INTER VIVOS: Between the living. An inter vivos gift is a gift made by a living grantor, as distinguished from bequests contained in a will, which pass upon the death of the testator.

IPSO FACTO: By the mere fact itself.

JUS: Law or the entire body of law.

LEX LOCI: The law of the place; the notion that the rights of parties to a legal proceeding are governed by the law of the place where those rights arose.

MALUM IN SE: Evil or wrong in and of itself; inherently wrong. This term describes an act that is wrong by its very nature, as opposed to one which would not be wrong but for the fact that there is a specific legal prohibition against it (malum prohibitum).

MALUM PROHIBITUM: Wrong because prohibited, but not inherently evil. Used to describe something that is wrong because it is expressly forbidden by law but that is not in and of itself evil, e.g., speeding.

MANDAMUS: We command. A writ directing an official to take a certain action.

MENS REA: A guilty mind; a criminal intent. A term used to signify the mental state that accompanies a crime or other prohibited act. Some crimes require only a general mens rea (general intent to do the prohibited act), but others, like assault with intent to murder, require the existence of a specific mens rea.

MODUS OPERANDI: Method of operating; generally refers to the manner or style of a criminal in committing crimes, admissible in appropriate cases as evidence of the identity of a defendant.

NEXUS: A connection to.

NISI PRIUS: A court of first impression. A nisi prius court is one where issues of fact are tried before a judge or jury.

N.O.V. (NON OBSTANTE VEREDICTO): Notwithstanding the verdict. A judgment n.o.v. is a judgment given in favor of one party despite the fact that a verdict was returned in favor of the other party, the justification being that the verdict either had no reasonable support in fact or was contrary to law.

NUNC PRO TUNC: Now for then. This phrase refers to actions that may be taken and will then have full retroactive effect.

PENDENTE LITE: Pending the suit; pending litigation under way.

PER CAPITA: By head; beneficiaries of an estate, if they take in equal shares, take per capita.

PER CURIAM: By the court; signifies an opinion ostensibly written "by the whole court" and with no identified author.

PER SE: By itself, in itself; inherently.

PER STIRPES: By representation. Used primarily in the law of wills to describe the method of distribution where a person, generally because of death, is unable to take that which is left to him by the will of another, and therefore his heirs divide such property between them rather than take under the will individually.

PRIMA FACIE: On its face, at first sight. A prima facie case is one that is sufficient on its face, meaning that the evidence supporting it is adequate to establish the case until contradicted or overcome by other evidence.

PRO TANTO: For so much; as far as it goes. Often used in eminent domain cases when a property owner receives partial payment for his land without prejudice to his right to bring suit for the full amount he claims his land to be worth.

QUANTUM MERUIT: As much as he deserves. Refers to recovery based on the doctrine of unjust enrichment in those cases in which a party has rendered valuable services or furnished materials that were accepted and enjoyed by another under circumstances that would reasonably notify the recipient that the rendering party expected to be paid. In essence, the law implies a contract to pay the reasonable value of the services or materials furnished.

QUASI: Almost like; as if; nearly. This term is essentially used to signify that one subject or thing is almost analogous to another but that material differences between them do exist. For example, a quasi-criminal proceeding is one that is not strictly criminal but shares enough of the same characteristics to require some of the same safeguards (e.g., procedural due process must be followed in a parole hearing).

QUID PRO QUO: Something for something. In contract law, the consideration, something of value, passed between the parties to render the contract binding.

RES GESTAE: Things done; in evidence law, this principle justifies the admission of a statement that would otherwise be hearsay when it is made so closely to the event in question as to be said to be a part of it, or with such spontaneity as not to have the possibility of falsehood.

RES IPSA LOQUITUR: The thing speaks for itself. This doctrine gives rise to a rebuttable presumption of negligence when the instrumentality causing the injury was within the exclusive control of the defendant, and the injury was one that does not normally occur unless a person has been negligent.

RES JUDICATA: A matter adjudged. Doctrine which provides that once a court of competent jurisdiction has rendered a final judgment or decree on the merits, that judgment or decree is conclusive upon the parties to the case and prevents them from engaging in any other litigation on the points and issues determined therein.

RESPONDEAT SUPERIOR: Let the master reply. This doctrine holds the master liable for the wrongful acts of his servant (or the principal for his agent) in those cases in which the servant (or agent) was acting within the scope of his authority at the time of the injury.

STARE DECISIS: To stand by or adhere to that which has been decided. The common law doctrine of stare decisis attempts to give security and certainty to the law by following the policy that once a principle of law as applicable to a certain set of facts has been set forth in a decision, it forms a precedent which will subsequently be followed, even though a different decision might be made were it the first time the question had arisen. Of course, stare decisis is not an inviolable principle and is departed from in instances where there is good cause (e.g., considerations of public policy led the Supreme Court to disregard prior decisions sanctioning segregation).

SUPRA: Above. A word referring a reader to an earlier part of a book.

ULTRA VIRES: Beyond the power. This phrase is most commonly used to refer to actions taken by a corporation that are beyond the power or legal authority of the corporation.

Addendum of French Derivatives

IN PAIS: Not pursuant to legal proceedings.

CHATTEL: Tangible personal property.

CY PRES: Doctrine permitting courts to apply trust funds to purposes not expressed in the trust but necessary to carry out the settlor's intent.

PER AUTRE VIE: For another's life; during another's life. In property law, an estate may be granted that will terminate upon the death of someone other than the grantee.

PROFIT A PRENDRE: A license to remove minerals or other produce from land.

VOIR DIRE: Process of questioning jurors as to their predispositions about the case or parties to a proceeding in order to identify those jurors displaying bias or prejudice.

Casenote® Legal Briefs